Reading Southern History

Essays on Interpreters and Interpretations

Edited by

Glenn Feldman

THE UNIVERSITY OF ALABAMA PRESS

Tuscaloosa and London

2 4 6 8 9 7 5 3 1
02 04 06 08 09 07 05 03 01

Typeface: ACaslon

∞

The paper on which this book is printed meets the minimum requirements of
American National Standard for Information Science–Permanence of Paper for
Printed Library Materials, ANSI Z39.48-1984.

Library of Congress Cataloging-in-Publication Data

Reading southern history : essays on interpreters and interpretations /
edited by Glenn Feldman.
p.   cm.
Includes bibliographical references (p. 311) and index.
ISBN 0-8173-1099-1 (cloth : alk. paper) — ISBN 0-8173-1102-5 (paper : alk. paper)
1. Southern States—Historiography. 2. Historians—United States—Biography.
I. Feldman, Glenn.
F208.2 .R43 2001
975'.007'2—dc21

2001002386

British Library Cataloguing-in-Publication Data available

For my parents, whom I love more than they know:
Julia Gárate Burgos Feldman and Brian Feldman

Contents

Acknowledgments

Debts are owed to many for their help with this book. I am grateful to a number of historians who provided valuable counsel on a variety of aspects of this project and conveyed confidence in the intrinsic merit of this idea: Robert H. Abzug, Ray Arsenault, Leah Rawls Atkins, Numan V. Bartley, Michael Les Benedict, John B. Boles, W. Fitzhugh Brundage, David L. Carlton, Dan T. Carter, Paul K. Conkin, Don H. Doyle, Robin F. A. Fabel, Michael W. Fitzgerald, Wayne Flynt, John H. Glen, Hugh Davis Graham, Dewey W. Grantham, Virginia Van der Veer Hamilton, David Edwin Harrell, James A. Hodges, Harvey H. Jackson III, Elizabeth Jacoway, Glen S. Jeansonne, Allen W. Jones, Charles Joyner, Peter Kolchin, J. Morgan Kousser, Shawn Lay, W. David Lewis, Leon Litwack, Robert C. McMath, Neil McMillen, Michael O'Brien, James L. Roark, William Warren Rogers, Sr., Charles P. Roland, Louis D. Rubin, Nick Salvatore, Anne Firor Scott, Jack Sproat, Martha H. Swain, J. Mills Thornton III, George B. Tindall, Eric Tscheshlock, Elizabeth Hayes Turner, Carol Ann Vaughn, Marjorie Spruill Wheeler, Joel R. Williamson, Margaret Ripley Wolfe, the late C. Vann Woodward, and Robert H. Zieger.

I am especially indebted to those scholars who actually took the time and effort to contribute to this book. This is particularly noteworthy during an era of information and communications revolution that seems to be distinctive for its remarkable ability to shrink our available time. We are all the better for their acumen and expertise. Our roster of contributors is, I believe, a good mix of accomplished senior historians, promising younger scholars, and a couple of genuine titans. I take full responsibility for whatever errors and shortcomings remain.

A special note of gratitude goes to Nicole Mitchell, director of The University of Alabama Press, and Suzette Griffith, assistant managing editor. Thanks also to my colleagues at the Center for Labor Education and Research (CLEAR) in the School of Business at the University of Alabama at Birmingham (UAB): Ralph Johnson, Ed Brown, Tracy Chang, and center director Judi King. I am grateful also to my dean at the UAB School of Business, Robert E.

Holmes, for fostering an atmosphere that is very supportive of research efforts. Charmagne Sturgis, Melanie Hightower, Alison Schmied, Diane E. Despard, and Terrence J. Weatherspoon also provided technical support at CLEAR that is much appreciated. A sincere and exceptional note of gratitude goes to Donna L. Cox, graduate student in history at UAB, for her expertise converting various word-processing software programs, and to Kathy Cummins, who did an excellent job as copy editor. My deepest thanks is due to my family, especially my indispensable wife, Jeannie, my precious daughters, Hallie and Rebecca, and my parents, to whom this book is dedicated.

READING SOUTHERN HISTORY

Introduction

The Pursuit of Southern History

GLENN FELDMAN

The South is a special place. Even now, after the turn of a new century and the dawn of a new millennium, the South is ever present in matters of American politics, American culture, and American life. It is difficult to foresee a time when things will be different. As I write this, a Texan and a Tennessean are struggling over Florida to decide who will succeed an Arkansan in the White House. The study of Southern history has long attracted a special kind of scholar and a special kind of scholarship. The beneficiary of, arguably, the most and the best attentions of professional historians of any of the nation's subregions, study of the American South has captivated generations of talented historical observers approaching the subject from a variety of intellectual and personal perspectives. This book is an effort to understand some of the best historical work ever produced on the region.

The format is an edited collection of essays on the most notable interpreters of Southern history. A sectarian approach has been consciously avoided in this work, largely in acknowledgment of the usefulness of other disciplines besides history to shed light on some of the most compelling themes currently and traditionally explored by Southern historians. Therefore, this volume includes chapters on several scholars who have made significant contributions to an understanding of the South's history from outside the discipline of history proper—specifically from the perspectives of political science, sociology, journalism, and economics.[1]

The essays here are primarily historiographical in nature. They seek to examine the major work or works of each scholar under consideration as well as that scholar's overall contribution to the study of Southern history. Of course, out of simple necessity, any good historiographical essay contains some biographical information. In fact, the biographical nature of some of these essays may be pointed to as a particular strength of this kind of approach because it sheds light on the history ultimately produced by our subjects. Not surprisingly, in a project in which nineteen different scholars contributed eighteen chapters, the essays vary in the extent of the biographical background that they include as well as in their degrees of criticism or praise. The volume explores a variety of subfields of Southern history as represented by the work and interests of the scholars under study in this book. Some of these topics include politics, religion, culture, class, identity, gender, race relations, civil rights, violence, honor, slavery, secession, war, labor, economics, industrialization, plain whites, Southern sociology, and sectional distinctiveness.

The collection makes no claim to be exhaustive or exclusive. Doubtless, there are more than a few historians who, for one reason or another—certainly not because they are undeserving—do not appear as the subjects of full chapters. Contemporary scholars such as Bertram Wyatt-Brown, Drew Gilpin Faust, Elizabeth Fox-Genovese, Eugene D. Genovese, Dan T. Carter, Wayne Flynt, John Shelton Reed, Jacquelyn Dowd Hall, Paul K. Conkin, Joel R. Williamson, Dewey W. Grantham, Numan V. Bartley, and James Cobb might have been included; older scholars like Joseph G. de Roulhac Hamilton, William E. Dodd, Phinzy Spaulding, Fletcher M. Green, Howard W. Odum, Herbert G. Gutman, and even several others might also have appeared. In fact, when taken together, the various references made in this volume to Eugene Genovese probably comprise enough material to constitute a full chapter. Still, several problems prohibited the formal inclusion of Genovese as well as others. It became increasingly clear, as I formulated the idea for this book and sought the counsel of many in the field, that to include some scholars who are still writing, and not others, might invite criticism of the work as the product of politics or popularity—charges of which I want this book to be free. Other problems are inherent in writing about historians who are still writing, namely those of perspective and completeness. For example, an essay completed today on Genovese, no matter how enlightening, would almost certainly be incomplete because the subject himself has probably not finished undergoing some very interesting permutations that will undoubtedly have a significant impact on the history that he has yet to write. The only reasonable solution, as I saw it, was to include chapters only on leading students of the South who are, for the largest part, finished with their careers or fairly set on their interpretive approaches to their subjects.

Other considerations influenced the choice of chapter subjects. Willingness and, even more important, the availability of expert students of Southern history to contribute chapters within a reasonable window of time were logistical but very real issues that had to be resolved. Of course, length was also a factor. To include a chapter about every historian who might have merited one would have simply made the length of this work prohibitive. It is thus quite possible that some of the giants of Southern history left out of this book might form the basis for a subsequent volume of *Reading Southern History*. Indeed, a strong case can be made for several historians who were not ultimately included in this volume.

It is my hope that this book will be useful, not only to specialists in Southern history, but also to those interested, more broadly, in American history and to graduate students and scholars from a variety of disciplines, to libraries, and to the ever-elusive, but certainly real, general educated readership. Thus far, the two principal historiographical works in the field of Southern history have been arranged by topic. In 1965, Arthur S. Link and Rembert W. Patrick's *Writing Southern History* appeared.[2] Twenty-two years later John B. Boles and Evelyn Thomas Nolen caught us up on two decades of historical innovation by giving us *Interpreting Southern History*.[3] While it would be presumptuous to suggest that this volume should share such illustrious company, I do hope that *Reading Southern History*, a historiographical work organized by author, will serve to complement the work that has come before.

That said, a number of themes emerge from the following essays. First, a concern with plain Southern whites appears over and over in the writings of many of our subjects. Junius P. Rodriguez specifically criticizes U. B. Phillips for not including plain whites in his analyses of the Old South, while Jacquelyn Dowd Hall tells us that Broadus Mitchell wrestled with his suspicion and fear of a Bleasite demagogy that pandered to poor textile workers and, consequently, placed his faith in a first generation of Carolina mill owners. This was a curious stance for a confirmed socialist to take and, as Hall demonstrates, Mitchell had increasing difficulty reconciling this faith with his private and deeply held beliefs. John Shelton Reed and Daniel Joseph Singal explain that Rupert Vance's interest in finding the causes and solutions of the South's regional problems (disease, poverty, cultural stagnation, et al.), many of which afflicted poor whites—as well as his frustration with a "cotton culture complex," monoagriculture, and a "colonial economy"—led him to strive for theory and generalizations, and to forsake mere description. Tony Carey credits Frank L. Owsley for stimulating and exciting the study of common whites; in fact, for redeeming the yeoman from the oblivion of historical obscurity. But Carey also strongly criticizes Owsley for disregarding race, minimizing class, being oblivious to gender, and thus painting a Pollyanna-type view of "economic democracy" in the Old South. Fred Arthur Bailey skillfully explores the influences of Theodore Bilbo's appeal to Mississippi's "rednecks" and "mudsills" in altering the history that Charles S. Sydnor ultimately produced. The extent of a rural survey project in New Deal Georgia on C. Vann Woodward's intellectual development is well known, but John Herbert Roper's probing essay more deeply demonstrates patrician Woodward's lifelong fascination with the South's rural plain folk and their periodic uprisings against their class "betters." One of W. J. Cash's most important contributions to Southern historiography, Bruce Clayton implies in his important essay in this volume, was the conception of a proto-Dorian consensus or bond, that is, the recurrent predilection of common whites to forsake biracial class action in order to ally with the South's "better" whites. Doing so, Cash argued (and others agreed) thus blinded these whites to their "real interests."[4]

Yet neither Cash nor many other historians of labor or plain whites (including Cash's most serious rival, C. Vann Woodward), have adequately considered the possibility that the "real interests" of common whites might have constituted more than just their class interests. The "real interests" of plain whites (poor whites, workers, yeomen, and tenants) might very well have been a broad and ever-shifting amalgam of class, racial, and even other interests that changed at any given time and place in Southern history. That is, in any specific time and place in the South, the "real interests" of plain whites may indeed have lain in making a common alliance with blacks against white bosses and planters. But, in other settings, plain whites may have consciously calculated that their "real" or genuine interests lay elsewhere; specifically, in the social and psychological acts of maintaining white supremacy, the racial status quo, Jim Crow, and even the perpetual repression of blacks. Plain whites, in other words, may have purposely calculated that racial solidarity was in their "real interests" more so than class solidarity that cut across racial lines—thus an alliance with their white "betters"—no matter how distasteful and disastrous such a course now appears to the historian. In those instances that they did (instances in which often the bosses profited more so than any other actors), plain whites were more the authors of their own eventual demise than the mere victims of circumstance. During these junctures common whites followed a conscious conception of what they considered to be their "real interests"—only it was an estimation of their real interests that might differ considerably from that of the historians.

Race is also a major theme, arguably "the" major theme, represented in the work, collectively speaking, of the South's notable interpreters here under review. It figures prominently throughout this volume in the works of Phillips, Coulter, Du Bois, Vance, Sydnor, Cash, Woodward, Key, Franklin, Potter, Donald, Stampp, Tindall, Scott, and Hill. U. B. Phillips, of course, addressed race in his exploration of slavery's incredible importance for the region in working out, during the antebellum era, the South's main characteristics and essential personality. He revisited the issue in his famous 1928 explication of race as the "central theme" of Southern history.[5] As Kari Frederickson reminds us, V. O. Key identified white supremacy and the place of "the Negro" as the most important element in the politics of the "Solid South." A concern with maintaining white supremacy was obviously a critical component for Cash and his proto-Dorian bond, as it was for Vernon Wharton's, Tindall's and Woodward's similar theses of Jim Crow's strange career, W. E. B. Du Bois's, John Hope Franklin's, and Kenneth Stampp's revisions of Reconstruction, E. Merton Coulter's and Charles Sydnor's early defenses of the South, and Samuel S. Hill's ongoing attempt to understand and explain Southern religion and its importance in the region's overall culture. As John White's essay relates, Franklin—despite his insistence, increasing over time, that he is a historian of the South, broadly understood—has clearly focused on the special problems, issues, and concerns of the black experience within the crucible of the American South.[6]

Relatedly, a race-versus-class debate underlies much of what is in the present volume, that is, an ongoing argument concerning the relative importance of race and class in influencing the course of Southern history in a variety of places and time periods. In matters of labor, ever since Herbert Hill's caustic 1988 attack on Herbert Gutman's romantic account of coal miner biracialism in the Deep South, a race-class debate has energized and almost characterized the subfield of Southern labor history. Following Gutman's lead, a good number of labor historians have defended a notion of Southern union biracialism that has some validity, but is still clearly romanticized as well. Compelling dissent has appeared not only in the form of Herbert Hill, but also in the works of Bruce Nelson, Nell Irvin Painter, Robert J. Norrell, and others (most recently David P. Roediger and the practitioners of an emerging school of "whiteness" studies). The argument is not likely to be resolved anytime soon, despite the appearance of more sophisticated and less exclusive ways of looking at the problem.[7] But the issue is present in the work of many of the masters of Southern history present in this volume—especially in matters of the Old South. Tony Carey, in his essay on Frank Owsley, instructs us in the Marxist arguments of class conflict identified with Eugene Genovese and Steven Hahn versus those that recognize the primacy of race: the works of Mills Thornton, James Oakes, J. William Harris, and Lacy K. Ford, Jr., for example. Carey criticizes Owsley for not putting *Plain Folk* at the center of such a debate, but Oakes is more forgiving of Kenneth Stampp's absolute renunciation of a place for race in his analyses of the antebellum South.

The history of the New South, the post-1865 South specifically, is of course influenced mightily by racial concerns. While race remains the most important key to understanding the region's history, the issue runs deeper and broader than that—solely. In fact, much of the post-1865 South can be understood in terms of the chronic appearance of what may be termed a *Reconstruction Syndrome*—a set of powerful negative attitudes that have shaped Southern history and culture for more than a hundred years. The attitudes that make up this syndrome, fortified by race, were originally born of the psychological trauma of military defeat, occupation, abolition, and the forcible imposition of a new political order. After the initial trauma, the syndrome has repeatedly manifested itself in the South—rising to the surface most clearly during times of acute stress. As a result, for more than a century after the Reconstruction trauma, the dominant white, Anglo-Saxon, Protestant South was largely distinguished and distinguishable by the syndrome's recurring component tendencies: very strong antiblack, anti–federal government, antiliberal, anti–Yankee, and anti–outsider/foreigner beliefs that translated into little tolerance for diversity. The Second Reconstruction cemented and personalized these beliefs in the minds of a new generation of white Southerners and their children. To a large extent, these unfortunate tendencies still persist at, or just under, the surface of the present-day South—shaping and coloring the region's approach to politics, economics, and social mores. Often, these tendencies appear in softer, sanitized, and more euphemistic forms. Yet appear they still do, as an almost manic concern for states' rights, local autonomy, individual freedom, political conservatism, sectional pride, traditional values, religion, and gender roles—in fact, reverence for all things traditional, including pride in the white race's leadership and achievements, disdain for hyphenated Americanism in favor of ethnic, racial, and cultural homogeneity: in sum, for all of the things that "made this country great."

Indeed, historians must continue to be aware of the vitally important relationship between race, class, and politics—especially in Southern history. Race and class have often been so closely bound in the region's history that to speak of them now as completely separate entities is to disentangle them with such force that the historian risks doing irreparable damage to both concepts—and thus speaking about what are basically artificial and incomplete constructs. As historians expand the scope of political inquiry to streets, stores, households, parlors, and train stations, they must continue to ask "who gets what, when, and how" and, perhaps most important, "why?" Southern history—including the recent Southern past and indeed the present—is largely distinguished by the skillful, in fact ingenious, manipulation of ingrained plain-white emotions (principally over race, but also *God and Country issues:* abortion, prayer in schools, patriotism, guns, the confederate flag, monuments, and others). We must keep sight of the fact that some Southerners—elite white Southerners—have proven more adept at using the regional preoccupation with race, Reconstruction, and related emotional issues to preserve their privileged status in a rigidly stratified and hierarchical society. Most recently this has been the province of the newly ascendant—even dominant—Southern GOP.

The staple of continuity versus discontinuity appears often in these pages in relation to whites and blacks, class and race, regional culture and sectional distinctiveness. Phillips, Mitchell, Cash, Owsley, and Key stand as monuments to the thesis of continuity while Woodward and Potter teach us that disunity, discontinuity, and even unpredictability have a strong tradition in the region's history as well. George Brown Tindall's work, as the essay by Susan Youngblood Ashmore demonstrates, embodied a profound appreciation of the dialectical nature of Southern history: the combination of both continuity and change as the result of periodic clashes between thesis and antithesis. Samuel Hill's career is also instructive. Ted Ownby's searching essay describes how the young Hill, so certain early on of religious continuity in Dixie, has, in recent years, come over more and more to a notion of change and, actually, of diversity.

The importance of mentorship and scholarly influence on these historiographical titans cannot fail to be impressed on any reader. All of the figures within this volume became influential through a combination of hard work, ambition, insight, perseverance, innovation, and brilliance at their craft. But it is striking that so many also benefited, especially early in their careers, from the springboard provided by an influential mentor: teachers who exercised influence both on the young scholar and the profession at large. It is difficult at best to have work appreciated, no matter how innovative, path-breaking, or valuable, unless a budding scholar is given a hearing. That point is nowhere more apparent than in Judith N. McArthur's exposition on A. Elizabeth Taylor. The advantage of influential mentors no doubt gained many of these young scholars an initial hearing for their bold and often irreverent theses. The rest was, of course, up to them, the quality of their work, and the open-mindedness of the profession. Still, the collective mentorship of our subjects here—an almost royal lineage—is striking: U. B. Phillips by Frederick Jackson Turner and William Archibald Dunning; Broadus Mitchell by Elizabeth Gilman; E. Merton Coulter by J. G. de Roulhac Hamilton and U. B. Phillips; Frank Lawrence Owsley by William E. Dodd; W. E. B. Du Bois by Max Weber and other German sociologists; Rupert Vance by Howard W. Odum, H. L. Mencken, and U. B. Phillips; V. O. Key by Charles E. Merriam and Roscoe C. Martin; John Hope Franklin by Arthur M. Schlesinger, Sr., and Paul Buck; Elizabeth Taylor and George Tindall by Fletcher M. Green; David Potter by U. B. Phillips; David Herbert Donald by Vernon Wharton, James G. Randall, and Allan Nevins; Anne Scott by Oscar Handlin; and Vann Woodward by virtually everyone—uncle Comer Woodward, Will Alexander, Glenn W. Rainey, Will T. Couch, Howard Odum and the Regionalists at Chapel Hill, Robert Penn Warren, Cleanth Brooks, and the Vanderbilt Agrarians, Howard K. Beale and Beardian analysis, and later through friendships with Langston Hughes, David Potter, Richard Hofstadter, Kenneth Stampp, John Hope Franklin, Reinhold Niehbuhr, and others. Jack Roper writes also in his chapter on Woodward of another side to this phenomenon: the importance of producing influential students in order to provide the air with which to keep one's kite high in the fickle skies of Southern and American historiography. Perhaps just as striking is the remarkable and persistent influence that Northern schools of higher learning have exercised on the study of Southern history—most notably Harvard, Yale, Columbia, Wisconsin, Johns Hopkins, and the University of Chicago.

Sheer longevity, in conjunction of course with incredible productivity, is also a hallmark found in these pages. Besides providing the physical opportunity for these ambitious scholars to achieve historiographical greatness, in many cases longevity also supplied our subjects with the advantages of perspective and the chance to observe and adapt to changing historiographical vogues and trends. In fact, of our eighteen subjects only W. J. Cash and, to a markedly lesser extent, V. O. Key and David Potter can be identified as having had their careers cut short by untimely deaths. In contrast, what is remarkable is how long most of these historians lived and, more important, how productive they managed to be for so long.

Unbounded passion for the historical subject of choice—with a frequent tendency to overstatement—also distinguishes our collection of notable interpreters of the South. This was not overstatement for the sake of overstatement, of course, but rather overstatement in order to make a point. Part of this derives from the intrinsic passion with which our subjects attacked their areas of interest, but it also stems from the nature of the historical beasts with which they wrestled. By and large these scholars were not echoing conventional wisdoms, nor were they engaged in what some have described as "historical landfill," the mere gathering of evidence for already-established interpretations. The vast majority of our subjects were dealing in revision; in some cases in the actual re-ordering of history. Naturally, recognizing excessive passion and overstatement in one another has proven to be much easier for our subjects than actually avoiding it in their own scholarship. The late C. Vann Woodward, in an oft-noted essay entitled "The Elusive Mind of the South," concluded that what W. J. Cash "at his best . . . was really . . . saying" was that despite the revolution—any revolution—Southerners, like the French, the English, and the Russians, remained Southern. "Only," Woodward lamented, Cash "rather overdid the thing." In a word, his argument was "extravagant."[8] The same, however, can just as easily be said about Woodward, not in his assessment of Cash as he may have feared, but in his own work on such matters as the extent of the Populists' liberalism on the race question and on the fluidity of race relations during the late nineteenth century (as his friend David Potter realized). A similar complaint can be lodged against U. B. Phillips for his reliance on race as a determinative factor, Kenneth Stampp for his choice of class, E. Merton Coulter for his slavish devotion to the mythology of the "Lost Cause," Frank Owsley for his somewhat idyllic depiction of plain folk, and Anne Scott for a too-flattering picture of the suffragists she studied. In fact, of all our subjects, as the perceptive essay by David and Jeanne Heidler makes clear, perhaps David Potter is least guilty of the charge of exaggeration. But, in retrospect, overstatement appears less a charge than a badge—a characteristic, an inevitable attribute of most of those who have contributed the greatest insight into our search for an understanding of the Southern past.

Perhaps as important as passion has been the power of the works here under review to inspire further inquiry. Because of the seminal nature of their work, and the works of some who were not included in this volume, there is no need to fear an end to Southern history anytime soon. Everything has not been worked out. New evidence, new techniques, new perspectives, new insights, new ways of looking at old evidence, new questions, and new concerns all guarantee that our understanding of the Southern past will continue to grow deeper, richer, and fuller with the passing of time.[9]

Civil rights historiography furnishes a good example in this regard. In recent years civil rights scholars, to their credit, have begun to realize that "the movement" did not begin with the 1954 *Brown v. Board of Education* decision, nor even with the 1955–1956 Montgomery Bus Boycott.[10] These events—tangible, visceral, concrete, dramatic—provide a tempting place of demarcation for scholars trying to make sense and order of a turbulent time. But recent scholars have traced the movement back at least to the 1930s, and some even earlier.[11] This "backing up" of the movement represents an advance in scholarship. But it is also readily possible to trace violent white supremacist reaction back to the 1930s and before. Traditionally, "civil rights" has been understood as the drive for increased rights among blacks, women, and ethnic, religious, and other minorities. But, actually, it is best understood as a two-sided coin: the drive for civil rights *and* the militant reaction against it, the *dark side of the civil rights coin*. It is difficult to understand either side fully without reference to the other. And it is difficult to understand the evolution of opposition to bigoted groups without also considering the parallel growth of societal tolerance of diversity.[12]

The future of Southern history guaranteed, it should also be said that the field would almost certainly profit from moving in the direction of greater inclusiveness of currently specialized fields of inquiry: women's history, black history, working-class history, ethnic studies, Native American studies, et al. Such specialized fields were, in large part, the children of the increased sensitivity and inclusiveness spawned by the 1960s reforms of women and African-Americans and an appreciation for cultural diversity, both very useful and necessary first steps in getting these fields inaugurated and established. The subfields were born with good intentions—to include important topics that had been all but ignored, to everyone's detriment, up until that time—and the results have been good. Southern history defined as white, male, Anglo-Saxon, Protestant history became exposed as limiting and delimiting during the 1960s. Women and men pioneered new and important avenues of research and inquiry that broadly and deeply expanded the limits of our knowledge, not only in Southern history but in all kinds of other history as well.

The challenge that awaits us now is to embrace these disparate subfields in a better and fuller sense—not just to tolerate the fact of their existence as separate routes of inquiry, even separate legitimate and mature routes. We need real inclusiveness: synthesizing the contributions of these subfields as part of a more comprehensive, general understanding of historical events and movements. Just as history should include more of the best that the social sciences can offer, history should not slight the best contributions of its own subfields. Left alone in magnificent isolation, specialized subfields invite eventual consignment to irrelevance, especially by those who are most hostile to them in the first place. That would be regrettable. As Southern history marches ineluctably forward, its students must be wary of the pitfall of continued balkanization of the field, or of any type of history for that matter. Such fragmentation, though certainly not the fault of the practitioners of the "new" histories, is the sign of a discipline not yet fully mature, and of understandings only partial. Southern historians should set as their goal as complete an understanding of the past as the discipline will allow, given the limits imposed on us by "soft sciences" such as the social science of historical inquiry.

Of the disparate post-1960s subfields, perhaps women's history and the "new Southern political history" have come further along the essential maturation process than any others, as revealed in the chapters in this collection on A. Elizabeth Taylor and Anne Scott. As Judith McArthur shows in her essay on Taylor, the first step in the pioneering process is trail-blazing a new field; staking it out as an area of legitimate historical inquiry; salvaging the parcel from the vast frontier of historical neglect. Such was the contribution of A. Elizabeth Taylor. Anastatia Sims's essay on Anne Scott delineates the next stage of the maturation process, the transcendence of hagiography, romance, and celebration of neglected historical actors to a more nuanced analysis that weighs their pros and cons, attributes, and shortcomings.

As Sims demonstrates, women's history has now been well assimilated into the mainstream of historical inquiry, besides staking out its own space as a legitimate and mature enterprise. Other subjects spawned by the 1960s "new social history" of neglected groups have not matured as quickly and are still marked by a rather defensive denial of the human nature (and shortcomings) of their historical subjects. The "new Southern labor history" has had a prolonged adolescence in this regard—most notably because of the militant refusal of many of its practitioners to admit the obvious (and, by the way, expected) shortcomings of its human subjects on matters such as racial enlightenment (or the lack thereof). In far too much of the new Southern labor history, we find competent studies of labor movements, but a distressing lack of awareness of, or refusal to note, even the most basic characteristics of *Southern* history, including an understanding of Southern distinctiveness and an acknowledgment of the vast importance of race. Because admitting Southern distinctiveness and the importance of race might, in some way, undermine the Marxist theory and economic determinism upon which so much of the new Southern labor history rests, too many of its practitioners have been loathe to admit the very human shortcomings of their protagonists.[13] But organized labor's struggle for enhanced industrial democracy was intrinsically noble. Noble enough, in fact, not to require embellishment now beyond the bounds of credulity—or reality.

More realism and less hagiography and romance is also to be hoped for as Southern historians confront the twenty-first century. Passion is essential to the writing of good history, as we have seen. But like anything else a delicate balance must be struck with detachment, objectivity, and perspective. It is difficult for the historian to view a subject with anything approaching objectivity if detached perspective is not also present. If the historian is too close to the subject, either in time or in sentiment, the degree of objectivity possible in a humanity/social science like history is lessened. The essential integrity of the enterprise runs the risk of being corrupted—or at least compromised. Studies of repressed or excluded groups are especially vulnerable on this score because many who write this kind of history are more homogeneous in their beliefs than scholars in other subfields. Quite often, practitioners are attracted to this kind of history in the first place because of definite beliefs and principles— prejudices and biases in less polite terms. They are convinced that the movements for greater and fuller inclusiveness were and are inherently good. Those convictions may make good politics and good social policy, but they do not always make good history. Some measure of detachment is fundamental. In Southern labor studies, for example, some counterpoint to the prevailing Marxist or neo-Marxist perspective by moderate, or at least traditionally liberal, voices is obviously needed. In its absence, there has been a tendency for practitioners to impose a canon of political correctness on the inquiry that performs a disservice to historical accuracy. A peril that is unfortunately all too pervasive is the "halo effect"; this is especially common in the study of traditionally repressed or ignored groups.

Relatedly, one thing that the essays in this volume should make fairly clear is that Dixie is a distinctive region from the rest of the country—an observation that is in some ways a built-in survival mechanism for the region's history. In this volume, the notion of Southern distinctiveness is perhaps most clearly illustrated in the chapters on Phillips, Cash, Woodward, Key, Tindall, and

Hill. As with England, there will always be an American South, whether it is understood as hotter, wetter, poorer, or more tragic, patriotic, militant, religious, polite, violent, conservative, honor conscious, or racially divided as well as racially cooperative than the rest of the country.[14] Southern distinctiveness may seem an obvious concept to many, but it will increasingly come under assault as the years pass and study of the region persists.

History's great weakness is a lack of theory—the tendency toward an ad hoc cataloguing of events that lends itself to a relativism of interpretations and a world where all conclusions are, at least potentially, equally viable. Southern history is no exception, although that is now changing. Its present and future practitioners must strive toward continuing to incorporate a more theoretical basis into the region's history, for without theory we lose sight of the exception that proves the rule. To this end, the South's historians should continue efforts to integrate history with sister disciplines such as sociology, psychology, anthropology, political science, economics, rural agronomy, geography, and demography. The great strength of history (detailed knowledge of past events and trends) must be matched with the great strength of the social sciences (theory and a general understanding of isolated events) in order to avoid the endemic weaknesses of both: history's lack of theory and tendency toward relativism and social science's identity crisis and unhappiness with not being as airtight a science as the "hard sciences." In a hard science (physics, biology, or chemistry, for example) one exception to the rule is devastating to that rule. If one apple refuses to fall to the ground after falling from a tree, the theory of gravity is seriously impaired, perhaps even invalidated. Not so in history. This is because in history we deal with innately different subject matter; in fact, subject matter that is "subjective"—human actors with an inherently unpredictable human will.[15] One exception, or two, or three, or even more may, in fact, serve to strengthen a general theory in the humanities and "soft" social sciences by illustrating just how accurate that theory is—in *most* cases.

Not only is the subject matter qualitatively different in a humanistic discipline such as history, but also the nature of the researcher—replete with bias, whim, predisposition, and caprice—holds the capacity for influencing the course and result of humanistic inquiry in a way altogether unlike inquiry in the hard sciences. Charles Sydnor intuitively realized that the biases of historical researchers exercised powerful influences on the choice of topics, evidence, character, and interpretation for all historians, including Southern historians. The process by which the historian is led to undertake the study of history, Fred Bailey quotes Sydnor elsewhere in this volume, "needs to be sketched . . . because whatever awakened his interest . . . may well have determined the nature and bent of that interest."[16] John Hope Franklin realized that this characteristic of historical inquiry held special relevance for Southern historians.

"Having failed to establish a separate nation and having gone down to defeat on the field of battle," John White quotes Franklin in his chapter of this book, "Southerners . . . turned their attention to their own past with a concentration so great that the cult of history became a permanent and important ingredient of the Southern culture. . . . [T]he writing of history became an act of sectional allegiance and devotion. . . . If the South has often reacted churlishly and shortsightedly, the fault does not lie with history itself, but with a distorted historical tradition of which even the South's historians have been victims, but which only they can correct."[17]

Technological and computer advancement is likewise not the salvation of Southern history nor any other type of humanistic inquiry. It is a tool, a valuable tool, a cliometric tool, a tool that can vastly enhance our understanding of social phenomena—but a tool nonetheless. As society's technological capabilities become even more impressive and more accessible, there will be a powerful temptation for scholars to utilize the latest information technologies simply for the purpose of utilizing them—or for the purpose of generating data with cutting-edge technologies. But if quantification becomes an end in itself, it will push history down a road of self-deception that political science and sociology have already traveled.

While Internet history discussion lists have allowed for the timely discussion of important topics and dissemination of news, information about professional activities, and findings, there is a definite downside. Too often the discussion of historical themes is thin, impressionistic, and self-promotional because of the pseudo-published nature of Internet communications. In an age in which technology now allows us to write "instant history" via the net, we must be aware that much of what makes it on to such lists lacks the rigor, carefulness, and evidentiary foundation of closely researched, detailed, documented monographic work. Yet Internet impressions are often stated, and sometimes received, with the same or even greater degree of assurance as the conclusions of scholars who have spent years unearthing and carefully analyzing primary documents.

These are some of the challenges that await present and future historians of the South—challenges that, it is likely, will eventually be met and overcome. In doing so, much solace and guidance can be taken from the subjects under review in this book. They too confronted the intimidating experience of dealing with seemingly overwhelming historiographical status quos as well as the daunting task of wrestling with unforeseen developments in historical methods and objectives. Accepting these challenges and working through them, as did our subjects here, can ultimately only increase the quality and depth of our understanding of the Southern past. And that is an end worth pursuing.

Ulrich Bonnell Phillips and the Beginnings of Southern History

JUNIUS P. RODRIGUEZ

According to William Shakespeare's account, friends and foes of Julius Caesar eulogized the fallen Roman leader in the wake of his murder at the hands of conspiratorial assassins. Mark Antony, a personal friend and admirer of Caesar, allegedly used his funeral oration to remark, "The evil that men do lives after them, the good is oft interred with their bones; so let it be with Caesar."[1] It matters not whether these remarks are authentic, apocryphal, or merely a fictive literary passage, for the salient truth found within this maxim resonates throughout time and the human experience. Unfortunately, the remembrance of one's failures and shortcomings all too often affects public consciousness to a greater degree than the inspiring legacy of past achievements. Memory, although the mother of inspiration, certainly has the capacity to sully reputations and diminish one's true importance over time.

Though it might seem unwise to compare the import of a departed historian like Ulrich Bonnell Phillips to that of a fallen Caesar, the unique qualities of the human condition do make such an assessment possible. The commonalties associated with the manner in which one's historical legacy endures beyond death do serve as a communal leveler linking the great and the small. In an ironic sense, the social egalitarianism that is often seemingly impossible to achieve in life finds expression in the silent domain of the departed.

To many in the historical profession, the death of U. B. Phillips on January 21, 1934, after an extended bout with throat cancer, marked not merely the passing of an eminent historian, but rather the demise of an interpretive school of Southern historiography that Phillips himself had created though his prodigious writings.[2] It quickly became fashionable for many historians to distance themselves from Phillips's ideas because blatant racism tinged his interpretations and his uncritical use of sources was called into question by some. For an entire generation after his death, Phillips was demonized within the historical profession by those who asserted that his scholarship had produced a one-sided, one-dimensional, distorted portrayal of antebellum Southern history. These a priori charges continued unabated until the December 1966 meeting of the American Historical Association when Eugene D. Genovese launched the scholarly resurrection of Phillips's work.[3]

Much like Saint Paul's admonition to early Christians that they must hate sin, but love the sinner, Genovese's challenge to the historical community in 1966 encouraged a continuing disavowal of Phillips's conclusions while urging renewed respect for the perceptive recognition of class differences found within Phillips's flawed interpretations. Much of the scholarship on race relations in the antebellum South produced in the past three decades has recognized the path-breaking ideas that Phillips first enunciated, but failed to develop adequately, in *American Negro Slavery* (1918) and *Life and Labor in the Old South* (1929). Despite the flawed racist interpretations that sprang from Phillips's methodology, Genovese maintained that Phillips might well have been the greatest American historian of the twentieth century. According to Genovese, "we may leave to those who live in the world of absolute good and evil the task of explaining how a man with such primitive views on fundamental social questions could write such splendid history."[4]

Much of twentieth-century scholarship of the history of the United States has focused on the question of race and its role in formulating and defining American society and culture. Perhaps as a natural corollary to this issue, much scholarship in recent generations has examined the institution of slavery and the consequences that it made manifest upon the social landscape of American history. Any effort to understand the merits of the historiographical debate that has resulted from this outpouring of research activity must be framed in an awareness of the basic presuppositions that were first formulated from the pen and the mind of Ulrich B. Phillips.

A constant theme that resonates in Phillips's work is the central notion that white supremacy and the ever-present nature of a biracial society are fundamental factors that define Southern identity and dictate power relationships in the region. Not only does Phillips view this as being central to Southern history, but he also posits this as an unchanging element embedded in the regional ethos of the South.[5]

As a result, subsequent scholarship on slavery and race relations has used Phillips's dogmatic "line in the sand" as a starting point from which to fashion revisionist interpretations that seek either to repudiate outright or to soften the certitude of Phillips's pronouncements. Scholars including Kenneth Stampp, Stanley Elkins, Eugene Genovese, John Blassingame, and others have found the genesis of their interpretations in a reconsideration and reevaluation of Phillips's ideas. Even C. Vann Woodward's introduction to *The Strange Career of Jim Crow* acknowledged the ubiquitous presence of Phillips's "central theme" in the intellectual origins of institutional racism in the twentieth-century South.[6]

The ideas of few historians can be described as being essential to an understanding of American life and culture, but U. B. Phillips's scholarship merits such an assessment. Accordingly, it is important to consider how his own social and intellectual growth contributed to the ideas that he enshrined in his works.

I

Phillips was born on November 4, 1877, in the west-central Georgia community of LaGrange. His family ancestry can be traced to antebellum-era slave owners as both of his grandparents had owned human chattel in Troup County, Georgia. One might argue that Phillips's birth in 1877, the year when the last federal troops left the South upon the conclusion of Congressionally mandated Military Reconstruction, marked the passing of an era, but such an assertion would belie the very fashion in which Phillips the historian would later view the South. Rather than debating subtle gradations of continuity and change that might mark passing eras, Phillips instead viewed the South as an unchanging, monolithic society that could be defined through constant themes within the social sciences. Accordingly, race relations was writ large in Phillips's mind as the dominant theme of Southern history, and he would use his scholarly career and the developing techniques of scientific historical inquiry to attempt to prove this thesis.[7]

Though he was a man of the New South, Phillips could never escape the aura of the Old South. He once remarked that "our minds are the resultant of the experiences of those who gave us birth and rearing."[8] Throughout his career elements of the mythic South permeated not only Phillips's scholarship, but also his very life. Friends and colleagues described him as a true gentleman of the Southern genteel tradition, some noted that he exuded an aristocratic sense of noblesse oblige in all public and personal affairs, and still others found him to be a bit of a dilettante. Although he eventually became a brilliant scholar with a work ethic that was certainly remarkable, there always seemed to be a sense of historical anachronism present that limited his greatness.

Phillips's love of the South was both real and symbolic. When he was twelve years old he took the name Ulrich because his given name, Ulysses, reminded him too much of the Northern commander who had been a scourge upon the South during the recent unpleasantness. Phillips had been named in honor of the doctor who assisted at his birth, but his sense of Southern honor, both real and imagined, would not permit any confusion on matters as important as regional allegiance. For Phillips, such a perceptive concern over a potentially symbolic affective response was indeed appropriate for one who was born and bred in the Southland and reared upon the ethos of a bygone era.[9]

II

Although the Phillips family was not exceptionally wealthy, and the brutal economic realities of the post–Civil War world taxed family resources even further, Ulrich's mother and father both recognized the value of a quality education and saw to it that their son received the best possible instruction. While Ulrich took his elementary training in the local school in LaGrange, his parents did not believe that such schooling would adequately prepare him for advanced study at the university level. Accordingly, at the age of fourteen Phillips left LaGrange to attend the Tulane Preparatory School in New Orleans, Louisiana, a boarding school that would give the young Georgian an intensive training in the liberal arts and sciences. Besides providing Phillips with skills in languages, mathematics, and composition, his two years of schooling in New Orleans provided him with a healthy spirit of independence and a more cosmopolitan, urbane outlook than he likely would have cultivated in rural Georgia.[10]

In 1893, Ulrich B. Phillips returned home to enroll as a freshman at the University of Georgia in Athens. It was at Athens that Phillips developed a passionate interest in history under the tutelage of Professor John H. T. McPherson, an early disciple of the methodology known as "scientific history." McPherson had studied at Johns Hopkins University under Herbert Baxter Adams, and he inspired his students to value the historical methodology of delving into primary materials, asking the perceptive questions, and cogently interpreting upon the basis of one's findings. McPherson found Phillips to be "progressive and ambitious . . . a young man of unusual promise," and he encouraged him to pursue work in history at the master's level when he completed his undergraduate studies.[11]

While at Johns Hopkins, McPherson had met a fellow graduate student named Frederick Jackson Turner, and both men earned doctoral degrees in 1890. In 1893, Turner presented a paper entitled "The Significance of the Frontier in American History" at the annual meeting of the American Historical Association, and the paper was published the following year in the *American Historical Review*. The sensational reception of Turner's work gave him instant celebrity within the profession and elevated the position of environmental determinism to newfound heights within the realm of historical causation. At McPherson's urging, Phillips became a willing disciple to Turner's methodology, and in response, Turner became a lifelong mentor to the budding young scholar from Georgia.[12]

III

Phillips began to correspond with Turner regarding the thesis topic that he was researching on politics in antebellum Georgia, and Turner offered perceptive advice on the subject. When Phillips learned that Turner would teach summer-term classes at the University of Chicago in 1898, he managed to find the resources to travel to Chicago to participate in a seminar and a course on frontier history. The bond that formed would last a lifetime, and in effect, Turner became a *de facto* adviser to Phillips as he completed his master's work at the University of Georgia. Phillips would later praise Turner by writing that his purpose "was to stimulate and exhilarate young scholars in a way to make them stimulate others, and so on in a ripple which though it must lessen in the lapse of time and the spread of space, never quite reaches an end."[13]

Phillips shared draft copies with Turner as he completed chapters of his master's thesis, and Turner offered suggestions that Phillips incorporated into his revisions. For example, it was Turner who suggested that Phillips use maps to offer both spatial and environmental insight into changing voting patterns from antebellum Georgia elections. In addition to drawing ideas and moral support from Turner, Phillips scoured the archival sources available at the University of Georgia to produce a thesis drawn almost entirely from primary materials. When Phillips completed his master's work and decided to pursue a doctoral degree, he relied heavily upon the advice that McPherson and Turner had to offer as to the best program in which he should enroll. Both men agreed that, while Johns Hopkins had an excellent program, Columbia University had established one of the preeminent history departments in the country. They suggested that Phillips apply there to continue his studies.

It was at Columbia that Phillips came into contact with another historian who would prove to have significant influence upon his career. William Archibald Dunning agreed to direct Phillips's dissertation, which was to be a study of antebellum Georgia politics. Dunning's primary research interest at the time involved a revisionist pro-Southern view of the Reconstruction era that he and his graduate students developed in the form of several state studies that appeared as monographs. So profound was his influence that the "Dunning School" of historiography dominated all studies of Reconstruction well into the mid-twentieth century.[14] Yet, Phillips had no particular interest in this period of history, primarily because he had already come to the conclusion that the antebellum era was the formative period in which all pertinent Southern attitudes and mores had come into existence. In Phillips's view, such studies of the Reconstruction era were somewhat superfluous, and, while he might agree with the findings of the Dunning-inspired scholars, it was Phillips's belief that the antebellum South was the area that needed to be mined with the tools of scientific historical methodology.

Phillips proved to be a capable graduate student, but he tended to devote his energies only to those issues and concerns that mattered to him. Dunning later observed that Phillips had a "tendency to slight work that is not just to his taste," but also countered that "he is most indefatigable in a field that attracts him." Phillips respected Dunning as a scholar and urged other students to take courses with him "for the sake of getting his method," but in Phillips's mind, Frederick Jackson Turner remained the single most important scholarly influence on his work.[15]

In 1901 Phillips completed his dissertation, "Georgia and State Rights," and at Dunning's urging, he submitted it for consideration for the American Historical Association's Justin Winsor Prize. Phillips won the prize and the association published the manuscript in 1902. With his Ph.D. in hand by 1902 and having won a major prize in the field, Phillips set out to find a teaching position where he might settle into the professional work of teaching, research, and writing for which he had trained so diligently.[16]

IV

The professional relationship that Phillips had cultivated with Frederick Jackson Turner over a six-year period proved to be a wise one when the University of Wisconsin-Madison hired Phillips to be a Lecturer in American History in 1902. There were many forces that drew Phillips to Madison. The state of Wisconsin and, in particular, the University of Wisconsin-Madison were the cultural center of American progressivism, and as a scholar who delved into the methodology of progressive or "scientific" history, Phillips believed that he had found the ideal institution to begin his professional career as a historian. Certainly the opportunity to work as a colleague in the same department with Turner, who was still the leading American historian of his age, was a calling that Phillips could not ignore. Additionally, Turner gave Phillips the latitude to create new course offerings including one of the first courses on Southern history ever offered at an American university. Phillips also found the archival holdings both of the university and of the state to be quite rich with materials pertinent to Southern history. As he had done earlier in Georgia, Phillips quickly mined these sources to find materials that could promote his research interests.[17]

At Wisconsin-Madison, Phillips was also a colleague of the noted sociologist Edward Alsworth Ross, who joined the university's economics department in 1906. Although entrenched attitudes of racial superiority were common to both scholars, there is little to indicate that either influenced the other's intellectual outlook. What is more likely is that Phillips learned from Ross the value of world travel as a means of collecting data to document theoretical formulations.[18] Ross, much like Columbia University's Franz Boas, the dean of twentieth-century anthropology, made the world his research laboratory and traveled quite extensively.[19] Phillips's eventual travels to Africa can thus be better understood as he claimed to observe "something of a primitive life . . . least disturbed [which] broadened my knowledge of Negro traits"—certainly a perspective unique to early twentieth-century American scholars of slavery.[20]

There is another important characteristic of Phillips's career as a historian that developed during his years in Madison. Phillips's familiarity with the source materials that he had at hand in Wisconsin is noteworthy in two particular respects. First, he used his skills at networking to make other scholars around the country aware of the materials that he had culled in his own research. In doing so, Phillips made himself not just another junior faculty member at another Midwestern university, but he quickly established a reputation for himself as a scholar who had connections and resources at his disposal. In essence, he found a way to make his mark on the profession. Second, it was through his experience in Madison that Phillips developed another skill at which his success became legendary. Phillips developed his skills as an antiquarian and eventually identified, purchased, and sold archival materials that for generations had remained in private hands. Phillips may well have been inspired to this task by his work with the Lyman Draper Collection that was housed at the Wisconsin Historical Society Library. Draper had scoured the country during the nineteenth century purchasing a wide variety of private papers that became the basis of the Society's archival holdings. Phillips found much in the Draper Collection that supported his research on the antebellum South, and he came to develop a careful eye for finding private papers that might have great value in an appropriate archival setting. Later in his career, Phillips occasionally spent summers doing cross-country travels during which he fashioned himself a manuscript collector.

From the time that he had been an undergraduate student, Phillips had always maintained an interest in political history and that interest continued into his master's and doctoral work, but the progressive mecca of Wisconsin would offer Phillips a new approach—the importance of economic causation in historical change. Phillips would incorporate economic history into his political studies as he began to look beyond the historical confines of Georgia and fashion a regional history of the antebellum South.[21] It was during his tenure at the University of Wisconsin-Madison that Phillips began the research and writing of *American Negro Slavery: A Survey of the Supply, Employment, and Control of Negro Labor as Determined by the Plantation Regime* (1918). This work, nearly fifteen years in the making, would eventually earn Phillips the reputation of being the greatest Southern historian of his time.

V

Phillips remained at the University of Wisconsin-Madison for six years (1902–1908) during which time he taught for several summer terms at other institutions including the University of Tennessee and the University of Kansas. Phillips generally pored through the archival holdings of the various institutions where he taught seeking materials that were of use to his work, and he used his summer travels to visit other archival depositories and, occasionally, to pursue his interest in antiquarianism by locating yet-undiscovered papers and manuscripts. Phillips recognized Southern history to be "almost a virgin field" and he viewed it as "one of the richest in the world for results."[22] He also recognized that what little history of the South had been written in the past was largely the domain of northeastern scholars who incorporated regional biases into their scholarship.[23] Phillips believed that it was time for the South to produce its own crop of historians who could set the record straight by countering the many fallacies that had found their way into standard historical interpretations of the South.

In 1908 Phillips returned to the South to accept a teaching position at Tulane University in New Orleans. Despite his previous experience in New Orleans, having attended the Tulane Preparatory School as a youth, Phillips did not believe that he would make his mark upon the historical profession through an extended tenure at Tulane, and he pondered future moves that he might make to advance his career. It was during this time that Phillips met Lucie Mayo-Smith while attending a December 1909 meeting of the American Historical Association in New York. After a brief long-distance courtship, the two were married on February 22, 1911.

In early 1911, Claude H. Van Tyne, who chaired the history department at the University of Michigan, contacted Phillips to inquire whether he might consider taking a position at Ann Arbor. Phillips accepted the position and returned to the North to continue his teaching and research on the antebellum South. He would enjoy his most productive years as a scholar during his tenure at the University of Michigan from 1911 to 1929. Phillips would eventually complete his professional career by teaching at Yale University from 1929 until his death in 1934.[24]

VI

Having been raised in the post–Civil War and post-Reconstruction era South, having experienced firsthand the workings of a society segregated by Jim Crow statutes, and having labored feverishly as a professional scholar trying to make sense of the South as he knew it, Phillips had much to say about the South and the powerful forces that had shaped its regional distinctiveness. Phillips believed that white supremacy was the one force that had created the American South and he believed that the origins of this ethos could be found in the plantation society that evolved in the antebellum era. Accordingly, an in-depth scholarly account of the institution and practice of slavery as it developed in the American South could illuminate the social and economic forces that had shaped Southern identity.

During nearly two decades of research Phillips had examined primary source materials from across the South from which he gleaned facts that he used to formulate his magnum opus of the antebellum South. The sheer volume of documentary evidence that Phillips used to base his argument is indeed impressive, but a closer and more critical examination of these sources indicates a problem that Phillips and his contemporaries failed to recognize. The sources that Phillips used presupposed the dominance of a plantation-centered Southern aristocracy that controlled the political, social, and economic development of the antebellum South. By examining plantation account books, diaries, bills of sale, and other private papers left behind by planter families, Phillips wrote the history of a truly mythic South in which poor white families and nonslaveholders were insignificant players in a plantocracy that determined the dominant social order.

The academic community later challenged Phillips's scholarship on the selective use of research data. The recognition that most slaves lived on small plantations and farms caused historian Richard Hofstadter to question the merits of any findings gleaned from the unrepresentative records of the South's planter elite. Nor were Phillips's economic interpretations universally accepted by scholars of his own era. Lewis C. Gray's *History of Agriculture in the Southern United States to 1860* (1933) argued vehemently against Phillips's position on the question of slavery. Later scholars like Frank L. Owsley in *Plain Folk of the Old South* (1949) would challenge the prevailing Southern social order that Phillips had fashioned.[25]

Even more disturbing than Phillips's planter-dominated South was the complete disregard that he exhibited toward Southern blacks, who constituted the bulk of the region's labor force in the antebellum era. While chattel slavery as an institution tended to dehumanize the slave by valuing his wealth as property rather than person, Phillips's patronizing treatment of Southern blacks also tended to objectify the race and, in so doing, deny a true historic role to Southern blacks and their forebears—slave and free.[26] Phillips's research trips across the South carried him through communities where thousands of former slaves resided, each harboring potent memories of the peculiar institution, but Phillips, like most of his contemporaries, failed to make use of this tremendous resource. Instead, he attempted to tell the story of the antebellum South from a singular, nonrepresentative perspective, and this decision necessarily flawed the interpretations that followed.[27]

In *American Negro Slavery,* Phillips's brand of paternalism was clear as he described the plantation as "a school constantly training and controlling pupils who were in a backward state of civilization."[28] Phillips maintained that the plantation economy that had developed in the South was indeed unprofitable, but that it continued to exist more as a means of social necessity than of economic prosperity. The slave, in Phillips's view, was an inferior creature who was the beneficiary of social order and the blessings of western civilization that were bestowed by the dominant planter class.[29] In a way almost reminiscent of the "white man's burden" mentality that was present in his day, Phillips's planters were portrayed as benevolent caretakers who did what was best for their less-than-capable slave laborers so that all might maintain a proper societal order.[30]

VII

In his efforts to maintain that the South was and should remain a region dominated by its white inhabitants, Ulrich B. Phillips either ignored or disregarded the controversial bits of evidence that he discovered that challenged his presupposed outcome. A careful reading of *American Negro Slavery* reveals several interpretive points that the author makes, but fails to develop in greater detail. Phillips refused to believe that Southern blacks were capable of being thinking, contributing members of a social order that could help to direct the South in any positive way, for to think otherwise would have shattered the racist assumptions upon which he based his entire argument. Yet, Phillips acknowledged that "the relation of planter and slave was largely shaped by a sense of propriety, proportion, and cooperation" without acknowledging that the implications of this statement belied the premise of his work.[31] Phillips also suggested that the antebellum South "was in fact shaped by mutual requirements, concessions and understandings, producing reciprocal codes of conventional morality," but he failed to attribute to black Southerners the elevated status that would be requisite to such a complex system of social and racial accommodation.[32]

Eugene D. Genovese has argued that Phillips's work should be a starting point for those historians who seek to examine the role of race and class in the history of the antebellum South. Though Phillips did not examine cogently all of the implications about class that can be drawn from his research, he is certainly one of the first American historians to recognize class distinctiveness and its role in the social and economic history of the antebellum South.[33]

VIII

The racist assumptions found in the work of Ulrich B. Phillips are indeed reprehensible and cannot be defended, but if one can look beyond these tremendous shortcomings, there is much in his work that should attract the attention of the modern historian. Phillips joined a profession in 1902 that was in the process of defining itself and the standards that he set as a teacher, a researcher, and a scholar helped to fashion the profession as one of the primary disciplines in the social sciences. Few had ever used primary materials to the degree or in the form that Phillips did, and generations of future scholars have continued down the path that he blazed.

Unfortunately, racism was the leitmotif of the Progressive era and Phillips's scholarship is replete with references and innuendo that assault modern sensibilities, but there are certain virtues that can be found in his method. It should not be all that surprising to find *American Negro Slavery* published in the same decade that produced D. W. Griffith's *Birth of a Nation* and that witnessed the rebirth of the Ku Klux Klan atop Stone Mountain in Georgia. That Ulrich Bonnell Phillips was a racist is indeed unfortunate—that he selectively culled evidence to support his prior assumptions is equally regrettable. The role of the historian should be to use the elusive power of interpretation to seek the truth regardless of where the facts may lead. George Washington Williams (1849–1891), one of the earliest African-American historians, once commented upon how he viewed his role as a scholar by saying "not as a blind panegyrist for my race, nor as the partisan apologist, but from a love for the 'truth of history' I have striven to record the truth."[34] Such should be the goal of all who aspire to record and interpret the historic past.

Still, there is much of value that can be found in the works of U. B. Phillips. He was the first scholar to study the plantation system as an economic entity in an effort to identify the inner workings of the Southern microeconomy that had sustained itself during the early generations of eighteenth- and nineteenth-century industrialization. Perhaps it was *because* of Phillips's views on race that he was able to look upon the plantation in a purely amoral sense to discover the mechanical processes that defined the economic lives of white and black Southerners in the antebellum era.[35]

We study historiography to determine the genealogy of ideas and the intellectual basis for revisionism. Anyone purporting to be a student of American race relations, the history of slavery, or of the American South must acknowledge the path-breaking contributions of Ulrich B. Phillips's scholarship in these fields. We are free to disagree with the presuppositions that influenced the theoretical framework of Phillips's work, but we must engage in scholarly consideration of the issues that he raised by recognizing his findings as fundamental to any reconsideration of these questions.

Broadus Mitchell

Economic Historian of the South

JACQUELYN DOWD HALL

Broadus Mitchell, economic historian and ardent socialist, died on April 28, 1988, at the age of ninety-five. Born December 27, 1892, in Georgetown, Kentucky, to Samuel Chiles and Alice Broadus Mitchell, he grew up in an academic family devoted to the "New South" panaceas of industrialization, education, and racial uplift. His mother was the daughter of the head of the Southern Baptist Seminary in Louisville. His father, who taught at Richmond College (later the University of Richmond), became president of the University of South Carolina in 1909, only to resign four years later when Governor Coleman L. Blease attacked him for favoring "blacks over white womanhood" because he recommended that a Peabody Fund gift be earmarked for black education to the state college for Negroes rather than the white women's college. Broadus was a senior at the university when this incident took place, and it encouraged his lifelong habit of standing on principle whatever the costs to his career. It also confirmed his faith in salvation through economic development, for the Mitchells saw Blease, spokesman for the up-country poor, as an ignorant, vicious opponent of progress and placed their hope in Blease's sworn enemies, the mill owners and their allies in the burgeoning towns.[1]

Broadus was torn between journalism and academics, between the roles of reforming publicist and methodical scholar. He first chose journalism, working off and on as a reporter between 1913 and 1918. When he pursued graduate work in political economy at Johns Hopkins, it was only to deepen his ability to write about the South's economic woes. His dissertation, completed in 1918 after a memorable trip along the route of the Southern Railway talking to the men who built the mills, was published in 1921 as *The Rise of Cotton Mills in the South.*

This essay first appeared as "Broadus Mitchell (1892–1988)" in the *Radical History Review* 45(1989): 31–38.

The book bore the mark of Mitchell's upbringing. Indeed, he claimed that his work represented "little more than illustration of [his father's] analysis of the past." The planters, in Mitchell's interpretation, had led the South to ruin through their choice of slave over free labor, and agriculture over industry. Under slavery, the poor whites had been squeezed off the land and into the ignorance and poverty that made them susceptible to Bleasite demagoguery. Slavery had, however, bequeathed one gift to the new order: an ethic of paternalism, which guided the leaders of the cotton mill building campaign as they brought disinherited poor whites back into "the Southern family" and rescued a society devastated by slavery and Civil War. The task since 1865 had been "to liberalize the South in thought, nationalize it in politics, and industrialize it in production."[2]

If Mitchell offered *The Rise of Cotton Mills* as a brief for his father's New South Creed, he also hinted at his own political evolution. By his second year at Johns Hopkins, he had been drawn into social work and socialism, in part through his association with Elizabeth Gilman, one of Maryland's leading reformers. Working with the Baltimore Family Welfare Association and the Christian Social Justice Fund, and talking to the peripatetic British and U.S. radicals who stayed at Gilman's home, Mitchell found refuge from the stultifying conventionality of academic life. He also developed an enduring commitment to socialism, pacifism, and workers education. Accordingly, *The Rise of Cotton Mills*, given over as it was to a celebration of the romance of Southern capitalism, also cautioned against repeating the mistakes of the antidemocratic past by allowing an "aristocracy of capital" to "preclude industrial democracy."[3]

Although Mitchell opposed the U.S. entry into World War I, he served a brief stint in the army. After the war, he joined the faculty at Johns Hopkins rather than returning to journalism. But he did not give up his yearning to be of broader social use. He took his students out of the classroom, guiding them on a trip to the Soviet Union, and using the city as a large laboratory for illustrating the contradictions of "poverty in the midst of plenty." Inspired by Marx's lectures at the London workingmen's club and by the British workers education movement, he conducted night courses for immigrant workers, tried in vain to start a Labor College at Johns Hopkins, and taught first at the Bryn Mawr Summer School and then at the Southern Summer School for Women Workers.[4]

Mitchell also used his journalistic skills to carve out a place as a harsh critic of the interwar South. In 1927, he published "Fleshpots in the South," a fierce assault on the textile magnates. Mitchell excoriated the second generation of mill owners for being "class-conscious and money wise," for sabotaging child labor legislation, squelching trade unions, and generally abandoning the noblesse oblige of their fathers without embracing the welfare capitalism appropriate to modern times.[5]

Mitchell turned more sharply to the left with the outbreak of the Depression, writing home to his father about the "approaching end of world capitalism. . . . We must have a new system, with production for profit abolished. I am giving my students socialism and communism hot and heavy." He went on the lecture circuit for the League for Industrial Democracy and became the first president of the Baltimore Urban League. His investigation of two lynchings on Maryland's Eastern Shore in 1932 received wide publicity and earned him a reputation in the black community as one of the few sparks of liberalism at "anti-Negro Johns Hopkins." In 1934, Mitchell ran for governor of Maryland on the Socialist party ticket against the Democratic incumbent who had failed to prevent the Eastern Shore lynchings or punish the protagonists. The only prominent Southern intellectual to run for public office in the 1930s, Mitchell captured 7,000 votes, hardly a threat to the major parties but twice as many votes as Maryland Socialists had ever won before. Over the next few years, Mitchell kept up a running critique of the New Deal. He condemned the Agricultural Adjustment Administration and the National Recovery Administration for trying to promote recovery through scarcity, opposed the Social Security Act in favor of the Lundeen Bill (which conceived of unemployment as a "disease of the capitalist system" and provided for full pay for the unemployed, funded by income and inheritance taxes), and called for public ownership of "the great means of production."[6]

By 1938, Mitchell's advocacy of socialism and racial justice had alienated some of his senior colleagues and won him the enmity of the Johns Hopkins administration. Without a hearing, the Academic Council censured him for using "vulgar epithets" in the classroom. A student apparently told his father that Mitchell had denounced the Supreme Court justices who were overturning New Deal legislation as "nine old bastards," and the father, a wealthy alumnus, had complained to the Board of Trustees. Mitchell defended his right to free speech and pressed ahead with a campaign to admit Edward S. Lewis, a prominent black social worker, to the graduate program in political economy. Summoned to Baltimore by one of Broadus's critics on the Board, his aging father, Samuel Chiles Mitchell, went directly to Isaiah Bowman, president of the university. Bowman pictured Broadus as a "wrong-headed nuisance," and the elder Mitchell came away from the interview convinced that his son's usefulness to the university was over. When Broadus confronted the president he was met with a "paroxysm of anger and abuse." He immediately wrote a letter of resignation, which was accepted by a department chair who had been his mentor and friend. Over the years, in interviews and memoirs, Mitchell returned to this decision to resign, sometimes blaming himself for impetuousness, sometimes blaming his father for imposing his nineteenth-century code of honor on his adult son's affairs. He linked his father's resignation from the University of South Carolina and his own departure from Johns Hopkins; in both cases, he felt, it would have been better to stay and fight.[7]

In 1935, three years before his troubles at Johns Hopkins came to a head, Mitchell's wife, Adelaide Hammond, whom he had married in 1923 and with whom he had two children, divorced him. A year later, he married Louise Pearson Blodget, a historian to whom he was devoted and with whom he collaborated on a number of his later works. In 1939, the couple left for Los Angeles—"a continent away from all our attachments"—where Mitchell had secured a job at Occidental College. They built a house and prepared to have a baby. But Broadus's reputation had preceded him, and when he opposed U.S. intervention in World War II and took public stands on other controversial issues, the president of the college refused to renew his contract. After two years at Occidental, the Mitchells found themselves back on the East Coast with no means of support. Lois McDonald, founder of the Southern Summer School for Women Workers, came to the rescue. She helped Broadus get a temporary job at New York University, and Louise began teaching at Mills College of Education. In 1943, Broadus took over the position of research director for the International Ladies Garment Workers Union while the director served in the army. When the war ended and the influx of veterans created new faculty jobs, Mitchell moved on to the economics department at Rutgers, where he taught from 1947 until he was forced to retire in 1958.[8]

By the time he settled in New York, Mitchell had concluded that he could never live in the South again, though he maintained close ties to the region through his brothers George Sinclair and Morris, both of whom devoted their careers to improved race relations and labor and education reform. World War II marked the end of the Socialist party as a force in American political and intellectual life, but Mitchell continued to think of himself as a leftist and refused to follow the path from socialism to anticommunism traced by many of his contemporaries. Indeed, soon after Mitchell's arrival at Rutgers, he found himself embroiled in one of the key academic cases of the McCarthy era.

In 1952, two Rutgers professors, M. I. Finley, an assistant professor of ancient history who went on to become an eminent classicist, and Simon Heimlich, an associate professor of mathematics, were identified as communists and called before Senator Pat McCarran's Internal Security Subcommittee. Both invoked the Fifth Amendment and both were fired by the Board of Trustees despite the unanimous recommendation of a Special Faculty Committee that they be retained. Mitchell was among the leaders of a small group that sought to rally the faculty against this clear-cut violation of academic freedom. The faculty response, however, was tepid, and the case set an unfortunate precedent for the purge of the academy that followed.[9]

Always an activist, Mitchell was above all an independent and dedicated scholar, and his work provides a fascinating, though idiosyncratic, counterpoint to his politics. All told, he wrote seventeen books counting those he coauthored and published numerous articles. During the 1920s, he wrote *Frederick Law Olmstead, A Critic of the Old South* (1924), which served as a vehicle for his own critique of the "Lost Cause," and *William Gregg, Factory Master of the Old South* (1928), in which he painted the antebellum industrialist as a kind of latter-day Robert Owen. With George Sinclair Mitchell, he published *The Industrial Revolution in the South* (1930), a collection of the brothers' previously published essays. Among his major later works were *American Economic History* (1947), with his wife Louise Pearson; *Depression Decade* (1947), a volume in a distinguished series on economic history; and a two-volume biography, *Alexander Hamilton* (1957, 1962).[10]

None of Mitchell's books has occasioned more criticism—and more longlasting attention—than *The Rise of Cotton Mills*, the dissertation he completed at the age of twenty-six. In *Origins of the New South* (1951), C. Vann Woodward suggested that Mitchell had underestimated the profit motive in his rush to paint the mill founders as selfless philanthropists. Yet Woodward also acknowledged that, thirty years after it appeared, Mitchell's study remained the basic monograph on Southern textile history. In 1982, David L. Carlton, a Woodward student, pointed out the conceptual problem at the heart of Mitchell's work. The mill builders, Carlton argues, may well have viewed themselves as community benefactors, but they identified the welfare of the community with the interests of their own class. Five years later, the authors of *Like a Family: The Making of a Cotton Mill World* sought to use the tools of social history to tell the story of the rise of the cotton mills from the workers' point of view. Mitchell saw himself as adhering to the rigorous standards of "scientific history" pioneered by German scholars and introduced to U.S. students at Johns Hopkins in the late nineteenth century. But he offered no evidence for his contention that first-generation workers reacted to exploitation with childlike gratitude. Where Mitchell relied on the self-representations of the powerful and the on-stage behavior of the powerless, *Like a Family* emphasized the offstage attitudes and strategies of both.[11]

Daniel Joseph Singal, in *The War Within* (1982), offers the only general assessment of Mitchell's career. Singal characterizes Mitchell as one of the "most intelligent, learned, and compassionate Southerners of his era," yet dismisses him as a "post-Victorian" unable to adapt to modernist trends by acknowledging the existence of evil (in the person of the planters and the mill owners) and the inevitability of class conflict. It is true that Mitchell was a social evo-

lutionist and that he was deeply—and permanently—impressed by the promise he saw in the first stage of the South's industrial revolution. It is also true
that there is little in his historical scholarship that betrays the passion of his
teaching and his political commentary. But the charge of insufficient modernism could not have surprised Mitchell more. He devoted his entire career to
the fight against what he saw as a backward-looking laissez faire individualism, whether espoused by the Southern Agrarians, by mill magnates who refused to "exchange a patronal relationship to their employees for a contractual
one," or by New Deal liberals with too much respect for property rights.[12]

Like many socialists, Mitchell pinned his hopes to technological progress.
Through collective ownership and planning, technology could be harnessed to
the goals of freedom and abundance for all. He saw peasant life as inherently
backward and antisocial. He could admit that the South's mill villages constituted a "benevolent despotism" and that a generation of farmers-turned-mill-
workers had been sacrificed to the cause of industrialization. But he justified
that sacrifice not only by reference to the region's desperate postwar needs but
by analogy to the Russian Revolution: "In Russia the Bolshevists have declared frankly that their autocracy is intended, that there must be strong leaders to assume responsibility if the new social venture is to carry through. Only
by such means can the democracy aimed at materialize." By the 1920s, the
Southern textile industry had overcome its New England rivals and pulled the
region out of poverty. But instead of sharing the wealth and allowing democracy to "materialize," a new generation of mill owners used the external forms
of paternalism to hide the inner reality of greedy individualism. Similarly,
Mitchell believed that by the 1930s the United States possessed the means of
providing leisure and prosperity for all its citizens, but instead production for
profit created an "economic jungle" in which productive capacity outran the
ability to consume. The New Deal responded to the crisis not by socializing
production but by creating artificial scarcity. In both cases, Mitchell saw the
behavior of the powerful both as tragic and morally wrong: like the Southern
planters before them, they stood in the way of history's grand design.
Mitchell's interest in Alexander Hamilton, which dated from the beginning of
his graduate career, reflected his consistent belief that democracy, industrialization, and a strong state went hand in hand.[13]

When he left Rutgers at sixty-five, Mitchell joined the economics department at Hofstra and accepted the challenge of teaching in the university's
experimental New College. Age did nothing to temper his iconoclasm. In
1959, he moderated a controversial forum on communism. He managed to
bring onto the faculty a kindred spirit named Dorothy Douglas, an economist
who had resigned from Smith when she became a target of red-baiting. When
he was awarded an honorary degree and was asked to deliver the commence-

ment address in 1967, he took the opportunity to speak out against the war in Vietnam.

In 1967, at the age of seventy-five, Broadus Mitchell retired once more. He spent the last years of his life in New York and on his beloved farm in Wendell, Massachusetts, where he continued to be a productive scholar, practiced his avocation as a "tolerable amateur carpenter," and entertained a stream of family and friends.

E. Merton Coulter and the Political Culture of Southern Historiography

FRED ARTHUR BAILEY

Honored to present the first presidential address before the Southern Historical Association, meeting in Birmingham, Alabama, on October 25, 1935, E. Merton Coulter lamented that the "North, having won the [Civil] war on the battlefield, immediately set out to win it again and consolidate victory on the printed page. . . . A new invasion was on, and the South must meet words with words—but words based on historical fact." For Southerners history assumed a "more practical character than had ever appeared before in all the annals of the South," he proclaimed. "It was the last stronghold of the South not for the defense of its nationality but for the protection of something more dear and sacred, its reputation." Coulter praised those Southerners who in the 1890s called for "impartial, and unpassioned" history to vindicate the South. That generation understood that "in this new struggle" historical "workers should march together no less surely than soldiers. . . . Thus, there was enacted the splendid spectacle of erstwhile warriors turned historians and conservers of history. Generals now became scholars."[1]

Coulter proudly listed himself among those scholar-warriors who not only defended the South of old, but also sought to preserve the essentials he deemed critical to its cultural future. Through ninety-one years his intellectual odyssey was chartered by the South's peculiar approach to its history. Immersed as a youth in the political culture of Southern historiography, he emerged in the 1930s in the van of the South's historical establishment, and in his declining years remained a faithful defender of its canted interpretation of the past. He stood with that generation of influential Southern historians— among them Frank Lawrence Owsley and Thomas Perkins Abernethy—who were convinced that their version of Southern history would insulate the South from would-be reformers within and without.[2]

Throughout Coulter's life the discipline of history served as a bulwark supporting the white South's values of race and class. Confederate patriotic socie-

ties, public school teachers and their textbooks, archivists, and university professors shaped and nurtured a historical monolith unshaken by challenges
from those scholars and other concerned individuals who wished for the
South a greater devotion to social justice. The region bore the burden of an
intellectual paradigm that was premised upon the seminal concept of man's
innate inequality and that assumed social order was best preserved when every
individual resided in his or her "proper" place.[3] If the Civil War had abolished
legal slavery, it little altered the reality of the South's unequal social structure
or the philosophy that supported it. As the nineteenth century merged into
the twentieth, Southern aristocrats regained their accustomed dominance over
the region's weal, reducing blacks to peonage, driving small white farmers into
tenancy, and restricting the civil rights of blacks and nonelite whites alike.

From his North Carolina birth in 1890, Coulter's life experiences formed a
dynamic microcosm of the impact Southern historiography had upon its political culture. While largely inarticulate nonelite whites and blacks struggled
with the detritus of the Civil War, the region's aristocrats, who retained their
control over the venues of public expression, articulated a response to the conflict to which all Southerners—white and black—were expected to conform.[4]

To the Southern patriciate the tragedy of the Confederacy's demise reached
beyond the unrequited sacrifice of loved ones or the loss of more than two
billion dollars in human property; it involved the collapse of a long-cherished
social order in which they had been its rulers, lesser whites its followers, and
African-Americans its slaves. By the century's end, Southern elites had defeated Reconstruction and the Populist crusade. Victorious on the field of
politics, the South's controlling class determined to prevent future challenges
by instilling Southern patrician values into all sectors of the next generation.
"The way for us to do [this] is to impress the facts of history upon the minds
of our young people," declared an official of the North Carolina Division
United Daughters of the Confederacy in 1906. "We propose to teach our own
children, of our own Southland, the facts about our own war in our own way.
For this is the only way we can rescue from infamy the memory of our fallen
heroes."[5]

Coulter grew up among a people conscious of these "fallen heroes" and
eager for cultural redemption. His home, his social environment, and his education nurtured his historical proclivities, molding him into a powerful apologist for the South's institutions of human inequality. Fourth among John Ellis
and Lucy Ann Propst Coulter's eight children, E. Merton Coulter was raised
in a financially comfortable family. His father owned extensive land holdings
in North Carolina's hill country, a successful lumber mill on a tract adjoining
the Henry River, and a prosperous hardware store in the community of Con-
nelly Springs, while investing heavily in livestock and agricultural ventures.

John Ellis Coulter also served as a justice of the peace, a long-term school board member, and a devout leader in his Lutheran congregation. Both his father and his wife's father had marched in the Confederate army, a fact that helped color his view of the past and frame his attitude toward the politics of the postwar South. E. Merton Coulter's maternal grandfather died at the Battle of Fredericksburg; his paternal grandfather was captured in the Gettysburg campaign and confined at the Point Lookout prison camp in Maryland. Following the war, he was accused of Klan violence in his native North Carolina, and, though acquitted of the latter by an all-black jury, he remained convinced that Reconstruction was aimed at humiliating whites by establishing black rule in the South, a view he bequeathed to his son John Ellis and his grandson E. Merton. "I am a 'good old rebel,'" proclaimed the historian in 1957, "both of my grandfathers having fought in the Confederate Army." Recalling fifteen years later Grandfather Coulter's "harrowing stories of the terrors of that hell-hole" Point Lookout prison, he reflected "that if some of our 'new light' young historians want to make a contribution to history, they should forget Andersonville for a spell and tell what happened at Elmira, Rock Island, Camp Douglas, etc."[6]

Enthralled by the passionate memories of his grandfather and other embittered Confederate veterans, young Coulter read enthusiastically the corpus of juvenile literature that had been carefully crafted by upper-class Confederate partisans. Rigorously inspected by the United Confederate Veterans, the United Daughters of the Confederacy, and the Sons of Confederate Veterans, his elementary textbooks painted a glowing portrait of the plantation South, a simplistic image of contented slaves, and a harsh assessment of misguided Northern abolitionists. These textbooks argued that an aggressive Yankee nation forced the Civil War upon the South, that the North's material advantages overwhelmed brave Southern patriots, and that Reconstruction served the cynical purposes of Radical Republicans intent on consolidating their power by stripping Southern whites of their fundamental civil rights and by gaining undue influence over easily duped freedmen. Coulter supplemented his classroom lessons by reading patriotic books for the young that spirited him back to the past and stirred in him a longing to have been in the grand crusade for Southern independence. Thomas Nelson Page's *Two Little Confederates,* a fictional account of the author's experiences in Civil War Virginia, especially moved Coulter. When presented a copy of the volume as a gift in 1969, the appreciative historian glowed: "I am pleased to no end with my *Two Little Confederates.* It ought to be required reading for every boy in America—and man, too."[7]

Although John Ellis Coulter hoped his son would embrace the Lutheran ministry, E. Merton entered the University of North Carolina in 1910 intent upon a career in history. The Chapel Hill community, the university, and es-pecially the university's history department were closely linked to the preser-vation of Confederate heritage. During the course of his studies, Coulter at-tended reunions of Confederate veterans, applauded the construction of a campus monument to their memory, and listened with rapture to various no-tables who praised Robert E. Lee and other Confederate icons. He even wit-nessed the mutiny of medical students who refused to violate the donated body of an indigent veteran. "One fellow," Coulter wrote to his father, "said his 'dad' would give him a whipping if he would dissect a Confederate Soldier."[8]

Coulter relished classes under J. G. de Roulhac Hamilton, a disciple of Co-lumbia University's William Archibald Dunning. Hamilton dutifully echoed his mentor's pronouncements on the Civil War and Reconstruction era, dog-mas that had in fact been developed by the Confederate patriotic associations long before they were repeated in Dunning's graduate seminars. Although Coulter praised Hamilton as "the most active man in the History Depart-ment," he was somewhat taken aback by the professor's "slightly snobbish" de-meanor; but doubtless he enjoyed Hamilton's well-regarded lectures on Negro venality.[9]

In spite of careful adherence to regional political correctness, Hamilton and his department were nonetheless subject to constant scrutiny from Southern censors. In May 1911, Rebecca Cameron, historian-general of the North Caro-lina Division United Daughters of the Confederacy, demanded to know why the University of North Carolina, Trinity College (now Duke University), and Davidson College assigned Henry W. Elson's *History of the United States,* a textbook her organization branded Yankee biased. That fall Cameron reported to her constituency that Hamilton, along with officials of the other schools, had purged the offending volume and had assured her that whenever "sec-tional questions came up in the class room the students were taught the truth from the Southern standpoint."[10]

Graduating from the University of North Carolina in 1913, Coulter dedi-cated one year to high-school teaching in the mountain community of Glen Alpine and then enrolled at the University of Wisconsin, Madison, to further his goal of teaching and writing about the South. Although this Northern state's political and social climate might at first seem uncongenial to Coulter's ideological inclinations, he soon developed a support group that reinforced his belief system. Coulter served as entertainment chairman of the Dixie Club, which he described as "quite a crowd of 'Rebels' who braved the [Wisconsin] weather's peril" to savor "peanuts and lemonade" and to reminisce about their native land's warmer environs. For Coulter and his friends in the Dixie Club, the showing of David W. Griffith's epochal film *Birth of a Nation* proved memorable. Based on Thomas Dixon's *The Clansman,* a racist novel slanted to the white South's interpretation of the Civil War and Reconstruction, it fascinated the university's Southern expatriates and hardly bothered a history faculty largely sympathetic to their views. Among the latter, historian Carl Russell Fish, whose mother was from Georgia, became Coulter's major professor, guided him through his duties as a graduate assistant, and directed his dissertation on the Civil War and Reconstruction in Kentucky.[11]

With Coulter's interest in the Bluegrass State and a family tradition linking his ancestry with the legendary Daniel Boone, he entered the job market in 1917 hoping for a position at the University of Kentucky, but the exactitudes of world war had greatly reduced the college population, shrinking employment opportunities. Coulter settled for a brief appointment at Marietta College in Ohio; two years later he moved on to a post at the University of Georgia where he would become both a highly respected scholar and a campus legend.[12]

Just over six decades of productive work lay before Coulter, divided into two well-defined periods. Prior to 1947, he was a champion among the Southern intelligentsia that provided intellectual legitimacy to the region's institutions of inequality. But by the late 1940s, reformers associated with the civil rights movement had commenced the crusade that eventually overwhelmed the South's established sages by challenging their assumptions and winning converts to democracy and racial justice. Coulter, allied with the old order, led a rear-guard action by writing books and articles trumpeting long-cherished interpretations of Southern history, even as he damned "deviant" scholars of the South—white and black historians—who, in his view, corrupted both the interpretation of the past and the value system that had been built upon it.[13]

Writing with purpose and teaching with passion, Coulter emerged as a leader of that between-the-World Wars generation of Southern historians who posited historical "truth from the Southern standpoint"; in the process he created a legacy of scholarship and achievement rarely equaled. He taught at the University of Georgia from 1919 to 1958 (serving as its chair from 1940 until his retirement), edited the *Georgia Historical Quarterly* for over fifty years, and wielded a fecund pen dedicated to Southern themes. Twenty-six books and ten edited volumes, one hundred three articles, and unnumbered book reviews and newspaper columns bore his name; and he was a founding father of the Southern Historical Association, serving as its first president and nurturing it through its infancy. Warm in spirit, enthusiastic for his chosen discipline, and unfailingly kind to those who shared his values, he was popular with his students, his professional peers, and his admiring readers. For while Coulter's scholarship was impressive in bulk, it was also thoroughly orthodox. He, along with the vast majority of his fellow Southern historians, faithfully repeated the dictums learned in their youths. These scholars, frozen in time, simply added their professional prestige to already developed themes and ideas designed to bolster a society dedicated to the preservation of a highly articulated social order. Segregation, the denial of voting rights to blacks and large numbers of whites, and the sustaining of elite rule were grounded in their historical interpretations. "Let me call your attention to E. M. Coulter, of Georgia," wrote J. G. de Roulhac Hamilton to his friend Ulrich B. Phillips in 1929. "He comes as near matching my interests and yours as any youngster I know."[14] Though by then hardly a youth, Coulter merited this recognition from an aging apostle of the Old South.

Coulter's writing style blended simple direct narrative with moderate humor to produce pleasing texts that both delighted and informed his audiences. His subjects varied from singular topics tightly focused on Southern culture to engaging biographies to broad surveys.[15] Throughout all his books and articles, he remained true to that version of Southern history whose essential elements had been fixed long before he commenced his fruitful career. He was a latter-day prophet urging Southern whites to remain faithful to their heritage.

First published in 1933, Coulter's *Georgia: A Short History* captured his fundamental themes; it also showcased his engaging style and his fidelity to historical truth from a white Southern perspective. Both read for enjoyment by the general public and studied as a textbook by university students, it strongly impacted several generations indoctrinating them with images of an Old South of stately plantations, sagacious masters, and humble slaves, and with presentations of sordid Yankees—fanatical and unreasoning abolitionists, cruel and morally debased invaders, and corrupt and ill-informed reconstructionists.

"The planter aristocracy," Coulter wrote, descended from the "nobilities and aristocracies" from "ancient times" who "when their representatives came to America . . . found Georgia and other Southern states a society which made them feel nearest at home. Their culture was genuine, and their manners were easy and unassuming. They took pride in their homes, they were hospitable; they bought many books and read them. Plantation life on the sea islands and the coast early took on a glamour which lasted until the economic organization which made it possible was smashed in the Civil War." Deeming the peculiar institution a burden for whites and a blessing for blacks, Coulter reflected that the Southern aristocracy "deserved a better fate" than to rest its culture upon "the insecure foundations of slavery." Disdaining to describe the life-style of the slaves, he simply noted that they "were treated no better or no worse than their economic well-being demanded," but, he emphasized, "the plantation could not have lasted so long if inhuman treatment of the slave had been the rule." The institution "carried with it many attendant problems," he reflected, chief among them a growing population of "free Negroes, and the Pandora's box which the abolitionists flung open."[16]

In Coulter's paradigm, abolitionists, Yankee soldiers, and Northern reconstructionists allied with ignorant blacks to form the coterie of villains that destroyed the South's once-great civilization. In the early 1830s "there arose with little warning one of the strangest phenomena in history," he averred. "For two hundred years slavery had existed in English America and there had been few voices in North or South raised against it; but . . . the thoughtful emancipation movement suddenly swept into a violent abolitionist crusade." William Lloyd Garrison, its virulent leader, "advocated action without compromise" and "spurred the government which permitted slavery by publicly burning a copy of the constitution of the United States and declaring it was 'a covenant with death and an agreement with hell.'" The hatred unleashed by Garrison and his ilk reached its inevitable climax in 1859 when "John Brown made his insane attempt to free the slaves through force, by seizing Harper's Ferry." To Coulter, "no more successful act could have been devised to cut the last ties of friendship which bound the South to the North."[17]

True to the version of Southern history promoted by the United Daughters of the Confederacy and like associations, Coulter affirmed that slavery alone was not responsible for the Civil War. Georgians pledged their lives "not so much to defend slavery as to protect the social and economic order which slavery made possible." Without it, he reasoned, "there would be a race problem; and the realization of this fact tied . . . both slaveholder and non-slaveholder alike, and explains why all fought with equal bravery in the war that came." Thus when "the day of argument gave way to bloody warfare, Georgia plunged into the midst of it with as much enthusiasm and determination as any other state in the Confederacy." Such "enthusiasm and determination," however, would not prevail. Georgia's defenders succumbed to Union General William Tecumseh Sherman, whose drunken minions burned Atlanta before marching eastward to cut a swath of destruction to the ocean. "The great Southern adventure had . . . ended in disaster," Coulter grieved. There "awaited Georgia and the other Confederate states rigors which they had pictured in their efforts to hold up the Confederate morale, but which they never honestly believed could happen."[18]

If Coulter lamented the lost dreams of the Confederacy, he raged at what he considered the nightmare of the postwar epoch. He carefully identified the South's tormentors during Reconstruction, and by implication suggested that the same groups and institutions retained the potential to bedevil the South in his own time. Even as "the Southerners," by whom Coulter always meant whites, sought to integrate freed blacks into the postbellum economic order, "the United States government and Northern organizations . . . greatly complicated" the problem. "The North," Coulter charged, "appeared to be more interested in the social and political construction of the Negro than his economic welfare." This was ill-advised because to blacks "liberty meant license and freedom from all restraint, and to many it meant surcease from all work." Thousands abandoned the fields and to the cities "came wandering and wondering Negroes, there to produce in good times slums for the social workers and crimes for the police."[19]

Coulter interpreted Reconstruction-imposed reforms as direct assaults upon the white man's natural dominion over blacks. "The supremacy of the white people in the South was threatened by the coming of . . . the Loyal or Union League and the granting of suffrage to the Negro," he stressed. "Under the control of designing Northern adventurers," abolition and suffrage "instilled into the Negro dangerous notions of his supremacy over his former white master." Suffering under the oppression of Yankee and African rule, white Georgians responded with appropriate force. "The white people . . . called to their assistance the Invisible Empire of the Ku Klux Klan, and the best elements in the state entered into its secret confines." Its "most spectacular work was done in convincing the Negroes that politics was a game reserved exclusively for the white man." Coulter rejoiced that by 1877 Georgians had thrown off "the foreign yoke" of Yankee rule, had laid the "foundations for new times which should be unhampered by Federal bayonets," and had commenced the march toward political, social, and economic recovery.[20]

The stirring assessments of the Old South, Civil War, and Reconstruction contained in Coulter's *Georgia: A Short History* (and his like-themed books and articles) serviced the Southern political establishment by contributing to the intellectual justification of a highly articulated social structure and by validating for Southern whites a deeply rooted resentment toward both Northern society and the federal government. Coulter's fifty-year editorship of the *Georgia Historical Quarterly* also represented his dedication to the creation and maintenance of a historical infrastructure that perpetuated the South's slanted social and political values. In the journal he published manuscripts congenial to his interpretation of the Southern experience, contributed his own articles coloring the South's past, and, throughout the 1930s and 1940s, wrote the vast majority of its book reviews.[21] The last became a sounding board from which he carefully indoctrinated his readers, informing them which works were acceptable and unacceptable interpretations of the past and, more important, instructing them on the criteria by which they were to assess the virtues of various types of authors.

Coulter particularly praised those authors whose views coincided with his own and took special delight in extolling Northern writers whom he deemed enlightened in their attitudes toward the South. He lauded Claude Bower's *The Tragic Era: The Revolution after Lincoln* as a book written "with consummate skill" that held up the Reconstruction era for "the present generation" to see "the untwisted truth of that disgraceful period in all American history." The book's value was enhanced, Coulter declared, because it was authored by "an Indiana Democrat living in New York City, [who] cannot be charged with being a Southern unreconstructed rebel." With equal joy, Coulter endorsed *The Epic of America* by New Yorker James Truslow Adams. He considered Adams's assessments of Reconstruction especially cogent. His "vigorous thinking and modern point of view stand forth clearly in some of the bold characterisations which may be noted," Coulter wrote: "Speaking of John Brown, [Adams said] 'perhaps no man in American history less deserves the pedestal of heroism on which he has been raised' . . . of Thaddeus Stevens, 'perhaps the most despicable, malevolent, and morally deformed character who has ever risen to high power in America' . . . of the North following the Civil War, 'No civilized victor was ever more ungenerous. The war left the South prostrate; Reconstruction left it maddened.'" Coulter concluded that "it should not be necessary to say that this book is vastly worth while."[22]

Coulter regularly highlighted those books and authors whose writings supported his historical model. Orland Kay Armstrong's *Old Massa's People*, based on the author's personal interviews of former slaves, revealed, Coulter wrote, that "few of the old slaves . . . remembered aught but the pleasant and romantic." The book made "vivid and clear the everyday life of the slaves" and came "about as near as possible to restoring the atmosphere of slave days in the antebellum South." John D. Van Deusen's *Economic Bases of Disunion in South Carolina* proved that when "Southerners, principally the unreconstructed and their sons and daughters, have blandly said that slavery was not the cause of session . . . they spoke the truth. . . . Slavery was merely a thread in the economic warp and woof of the Old South." Henry Lee Swint's *The Northern Teacher in the South* documented that post–Civil War Yankee concern for educating the former slaves "was based on the feeling that an educated Negro would buy more Northern goods than an uneducated one" and that properly instructing blacks would "convert the Freedmen to Republicanism." And, Paul Lewinson's *Race, Class, and Politics: A History of Negro Suffrage and White Politics* demonstrated the essential evil of African-American enfranchisement. "The rise of the Farmers' Alliance and the Populist Party," Lewinson wrote, "emphasized the danger of the negro vote always settling any quarrel within the white man's party, and there resulted the disfranchisement movement of the 1890's and 1900's."[23]

Coulter also warned his readers against those authors whose musings threatened to undermine the region's contemporary established order. He looked askance at the writings of both black scholars and Marxist historians, finding in them the seeds of a future and undesired social revolution. Believing that African-American authors possessed an inborn bias (such as he never discerned in whites), he strongly hinted that this tempted blacks to fundamental misinterpretations of the past. Although most of Coulter's reviews of books by blacks were favorable, he always used the opportunity to warn his audience of the dangers inherent in scholarship conducted by members of the Negro race. Coulter noted that one author, "who is a Negro teacher . . . writes with clarity and ease, and . . . almost forgets the racial slant." Another was described as "a Negro . . . [who] has the characteristic rare among writers of his race, of being able to write without a racial bias," and still another was presented as a "negro [who] writes with detachment and freedom from a crusading complex." Reviewing Charles H. Wesley's *The Collapse of the Confederacy*, Coulter complimented the author as "a Negro [who] lets the racial feeling touch and color his writing slightly, but it is so little as compared with Negro writers in general that he should be commended."[24]

However much Coulter disdained black scholarship, he took seriously the efforts of Marxist historians, seeing in their works a malevolent force threatening Southern social stability. While he found in the Marxist interpretations of W. E. B. Du Bois and James S. Allen a perversion of the historian's craft for political purposes, he shuddered at the revolutionary implications of Herbert Aptheker's works chronicling the black experience in America. Reviewing Du Bois's *Black Reconstruction,* Coulter warned in 1937 that "it is not straight forward history, but rather a polemic work interspersed with history." Du Bois "has a message that burns its way out in language which now and then is filled with bitterness—a bitterness born of the lost opportunities and thwarted hopes of the colored people and the working class." Two years later, the Georgia editor warned his readers that James S. Allen's *Reconstruction: The Battle for Democracy* was "written from the standpoint of the Marxist-Leninist" and that given Allen's sympathy with the concept of class struggle in America, "it is evident from the beginning that there must be much straining of points and forced interpretations to produce such a work."[25]

Although Du Bois and Allen's volumes mildly unsettled Coulter, Aptheker's writings he viewed as an evil harbinger of future revolution. He saw in Aptheker's *The Negro in the Civil War,* published in 1938, a bald attempt to radically alter Southern racial customs. Coulter branded the work "an absurd bit of propaganda, based on a perversion of historical facts," whose purpose was "to show the Negroes today that they were not in slavery a meek servile people, but that they then showed and still have the vigor necessary to complete the revolutionary Reconstruction they were denied following the Civil War." When Aptheker vehemently protested this damning review, Coulter heatedly responded: "When you establish by sound historical work your right to dismiss cavalierly [Ulrich B.] Phillips and other standard American historians, I shall be glad to enter into an argument with you. . . . [Meanwhile,] I'll admit it was foolish to dignify your propaganda pamphlets by noting them in the *Quarterly.*" Perhaps because of this, in 1947 Coulter assigned himself the task of reviewing Aptheker's *Essays in the History of the American Negro.* The author's "uncontrollable zeal for Karl Marx makes him forgetful of the restraints which should surround the true searcher after knowledge," Coulter charged. "His purpose is to show the Negroes that they had been a holy terror throughout their lives as slaves in America; and the implication is left that they should get properly excited over their present status."[26]

Coulter had good reason to fear that black Southerners might get "properly excited over their present status." Rather than analyze this status, though, in large measure Coulter blamed the discontent upon a rising generation of revisionist historians who challenged the long-established theories of Southern history in general and Coulter's work in particular. Respected as a master scholar in the field of Southern history, and especially the Reconstruction epoch, he was in 1947 ill-prepared for the wave of criticism that awaited him following the much anticipated publication of his seminal work *The South during Reconstruction.* The inaugural volume in the History of the South series jointly sponsored by Louisiana State University Press and the Littlefield Fund for the Study of Southern History of the University of Texas, this book, the series, and Coulter's role in it illustrated the restrictive nature of Southern historiography during the first half of the twentieth century.

The ten-volume History of the South project had its genesis in the somewhat less than altruistic benevolence of George W. Littlefield, late major in the Confederate Army, wealthy Texas banker, and member of the University of Texas's Board of Regents. Between 1911 and 1913, he and his fellow members of the John Bell Hood Camp, United Confederate Veterans, had bullied the university's Department of History into removing two textbooks they condemned as unsuitable for Southern youths. Turning adversity into advantage, Eugene C. Barker, chair of the Department of History, convinced Littlefield that proper textbooks sympathetic to the Southern version of truth did not exist, that the University of Texas should take the lead in training historians who would write worthy works on Southern topics, and that the university should establish an archival collection sufficient to support research into Southern themes. In 1914, Littlefield made his initial donation for the acquiring of primary materials on Southern history and for the publication of a "history of the United States with the plain facts concerning the South . . . fairly stated that the children of the South may be truthfully taught."[27]

University of Texas historian Charles W. Ramsdell, a disciple of Columbia University's William Archibald Dunning, accepted oversight of the Littlefield Fund, supervised the collection of materials that became the foundation of the university's Eugene C. Barker Center for the Study of American History, and in 1937 proposed the publication of a multivolume series on the South suited to Littlefield's wishes. Meanwhile, Wendell Holmes Stephenson, then a professor at Louisiana State University, had urged his school's press undertake a similar project. Given the essential harmony of the two proposals, Ramsdell and Stephenson combined their efforts with the two of them designated co-editors. They searched for scholars faithful to the Southern version of historical truth and selected Ramsdell to write the volume on the Confederacy and Coulter to develop that on Reconstruction. Following Ramsdell's death in 1942, Coulter assumed his duties as coeditor of the History of the South series and took on the additional responsibility of composing the Confederacy volume. Shortly after the publication of Coulter's *Confederate States of America* in 1952, Stephenson wrote his friend and co-laborer indicating the degree of regional chauvinism associated with the project: "I get pretty enthusiastic when I think of all you have done for Southern historiography. If you were connected with one of the schools in the (Poison) Ivy League rather than a Southern university, you would have been president of the American Historical Association long ago, though I am not sure just how much of an honor that distinction would be."[28]

Although Stephenson avowed his enthusiasm for Coulter's contributions to Southern historiography, other scholars were less enchanted and Coulter's initial contribution to the series drew academic fire. Alert to post–World War II changes in ethnic attitudes, his critics challenged the racism evident in his *The South during Reconstruction*, suggesting that he was as insensitive to current revisionist literature on the topic as he was unresponsive to the evolving social conditions extant in the contemporary South. "It is a standing joke among historians," wrote Columbia University's David Donaldson, "that what this country needs is an impartial history written from the Southern point of view. Professor Coulter's *The South during Reconstruction* . . . precisely fills the bill." Donaldson focused on the "unfortunate sectional attitude" apparent in Coulter's discussion of the freed black: "It is distressing to read that the nation owed Southern whites an 'unpaid debt' for emancipated slaves, that the freedmen 'spent half their earnings for liquor,' that the Negro's 'religion had no relation to morality,' and a score of other statements with similar bias." Thoroughly dissatisfied with the work, Donaldson prayed "for a more objective approach in the succeeding volumes of this important series."[29]

However much Donaldson's criticisms and other negative assessments may have stung Coulter, he doubtless enjoyed the endorsements given by white historians in the South. Not surprisingly the superannuated J. G. de Roulhac Hamilton proclaimed Coulter's book "a significant contribution" and said of it "too high a praise cannot be given [Coulter's] calm and dispassionate treatment of the whole subject." Coulter's friend and Vanderbilt historian Frank

Lawrence Owsley echoed this view. The work's emotionally charged subject "gives the book a sharp and bitter tone," he explained, but then cautioned that this "must not be confused with the author's outlook; there are few historians today whose approach is more impartial and unemotional than Coulter's."[30]

One Southern historian, however, took a dramatically different approach in his evaluation of both Coulter and his interpretation of Reconstruction. John Hope Franklin, who Coulter would later describe as a "Negro [who] writes with much less race consciousness than is the case with most Negro authors," raged at the book's antiquated methodology. Repelled by its consistently negative treatment of newly freed African-Americans, he accused Coulter of ignoring black primary sources, of drawing illustrations of the Freedmen's Bureau, black legislators, and emancipated slaves from Negrophobic newspaper accounts, and of discounting modern authors whose revisionist writings cast Reconstruction in a light less favorable to the white South. In the end, Franklin counted Coulter's work as "valuable in the history of history as it is in the history of Reconstruction," serving as a marker from which other scholars should depart seeking new and more enlightened paths.[31]

To Coulter, Franklin was but one of several Southern historians who not only departed from established truth, but also moved the South in directions he deemed inappropriate. "History . . . makes me a conservative," he admitted in one of his letters. "It makes others radicals. . . . Too many people today bend history to suit their purposes, they make it a propaganda tool. . . . Much of this 'revisionism' is nothing more than propaganda for this or that." More to the point, he explained to his sympathetic friend Thomas Perkins Abernethy that "[modern] scalawags irk me, because I think they are pursuing that line for the same reason which actuated their antecedents who made that name current."[32] In his private correspondence, Coulter singled out three Southern historians—John Hope Franklin, C. Vann Woodward, and James W. Silver—as intellectuals threatening the Southern weal.

Coulter especially resented Franklin's attacks upon his own works, seeing in this scholar a lack of deference and a standard of aggression that must not be tolerated in a rightly ordered South. "Franklin has some ability but not nearly as much as he thinks," Coulter wrote in exasperation. "Were we not using him as an exhibit in our counter moves against the communists, showing how we draw no racial lines and how much we appreciate our colored people . . . I say had Franklin not had all this in his favor (in other words had he not been a Negro), he would likely never or little been heard of. The to-do over him because he is a Negro has gone to his head and made him really obnoxious." Franklin, Coulter went on, "is very plausible and ingratiating, but in his writings he cannot forget that he is a Negro."[33]

Coulter thoroughly disliked C. Vann Woodward's tradition-challenging

Origins of the New South and regretted that as a latter-day editor of the History of the South series he could not prevent its publication. Initially Ramsdell and Stephenson chose Burton Kendrick of the Woman's College of the University of North Carolina, Greensboro, for the New South volume, but he soon declined and recommended Woodward as his replacement. Neither Ramsdell nor Stephenson was pleased with the nomination, seeing in Woodward both an author new to the craft and a scholar tinged with radicalism. They leaned toward Holland Thompson, a professor of history at the College of New York City, whose post-Reconstruction volume in the Yale Chronicle series struck Stephenson as politically reliable. Concerned with Thompson's advanced age and ill health, Stephenson sought Coulter's council. The Georgia historian voted in Thompson's favor. "I believe Woodward could do it," he explained, "but he is still quite young and has some distance to go." In the end Thompson's death settled the matter, and Woodward produced a path-breaking volume as critical of Southern elites as it was sympathetic to the South's inarticulate masses—white and black. "As one of the editors of the series I would have objected to the MS, if there would have been any way to bring it more into line with the facts," Coulter lamented in 1961. "But the point of view permeated the whole. And so we could not afford to reject the MS, which, by the way, put C. Vann on the pinnacle in Yankeeland."[34]

While Franklin's and Woodward's scholarly endeavors provoked Coulter, the actions of the University of Mississippi's James W. Silver directly threatened Coulter's reason for being. Appalled by the violence associated with James Meredith's integration of the university in the fall of 1962, Silver, who befriended 'Ole Miss's first African-American student, determined to expose the forces that had corrupted the state's intellectual environment. As president of the Southern Historical Association, he had originally intended in his presidential address to speak on the tragic limitations of antebellum Southern leadership, but the traumatic events current in his home state led him to a more contemporary topic. His address, "Mississippi: The Closed Society," delivered in Asheville, North Carolina, on November 7, 1963, stunned the audience, which at its conclusion gave him a standing ovation. "The search for historical truth has become a casualty in embattled Mississippi," he began. "Neither the governor nor the legislature . . . indicates any awareness that Mississippians were Americans before they were Southerners." He saw this as a result of "the romanticism associated with the Old South, the glorification of the Confederacy, and the bitter remembrances of Reconstruction" all of which played "their witless role in preserving a social order based on neither fact nor reason." The result, he proclaimed, was that "today the totalitarian society of Mississippi imposes on all its people an obedience to an official orthodoxy almost identical to the proslave philosophy."[35]

Absent from the Asheville meeting, Coulter read accounts of the speech in the *New York Times* and immediately registered his protest. "Jim's address would have fit a soap box better than the platform of a historical society," he wrote an official of the association. "I doubt not his sincerity for reform, but it was a most unwise address before a historical society. There was nothing historical about it." Ironically, Coulter found at least one good in its appearance in a Northern newspaper. That, he said, "could relieve the *Journal [of Southern History]* from publishing it, now that the newspapers have taken it up as part of their propaganda line."[36]

Coulter's anger was understandable, for he was one of the romanticizers of the Old South, the Confederacy, and Reconstruction who contributed to Mississippi's and the South's closed society, and he consciously employed his skills as a historian to bolster the white South's rejection of social justice for blacks. Standing before the University of Mississippi's Claiborne Society in March 1958, he had declared that the "spirit of the Abolitionists which whipped up the bitterness leading to the Civil War was transmuted into Northern Radicalism after the war to belabor and humiliate" the defeated South. He then moralized that there "are agitators and reformers today who are the lineal descendants of the Abolitionists of ante-bellum times and of the Radical during and after the Civil War. And they get as much pleasure out of making the South their whipping boy as ever their ancestors did in Reconstruction." But there was one difference. Prior to the Civil War abolitionists condemned the Supreme Court for its support of the Constitution and slavery. "Today," he argued, the hypocritical descendants of abolitionists defend the court and its support of Negro rights, "hold it sacrosanct and infallible," and proclaim that to protest the court "is next to treason if not treason itself."[37]

A year later Coulter repeated these themes in his address to the summer graduates at the University of Georgia. "It has been an age-old habit with certain people to make the South a whipping boy," he observed. "This attitude was basically the cause of the development of that bitterness and misunderstanding between the North and South that brought on the Civil War." There was nothing new in the "sectional attitudes of various people and newspapers in the North toward the South," he reasoned. In the present age, the North, allied with the Supreme Court, still sought to impose its will upon the American South. When Richard Russell, Georgia's segregationist United States senator, ordered Coulter's graduation address read into the *Congressional Record*, the professor expressed his delight. "Had I thought in the least that it would ever be published I might have been more restrained or might not have written it at all," he confided to a close friend. "But now I am glad that I did not have those inhibitions and did say exactly what was on my mind—and has been there for a considerable time."[38]

Serving the anti–civil rights cause, Coulter exercised his historian's insights before audiences far larger than university students and faculty. In an ongoing crusade to properly indoctrinate the South's youth, Coulter joined two other Georgia historians to write the junior high–level textbook *History of Georgia.* Published in 1954, the book claimed that in the decades prior to the Civil War "many of the Northern people were beginning to say that the Southern people were bad because they owned slaves. These . . . were called 'Abolitionists,' and they said that the South must get rid of its slaves; and if it did not Abolitionists would do it for them." Of course, Southern slaves were far from discontented. They lived in small cabins that kept them warm and dry, had plenty of food to eat, and were often treated by their masters to barbecues and picnics at which "they had a great frolic." During the Civil War, the slaves remained loyal to their owners, and stayed at home and "helped raise food for their masters and for the [Southern] soldiers. So, when the war was over, nearly everybody felt thankful to the Negroes." But freedom altered the South's social order. Negroes refused to work because it reminded them of slavery, they depended upon the charity of the Federal government in the form of the Freedmen's Bureau, and they were foolishly given the right to vote. "People in the South did not believe the Negroes, who had been slaves only a short while before and had no education, would know how to vote, at least until they had learned to read and to write," stated the *History of Georgia*. Because the Negroes often "sold their votes to dishonest people who wanted to win elections," the people of Georgia determined that the "worthless Negroes" should not participate in elections. By the opening of the twentieth century Georgians had "worked out a special plan" that kept most of the Negroes from voting. It did not, however, keep "good Negro citizens" from participating in government.[39] Written in the same year that the Supreme Court handed down the *Brown* decision mandating desegregation of schools with all deliberate speed, this textbook set the tone for a developing generation of white Georgians who would have to live with circumstances imposed by the Federal government.

The passage of the Civil Rights Act of 1964 and the Voting Rights Act of 1965 greatly altered Coulter's South, advancing a social revolution that had been defeated in the Reconstruction era he so loved studying. But he remained unreconstructed. Even as black suffrage loomed inevitable, Coulter published six articles in the *Georgia Historical Quarterly* exposing the villainy of three black legislators during the period of Georgia's Reconstruction, Henry M. Turner, Aaron Alpeoria Bradley, and Tunis G. Campbell, and strongly hinting that they were but harbingers of black rule in the modern South. Having completed his essays in 1968, he republished them in book form adding a concluding chapter that drove his point home. Turner was "guilty of immorality, forgery, and theft, also a preacher of the Gospel; Bradley, guilty of seduction, disbarred from the practice of law in Massachusetts, punished for inciting Negroes to riot and revolt, irrepressible in the legislature and twice expelled from this body; Campbell, guilty of malpractice, of false arrest and imprisonment for which he was sentenced to the penitentiary for a year, inciting Negroes to riot, and also a preacher of the Gospel." Such was to be expected of a class of voters loyal only to their race and impervious to all other considerations. "Just a century later," Coulter pontificated, "Adam Clayton Powell, Jr., with his amazing career of reputed immorality, arrogance, forgery, and theft of public money, albeit a preacher of the Gospel, was returned to Congress time after time by his adoring Harlem constituents." Little wonder, he concluded, that "Georgians a century ago should have done whatever they could to prevent Negroes voting and sending such representatives to the legislature."[40]

Coulter retired from the classroom in 1958 and stepped down as editor of the *Georgia Historical Quarterly* in 1973. He remained in good health and good spirits almost until his end, and took a genuine interest in the graduate students at the University of Georgia and encouraged them in their pursuits of historical knowledge. Nonetheless, in his life's waning years, his historical interpretations passed out of vogue, made old fashioned in a South sensitive to the civil rights of all her citizens—black, white, and other. John Hope Franklin had observed that Coulter's writings on the Reconstruction epoch were more valuable "in the history of history" than "in the history of Reconstruction." True enough, but in a larger sense the entire corpus of Coulter's scholarship goes beyond the writing of history for history's sake. It illuminates the profound nexus between the interpretation of the past and the perception of the present. His works and the works of his allies among Southern historians justified an articulated society rigidly stratified by race and class.

Coulter was disenchanted with the South of his closing days and doubtless looked back with longing to a time more suited to his values. By his death in 1981 he had lived well beyond the time when his works bolstered his vision of the South's proper social order. To him, this historiographical change was the ultimate tragedy, for decades before he had proclaimed with fervor: "In my teachings I am still trying to re-establish the Southern Confederacy."[41]

Frank L. Owsley's *Plain Folk of the Old South* after Fifty Years

ANTHONY GENE CAREY

At a meeting of the Southern Historical Association several years ago, a crowd of tweed-coated and blue-blazered men, and women in dark dresses, packed a large room for a session on plain whites in the Old South. About midway through the proceedings, a telephone mounted near the door buzzed loudly, turning heads and engendering chuckles. Just as the first ring faded, one presenter quipped, "It's Frank Owsley!" Tittering gave way to roars of laughter, which continued as the audience began to appreciate the whole joke. Not only did it seem appropriate that Owsley, the scholar who did most to lift Southern (white) plain folk from obscurity, should be on the wire, but also the assembled historians could easily imagine Owsley denouncing the critical, sophisticated approaches to plain folk on display in the session. A laugh line drove home a serious point: Owsley and his brand of Southern history had long since passed away.

Frank Lawrence Owsley's productive, multifaceted, and often controversial career earned him a lasting place in the pantheon of Southern historians. His early work on discord in the Confederacy and on Confederate diplomacy is still cited, and he will forever be remembered as one of the Vanderbilt Agrarians. Above all, however, his renown rests on the scholarship on plain folk produced during the 1930s and 1940s by him, his wife, Harriet Chappell Owsley, and their students and assistants. *Plain Folk of the Old South*, published in 1949, was one among several studies, but it alone is widely and rightly regarded as a landmark work.[1]

Insofar as Owsley wrote *Plain Folk* to demonstrate that ordinary, landholding farmers were historically important and to encourage serious study of them, he fulfilled his mission. Over the past three decades, increasing numbers of historians have been attracted to common whites as subjects of research. It is still possible to claim that too little has been done on common whites, but it is no longer plausible to claim, as Owsley did, that nothing has been done.

Owsley's successors, however, do not investigate plain folk in the ways or for the reasons that Owsley did; recent writers draw their inspiration more from the various types of "new" history that have arisen since the 1960s than from Owsley's work. While aspects of Owsley's interpretive themes are still echoed and some of his most basic contentions have become conventional wisdom, *Plain Folk* is, on the whole, of limited and diminishing relevance to late twentieth-century historians of the Old South.[2]

Frank Owsley's interest in Southern plain folk stemmed from several sources. His boyhood in central Alabama familiarized him with rural folk, introduced him to Confederate veterans, and formed his Southern identity. In the 1910s and 1920s, Owsley attended Alabama Polytechnic Institute (later Auburn University) and ultimately received his doctorate in history from the University of Chicago. Owsley also served in the armed forces, married Harriet Chappell, and taught history at Alabama Polytechnic and Birmingham-Southern College. He took a position at Vanderbilt University in 1920, rose to full professor in eight years, and remained at Vanderbilt until 1949. During his days in graduate school and in his early years as a professor, Owsley was increasingly exposed to what he considered a biased, Yankee-constructed view of Southern history, which blamed white Southerners for the Civil War and pictured the Old South as a slavocracy dominated by rich planters. Even Owsley's mentor at the University of Chicago, William E. Dodd, though himself a native North Carolinian, depicted the Old South as a class-ridden society rife with conflict between common whites and lordly slaveholders. Owsley came to believe that prejudice against the South permeated scholarly writing and warped outsiders' perceptions of his region, and he dedicated himself to presenting a more positive—to him more accurate—view of the Southern past. Owsley's early efforts at reinterpretation partly involved fastening responsibility for the Civil War on Northern abolitionists and irresponsible politicians. His immersion in the Vanderbilt Agrarian movement of the 1930s intensified his conservative political and racial views and identified him as a prominent defender of Southern and rural values against Yankee ways and modern industrialism. Owsley, by that time, had embarked on the research that led to *Plain Folk*, and he had already adumbrated the major themes of his magnum opus. Both unconsciously, in the day-to-day unfolding of his life, and consciously, as evidenced by his private correspondence and published work, Owsley was preparing to write *Plain Folk* for decades before the book appeared.[3]

The first lines of *Plain Folk* mark it as an adversarial work. Nineteenth-century travelers, commentators on the sectional conflict, and Northern-born historians had, Owsley was convinced, wrongly dismissed and unjustly despised common whites, slighting their role in antebellum Southern society and misunderstanding their character. Even native Southerners—such as Ulrich B.

Phillips, whom Owsley never cited in *Plain Folk*—had erred in emphasizing plantations, planters, and slaves, and Owsley intended to correct the record.[4] In a definition partly economic, partly geographic, and partly moral, Owsley identified those he hoped to rescue from neglect:

> It is the plain country folk with whom I am most concerned here, that great mass of several millions who were not part of the plantation economy. The group included the small slaveholding farmers; the nonslaveholders who owned the land which they cultivated; the numerous herdsmen on the frontier, pine barrens, and mountains; and those tenant farmers whose agricultural production, as recorded in the census, indicated thrift, energy, and self-respect.[5]

The forebears of plain folk, Owsley asserted, had tilled the soil or tended stock for countless generations. Immigrants to the South had crossed the ocean seeking productive freeholds. Some had failed in their quest, and their descendants existed as impecunious squatters or tenants. Most obtained land and prospered, however, and these fortunate ones possessed all "the solid virtues: integrity, independence, self-respect, courage, love of freedom, love of their fellow man, and love of God."[6] Instead of appearing as degraded and marginal, plain folk emerged in Owsley's work as quintessential Americans, whose hard work, sound morals, and solid accomplishments defined Southern society and exemplified the best values the nation had to offer.

Owsley's account of how plain folk peopled the South owed something to Frederick Jackson Turner—also uncited—and more to what Owsley considered common sense. People moved west for mundane reasons, ranging from a desire for fresh lands to a distaste for jail. Herdsmen, the frontier vanguard, were displaced over time by farmers in a relatively straightforward two-stage pattern of development. Agriculture, not slavery, Owsley insisted, "drove the herdsmen from frontier to frontier and finally into the pine barrens, hills, and mountains," much as farmers pushed cattlemen across the Great Plains in a later era.[7] Piney woods and mountain folk continued—largely by choice, Owsley stressed—to live by stock-raising and hunting, a mode of subsistence that Owsley romanticized to counter long-standing stereotypes that branded common whites in these regions as ignorant and impoverished. Although Owsley's sources on herdsmen were thin and his discussion general, his central point, that stock-raising was an integral part of the Old South's economy, was unquestionably correct and has been supported and elaborated by subsequent research.[8]

In tracing the migration of farmers, Owsley extended his depiction of a conflict-free frontier. Farmers "settled where they chose and stayed as long as it suited them"; they located "in considerable numbers on every type of soil adapted to agricultural uses except the swamp and river lands," which plain folk avoided because of diseases and the cost of clearing fields.[9] Large slave-holders did not force plain folk off the best lands. Rather, farmers sensibly elected to settle on lands and in climates similar to those they had left behind, which allowed them to pursue old habits and benefit from acquired skills. Mi-grants did not necessarily seek prime cotton soils; each family had its own purposes and predispositions. Migration generally followed lines of latitude: Virginians looked to Kentucky and Tennessee first, while Carolinians set out for Georgia and Alabama. Frontier patterns, such as the tendency to settle near kin or the propensity to relocate several times over the years, applied to rich and poor migrants alike. Distinctive Southern regions thus developed, for Owsley, out of nature, human choices, and luck.[10] Settlers "who moved into the rich lands were most fortunate"; nearly all could have and many did be-come wealthy from cotton and other staple crops. The larger portion of mi-grants, though, let longings for familiar surroundings guide them toward infe-rior soils, which ultimately limited their economic prospects.[11]

Themes of pluralism (different people pursuing diverse interests) and vol-untarism (decisions being freely made) thus dominated Owsley's version of the making of the Old South. Owsley not only overlooked involuntary mi-grants, slaves, American Indians, and many white women, but he also disre-garded disparities in power among white men. So focused was Owsley on smashing the myth of a tripartite South composed of planters, slaves, and poor whites, that he constructed a South without classes or coercion, in which op-tions were open—some simply chose more prudently than others—and re-wards were distributed justly, if unevenly. In Owsley's Old South, the ideals of the Declaration of Independence were translated into everyday practice; free-dom and opportunity ensured that plain folk could pursue happiness as they defined it.[12]

Owsley relied on precinct maps of Greene County, Alabama, prepared by Harriet C. Owsley, to clinch his contention that Old South neighborhoods were not segregated by class, that the landholdings of slaveholders and non-slaveholders, wealthy planters and common farmers, were "thoroughly inter-mingled."[13] The maps, to be sure, show that the precincts were not monolithic: instances of planter–plain folk proximity were numerous. Here Owsley rested his case, without exploring other equally or more obvious features of the maps. Imperfect but definite clusterings of similar holdings can be seen, although whether this tendency predominates over scattering depends partly on which map is considered and partly on the eye of the beholder. To the extent that Owsley recognized such clusterings, he attributed them to free choice; in other words, Owsley interpreted both scattering and clustering as supportive of his argument. More important, although Owsley drew attention to a handful of conspicuously large parcels owned by nonslaveholders, he otherwise ignored enormous differences in the size of landholdings. It is readily apparent from the maps that slaveholders owned the vast majority of the acreage in these precincts, and that a small planter minority owned huge tracts of land. Owsley's narrowly focused discussion of the maps, in conjunction with his previous remarks on settlement habits, invited readers to conclude that plain folk not only preferred to settle on poorer lands, but for some reason also preferred to let others hold the lion's share of acreage.[14]

Even more than maps, numbers provided key evidence in *Plain Folk*. For its day, Owsley's analysis of landholding in 1850 and 1860 was remarkable, path-breaking, even awe-inspiring. The immense labor involved in gathering the data was, as noted above, to a great extent performed by Harriet Owsley and others. Later Southern historians who have used the United States Census to study plain folk remain in Owsley's debt, and some of his factual contentions are incontrovertible. Most Southern whites were not landless poor, and wealthy planters did not control all the land or every slave. Landholding families usually formed a majority, often a substantial majority, of the white agricultural population in counties across the South. Most landholders were small landholders, and most slaveholders were small slaveholders. These and kindred truths that Owsley helped bring to light are now emphasized in any respectable American history textbook or survey of the Old South.

Yet, despite the impressiveness and usefulness, for some purposes, of the eighty pages of statistics in the closing chapter of *Plain Folk*, Owsley's arrangement of the numbers and his commentary on the tables displayed consistent biases and significant omissions. None of the statistics measured the value of landholdings or slaveholdings, making a determination of the distribution of wealth impossible. Although Owsley compared landownership among slaveholders and nonslaveholders, he invariably minimized differences.[15] To take just one representative example, Owsley stated that in the Georgia black belt in 1850 fifty percent of nonslaveholding farmers owned land, compared to ninety-one percent of slaveholders; the figures for 1860 were fifty-eight percent and ninety-two percent, respectively. Considering this gap in levels of landownership undeserving of remark, Owsley emphasized the gain in landholding among nonslaveholders during the 1850s.[16] Turning to the size of landholdings, Owsley used the fact that virtually all nonslaveholders and somewhat fewer than two-thirds of slaveholders owned fewer than fifty acres to argue that most agriculturists "were farmers rather than planters."[17] Along with objecting that any category that lumps together owners of five and five hundred acres is too broad, one might suggest an alternative perspective on the numbers. A table for 1860 shows that more than three-fourths of nonslaveholders owned less than 201 acres while more than three-fourths of slavehold-ers owned 201 acres or more.[18] Regardless of whether one calls them farmers or planters, slaveholders in the Georgia black belt owned far more land in considerably larger tracts than did nonslaveholders. Owsley was eager to show that plain folk were on the economic ladder, but he was unwilling to note that their feet rested on the bottom rungs.

The failure of Owsley and his students to confront the problem of unequal distribution of land, slaves, wealth, and power offered a wide opening for crit-ics.[19] Economist Gavin C. Wright, in one of his several extensive and sophis-ticated analyses of the distribution of wealth in the cotton South, contends that slave ownership was a more accurate determinant of economic position than landownership, and that merely documenting the existence of large num-bers of small landholders in the South proves little about the region's social structure. Landholding was, Wright demonstrates, more concentrated in the cotton South than in Northern states. When farm value instead of simply acres owned is considered, the richest five percent held over thirty-nine per-cent of the total farm value, while the poorest fifty percent held less than eight percent of the total farm value. The distribution of slaves was still more un-equal, and the share of slaves held by small farmers shrank during the 1850s.[20] Owsley and others, Wright charges, "either failed to use the relevant statistical criteria to test their hypotheses, or altered the hypothesis itself into an irrefu-table triviality, or, finally, relied on ad hoc explanations to dispense with that portion of their own evidence which pointed in the opposite direction."[21]

Not all of Owsley's critics are so harsh; some even lend him substantial support. Taken collectively, studies of Texas, Tennessee, Kentucky, and Arkan-sas show that vast disparities in wealth existed, that planters increased their shares of wealth over time, and generally, as Donald Winters phrases it, that "planter economic dominance rather than economic democracy characterized the antebellum South."[22] But Owsley did not, after all, claim that wealth was distributed *equally* in the Old South; rather, he argued that wealth was distrib-uted *widely* and *sufficiently* among the white agricultural population to allow most farmers to make a decent living by their own standards. The aforemen-tioned studies document high levels of landownership, opportunities for up-ward mobility, and general increases in wealth among plain folk during the 1850s. Plain folk lost ground, relatively, over time to large landholders and slaveholders, a fact that Owsley either did not recognize, chose to suppress, or thought immaterial. Small farmers were not, however, being driven off the land or being reduced to penury—precisely the points Owsley frequently reit-erated in *Plain Folk*.

More statistical studies of more counties will not reconcile differing recon-structions of the Old South's white social pyramid. Owsley's pyramid had a broad base that tapered toward a remote pinnacle, the planter elite. Each uniform stone represented one white family, the stones of landholders far outnumbered the rest, and the pinnacle could fall without disturbing the foundation. The pyramids of other historians are built of precisely hewn stones, scaled according to the wealth of the families represented. These inverted pyramids teeter on a tiny flake of rock, representing all the landless, slaveless whites of the Old South. The stones of the elite, weighing tons, overshadow all below them and press down with immense force—collapse impends.

Owsley's pyramid required no maintenance; each stone bore its proper burden and all were locked securely together. In considering interactions among whites, Owsley announced that plain folk "were not class conscious in the Marxian sense, for with rare exceptions they did not regard the planters and men of wealth as their oppressors."[23] Unfortunately, Owsley examined the issue cursorily, advanced two somewhat contradictory lines of argument, and presented no meaningful evidence to support his conclusion. Owsley contended that plain folk admired planters and hoped to emulate them, and that abundant opportunities—cheap land, high crop prices, and a fluid social order—made ambitions for upward mobility realistic. Having said that, though, Owsley also opined that few common whites "had a desire to become wealthy."[24] Instead, plain folk sought agricultural self-sufficiency, shunned debt, treasured family independence, and lived contentedly on humble homesteads. Owsley, for the most part, portrayed plain folk as plucky survivors, who "by ingenuity, heartbreaking toil, patient endurance, self-denial, and physical toughness" endured the horrors of Civil War and Reconstruction and afterward rebuilt the shattered South.[25] Perhaps hoping for more, but determined at least to keep what they had, plain folk allegedly were too busy running farms and grazing livestock to waste time reviling their economic betters.

On the strength of three reminiscences, two monographs, and an article, Owsley briefly characterized the Old South as a vibrant democracy. Coercion, whether economic, physical, or legal, was impossible in close-knit communities of independent men. Planters ruled, to the limited extent they did, by the power of reputation and by the art of persuasion. Adult white men had the ballot, were politically astute, and forced political parties to battle for their allegiance. Leaders in politics, planting, or the professions frequently rose from plain folk ranks and retained the common touch.[26] Owsley's interpretation of politics reflected his overarching conception of the Old South as an essentially changeless, harmonious society, in which power resided ultimately in the plain folk.

In his summary judgments regarding the mindset of plain folk and the power of white solidarity, Owsley touched on issues of enduring significance. A host of works written during and since the 1960s seek to explain, in one way or another, what Owsley intuitively understood: the bonds among white Southerners that cemented the Old South's social order. This rich historiography can be divided, essentially, into two schools. One, composed of historians influenced by Marxism and its variants, emphasizes the distinctiveness of the Old South, the peculiar nature of its society and its class relationships, and the ambiguous position of plain folk within a market-oriented, yet fundamentally noncapitalist, slave society. The other school, a more heterogeneous group, stresses white consensus on core values, highlights the importance of slavery, race, and racism in shaping white society, and sees many similarities between the Old South and the rest of the nation.

At the head of the line of Marxist interpreters of the Old South stands Eugene D. Genovese, whose corpus includes several of the most influential works on Southern history ever written. Genovese's sweeping, nuanced, and controversial interpretation of a noncapitalist Old South ruled by a planter class possessing hegemonic power has challenged and intrigued historians for more than thirty years. Slavery, peripheral in *Plain Folk,* is for Genovese the Old South's defining institution and the root cause of regional distinctiveness. So vast is the gulf separating Genovese from Owsley that one can hardly imagine how the latter would have reacted to, for example, *Roll, Jordan, Roll.* Would Owsley have even recognized such a book as history? Oddly enough, though, Owsley's and Genovese's descriptions of daily life in the Old South display similarities; Genovese's famous article on yeomen, particularly, contains numerous Owsley-like passages. Both contend that overt conflict among whites was limited and relatively infrequent, that planters and plain folk mostly got along. Genovese's explanation for this tranquility, planter-class hegemony, differs from Owsley's consensus argument as night does from day, yet on the bare fact of white unity they are in agreement—Genovese's far more numerous qualifications notwithstanding.[27]

While Genovese focuses on planters, Steven Hahn provides a sophisticated Marxist interpretation of the Southern yeomanry. Hahn's plain folk resemble Owsley's in several respects. Up-country Georgia farmers were proud, independent landholders intent on achieving family self-sufficiency; they feared debt, resisted the intrusions of the market, and had no desire to ape planters. Fiercely egalitarian and suspicious of change, yeomen espoused republican values—the republicanism paradigm, of course, had not yet been "discovered" when Owsley penned *Plain Folk*—and struggled to maintain autonomy. Fundamental differences nonetheless distinguish Hahn's work from Owsley's. In Hahn's view, yeomen resented the power of black belt planters and sometimes engaged in class skirmishes. If not quite class-conscious, Hahn's yeomen certainly harbored animosities and perceived white social divisions. Hahn's emphasis on yeomen's aversion to the market economy and capitalism obviously runs counter to one of Owsley's themes, plain folk as upwardly mobile American strivers. Most important, Hahn's work is modeled on the "new" social history and rests on a body of literature—studies of peasant cultures, Northern farm families, and Marxist theory—utterly foreign to Owsley. Despite some coincidence in conclusions, to speak of the meaningful influence of Owsley, who adamantly denied the existence of class or class-consciousness, on Marxist historians is to talk nonsense.[28]

Prominent non-Marxist historians of the Old South can more plausibly be linked to Owsley. James Oakes, Lacy K. Ford, Jr., J. Mills Thornton III, J. William Harris, and many others have constructed a composite interpretation of Southern society that incorporates many of Owsley's key points. James Oakes portrays small slaveholders as acquisitive capitalists on the prowl for the main chance. Lacy Ford largely supports—with modifications appropriate for up-country South Carolina—Owsley's analysis of a plain folk farm economy centered around family self-sufficiency, and Ford roots South Carolina's famous radicalism in widespread allegiance to republican precepts. Owsley surely would have understood politics in Mills Thornton's Alabama, where plain folk backed politicians who vowed to protect liberty and thwart the powerful. And J. William Harris's book on the area around Augusta, Georgia, expands greatly on Owsley's explanation of the forces that unified Southern neighborhoods and inhibited class conflict. Claims of white consensus, albeit more guarded than in *Plain Folk*, thus underpin much recent scholarship, and echoes of Owsley can be distinctly heard.[29]

Had Owsley not disregarded the role of race in shaping white consensus, *Plain Folk* might be nearer the center of ongoing debates. As it is, however, various formulations of the thesis that the Old South was a "herrenvolk democracy" dominate current non-Marxist historiography, and *Plain Folk* is relegated to the margins. George Fredrickson and many others emphasize that the lines separating races mattered most in the Old South. Social logic dictated that whites were free and blacks were slaves; free people of color constituted, from the white perspective, a troublesome exception to the rule. White skin was the most precious possession; whiteness overrode distinctions of wealth and made all white men, in the most crucial respect, equal. Whites valued liberty more because of the constant presence of its antithesis, slavery. All whites had a stake in preserving the peculiar institution, the foundation of the Old South's racial order. Southern politics revolved around the celebration of white democracy and the protection of slavery within the Union.[30]

Owsley made none of these arguments in *Plain Folk*. Instead, he implied by omission that plain folk lived and died in a slave society without being appreciably influenced by the presence of millions of African-Americans. African-Americans appear in *Plain Folk* almost exclusively as objects, as a mass of property possessed by slaveholders. The only substantive reference to black-white interaction in the entire book comes in an undocumented passage devoted to the origins of the Southern drawl, in which Owsley speculated that whites developed the drawl, while blacks merely mimicked it and helped diffuse it.[31] Needless to say, the remarkable work on race, slavery, and African-Americans that over the past forty years has transformed scholarly and popular understanding of American history owes nothing to *Plain Folk*, except insofar as Owsley's book was a single volume within a vast racist historiography that ultimately provoked a needed reaction.[32]

Owsley was undoubtedly aware of the significance of race; it counted as a factor in his other scholarly and polemical works, and he responded sharply to threats to segregation in his own time.[33] For several reasons, though, highlighting race in *Plain Folk* would have thwarted Owsley's purposes and played into the hands of his adversaries. Owsley thought that Northern interpreters of the Civil War had already said more than enough, much of it slanderous, about slavery and white racial prejudice in the Old South, and Ulrich B. Phillips had long before identified the determination to maintain white supremacy as the central theme of Southern history.[34] Owsley, who wanted to slay these messengers, could not parrot them. Discussing slaves, even as objects of fear and loathing, would have weakened Owsley's focus on the slaveless white majority and disturbed his image of a pacific South. Interpreting the Old South more as a racist and less as a rural society would also have problematized Owsley's contentions that plain folk exhibited the most admirable traits of Americans and that the South's history was a bright thread in the national narrative.

It thus was more appealing and, Owsley believed, accurate to attribute white consensus to common Southern folkways. Although Owsley consulted a few county histories and antebellum accounts for material, including a number of lengthy quotations, on folkways, he seemingly drew mostly on his own background and personal knowledge of the South to present a nostalgic portrait of life in the field and at the fireside. Innocuous generalizations abound in the most forgettable chapter in *Plain Folk*.[35] White folkways were, Owsley judged, partly rooted in the culture of the British Isles and partly "an indigenous growth of the South."[36] Families were close and kin relationships important. Religion was central; camp meetings were colorful. Communities enjoyed house-raisings and corn-shuckings; men relished court days and elections; and singings and weddings were grand social occasions. Men of the Old South, of course, rode as if born on horseback and always shot straight; their "average skill in the use of firearms has probably never been equaled and certainly never surpassed."[37] To rehabilitate plain folk and refute their detractors, Owsley banished both class and race from the Old South, and created a Dixie arcadia filled with joyous commoners whose greatest earthly worries were missing a squirrel or burning the fried chicken.

Owsley's discussion of Southern folkways was, like the rest of *Plain Folk*, correct to a point but incomplete and misleading. As the most recent work on plain folk makes clear, common whites experienced hunger, misery, and grief, which they did not always bear with quiet fortitude. Conflict among whites was far more pervasive than Owsley allowed, even if it normally was contained within bounds that did not fundamentally challenge the social order. Hard feelings between neighbors, resentment of arrogant local grandees, disputes within churches, and contests over land, to mention just a few matters, seriously disturbed the peace of plain folk. In ways Owsley never conceived of, male domination and gendered power structured the lives of white Southerners and other Americans. As Stephanie McCurry demonstrates so remarkably, both race and sex privileged white men as rulers over African-Americans and over the women and children in their own households. And, she argues, the status and interests that white men shared as masters of households bound them together and proved critical in creating and maintaining planter hegemony. Studies of power relations within and between Southern households that are sensitive to questions of race, class, and gender have already revolutionized Southern history and will be at the forefront of the field in the future.[38]

Plain Folk provided a valuable corrective to the views prevailing in 1949; Owsley accomplished much and told a part of the history of the Old South well. Had subsequent historians confined themselves to confronting Owsley on his own terms, *Plain Folk* probably could have withstood the assault. But events and intellectual developments since Owsley's death in 1956 have made it impossible for most historians to adopt or to sympathize with Owsley's perspective on Southern history. *Plain Folk*, dismissive of class, mute on race, and oblivious to gender, would never reach print today without drastic revisions that would alter it beyond recognition. Owsley cannot, of course, be blamed for lacking prescience or for not advancing arguments that he either was unacquainted with or abhorred. Nor can he be condemned, personally, for his biases, any more than can other historians who are, as Owsley was, products of their times and backgrounds.

But one can fairly say that *Plain Folk*, after fifty years, resembles a log cabin that has outlasted its usefulness. When raised amid the wilderness, the cabin provided welcome shelter and a nucleus for a community. As the neighborhood expanded and developed, however, newcomers with ambitious designs and refined materials fashioned larger, sturdier, and more impressive structures. The first cabin, still standing but uninhabited since the children of the original family moved away, continues to remind succeeding generations of their origins, even as time transforms landscapes and assumptions. The cabin and its builders are honored in memory and ritual, but the concerns of the present are not those of the past, and the heirs of the pioneers concentrate on constructing their own world and own history.

5

W. E. B. Du Bois

Ambiguous Journey to the Black Working Class

JOE W. TROTTER

W. E. B. Du Bois is a pivotal figure in the study of African-American life during the late nineteenth and early twentieth centuries. His intellectual, cultural, civil rights, and political activities influenced virtually every facet of the black experience, North and South. While scholars have written extensively about Du Bois's contributions to African-American studies, his scholarship on Southern and U.S. labor and working-class history is less fully appreciated. This gap in our knowledge is understandable. Du Bois only gradually moved the black working class to the center of his analysis of African-American and U.S. history. In his earliest writings, he emphasized the use of "social scientific" research to address issues of "race and reform" and gave primacy to the leadership of educated black professional people.[1]

By the early 1930s, while Du Bois retained his commitment to the employment of social science research to address contemporary problems, he accented the role of class conflict and the need for "social activism." Moreover, he increasingly linked the struggle to liberate African peoples in the United States to similar efforts around the world. In this global struggle for social change, Du Bois treated black workers as the vanguard, but retained the notion that they would be led by an "intelligent" and formally educated black leadership. Accordingly, this essay not only assesses Du Bois's principal sociological and historical writings within the context of his own changing life experiences in the Jim Crow North and South, but also emphasizes his ambiguous journey from a focus on elites to a focus on black workers as the primary force in African-American, Southern, and U.S. history.[2]

W. E. B. Du Bois was born in Great Barrington, Massachusetts, just a few years after the Civil War and the legal emancipation of all African-Americans. The only child of Alfred and Mary Burghardt Du Bois, the young Du Bois would later say that he was born "with a flood of Negro blood, a strain of French, a bit of Dutch, but thank God: no Anglo-Saxon."[3] Like other "Yankee

Protestants," however, Du Bois "cordially despised" the poor Irish and South Germans who worked in the local mills and on the railroads. Nonetheless, during his high-school years, Du Bois experienced an abrupt racial awakening when a white girl refused his offer to exchange cards: "I remember well when the shadow swept across me. . . . The exchange was merry till one girl, a tall newcomer, refused my card—refused it peremptorily, with a glance. Then it dawned upon me with a certain suddenness that I was different from the others . . . shut out from the world by a vast veil. I had thereafter no desire to tear down that veil, to creep through."[4]

Du Bois's encounter with racism reinforced his desire to excel in his school-work. Although he desired to attend nearby Harvard University, financial difficulties forced him to attend Fisk University, an all-black college established in 1866 in Nashville, Tennessee. Before graduating from high school with honors in 1884, Du Bois had made only two short trips out of Great Barrington. On one occasion, he had visited his uncle in New Bedford, Massachusetts, but a trip to Providence, Rhode Island, had the greatest impact on his thinking about black people. Du Bois attended a picnic on Narragansett Bay, at which black people from three different states came together. As he put it, "I was astonished and inspired. I apparently noted nothing of poverty or degradation, but only extraordinary beauty of skin color and utter equality of mien, with absence so far as I could see of even the shadow of the lines of race."[5]

At Fisk, Du Bois observed the rising tide of racial violence, intimidation, segregation, and disfranchisement in the post-Reconstruction South. In Nashville, he early encountered Southern racism as he walked along a city street. Again, as during his high-school days, his experience involved the cross-cutting issues of gender and race. Just as he approached a corner, a white woman suddenly appeared and brushed against him. When he tipped his hat to her and politely said, "I beg your pardon, madam!" the woman angrily retorted: "How dare you speak to me, you impudent nigger!"[6]

As a result of his Southern experience, Du Bois later said that he realized in no uncertain terms that "henceforward I was a Negro." He soon immersed himself in the academic life of Fisk and received extraordinary encouragement from his teachers. Du Bois edited the school's newspaper and used it to indict racial inequality. In "An Open Letter to the Southern People," the young Du Bois criticized whites for erecting a color line that excluded blacks from equal access to education and then justifying disfranchisement on the premise that blacks were "ignorant."[7]

After graduating from Fisk in 1888, Du Bois received a fellowship to pursue graduate studies at Harvard. He earned a second bachelor's degree in 1890, a master's degree in 1891, and his doctorate in history in 1895.[8] Between 1892 and

1894, however, Du Bois studied abroad at the University of Berlin, the seat of the emerging professionalization of historical scholarship. He deepened his study of economics, history, and especially sociology. Under scholars like Adolf Wagner, Heinrich von Treitschke, Gustav Schmoller, and Max Weber, Du Bois gravitated increasingly toward the use of scientific methods of social research and the emerging field of sociology. He later recalled very positive interactions with Europeans and dreaded his return to the United States: "As a student in Germany, I built great castles in Spain and lived therein. I dreamed and loved and wondered and sang; then after two long years I dropped suddenly back into 'nigger'-hating America!"[9]

Upon his return to the United States in 1894, Du Bois could not find a job in white universities despite his stellar credentials. Even black colleges like Fisk, Atlanta, and Tuskegee informed him that all posts were filled. Du Bois finally received an offer from Wilberforce College, an African-American Episcopal Church school in Ohio. Even here he received an offer to teach classics rather than his primary areas of interest and training—history, political economy, and sociology. Nonetheless, Du Bois eagerly accepted the position while simultaneously completing work on his doctoral dissertation, *The Suppression of the African Slave-Trade to the United States of America, 1638–1870.*[10]

A revised and enlarged version of his master's thesis, Du Bois's doctoral dissertation was published in 1896—the first monograph to appear in the new Harvard Historical Studies series in the Department of History and Government. Considering the sway of white supremacist ideas in the academy at the time, Du Bois's book received good reviews in the *American Historical Review,* the *Annals of the American Academy,* the *English Historical Review,* *Atlantic Monthly,* and *Nation,* all in 1897. The reviewer in *Nation* correctly predicted that Du Bois's book would "long remain the authoritative work on the subject."[11] Although Du Bois would later lament his failure to appreciate the theories of Karl Marx and Sigmund Freud, his Pulitzer Prize–winning biographer, David Lewis, concludes that his book remains "a useful classic."[12] From the vantage point of the use of primary documents and original research, Du Bois's study of the African slave trade was his most significant historical work. His subsequent historical writings were chiefly works of synthesis and interpretation, while his subsequent scholarship employing primary documents was mainly sociological.[13] Taken together, these studies not only highlight Du Bois's contributions to Southern labor history, but also his ongoing struggle to reconcile the profound tensions of class and race in his scholarship, thought, and policy injunctions.

Based mainly on official government reports, maritime records, personal diaries, and the papers of abolition and anti-abolition societies, *The Suppression of the African Slave-Trade* explored the shifting currents of antislavery thought and practice in the slave trade from the colonial era through the emancipation years. Du Bois concluded that the abolition of slavery required a bloody Civil War because Europe, the colonists, and later the new nation regarded this land as existing chiefly for the benefit of whites, "and as designed to be exploited, as rapidly and ruthlessly as possible" (p. 194). The nation lowered its moral standard for the sake of material advantages. Even in the wake of the American Revolution, when new opportunities for abolition presented themselves, "energetic efforts were wanting and, before the nation was aware, slavery had seized a new and well-nigh immovable footing" in new land in the southwest (p. 194).

Although Du Bois accented the moral imperative, he nonetheless probed restrictions on the slave trade within the larger context of economic change and the shifting uses of slave labor. He examined the subject, respectively, in the planting, farming, and commercial regions of the South, mid-Atlantic, and Northeast during the colonial era, and looked at the rise of the cotton kingdom during the antebellum years. Though only briefly, Du Bois noted the impact of economic and technological innovations like the cotton gin in the growth, manufacture, and marketing of cotton products. Indeed, Du Bois suggested that "the development of Southern slavery has heretofore been viewed so exclusively from the ethical and social standpoint that we are apt to forget its close and indissoluble connection within the world's cotton market" (p. 152).

Du Bois emphasized the actions and power of planters, commercial elites, and the state, but he indirectly (and occasionally directly) illuminated the role of blacks in limiting the slave trade. From the outset of the colonial period, he noted the planters' fear of slave insurrection as a deterrent to unlimited importations of Africans. As the number of slaves escalated, planters expressed growing fear of being "cut off by their own negroes" (p. 6). As Du Bois put it, "This condition of vague dread and unrest not only increased the severity of laws and strengthened the police system, but was the prime motive back of all the earlier efforts to check the further importation of slaves" (p. 6). References to black self-activity were not limited to mainland insurrections like the 1740 Stono Rebellion in South Carolina. Du Bois also emphasized the impact of Toussaint L'Ouverture and the Haitian Revolution during the 1790s and early 1800s. L'Ouverture represented the "age of revolution in America." "He rose to leadership through a bloody terror, which contrived a Negro 'problem' for the Western Hemisphere, intensified and defined the anti-slavery movement, became one of the causes, and probably the prime one, which led Napoleon to sell Louisiana for a song, and finally, through the interworking of all these effects, rendered more certain the final prohibition of the slave trade by the United Sates in 1807" (p. 70).

Despite Du Bois's emphasis on the self-activity of slaves and the role of economic forces in the spread of human bondage, he aimed first and foremost to use his training in the new "scientific history" to illuminate the nation's "moral" failure to eradicate the institution of slavery. As he repeatedly stated, in varying ways, "It was the plain duty of the colonies to crush the trade and the system in its infancy. . . . It was the plain duty of a Revolution based upon 'Liberty' to take steps toward the abolition of slavery. . . . It was the plain duty of the Constitutional Convention [not] . . . to compromise with a threatening social evil" (p. 198).

Du Bois's emphasis on moral imperatives was partly a product of his graduate school training in philosophy. Only slowly did he move from what he called the "sterile land of philosophic speculation, to the social sciences as the field for gathering and interpreting that body of fact which would apply to my program for the Negro."[14] In other words, Du Bois said, "I conceived the idea of applying philosophy to an historical interpretation of race relations. . . . I was trying to take my first steps toward sociology as the science of human action."[15] According to Lewis, had Du Bois systematically followed up on the insights of economic factors, he "would have sensed that by reducing morals exclusively to a function of profits he would be nullifying the major African-American strategy for improving race relations through leverage on the national conscience."[16]

Du Bois's moral engagement with the slave trade was not only a consequence of his professional school training and his determination to awaken the conscience of the nation. It was also a product of his engagement with the search for the essential spirit of "the race." Even as he conducted his careful historical research, Du Bois retained a strong commitment to what he perceived as the core ideas, beliefs, and "soul" of black people. In 1897, he delivered a paper to the inaugural meeting of the American Negro Academy entitled "The Conservation of the Races." He argued that African-Americans were Americans by birth, citizenship, political ideas, language, and religion, but "farther than that, our Americanism does not go." African-Americans were more than merely Americans. They also had a special relationship with African peoples around the globe: "We are Negroes, members of a vast historic race that from the very dawn of creation has slept, but half awakening in the dark forests of its African fatherland. We are the first fruits of this new nation, the harbinger of that black tomorrow which is yet destined to soften the whiteness of the Teutonic today. We are that people whose subtle sense of song has given America its only American mad money-getting plutocracy."[17]

In other words, Du Bois's work on the suppression of the slave trade was intertwined with his larger project of "race-making." No less than his effort to awaken the moral conscience of the nation, however, Du Bois's program of "race-making" only gradually acknowledged the black workers as the keystone in their own, black America's, and the nation's development. As we will see in our assessment of *The Philadelphia Negro,* Du Bois's "program for the Negro" exhibited little confidence in the capacity of poor and working-class blacks to take charge of their own lives and make their own history.

After teaching at Wilberforce for one year, Du Bois received an invitation to go to Philadelphia to undertake a systematic study of the city's expanding black population. Because Wilberforce officials exhibited little interest in his research, Du Bois enthusiastically accepted a temporary appointment as assistant instructor in the Department of Sociology at the University of Pennsylvania. For the next two years, he studied Philadelphia's black community, systematically using maps, census data, descriptive statistics, and in-depth interviews. Moreover, while this was mainly a sociological study with an attenuated temporal framework, Du Bois developed his research against a solid historical backdrop. Published in 1899, *The Philadelphia Negro* helped to set the standard for urban community studies, which proliferated with the emergence of the Chicago School of Sociology during the 1920s. Unfortunately, while liberal historians and some journalists praised *The Philadelphia Negro,* mainstream urban sociologists largely ignored Du Bois's contribution to the field.[18]

Although *The Philadelphia Negro* focused on black life in a Northern city, it is a key study of Southern black migration, labor, and community life. The Seventh Ward, the site of massive in-migration of Southern blacks, emerged at the heart of Du Bois's research. Du Bois examined two major waves of Southern black migration into the city. The first emerged during the antebellum years when large numbers of free blacks and fugitive slaves entered the city, while the second came in the wake of the Civil War and Reconstruction. In both waves, blacks from upper South and border states comprised the bulk of newcomers (pp. 25, 77–78). For the antebellum and postbellum years, he concluded that black population movement "proved disastrous" for the city's black "better class." Since the city's white population refused to draw class distinctions among blacks, old Philadelphians "could not escape into the mass of white population and leave the new Negroes to fight out their battles with the foreigners" (pp. 25–26).

By analyzing black migration primarily from the vantage point of Philadelphia's established black elite, Du Bois treated Southern blacks as the chief problem in African-American work, institutional, and political life. In his view, the "Philadelphia Negro" faced two prominent difficulties as a worker. First, he said, "training as a slave and freedman" made the black worker a less "efficient and reliable workmen" than the "average native American or . . . many foreign immigrants." Second, according to Du Bois, black workers were "as a rule, willing, honest, and good natured," but "as a rule, careless, unreliable and unsteady" (p. 97). At times, Du Bois seemed to dismiss the exclusionary practices of white workers as factors limiting the job opportunities of black artisans. I here cite his analysis at length:

> What the trades unions and white workmen have done is to seize an economic advantage plainly offered them. . . . Here was a mass of black workmen of whom very few were by previous training fitted to become the mechanics and artisans of a new industrial development; here, too, were an increasing mass of foreigners and native Americans who were usually well fitted to take part in the new industries . . . they were by previous training better workmen on the average than Negroes; they were stronger numerically and the result was that every new industrial enterprise started in the city took white workmen. . . . The supply of Negroes for such trades could not keep pace with the extra-ordinary growth of the city and a large number of white workmen entered the field. They immediately combined against Negroes primarily to raise wages; the standard of living of the Negroes lets them accept low wages, and, conversely, long necessity of accepting the meager wages offered [has] made a low standard of living. (pp. 126–27)

The Philadelphia Negro offered a class analysis of African-American churches, fraternal orders, leisure, and politics. Du Bois carefully differentiated the experiences of the middle class and its small elite; the members of what he called the "respectable working-class"; the "moral" but "not always energetic or thrifty" poor; and what he termed the "submerged tenth," that is, the "lowest class of criminals, prostitutes and loafers" (pp. 310–11). Southern migrants stood at the center of his portrait of the most problematic dimensions of life among the working class and poor, which in turn affected the lives of blacks at the upper end of the class structure. Du Bois continually reiterated the point: "Usually they are not natives of the city, but immigrants who have wandered from the small towns of the South to Richmond and Washington and thence to Philadelphia" (p. 313). According to Du Bois, the experiences that these migrants accumulated from such "wanderings" helped "to swell the numbers of a large migratory criminal class who are often looked upon as the product of particular cities, when, as a matter of fact, they are the off-scouring of country districts, sharpened and prepared for crime by the slums of many cities through which they have passed" (pp. 76–78).

In Du Bois's view, migrants not only placed extraordinary pressure on the material resources of established black institutions, but they also weakened the community's influence on municipal politics. Pennsylvania disfranchised black citizens in 1837. Du Bois not only related disfranchisement to the growing antebellum controversy over slavery, but also accented the role of "ignorant and dangerous elements" of Southern black migrants who entered the city in

rising numbers (p. 370). Similarly, during the onset of Southern disfranchisement of blacks during the 1890s, Du Bois again related the phenomenon
to the presumed "ignorance" of the Southern ex-slaves: "The indiscriminate
granting of universal suffrage to freedmen and foreigners was one of the most
daring experiments of a too venturesome nation" (p. 368). Du Bois advocated
"educational and property qualifications impartially enforced against ex-slaves
and immigrants" (p. 368). Indeed, he justified a less democratic approach to
black working people and the poor as a measure to ensure the rights of educated black elites. In the absence of a nonracial education and property re-
quirement for voting, he argued that it was certainly "more just to admit the
untrained and ignorant than to bar all Negroes in spite of their qualifications;
more just, but also more dangerous" (pp. 368, 373).

As harsh as Du Bois seemed in his judgment of black workers and the poor,
he insisted on the role of racism in limiting their economic and educational
opportunities. His emphasis on white workers' efficiency and their ability to
out-compete blacks highlighted and buttressed his call for an end to discrimination. "It is sufficient to say in general that the sorts of work open to Negroes
are not only restricted by their own lack of training but also by discrimination
against them on account of their race; that their economic rise is not only
hindered by their present poverty, but also by a widespread inclination to shut
against them many doors of advancement open to the talented and efficient of
other races" (p. 98). At another point, Du Bois went a step further and refuted
the notion of free labor competition in a market economy: "In many cases men
will not do this [hire blacks] if it involves association, even in a casual and
business way, with Negroes" (p. 146). Economic discrimination, he said, represented "the centre and kernel of the Negro problem so far as the white people
are concerned." Such discrimination, he exhorted, was "morally wrong, politically dangerous, industrially wasteful, and socially silly" (p. 394).

Du Bois's portrait of black migrants was considerably modified in his detailed social study of blacks in Farmville, Virginia. As he neared completion of
The Philadelphia Negro and the end of his instructorship at the University of
Pennsylvania, Du Bois conducted the Farmville study under the auspices of
the U.S. Commissioner of Labor. Released in January 1898 as Bulletin No. 14,
his Department of Labor study offered a more nuanced and complex portrait
of Southern black workers than appeared in The Philadelphia Negro. Du Bois
not only talked about the men who easily lapsed "into the habit of working
part of the year and loafing the rest"; he also talked about the motivation of
the "really industrious man" who desired to work but faced recurring bouts of
unemployment. Southern black institutional and cultural life also gained
highly favorable comment in the Farmville study.[19]

In The Philadelphia Negro, Du Bois downplayed the range of Southern black experiences and their impact on the city partly because he aimed to develop a program of interracial reform that privileged interactions between black and white elites. Du Bois urged sympathetic whites, particularly industrialists, to recognize the existence of "the better class of Negroes" and "gain their active aid and cooperation" in "uplifting" the mass of working-class and poor blacks (p. 396). As a class, Du Bois believed that employers represented "the best average intelligence and morality of the community" (p. 129). Thus, he held out few prospects for interracial cooperation in the labor movement. Within a few years, however, black workers and their relationship with the predominantly white labor movement would take on greater significance in Du Bois's historical and sociological writings.

Following his work on *The Philadelphia Negro*, Du Bois accepted an invitation to join the faculty of Atlanta University. Influenced by Booker T. Washington's Tuskegee conferences on black life in the rural South, university president Horace Bumstead hoped to make Atlanta the center of social scientific research on urban blacks. Thus, he invited Du Bois to head the university's annual conferences on "urban Negro problems" and to supervise the university's sociology program. When Du Bois accepted the assignment in 1897, the university had already staged its first two conferences and published the proceedings for 1896 and 1897. Under Du Bois's leadership, however, Atlanta University "tightened up the series and set up a long-range, more intensive research program, and made the studies as thorough [as its limited resources permitted]." Between the series inception in 1896 and its demise in 1914, the Atlanta University Publications produced eighteen monographs. While the later studies sometimes repeated the findings of earlier ones, the published proceedings of the famous Atlanta University Conferences and Publications not only helped to establish the foundation for the broader field of African-American studies, but they also established the groundwork for the special field of African-American labor and working-class history.[20]

Du Bois's growing disenchantment with Booker T. Washington's leadership shaped his approach to the Atlanta University Conferences and Publications. When Washington delivered his famous Atlanta Cotton Exposition address in 1895, Du Bois agreed with his gradualist perspective on improving race relations in the Jim Crow South. By the early twentieth century, however, as public opinion makers, philanthropists, and industrialists ignored the fruits of his social scientific studies, and the conditions of black people continued to deteriorate, Du Bois exhibited growing impatience with Washington's effort to work within the existing legal and institutional framework of the segregationist South.[21] In 1903, he published *The Souls of Black Folk* and clearly spelled out his differences with Washington. As he put it, "So far as Mr. Washington preaches Thrift, Patience, and Industrial Training for the masses, we must hold up his hands and strive with him. . . . But so far as Mr. Washington apologizes for injustice, North or South, does not rightly value the privilege and duty of voting, belittles the emasculating effects of caste distinctions, and opposes the higher training and ambition of our brighter minds—so far as he, the South or the Nation, does this—we must unceasingly and firmly oppose them."[22]

Two years later Du Bois issued a call for a meeting to chart a new course for the civil rights movement. Twenty-nine leading black professional men answered Du Bois's call and, meeting on the Canadian side of Niagara Falls, launched the Niagara Movement, which resulted in the formation of the interracial National Association for the Advancement of Colored People in 1909. The Niagara Movement and its successor NAACP demanded an end to lynchings, disfranchisement, and segregation in American life. In 1910, when the NAACP selected Du Bois to edit *Crisis* magazine, its principal organ of public opinion, he resigned his position at Atlanta University and moved to New York. Under the influence of white socialists—including Mary Ovington, William English Walling, and Charles Edward Russell—Du Bois joined the Socialist party the following year, but he resigned in 1912, when his comrades vehemently opposed his support of Democrat Woodrow Wilson for president. In the meantime, Du Bois exhibited a growing interest in the plight of black workers.[23]

Du Bois's shifting ideas on race, class, and labor gained articulation in *The Negro Artisan*. Published in 1902 and revisited with Augustus Dill in 1912, *The Negro Artisan* emphasized the discriminatory attitudes and behavior of white workers, employers, and the state. Du Bois now strongly rejected the racist perceptions of black workers as inefficient, lazy, incompetent, and "incapable of filling a place in modern industrial organization" (pp. 22–23, 153–54, 155–88). He not only defended black workers against charges of inferiority by highlighting the role of racial discrimination and prejudice in the present, but he also used history to provide a more positive view of the black workers than theretofore presented. He opened his study with a discussion of the African artisan, emphasizing that "in practically all parts of the continent of Africa, we find concrete evidence of that ability which makes for artisanship" (p. 25). Moreover, while Du Bois downplayed the skills of the antebellum slave artisans compared with those of free whites, he nonetheless concluded with an emphasis on the prominence of the slave artisan in the Southern economy (p. 28). In his view, it was the tyranny of slave masters and later employers, combined with the enmity of white workers, that enforced the economic subordination of the black proletariat. Du Bois defended black workers against charges that they "carelessly threw away their monopoly of the Southern labor market and allowed the white mechanic to supplant them." Lack of political

rights, white worker competition, and development of new industrial processes all undermined the position of the black artisan in the emancipation era:
"He was enabled to maintain himself only by accepting low wages and keeping
at all hazards the good will of the [white] community" (pp. 1–28).

Du Bois also illuminated the experiences of black miners, sawmill hands,
teamsters, and rural and urban laborers of various types. He noted how op-
pressive conditions in postbellum Southern agriculture—including laws regu-
lating contracts, wages, and vagrancy—undermined the position of black rural
workers and forced them into "pauperism and crime" (p. 140). Consequently,
unlike his policy prescriptions in *The Philadelphia Negro*, he advocated voting
rights, more equitable laws, and expanded opportunities for education as solutions to the problems of black "common laborers." Du Bois now believed that
it was "impossible for these two million and more black workingmen to maintain themselves when thrust into modern competitive industry so long as the
state allows them no voice or influence in the making of the laws or the interpretation and administration of the same" (p. 142). Moreover, while he attacked the racism of white workers, he also affirmed the common interests of
all workers and concluded that "the salvation of all laborers, white and black,
lies in the great movement of racial uplift known as the labor movement. . . .
Let us black men fight prejudice and exclusion in the labor world and fight it
hard; but do not fight the labor movement" (p. 7).

Under the impact of World War I, the 1920s, and especially the early years
of the Great Depression, Du Bois made the transition to a more fully prole-
tarian approach to the black experience. Following Booker T. Washington's
death in 1915, he became the most prominent black public figure in the United
States. Before he could gain his bearings, however, he faced challenges from
new and more militant spokespersons. During the war years, the young socialist A. Philip Randolph criticized Du Bois and the NAACP for urging blacks
to "close ranks," support the war, and curtail their agitation for civil rights until
war's end.[24] During the early 1920s, the rise of Marcus Mosiah Garvey and the
Universal Negro Improvement Association eclipsed the prominence of Du
Bois and Randolph, until Garvey's imprisonment in 1924 and deportation in
1927. Garvey advocated a militant black consciousness and "Back to Africa
Movement."[25] Still, in the early postwar years, Du Bois regained his militant posture with his stinging *Crisis* editorial: "We Soldiers of Democracy return. . . . We return from fighting. We return fighting. Make way for Democracy! We saved it in Europe, and by the Great Jehovah, we will save it in the
United States of America, or know the reason why."[26]

Following his *Crisis* editorial, Du Bois extended his ideas of black nationalism, pan-Africanism, and the class struggle. He coordinated several Pan-
African Congresses—which met in European capitol cities including Paris,

Brussels, and London—to organize resistance against colonialism; he used the *Crisis* to promote Harlem Renaissance writers and artists; and he advocated the development of black consumers' and producers' cooperatives. Du Bois believed that such efforts would transform segregation into a potent weapon against racism in the predominantly white culture, capital, and labor markets. Under the impact of the Depression, Du Bois heightened his advocacy of "voluntary segregation" as a way to shield black communities against hard times. Coupled with the growing financial difficulties of the *Crisis*, this idea cut against the integrationist grain of the NAACP and precipitated Du Bois's resignation from the editorship in 1934.

After resigning from the *Crisis*, Du Bois returned to his job at Atlanta University and soon produced *Black Reconstruction*. As early as 1909, Du Bois had suggested a new interpretation of the Reconstruction era. In a paper delivered at the annual meeting of the American Historical Association in New York, Du Bois argued that "Negro rule" gave the South three things: "1. Democratic government. 2. Free public schools. 3. New social legislation." Published a year later in the *American Historical Review*, "Reconstruction and Its Benefits" became the first and only essay published by a black scholar in the nation's premier historical journal until the modern civil rights era. Yet, Du Bois's ideas on the centrality of black workers in the emancipation process had slowly taken shape in the wake of World War I when he started to read Karl Marx. His trip to Russia in 1926 deepened his understanding of communist ideology. Although he rejected "Communism of the Russian-type" for African-Americans, he did believe "that the solution of letting a few of our capitalists share with whites in the exploitation of our masses, would never be a solution of our problem."[27] More important, as Du Bois related in his autobiography, as the Great Depression took its toll on black and white workers, he "began to awake and to see in the socialism of the New Deal, emancipation of all workers, and the labor problem, which included the Negro problem."[28] Along with the devastating impact of the Depression on workers in America, particularly black workers, Du Bois's growing sensitivity to the struggles of working people helped to set the stage for *Black Reconstruction*.

Based upon established studies rather than a systematic examination of archival sources, *Black Reconstruction* reconceptualized the black experience in class terms and placed black workers at the center of the nation's history. According to Du Bois, black workers fueled the development of "modern industry" during the cotton revolution of the early nineteenth century in Europe and America. They also represented the central "problem of democracy" in the new republic. In other words, despite efforts to confine the Civil War to white men, sections, and classes, Du Bois convincingly argued, it was the black worker, "as founding stone of a new economic system . . . who brought Civil

War in America. He was the underlying cause, in spite of every effort to base the strife upon union and national power" (p. 15).

Du Bois not only reinterpreted the mass movement of black fugitives into Union lines as a workers' "general strike" against the Confederacy, but he also viewed it as a much needed addition to the Union Army and labor forces. Bondsmen and women helped to transform a war between the states into a war for their own liberation. Thus, they helped to forge their own transition from enslaved laborer to soldier-worker-citizen. As Du Bois put it,

> What the Negro did was to wait, look and listen and try to see where his interest lay. There was no use in seeking refuge in any army which was not an army of freedom; and there was no sense in revolting against armed masters who were conquering the world. As soon, however, as it became clear that the Union armies would not or could not return fugitive slaves, and that the masters with all their fame were uncertain of victory, the slave entered upon a general strike against slavery by the same methods that he had used during the period of the fugitive slave. He ran away to the first place of safety and offered his services to the Federal Army. So that in this way it was really true that he served his former master and served the emancipating army; and it was also true that this withdrawal and bestowal of his labor decided the war. (p. 57)

Black men made good on their citizenship rights. They allied with white Republicans and helped to write their citizenship rights into law. Under the guidance of a relatively well-educated and skilled black leadership, African-Americans helped to draft new constitutions that not only enfranchised male ex-slaves, but also initiated reforms that liberalized Southern laws and improved the social welfare and legal position of poor whites as well as blacks. Although Du Bois erroneously referred to the new interracial governments as "signs" of the "dictatorship of the black proletariat," particularly in South Carolina, he acknowledged the limited scope of interracial cooperation and offered telling insight into the resurgence of racial hostilities in the aftermath of Reconstruction (pp. 381–430). According to Du Bois, the old planter class increasingly merged "their blood so completely with the rising poor whites" that they virtually "disappeared as a separate aristocracy" (p. 54). As white elites disengaged from blacks and created alliances with poor whites, Du Bois persuasively argued, "lynchings, mob law, murders and cruelty" correspondingly intensified (p. 54).

In an illuminating chapter called "The Propaganda of History," Du Bois again linked his ongoing engagement with social scientific studies with his abiding commitment to social change. He dissected the racial biases of the prolific William Archibald Dunning and John W. Burgess School of Reconstruction historiography at Columbia University. According to Burgess, Dunning, and some sixteen studies by their graduate students, Reconstruction was a "tragedy" because it subordinated the interest of the white South to corrupt and "barbarous" black-Republican machines. These studies culminated in the publication of Claude Bowers's *The Tragic Era* (1927). While Du Bois acknowledged the "scientific poise" of some of these studies, he decried most as "thoroughly bad" or "openly and blatantly propaganda" (p. 720). In the case of Bowers's popular work, it was an "excellent and readable piece of . . . classic . . . historical propaganda of the cheaper sort" (p. 721).

Du Bois sharply decried the racist uses of history and reaffirmed the antiracist project of historical recovery and black liberation. In his view, the emancipation and Reconstruction years were a "magnificent" period in African-American, Southern, and U.S. history. African-Americans spearheaded "the finest effort to achieve democracy for the working millions which this world had ever seen. . . . Yet we are blind and led by the blind. We discern in it no part of our labor movement; no part of our industrial triumph; no part of our religious experience" (p. 727). Unlike Du Bois's earlier works, however, *Black Reconstruction* concluded with a call for a broader international consciousness that reached beyond pan-Africanism and embraced all the colonized and exploited peoples of the modern world: "Immediately in Africa, a black back runs red with the blood of the lash; in India, a brown girl is raped; in China, a coolie starves; in Alabama, seven darkies are more than lynched; while in London, the white limbs of a prostitute are hung with jewels and silk. Flames of jealous murder sweep the earth, while brains of little children smear the hills" (p. 728).

Scholars now acknowledge Du Bois's immense contributions to African-American, Southern, and U.S. labor and working-class history. His impact is also apparent in the growing "whiteness" studies of American labor and working-class history. According to historian David Roediger, a leading proponent of whiteness research: "No body of thought rivals that of W. E. B. Du Bois for an understanding of the dynamics, indeed dialectics, of race and class in the U.S."[29]

Du Bois's legacy is nonetheless the subject of ongoing debate and challenges. Perhaps the greatest challenge has emerged from women's, gender, and cultural studies. In her careful assessment of *The Philadelphia Negro*'s treatment of working-class women, historian Tera Hunter shows how Du Bois "recognized the structural problems of racial discrimination that perpetuated underemployment and unemployment" for black men and women, but criticized women who took work outside the home "for imperiling" the lives of "their unsupervised children."[30] In his groundbreaking cultural biography, *The*

Art and Imagination of W. E. B. Du Bois, Arnold Rampersad decries the narrow emphasis of existing scholarship on Du Bois's sociological and historical writings. In his view, Du Bois's "greatest gift was poetic in nature" and his "essentially poetic vision" fueled his "scholarship, propaganda, and political activism."[31] Similarly, historian Thomas C. Holt urges us to capture the "multivocality" of Du Bois's scholarly writings—"by turns lyrical, socio-historical, hortatory, self-revelatory."[32]

While Du Bois only gradually moved the black working class to the center of his scholarship on African-American life, his journey to the proletariat was nonetheless deeply rooted in his earliest research on the black experience. His book on the African slave trade helped to open the door to the problem of slavery, labor, and the development of the new republic. Although he emphasized the ways that the nation lowered its moral standard, enslaved millions of Africans, and allowed material advantages to dictate its development, he also noted the activities of slaves on behalf of their own liberation. Similarly, while *The Philadelphia Negro* elevated an educated elite to a favored position within black and white America, the "problems" of Southern black migrants buttressed his call for an end to economic discrimination against *all* blacks. In his view, policies designed to lift "the mass" were the principal aim of the "new social science of human action." Between *The Negro Artisan* and *Black Reconstruction,* Du Bois elevated working people to the center of his story and reinterpreted the experiences of blacks, the South, and the nation. Thus, even as historians turn to Du Bois's imaginative works, and deeply probe his treatment of gender and cultural issues, his myriad contributions to Southern, African-American, and U.S. labor and working-class history should remain instructive.

Rupert B. Vance

A Sociologist's View of the South

JOHN SHELTON REED AND DANIEL JOSEPH SINGAL

Rupert B. Vance was born in Plummerville, Arkansas, in the closing months of the nineteenth century. He died in Chapel Hill, North Carolina, three-quarters of the way through the twentieth. For him, the South was always home, and in his lifetime he saw the region transformed.

Vance's birthplace was a region still recovering from the Civil War. Its white citizens were suffering the consequences of defeat, occupation, and exploitation, and were engaged in inflicting some of the same experiences on Southern blacks. In 1900, close to ninety percent of Vance's fellow Southerners lived in the countryside, and the region's cities, with a couple of exceptions, did not amount to much. The vast majority of Southerners were farmers and farm workers; nearly all were supported, directly or indirectly, by agriculture. They were supported, as Louis XIV once put it, the way a hanged man is supported by the rope. Southern personal income, per capita, was roughly at the level of Trinidad's today—and was considerably less than half of the level in the rest of the U.S. Southerners, both black and white, were leaving the region in increasing numbers for employment, or the chance of it, elsewhere. When Vance was born, Southern state legislatures were busy transforming discriminatory custom into the formidable structure of Jim Crow law, designed to fix the Negro "in his place" for eternity. Informal efforts to the same end were commonplace: blacks were being lynched at an average rate of two a week.

When Vance died, his adopted hometown had a black mayor, who was soon to take a cabinet position in the state government of North Carolina. Within a year, the Democratic party would nominate for president a former governor of Georgia, a "born-again" peanut farmer–businessman, backed by Southerners of both races and a good many non-Southerners as well. From

This essay first appeared as "Rupert B. Vance: An Appreciation," in *Regionalism and the South: Selected Papers of Rupert Vance*, eds. John Shelton Reed and Daniel Joseph Singal (Chapel Hill: University of North Carolina Press, 1982).

the political left came warnings of a sinister entity called the "Sun Belt": this region, which combined the South and Southwest, was alleged to be draining population, wealth, and influence from the old Northeast and achieving a baleful dominance in national affairs from a base of "agribusiness" and extractive industry. Certainly the flow of population had reversed—more blacks and whites were moving to the South than were leaving it—and if per capita income in the South was still lower than that in the rest of the country, the gap had narrowed substantially. In absolute terms the great majority of Southerners led comfortable lives. Like the rest of the United States, the region had become an urban society. By 1975, less than a third of its people were rural, and fewer than one in a dozen actually worked in agriculture. For better or for worse, Atlanta had become the model of the "New South," a hackneyed phrase popularized by an Atlantan over a century before.

Rupert Vance came to Chapel Hill in 1926 to join the Department of Sociology and the Institute for Research in Social Science at the University of North Carolina, both of which had been founded a few years earlier by Howard W. Odum. For the next half century, the South, its problems, and the changes taking place there occupied much of his attention. In a half-dozen books and scores of articles, in his classroom teaching and his work with graduate students, in lectures to varied audiences throughout the South and beyond, Vance applied his intellect and the tools of his discipline to the problems of his native region and, with Odum and his other colleagues, developed the intellectual apparatus of "regional sociology."

Although Vance is probably best known as a student of the South, he easily ranked among the leading sociologists of his generation not only in the South but in the nation and, for that matter, in the world. In 1944, he was elected president of the American Sociological Society (now Association). The depth, quality, and encyclopedic range of his work set a standard for Southern sociologists that has never been equaled.

The breadth of his interests was especially striking. He began by writing the definitive study of the South's cotton tenancy system, moved on to a magisterial portrait of the region from the standpoint of human geography, then to studies of its complex population problems, and finally to examinations of the process that had transformed it from an agrarian to an urban and industrial society. Along the way, he found time to compose remarkably insightful essays on the South's politics, culture, and history, as well as more general contributions to sociological and demographic theory. Unlike the work of many scholars, Vance's has never seemed dated: his masterpiece, *Human Geography of the South*, can be read with almost as much profit today as when it first appeared in 1932.[1] His accomplishments also included over forty years of teaching and directing graduate studies at the University of North Carolina in Chapel Hill, where he was made Kenan Professor of Sociology in 1946, and service as a consultant to innumerable government commissions and agencies and to the United Nations (on international migration).

Vance's achievement is all the more noteworthy because he worked throughout his career with a severe physical handicap. Born in 1899 in a small central Arkansas town, he contracted polio at the age of three and soon lost the use of both legs. Unable to obtain treatment or even proper diagnosis in his hometown—"It was hell to live in the backwoods then," he would recall—he and his mother spent two years at the McLean Orthopedic Hospital in St. Louis, where he learned to walk with the aid of crutches. Although the affliction kept him from entering school until age ten, he was able to enter in the fourth grade and promptly rose to the top of the class; thereafter, his paralysis had no significant effects on either his education or his career. Colleagues would later marvel at how Vance kept up a full round of professional activities, including a busy schedule of travel to meetings and conferences. Nor did his handicap exclude him from the normal boyhood pastimes: a 1950 profile in the *Raleigh News and Observer* reported that he often served as umpire for youngsters' baseball games. "He stood on crutches behind the pitcher," it noted, "and he never reversed a decision."

Like his mentor Odum, Vance grew up in a rural community typical of the South in that day. His grandfather was a Confederate veteran; his father a New South–style cotton planter, who managed his work force of sharecroppers from behind the counter of his general store. Several times, the elder Vance tried to escape the narrow confines of the cotton system by raising peaches, cantaloupes, or livestock, but each time the vicissitudes of the national market brought financial disaster. His efforts to prosper growing cotton also met repeated failure owing to the sharp fluctuations in the price of that staple. During the agricultural depression of the early 1920s, he finally went bankrupt and lost all his land. To his son this spectacle of hard work and initiative culminating in failure came to epitomize the overall plight of the South. Why, he asked himself, were capable Southerners like his father forever frustrated in their desire to improve themselves? Was something grievously wrong with the South's culture, or economy, or social system, or perhaps with the genetic makeup of its people?

His education had given him a broad background to draw upon in his search for an answer. Taught to read at age four by his mother, he soon developed an appetite for books that his family found hard to satisfy, even though they purchased Dickens, Irving, and Scott by the set. The results of this early exposure were later reflected in his own writing, which was always clear (and not just "for a sociologist") and often elegant. He attended college at Henderson Brown, a small Methodist school in Arkadelphia, where he edited the college paper and yearbook, was president of the Young Men's Christian Association, and served as class valedictorian. Although he majored in English, his first love, he also encountered a gifted teacher named B. S. Foster who introduced him to social science. Intrigued by the new field, he accepted a scholarship to Vanderbilt University to study for a master's degree in economics. His studies there with Augustus Dyer, a stodgy and resolute exponent of classical laissez-faire, left him little taste for economics unleavened by sociological analysis. He found the double-distilled Southern progressivism of Edwin Mims (who later wrote *The Advancing South*) more attractive, though, and he was exposed to such fellow students as Ralph McGill (about whom he was later to tell some hilarious stories) and some young literati who were later to number among the Vanderbilt Agrarians.[2]

After Vanderbilt, still unsure of his choice of profession and unwilling to enter law school (as his father advised), Vance entered a period of apparent drift, but one in which his social views were in actuality maturing rapidly. He took a job for two years as principal of a small Oklahoma high school and then taught English for three years at South Georgia College in McRae.

Vance later attributed much importance to his time in McRae. His social views were developing, he recognized, in a liberal direction, and while they had been fairly unremarkable in the Southwest and, to some extent, at Vanderbilt, they were enough out of place in south Georgia that his colleagues sometimes accused him of being a disguised Yankee. (This experience almost certainly had something to do with his lifelong interest in subregional differences, an interest he turned to good account in his *Human Geography of the South*.)

All the while, he was avidly reading many books and periodicals, especially H. L. Mencken's iconoclastic *American Mercury*. (Until he met Mencken, Vance said, he had always assumed that the man ate little children for breakfast.) It was during this period that he also discovered Howard Odum's *Journal of Social Forces*, with its hard-hitting editorials cataloging the South's ills and proposing programs of action to address them. This kind of engagé academic sociology appealed to Vance because it provided a way both to implement his commitment to reform and to satisfy his intellectual curiosity. After considering Columbia University and the University of Chicago, he chose Chapel Hill as the place to do his graduate work, primarily because of the chance to work with Odum.

A young and energetic Southern-born sociologist, Odum had come to Chapel Hill in 1920 to found an academic empire. He came as first director of the university's School of Public Welfare and as chairman of its new sociology department (the only one in the South). Two years later he began the *Journal of Social Forces*, with himself as editor, and in 1924, with support from the Laura Spelman Rockefeller Memorial, launched the Institute for Research in

Social Science. His two basic goals were closely related: he wished to promote the scientific study of Southern society so that people in the region could begin tackling their immense problems in constructive ways, and he hoped to provide an opportunity for talented Southerners to train in the new social science disciplines unhampered by financial cares or constraints on their freedom of inquiry. To those ends, the institute offered fellowships to promising graduate students willing to investigate aspects of Southern life. The stipends were high, the length of tenure was open, and there was no obligation to teach. Vance was one of the first to take advantage of these attractive terms, and so began an extraordinary association that was to last until Odum's death nearly thirty years later.

Odum was in his early forties when Vance came to Chapel Hill at age twenty-seven, and from the start relations between the two men were warm and mutually admiring. Keenly aware of Odum's sensitivities, Vance always maintained the humble role of student, of the loyal disciple both grateful to and slightly in awe of his master. And there was much to be grateful for. Odum provided Vance not only with institutional support and personal encouragement but, just as importantly, with the drive to theorize and to generalize that would ultimately raise Vance's work well above simple description. In addition, Odum reinforced Vance's sense of mission about the South, an unapologetic assumption that something *must be done* about the problems they were studying. Vance always acknowledged his intellectual debt to Odum: one of his last published articles was, in effect, an act of homage to his mentor, an attempt to restore one of Odum's neglected concepts to use.[3] For his part, Vance contributed as much as anyone to realizing Odum's vision of Chapel Hill as a center of regional scholarship and what is now called "policy research." In both volume and quality, his publications helped put North Carolina on the national academic map.

Yet Vance proved to be different in many ways, both temperamentally and intellectually, from his master. Odum's training had been in the organicist brand of sociology that was dominant before World War I. As a result, he tended to view the ideal society as a seamless web in which all groups and social institutions functioned harmoniously with one another. Odum regarded any sign of conflict as aberrational and potentially dangerous—political conflict as the worst. Thus, his ideology of "regionalism" included a blueprint for Southern society in which consensus was so strong that the projects of academic social planners and the desires of the common folk would be instantly and automatically reconciled.

More solidly grounded in the newer developments in social science, Vance had no such illusions. For him, conflict was at least a given, if not a positive good, as evidenced by a memorandum he wrote to Odum after reading the manuscript of Odum's *American Social Problems*[4]:

> I believe I must be wanting a more hard-boiled view of social conflict. Conflict we will always have with us. How does Regionalism take [sectional conflict] out of the realm of hard knocks and place it in the realm of discussion and reasonable "due process" of policy-making? And what about class conflict? . . . Maybe it comes down to this, that we can't take a point of view with-out taking sides. Still, I have the feeling that we need to be sure of the alternatives, if necessary to argue one side and then the other, show the interest involved.

Vance's graduate school paper on "Stuart-Harmon" (a thinly disguised picture of McRae, Georgia) contains a forthright treatment of class, racial, and generational conflict, and his dissertation, while it makes a scapegoat of no one, nevertheless recognizes that tenant and landlord necessarily have some divergent interests.[5]

Vance's fascination with Southern politics, a subject not for those squeamish about conflict and one that Odum largely ignored in his own work, led him to undertake a series of articles on populist-style Southern politicians, beginning with a sketch of Jeff Davis of Arkansas entitled "A Karl Marx for Hill Billies," published in *Social Forces* in 1930.[6] This article, perhaps more than any other, shows Mencken's influence. Vance was not the only reform-minded young Southerner to read the *American Mercury;* as Fred C. Hobson, Jr., has pointed out, Mencken was something of a hero to many. Having flayed the South in his famous essay "Sahara of the Bozart," Mencken was encouraging the Southerners who were trying to remedy the situation that he had (exaggeratedly) diagnosed, and he published works by many of them in his magazine.[7] His relations with Odum and his students were warm and supportive, and Vance admitted in later years that his piece on Jeff Davis was written with the *American Mercury* in mind. Still, it appeared in Odum's journal, not Mencken's.

Vance also differed from Odum in the style and approach of his writings. What someone once said of Kant could be said as well of Odum: he was both like and unlike Jehovah—he spoke through a cloud, but without the illumination of the thunderbolt. Vance's work, on the other hand, was always lucid and well organized, proceeding through clear-cut logical analysis to an identifiable conclusion. In some ways, Vance served as an interpreter for Odum, by clarifying and substantiating the latter's ideas on regionalism, making them comprehensible to readers who could not pin Odum down in person for an explanation. On at least one occasion, Vance even tried valiantly to repair Odum's prose, after plowing through the draft of a 1938 book:

> My first impression [wrote the former English teacher] was that the materials were undigested and the manuscript was rather hastily done. [For example,] I look for a resolution, a point of view or a summary at the end of many chapters, and I find sometimes an abrupt conclusion and sometimes a quotation. . . . I would like to see [in] the manuscript the emergence of what might be called a point of view. Some of the most original and challenging of your ideas are stated as assumptions rather than emerging from the discussion as conclusions. Again, I see certain slants that are taken without being explicitly defined or argued.

This memorandum (which goes on) tells us something of the nature of the relationship between the two men. So may the fact that Odum apparently left the manuscript unrevised.

These contrasts between the two were apparent in Vance's *Human Factors in Cotton Culture,* a revised version of his doctoral dissertation published in 1929.[8] Whereas Odum's writing on the South tended to be upbeat and optimistic, Vance's portrait of how Southerners were trapped by what he called "the cotton culture complex" was strongly pessimistic. Ever mindful of his father's experience, he stressed the ruinous unpredictability of the system by emphasizing how the cycles of the cotton market or the vagaries of the weather could destroy men's livelihoods virtually overnight and lead them to irrational behavior. He employed statistics and graphic literary detail to depict the lives of ordinary tenant farmers, again drawing on his personal recollections, and presented anything but a pretty picture. The resulting book was, as one reviewer aptly put it, "a rare combination of sound economics and human interest."

The book eschewed easy solutions. Far from holding out hope for reform, Vance concluded that the dependence on King Cotton led to a "vicious circle" almost impossible to break, a system whose participants "form an economic harmony that often benefits all except the producer, a complex whole that is so closely interconnected that no one can suggest any place at which it may be attacked except the grower; and the grower is to change the system himself, cold comfort for advice." The book introduced a needed note of sober realism to subsequent discussions of the South's problems in the 1930s.

Still, in *Human Factors,* Vance did not really answer his basic causal question of what had gone wrong in the South; that answer came in his *Human Geography of the South,* which appeared in 1932. This massive work, with a bibliography long enough to impress even the most compulsive scholar, surely belongs among the classics of American social science. Borrowing techniques from the French school of human geographers and from the new science of ecology, Vance tried to see if some natural factor—some inescapable attribute of the physical environment—could account for the ills of Southern life. Methodically, he reviewed the region's physical features as they had interacted with its social development, only to conclude that all, from topography and soil content to water supplies, had been sufficient for prosperity. An especially provocative chapter on the Southern climate showed that, if anything, the region's weather should have given it a clear advantage over the North in industrial production. Chapters on the supposed biological inferiority of the Southern people demonstrated that what many observers had described as "laziness" could more accurately be attributed to inadequate diets and endemic diseases such as hookworm and malaria. The South's plight was not the fault of nature, then, but was in fact man-made. Natural forces may have played a role, but in the end, Vance insisted, "history, not geography, made the solid South."

More precisely, according to Vance, history had left Southern society arrested in the frontier stage. Adapting his thesis from the work of the historian Ulrich B. Phillips—whose influence on Vance was second only to that of Odum—he maintained that the social and economic patterns of the South had been shaped essentially by the plantation, a frontier institution that produced cotton by almost literally mining the soil. During the nineteenth century, the rest of the country shed its colonial status as an exporter of raw materials to become an industrial society. Because of its dependence on the plantation system and, later, the devastation of the Civil War, the South failed to keep pace. The region never built up a capital supply of its own and remained backward in technology and industrial skills. The result, Vance argued, was a "colonial economy" frantically exploiting its natural resources to pay for manufactured goods produced elsewhere. The North (he quickly added) was not to blame; rather, the tragic course of Southern history had condemned the region to its poverty and dependence. To escape this fate, Vance believed, Southerners would have to strive consciously for urbanization and industrialization and for a more diversified agricultural system that was less dependent on staple crops. More cautiously than Odum, he endorsed regional planning as the quickest and most efficient route to a mature economy, but he characteristically pointed out that any such program would have to take into account the entrenched folkways of a people still under the sway of the plantation mentality.

The publication of *Human Geography of the South* cemented Vance's reputation as a leading figure in sociology. Invitations began pouring in for him to serve as consultant on various projects, both scholarly and governmental, and Vance was usually quick to take them up. He actively lobbied for passage of the Bankhead-Jones Farm Tenant Bill and, after its enactment in 1938, frequently acted as advisor to the Farm Security Administration, which was created by the new law. In addition, he was among the founders of the Southern Sociological Society in 1935 and became its third president in 1938. His most important contribution to the organization, he liked to recall afterward, was seeing to it that the society met from the start only in hotels where its black members could attend all functions, including formal dinners. Finding such facilities in the South of the 1930s was not always easy, but Vance and others persisted in this policy, with the result that some other professional associations then getting under way in the region followed suit.

At the same time, Vance was becoming increasingly interested in the fledgling field of social demography. In 1938 he published *Research Memorandum on Population Redistribution within the United States,* for the Social Science Research Council, attempting to set forth an agenda for research in an area whose importance was just beginning to be recognized by sociologists generally.[9]

In fact, by the mid-1930s Vance had begun to view population as an alternative explanation of the South's dilemma. The solid, scientific feel of demographic theory strongly appealed to him; it was hard to argue against numbers. More important, as Vance was to demonstrate in *All These People: The Nation's Human Resources in the South* (his next major study, published in 1945), there could be no question that the South since the Civil War had been dramatically overproducing people.[10] Again the fault seemed to lie with the system of staple crop agriculture, which encouraged families to have as many children as possible in order to have hands available for field labor. But, as Vance showed, whatever the short-run advantages for individual families, this system led to long-run disadvantages for the region and nation, since the huge reservoir of underemployed workers that resulted kept wages in the South at a bare subsistence level. Here, Vance thought, was the root cause of Southern poverty. His solution once more was industrialized and urbanized society, arrived at through planning, precisely because urban life and higher living standards would of themselves help to lower the birthrate and thus to solve the South's population problem. He had only limited faith, however, that such planning would actually come about. More realistically, as early as his 1936 article "The Old Cotton Belt," Vance foresaw the process in which the South would export its surplus population to the urban slums of the North, with tragic consequences for the country as whole.[11]

Vance continued his interest in demography, becoming president of the Population Association of America in 1952, but in the latter part of his career he focused his attention primarily on the subject of urbanization itself. In a 1955 article he claimed, accurately as it turned out, that a major "breakthrough" had taken place in the South around the middle of the preceding decade: the cities rather than the countryside had finally come to dominate the society.[12] For Vance, the main significance of this development was its meaning for the South's relationship to the rest of the nation. As he observed in *The Urban South*, a symposium he edited at this time with a Chapel Hill colleague, Nicholas Demerath, the South in one critical area after another was finally catching up with the other regions.[13] The indices of Southern deficiency that he and Odum had charted for years were at last disappearing. Put another way, the circumstances that prevented members of his father's generation from succeeding, despite their best efforts, appeared to be past.

Although this view was correct as far as it went, it clearly failed to take into account the other major change that was occurring in Southern life during these years, namely, the civil rights movement, which in 1954 and 1955 saw the Supreme Court decision in *Brown v. Board of Education* and the Montgomery bus boycott. Vance may well have hesitated to trespass in an area he regarded as the domain of his friend and colleague Guy Johnson, but in any case, despite his own liberal racial views, the changing structure of Southern race relations simply did not receive the attention in his published work that, in retrospect, it clearly deserves in any account of the South's modernization.

Another difficulty the contemporary reader may find in Vance's work is the concept of regionalism itself. To a greater extent than is usually recognized, Vance was as much the father of regional sociology as was Odum. Indeed, Vance's explorations in human geography, his charting of subregions and resources, led directly to Odum's pointillist portrait of the South in *Southern Regions*, an imposing study published in 1936.[14] Vance was always far more conversant with modern social theory than was his mentor, and the gap between that theory and regionalism troubled him. To the charge that regionalists were engaged in "mere description" of particular locales rather than in the attempt to build a general science of society, Vance replied that description was a necessary preliminary operation: "The truth in the statement I do not find too disturbing provided one can go from description to generalization by good empirical methods. There are certainly sufficient regions and sufficient societies to offer basis for valid generalization." To the accusation that regionalists in attempting to understand a region by dabbling in history, geography, and economics were doing everything *but* sociology, Vance replied ruefully: "I have sometimes said that it must be fun to be a dilettante, but dilettantes are not supposed to work very hard." He added: "Regionalism focuses many disciplines on the one area under study, and anyone who follows this line takes a calculated risk that leads to trespassing on other people's preserves."

Nevertheless, he acknowledged (in a 1948 letter) that "all of these things [his extrasociological interests] have enabled me to examine one region from different facets, but they have not brought me much closer to the core and essence of sociology." This lack of connection still troubled him over a decade later. In 1960, he was writing that "regional sociology has been much better at taking in other people's washing, relating its contributions to those of geography, economics, political science, and so forth than it has been in relating regionalism to its own domain, that of general sociology."

This uneasiness may have been aggravated by the postwar development of the South. Since its origins lay in a concern with the economic and social problems of the region, regionalism faced a dilemma when those problems appeared to be on the way to solution. Vance was delighted with the South's modernization but realized its consequences for his own style of research. As he put it in 1960: "The New Deal has been dealt. . . . As the affluent society crosses the Mason-Dixon line, the regionalist of the 1930s turns up as just another 'liberal without a cause.'" Whatever the reason, it is ironic that by the early 1950s, when Vance produced for a symposium on regionalism what is probably the clearest statement available of what the regional sociologists were up to, his own work had largely left regionalism behind. As something of a valedictory gesture, although it may not have been intended as such, he and Charles Grigg presented a paper to the American Sociological Association in 1956 that proposed a synthesis of the declining subdiscipline of regional sociology (purged of its particularistic emphasis on the South) and the ascendant one of human ecology. Unlike corporate mergers, intellectual ones are not a matter of public record, but if this one took place, it resembled many corporate mergers in that the smaller party effectively vanished. Still, the student of intellectual life who is looking for regionalism's impact on its parent discipline of sociology must seek it in the work of present-day human ecologists. If regionalism produced a third generation, it is effectively disguised.

In the years after 1960, however, Vance's attention did return occasionally to the South in papers dealing with aspects of the region's social structure and "quality of life" more subtle than those linked directly to per capita income: education, family life, high culture. In addition, Vance became concerned with Appalachia, which was largely bypassed by the urbanization and industrialization that transformed the rest of the South. Appalachia's problems were much like those of the South as a whole thirty years earlier and seemed susceptible to study and treatment in the old regionalist framework.

But if the relation of Vance's interests to one another and to those of his discipline of sociology occasionally troubled him, it need not concern his readers. When he "trespassed" on other disciplines, he did well, and the natives recognized that. Although he never studied human geography, population, human ecology, and social structure in the classroom, his authority in these areas was recognized. Although affiliated with a sociology department, he was always being mistaken—flatteringly, he said—for something else. "O. E. Baker nominated me to the Association of American Geographers. . . . Carter Goodrich thought I was an economist when he asked me to work with the Study of Population Redistribution. There was a time when work in tenancy led some to classify me with the rural sociologists. The editors of the *History of the South* persuaded me to attempt the last volume for their series [an attempt later abandoned]."

These confusions and problems of classification are testimony to the range of Vance's interests and the caliber of his mind. In his works on the South, we see a vigorous and well-informed intellect addressing some of the most pressing problems of his day. In the works on regionalism, Vance pondered the question of how to bring together many disciplines without becoming undisciplined altogether, of how to study a region "as a whole" without simply studying *everything*—questions still vital to all interdisciplinary enterprises.

Vance was very much a man of his time. As the citation accompanying his honorary degree from the University of North Carolina accurately observed, he "contributed not only to the understanding of the human problems of this century, particularly those of his native South, but to the solution of many of them." In doing so, however, he also exemplified some virtues of an earlier time. Like others of his colleagues at Chapel Hill, Robert Coles has observed that the "narrative power" of Vance's work carried on "an older tradition of social science, and a Southern one." When Gunnar Myrdal made a related point, in *An American Dilemma,* he undoubtedly had Vance and his colleagues in mind: "Social science in the South has never, as in the North, lost the tradition of reasoning in terms of means and ends. . . . The significance for human happiness in the problems under study is always a present thought in the South."

But if Vance addressed the problems of his day in a style recognized even then as an "older" one, he was also, in an important sense, ahead of his time. Whatever the final verdict on regionalism, Vance's excursions into geography, history, economics, and political science evidence his vision of a unified social science, his conviction that a complicated modern society like the American South cannot rightfully be vivisected for the convenience of academic departments. It is a measure of his foresight that this fact is only now becoming obvious to the rest of us.

Charles S. Sydnor's Quest
for a Suitable Past

FRED ARTHUR BAILEY

Governor Theodore S. Bilbo ruthlessly purged the University of Mississippi's faculty in 1930, ridding it of professors deemed unsupportive of his distinctive vision for the state's intelligentsia. While the pogrom shattered many carefully nurtured academic careers, historian Charles S. Sydnor and the department he chaired weathered the disaster that swept away the school's president and perhaps a quarter of its faculty. Sydnor emerged from the crisis with a sharpened awareness concerning the South's intense class struggle and its disruptive potential. The affair reshaped his life's work, stirring in him an unwonted vigor and reawakening his sense of academic purpose.[1]

Bilbo, the quintessential Southern demagogue, had championed the cause of Mississippi's white underclass, impoverished pinewoods farmers and oppressed cotton-land sharecroppers who resented the aristocratic hauteur and economic privileges of the planter elite. To them, the University of Mississippi stood as a bitter symbol of the state's patrician establishment. Bilbo demanded educational reform, insisting that the state's principal university become more sensitive to the common man's needs; when the school's faculty and administration refused, he wreaked vengeance upon them.[2]

Sydnor had sprung from an element of Southern culture far removed from hill country cabins and Delta shacks. Raised the son of a cultured Presbyterian minister, he had benefited from a superior Southern education and unquestioningly accepted that the sagacious leadership of an enlightened few leavened the whole of society. Before Bilbo, Sydnor had developed into a somewhat erudite teacher, content to uplift his students and make modest but carefully informed contributions to his discipline's body of literature. Bilbo's assault became Sydnor's crucible, the defining moment that changed his life. He was shaken that the careers of his friends had been destroyed to satisfy the fickle whims of the ignorant and anarchistic masses. This not only offended his sense of order, but also, more important, transformed him from a pedantic professor of history into a passionate chronicler and champion of Southern culture.

Ten years beyond this trauma, Sydnor's historian peers endorsed his leadership by electing him president of the fledgling Southern Historical Association. Introspective by nature, he wondered aloud what prompted scholars to study the South and how their motives might have shaped their particular interpretations. The process by which the historian was led to undertake the task of revealing the South "needs to be sketched," he reasoned, "because whatever awakened his interest . . . may well have determined the nature and bent of that interest."[3] This reflected Sydnor's personal journey as he followed his own distinctive course in Southern scholarship, developing insights others failed to see, and yet he died at the critical moment when his teachings might have led his native land along more progressive paths.

Sydnor had by 1940 emerged as one of the academy's leading lights, an earnest searcher for truth who dared explore corners of the South's past largely ignored by his peers. To a great extent his generation of Southern historians— among them Frank Lawrence Owsley, E. Merton Coulter, and Thomas Perkins Abernethy—clung to comfortable legends of the Civil War, focused their attentions on the Old South, the Confederacy, and Reconstruction, and produced a historiography that amounted to little more than an apology for a romanticized land of spreading plantations, paternalistic aristocrats, and contented slaves. In common with his contemporaries, Sydnor grew up in a region in which the bitterness of defeat fueled a sense of indignation and gave rise to scholars who championed their ancestors' actions even as they defended the social inequities of the modern South.[4]

By the time of his presidential election, however, Sydnor had begun to distance himself from the neo-Confederate polemics of his historian peers. He sought to lift a voice of moderation within a generation of Southern scholars who retained a powerful sense of regional ethnocentrism, who resented slights —real and imagined—from Yankee academicians, and stoked the flames of sectional bitterness. Sydnor disdained those practitioners of the past who desired "to prove that the South was right or wrong in its controversy with the North" or who employed "history to support the racial prejudices" that marred the land. Rather, he celebrated the Old South's cultural diversity that "included . . . tidewater and piedmont, cotton kingdom and tobacco land, Democrats and Whigs, country and town, planters and non-slaveholders, the liberalism of Jefferson and the conservatism of Calhoun." Such a rich heritage surely placed upon historians a heavy burden compelling them to reach their own decisions as to how to write about the South in such a way as to "to treat it as a coherent whole without denying the presence of its many diversities."[5]

The process by which Sydnor matured as a scholar arose from circumstances that would separate him from the neo-Confederate radicalism of his academic peers and shape the "nature and bent" of his own writings. Although his familial ancestry was rooted in the cultural dynamics of the Old South and his forebears willingly sacrificed for the Confederacy, this hardly informed his intellectual development.[6] Twentieth-century political anarchy, not nineteenth-century rebellion, inspired his scholarship. Offended by the less-than-exemplary Southern society of his own time, he searched the past for a model that would lead his native region to a virtuous renaissance.

Sydnor was born into a proper Presbyterian family in 1898. His father held a prestigious pulpit in Augusta, Georgia, placing him as a respected member of that element of Southern society then referred to as the "better sort of people." Considering themselves apostles of culture and decorum, they strove to preserve established mores and promote social stability. Drawn largely from the professional classes such as attorneys, physicians, teachers, and ministers, they disdained the vulgar amusements of the masses and judged dignity, order, and manners essential to Christian civilization. They saw themselves as the natural, even God-ordained, leaders of society, deemed public service the customary obligation of their class, and took offense whenever the unwashed mob failed to demonstrate proper deference or, even worse, challenged perceived entitlements. Thoroughly inculcated with these values, Sydnor cultivated personal attributes that combined modesty and moderation with a quiet interest in things intellectual.[7]

As the nineteenth century merged into the twentieth, Sydnor's South husbanded bitter memories of the Civil War. Patriotic societies—the United Confederate Veterans, Sons of Confederate Veterans, and United Daughters of the Confederacy—determined to preserve their history of the "Lost Cause," defend the South of slavery and aristocracy, and perpetuate not only the reshaped memory but also the reinterpreted values of the Old South. From Virginia to Texas, these groups targeted Sydnor's generation, pushing through state legislatures textbook adoption laws that enabled them to regulate school curriculums ensuring that children would learn the story of the past from only an upper-class Southern perspective. In the Georgia of Sydnor's youth, Mildred Lewis Rutherford, historian-general of the United Daughters of the Confederacy, largely dictated the essential elements taught in classrooms across the state and even the South. She led the South-wide crusade to promote historical censorship, wrote pamphlets outlining the acceptable interpretations of the past, and applauded those individuals and groups that banished, and even burned, Northern-biased materials. These foundational efforts gained reward in the unrelenting chauvinism characteristic of most Southern historians from the 1920s through the 1960s.[8]

Unlike many of his fellow adolescents, Sydnor seemed little touched by the dominant historical spirit of his youth. While other boys might thrill at martial tales spun by aging Confederate soldiers and dutifully repeat classroom lessons designed to contrast Southern virtues with Northern venalities, he moved in other directions. Sydnor early evidenced a bookish inclination, but his interests were eclectic, unfocused. Although this hardly indicated a future as a scholar of the American South, the lack of specific interest did insulate him from the pervasive historical themes of his childhood, freeing him as an adult scholar to take a more detached view than that held by historians more thoroughly indoctrinated by the Confederate societies. Sydnor's self-proclaimed dispassionate approach toward Southern history placed him at odds with his peers. "If anyone wishes to test his own capacity for objectivity," he reflected in 1940, "he might try his hand at writing Southern history or reviewing what others have written."[9]

In 1901, the Sydnor family moved to Rome, Georgia, where young Charles enjoyed a privileged childhood. He attended the Darlington School, a quality preparatory institution, whose headmaster, James R. McCain, taught history and planted in the youth an almost subliminal interest in the discipline that would slowly germinate into his lifetime career. Graduating in 1915, Sydnor, encouraged by his father, entered Hampden-Sydney College, a Virginia school long associated with the Presbyterian Church. Steeped in traditions that reached back to its eighteenth-century origins, the college clung tenaciously to its liberal arts curriculum. Sydnor flourished in its genteel ambiance, relished its "old-fashioned classical course," and studied diligently Greek, Latin, and mathematics. A history major was not an option, he later recalled, "the classical course of that day not having such things as majors."[10]

Having tested out of freshman requirements, Sydnor entered Hampden-Sydney as a sophomore. He was popular with fellow students, excelled in debate, edited the college magazine, and served as class historian. In the evenings, he entertained his housemates "playing on his mandolin some soft and tender melody of love or lending his mellow voice to the accompaniment of his guitar." He also demonstrated academic excellence. Noting that the "hard work of [his] fertile brain has enabled him to accomplish [in three years] what it takes most of four years to do," the editor of the college yearbook proclaimed that he "possesses the qualities of stability and determination which always assures success."[11]

The shattering events of World War I impacted even isolated Hampden-Sydney College. Joining his fellow seniors in the Reserve Officers Training Corps, Sydnor earned a commission and served briefly stateside. In 1918 he mused that for him and his classmates "the opportunity of making history worth recording is not yet past," as he envisioned a future "fraught with many opportunities." Ironically, Sydnor would devote a lifetime to the recording of history, but in the midst of war-making events there was little to indicate that he would answer Clio's calling and emerge as one of the South's more eminent historians.[12]

Initially Sydnor taught high-school mathematics, first at Rome, Georgia, in the spring of 1919 and then at the McCallie School, a private academy in Chattanooga, Tennessee, in 1919–1920. At the latter, he made three seminal decisions. He commenced his courtship of Betty Brown, whom he married in 1924; he found that he wished to work with more mature students than those on the secondary level; and he concluded that he would teach something more exciting than algebra, geometry, and calculus. Although Sydnor always credited high-school teacher James R. McCain's enthusiasm for awakening his interest in history, he was also stirred by Hampden-Sydney's president Ashton W. McWhorter, who combined his extensive administrative duties with classes in history, English, and political science. McWhorter had earned his doctorate at The Johns Hopkins University; Sydnor emulated his mentor by enrolling at the same institution in 1920, his mind focused on a career as a college professor.[13]

A man of talent and intellectual depth, Sydnor had difficulty deciding upon an academic discipline suited to his personal temperament; he more drifted into history than embraced it. Thirty years later he reflected: "I decided to go to graduate school and be a professor. What to profess was least important at the time." Hampden-Sydney's classical emphasis had awakened in him an antiquarian taste for studying the past for the past's sake. This melded well with the academic traditions of Johns Hopkins's Department of History. Long after other programs had abandoned the scientific school of historiography, it remained committed to it. Emphasizing an unrelenting faithfulness to precisely documented fact and a careful reconstruction and passionless interpretation of past events, practitioners of this school crafted massive, spiritless tomes, devoid of the human context and focusing primarily on political and economic events, constitutional developments, and military campaigns. They deemed historians little more than chroniclers and laid the interpretations of the past, if any, at the reader's feet.[14]

Throughout his early works, Sydnor remained faithful to both the letter and the spirit of these dictums, and even after his writings had evolved into more modern thesis-oriented presentations, he still professed a commitment to the scientific ideal. Interviewed by a reporter in 1948, Sydnor emphasized his distaste for the "'apologetic' historian who uses history only to defend and excuse iron-clad convictions he refuses to modify" and proclaimed his intent to develop in his students "a respect for the facts 'whether they hurt or not.'"[15]

At Johns Hopkins, Sydnor studied English and medieval history, subjects that complemented his undergraduate grounding in the classics. Completing a dissertation titled "Press Censorship in England, 1534–1603," he earned his degree in the spring of 1923. Decades later he judged that his scientific training and his examination of historical subjects far removed from his native culture contributed to his sense of objectivity, that he had learned to set aside his personal experiences and to see society from a detached perspective. "That's not a bad background for a man in American and Southern history. We historians have to fight our prejudices, which grow out of our own life and contemporary world. We [can] have no prejudice which would affect us."[16]

Only twenty-five years old and certified by a doctorate from one of the nation's more prestigious graduate schools, Sydnor happily accepted the newly created post of professor of history and political science at Hampden-Sydney College.[17] His alma mater suited his cultured taste. Isolated in the rolling hills of south-central Virginia, its wooded campus, classical traditions, and stately Victorian architecture made it an island of civility set apart from the world of the mundane. Sydnor was firmly committed to its elitist Presbyterian heritage, its ideals of liberal education, and its determination to educate properly the embryonic leaders of the future South.

Sydnor had set himself on a life course to become an American version of an English don, a somewhat erudite scholar shepherding young men dedicated to life's higher callings. Reality soon intruded. Throughout his tenures at Hampden-Sydney, later at the University of Mississippi, and finally at Duke University, the South's cruder nature invaded his comfortable world, forced him to confront the dark realities of his native land, and then led him to the production of insightful and useful interpretations of the South's cultural heritage.

Hampden-Sydney's institutional penury induced the first crisis of Sydnor's academic career. Its woefully inadequate library precluded significant research into his chosen area of scholarly interest—English and medieval history—and thus for no more profound reason than that needful primary and secondary sources were close at hand, Sydnor moved away from the Old World to historical explorations of the American South. The school's failure to regularly meet its faculty's payroll or at best to fund only a portion of promised stipends also burdened the newly married professor. Although Sydnor always remained a loyal friend and supporter of Hampden-Sydney College, by the spring of 1925 desperation forced him to seek more lucrative employment. That fall he and his bride moved to Oxford, Mississippi, where he became chair of the University of Mississippi's Department of History.[18]

'Ole Miss shared Hampden-Sydney's mission to educate the South's elites. From its opening in 1848, the university catered to the sons of the state's planter-establishment and perpetuated appropriate values deep into the twentieth century. In the 1920s, its chancellor, Albert Hume, deemed higher education the special prerogative of the South's upper classes. A loyal Presbyterian elder of conservative temperament, he held as a matter of faith that the enlightened leadership of the privileged few uplifted the whole of society. Sydnor thrived in an academic community dedicated to this mission, but in time he discovered that the university was hardly a cloistered institution. The powerful Confederate patriotic societies insisted that the university in general and the Department of History in particular affirm loyalty to the elite South's historical ideology, while Mississippi's white underclass demanded that the school become more sensitive to its own social and economic needs. All of this weighed heavily upon the bookish professor, severely undermining his personal felicity.[19]

However much Sydnor cherished his sense of academic objectivity, he had inherited a department of history that conformed to the dictates of the Confederate societies. These powerful forces of oppression discouraged free inquiry, demanded that teachers on every level swear their fidelity to the late Confederacy, and vowed to remove any educator unfaithful to their definition of Southern virtue. At the century's opening, Stephen D. Lee, ex–Confederate general and founding president of the Mississippi Agricultural and Mechanical College, chaired the United Confederate Veterans' history committee, and from that post railed against Yankee-biased textbooks, demanding that Mississippi and the South create a historical infrastructure dedicated to the singular purpose of perpetuating an aristocratic image of the Old South and the Confederacy.[20]

At the University of Mississippi, Lee's friend and professor of history Franklin L. Riley not only painted a felicitous picture of antebellum plantation society in his elementary textbook *School History of Mississippi*, but he also worked closely with the University of North Carolina's J. G. de Roulhac Hamilton to write *Our Republic*, a high-school textbook whose themes conformed to neo-Confederate interpretations. Well versed in the politics of Southern scholarship, he employed his considerable connections among the Confederate patriotic societies to secure statewide adoptions of *Our Republic* in Mississippi, North Carolina, and Florida. Even after Riley left Oxford to teach at a Virginia college, the department remained conscious of its limited academic freedom. From her home in Jackson, Mississippi, Eron Rowland, wife of state archivist Dunbar Rowland, carefully scrutinized the work of the university's historians and exercised her considerable leverage within the Mississippi division of the United Daughters of the Confederacy to intimidate any who strayed from its prescriptions. As she confided to a professor in 1914, her "special object" was "to refute the historical perversions and grave injustices to the south of northern writers."[21]

Caught up in this sere intellectual climate, Sydnor produced his first two books: *Mississippi History* (1930), a textbook suited for use in the sixth and seventh grades, and *Slavery in Mississippi* (1933), a massive tome intended for more mature audiences.[22] Stultifyingly dull, both were laden with the carefully worded, sterile prose of the scientific school and both conformed to conclusions amenable to the region's guardians of historical orthodoxy. While in time Sydnor came to recognize the Confederate societies' negative impact upon the Southern mind and condemned publicly their use of history for political purposes, these early works served their will, buttressing their positions with the prestige of a respected academician.

Mississippi History kept faith with the scientific school's rule that an author must simply lay the facts before his readers. Sydnor seemed not to have appreciated that the facts chosen and their manner of presentation often constituted an unintended polemic, in this case a defense of slavery, a condemnation of abolitionists, a reaffirmation of the rationale for secession, and a castigation of Yankee invasion and subsequent Reconstruction. Essential elements in neo-Confederate apologetics, such interpretations had long served as the foundations upon which the defenders of the South's unequal social system induced a fear of Northern society, a disdain for African-Americans, and a chauvinistic faith in "Southern" virtues.[23]

With *Mississippi History* Sydnor sought to equip young Mississippians for good citizenship, believing also that a "sympathetic interest in the past" of their state would give them a "greater faith in its future possibilities." The "sympathetic interest in the past" included a happy image of slavery in which "negroes were well cared for, given enough food and clothing, and not required to do more than a reasonable amount of work. . . . There was a friendship with other slaves, fishing now and then . . . religious meetings, and occasional merrymakings, all of which made the life of a slave pleasant." To be sure, there were "some negroes whose owners were cruel men." But, Sydnor asserted, "even such owners generally gave their slaves fairly good care. A slave was worth a great deal of money."[24]

From a defense of the peculiar institution, Sydnor moved to criticism of those who opposed it. "There were many people in the North who believed that all slaves should be set free at once," he told Mississippi's youth. These abolitionists did not realize "all the difficulties in the way of setting free all the slaves at once, [and] they worked night and day to make other people believe as they did." Not only did these misguided souls urge Congress to pass laws against slavery, but they also failed to "help Southern masters recapture runaway slaves, and sometimes they even helped the slaves to escape." These Northern misdeeds, he concluded, "were some of the ways in which the people of the South felt that they were being mistreated" and because of which they eventually justified secession.[25]

In its graded vocabulary *Mississippi History* led its young readers through the rationale for disunion, the travail of civil war, and the oppression of Reconstruction. "Did a state have the right to leave the Union?" Sydnor asked in bold letters, then answered with a Calhounian logic. The only way to have peace, Southern leaders believed, "was to separate from the North." They reasoned that "when the thirteen colonies won independence they . . . had decided to join one another and form a Union." Since "no colony was forced to join unless it wanted to do so," every state had the right to dissociate at will. "At different times," Sydnor lectured, "some of the northern states" had held to that position. "The belief that a state could leave the Union when it desired to do so was called the doctrine of secession."[26]

If departure from the Union was deemed necessary to protect the Southern weal, Sydnor's *Mississippi History* lamented that the Yankee invasion and consequent Northern-imposed Reconstruction together prostrated the region. Mississippi and its citizens suffered at the hands of both blue- and gray-coated soldiers who came "to the towns and plantations, taking the horses and food and whatever else was needed for the armies." Across the state "many homes were burned, and some towns were almost completely destroyed by fire. A traveler could hardly have found it possible to believe that this country had once been happy and prosperous."[27]

However egregious the impact of war upon Mississippi and the South, Sydnor painted Reconstruction in still darker hues. Defeated Southern soldiers trekked homeward to a devastated land whose "broad and rich fields were uncultivated" and where its black laborers "had been freed and could no longer be forced to work." Few former slaves "could be hired even for high wages, because they expected the government which freed them would also care for them." Therefore Southern white legislatures, Mississippi's included, enacted the "Black Codes," rules that required all former slaves to sign contracts that legally bound them to work. After all, blacks "had always been slaves and had been forced to work, and now that they were free they did not know how to behave." Unfortunately, Northern Republicans misinterpreted these laws, thinking that "making a negro work whether he wanted to or not amounted to making him a slave again." This became the "argument for not permitting the South to govern itself."[28]

Uninformed about the true nature of Southern society, the Northern-dominated Congress seized control of Reconstruction, placing Mississippi under military occupation and denying the franchise to whites who had supported the Confederacy while granting it to the former slaves. This created a social and political climate ripe for disaster. Sensing opportunity in anarchy, Northern carpetbaggers and Southern scalawags snatched the reins of government. "They did not love the state," Sydnor sneered; they "sought office because of the salary and the chance to rob the state." Mississippi's ignorant blacks became their willing minions: "These white men taught the negroes to hate their former masters, and to believe that the Republican party was their friend." When the illiterate and sometimes befuddled blacks proved difficult to train, the Republicans organized the "Loyal League," encouraged all black men to belong, and then employed the organization to intimidate any black who refused to do its will. "Each negro was told that if he failed to do as he promised he would receive fifty lashes on his bare back. For a second offense the punishment was a hundred lashes, and for a third he would be killed secretly. By such methods the white men ruled negro voters." Almost as an afterthought Sydnor added that the federal government created the Freedmen's Bureau, which also "helped control the negroes."[29]

Sydnor pontificated that the misdeeds of Reconstruction aroused a hatred "between the races that had not been known in the days of slavery." Because the state government no longer protected its white citizens, they soon formed the Ku Klux Klan whose hooded members rode "by night to the homes of negroes and carpetbaggers who were causing trouble, and warned them to behave." More often than not, the Klan "was able to frighten the negroes into better behavior. If they continued to act in a disorderly way, on the next visit the whip was used. Some negroes and some of their white leaders were hanged or shot." Sydnor admitted that such actions were technically illegal, but he assured his youthful readers that "most of the acts of the Klan can . . . be justified on the grounds of grim reality." By 1875 the "white people of Mississippi [had] regained control of the government" and brought an end to Reconstruction's corruption. But the ill will generated by the experience would long remain, perhaps still remained, Sydnor added poignantly, for "it has been said that the South suffered more from reconstruction than from the war."[30]

Mirroring similar textbooks published from Virginia to Texas, Sydnor's *Mississippi History* was hardly unique in its scope or content. Schoolbooks across the South all conformed to essential elements designed to create among white Southerners an intense fear of Northern-imposed ideas and a justification of those Southern customs that denied civil rights to large segments of the population. These textbooks of the "Lost Cause" not only produced in the minds of Southern youth a canted image of the past, but they also prophetically girded them for battle against some future time when "misguided and misinformed" Northern reformers might once again threaten well-established Southern mores.[31]

If Sydnor's *Mississippi History* prepared young white Mississippians to face the vicissitudes of an uncertain future, his second book, *Slavery in Mississippi*, served as a foundation document, framing for seasoned scholars and more mature students favorable impressions of the peculiar institution. While the work's narrative largely conformed to the scientific school's rigid emphasis upon a descriptive style, in broaching the controversial topic of slavery, it called forth value judgments and other assessments usually alien to those trained in that particular academic discipline. Sydnor determined that the Gulf states had been "less closely studied in respect to slavery than the upper slave States," leaving a vast gap in the historical record and necessitating a thorough investigation of the topic. He set forth as his limited purpose to explore the daily lives of Mississippi slaves, to describe their work habits, food, clothing, shelter, physical condition, and social parameters, but he also acknowledged that he could not divorce his work from the political and historiographical debate that had long surrounded the topic. "Any consideration of the ethics of slavery is closely related to the question of slave treatment," he pointed out in his preface. This "in turn is an important index to the character of the dominant slaveholding class of the Old South."[32]

Sydnor approached *Slavery in Mississippi* as a journeyman working confidently through a complicated historical problem, thoroughly studying available primary sources (largely produced by proslave whites), and in the end he drew conclusions that confirmed rather than challenged the prevailing views of his own time. He set down the appropriate facts relating to Mississippi slavery in a straightforward fashion—simple in organization, careful in vocabulary, cogent in examples. Each chapter focused on a specific element of the subject, led the reader through logical subdivisions, and then ended abruptly without drawing conclusions or even adding a summary statement that might be deemed argumentative or assertive. And yet, each chapter and each of its elements placed before the reader the mildest images of slavery and, by inference, the most benign pictures of the master class. "The average slave did not perform an unreasonable amount of work in a day," Sydnor wrote at the book's end. "Except for the omnipresent danger of being sold—and no slave was beyond the shadow of this—being a slave was not for the average negro a dreadful lot. Most strangers who witnessed slavery for the first time were surprised at the cheerfulness of the negroes."[33]

With the writing of *Mississippi History* and *Slavery in Mississippi* Sydnor had settled himself into a comfortable niche in a well-regarded profession. Given the context of Sydnor's South, his future seemed secure; before him lay, apparently, a life of respected rectitude, fellowship with congenial colleagues, and moderate challenges from acceptable students in a Mississippi classroom. He had not reckoned with Theodore Bilbo.[34]

Sydnor's perspectives had until then never reached beyond the privileged classes of the South. He had failed to see white tenants, black sharecroppers, or any others trapped in the hard-scrabble life; they had no particular relevance to his personal well-being or to the comfort of his limited circle. But

Bilbo's redneck assault upon the quiet halls of academia drove Sydnor not only to confront his own place in the world of the American South, but also to assess the complicated relationship between the region's "better sort of people" and the underclass that labored under their discriminating leadership.

A Negrophobic champion of Mississippi's underprivileged white laborers and hill country farmers, Bilbo was the product of a social environment foreign to Sydnor's cultured Presbyterian upbringing. He was a short, stocky man given to garish clothes, rustic wit, and fiery oratory learned at the feet of hell-baiting Southern Baptist preachers. In a mercurial political career, he shuttled in and out of elective office as for the better part of a half century he pitted his followers against the Delta aristocracy and its conservative minions. His pathological racism aside, Bilbo was at heart a Southern liberal who raged at the oppression of the white masses and who determined to right wrongs long inflicted upon them.[35]

By 1930 Bilbo was well into his second term as governor and thoroughly frustrated by reactionary enemies ensconced in the state's Delta-dominated House of Representatives. Unable to push his social agenda through the legislature, he was in no mood to tolerate Mississippi's intransigent higher education establishment, nor to acquiesce in its opposition to his plans for remodeling the state college system along democratic lines. Long association with the Mississippi aristocracy gave the state colleges—especially the University of Mississippi—a sense of invulnerability. Thus Chancellor Hume and his cohorts at the state's other public colleges had assiduously ignored calls for reforms that would make their campuses more accessible to plebeian students. In 1927, Governor Henry Whitfield, Bilbo's predecessor, had organized a commission of professional pedagogues to scrutinize public education in Mississippi and make recommendations. Their findings, termed the O'Shea Report, called for the consolidation of most of the functions of the University of Mississippi, Mississippi College for Women, and Mississippi State College into a "greater university" to be located in Jackson. The older campuses would then be reduced in status to normal colleges training teachers for the woefully understaffed public schools.[36]

When in 1928 Bilbo announced his intent to implement the O'Shea recommendations, Chancellor Hume employed his considerable political acumen to frustrate the governor's will. In early February the university, along with leading citizens of Oxford, hosted a banquet to entertain Mississippi legislators and to properly inform them of the school's honored place in the state's heritage. "Gentlemen, you may move the University of Mississippi," Hume protested. "You may move it to Jackson or anywhere else. You may uproot it from the hallowed ground on which it has stood for eighty years. You may take it from these surroundings that have become dear to thousands who have gone before. But, gentlemen, don't call it 'Ole Miss.'" Rallying to such sentiment, the lawmakers returned to Jackson, rejected Bilbo's proposals, and voted appropriations for new buildings, scientific equipment, and other needful improvements.[37]

Infuriated, Bilbo counterattacked. Over the next two years, he appointed his loyalists to the University of Mississippi's Board of Trustees and in June 1930 they fired its chancellor, whom the governor deemed "temperamentally unfit," and purged thirty-one teachers judged academically unqualified. Although this action elicited cries of outrage from within the university, from alumni throughout Mississippi, and from academicians across the South, in time the school benefited. Almost every terminated faculty member was replaced by an individual with stronger scholarly credentials and specializations more appropriate to a major state university. This, however, brought no solace to those cast off in the context of the Great Depression's worst years and at a point in the academic calendar when employment opportunities hardly existed. Most never resurrected their careers.[38]

Morale among the remaining faculty reached a nadir. Fearful that they too might be counted in the ranks of the unemployed, they stilled the urge to voice public criticisms but in private raged at the plebeian governor and the vulgar mass that adored him. Along with the other survivors, Sydnor despised life under "Bilbo's dictatorship." Six years later he confided to a close friend that "our professor of English, as fine a man as I know, was dismissed because a student who once failed to pass his course was a member of the Bilbo board. About ¼ of our faculty was dismissed in this one pogrom."[39]

Yet Sydnor's discontented Mississippi years fueled an intellectual awakening that dramatically altered his historical interests. His earliest writings—*Mississippi History* and *Slavery in Mississippi*—had been pedestrian works, competent, and scholarly, but uninspired, the product of a contented academician little inclined to challenge his circle's narrow cultural assumptions. Sydnor had not yet developed what he would later call a "wholesome skepticism" necessary to throw "light on the process by which mankind has been fragmented into differing civilization."[40]

Bilbo's assault upon Mississippi aristocracy in general and the University of Mississippi in particular shocked Sydnor into a recognition that Southern civilization encompassed far more than the cultured purview of a favored few. It was intensely divided, fractured into warring elements characterized by race and class. This profoundly troubled Sydnor who by nature preferred consensus to conflict. While he resented and even feared Bilbo's demagogic stirring of the unlettered masses, he had also become disenchanted with the South's so-called "better sort of people," whose narrow interests he had come to serve. Their crusade to restore the antebellum epoch of slavery and aristocracy oppressed the white underclass as well as the struggling descendants of slaves. His contemporary South hardly validated the concept of inevitable progress popular among American scholars as a whole. "Historians of the Old South have been generally able to study change without labeling it progress," he lectured a gathering of Northern students. "If their work can be continued in this mood . . . with a diminution of prejudices arising from race and place," then, he believed, Southern scholars "may yet have more and wiser things to say."[41]

Sydnor deemed himself among those students of the Old South who had "more and wiser things to say." He searched the past to find an idyllic time when the region produced far better leaders than the rude Bilbo or the thoughtless representatives of Mississippi's overbearing aristocracy, and he especially resented the constrictions that patrician guardians of "truthful history" imposed upon open inquiry and free speech. When in 1937 Eron Rowland—a champion of the state's United Daughters of the Confederacy—applied for her late husband's position as director of the Mississippi Department of Archives and History, Sydnor immediately posted a strong letter of protest to Alfred Stone, president of the powerful Mississippi Historical Society. "I would consider [her election] a very great catastrophe," he explained to a colleague at the University of Mississippi and he urged that colleague along with professional historians across the state to echo his opposition. To his relief, she failed in her quest for office.[42]

In Sydnor's mind there had once existed a golden epoch before the hysteria of secession, before the defeat and destruction of a well-nurtured culture, and before the South's vanquished upper class insisted upon a narcissistic defense of its civilization to the exclusion of the needs of all others. From the mid-1930s onward he endeavored to revive what he believed to be a vanished tradition of enlightened aristocratic statesmen who had created a model society beneficial to those of high estate and low. While composing his manuscript on Mississippi slavery, Sydnor had considered moving from his discussion of that topic to an analysis of the experiences of free blacks in the antebellum era, but as he later explained to the editors of the *American Historical Review:* "I am now far more interested in Southern political leadership. Some day I hope to publish something on the procedures by which Southern political leaders have been advanced to power or have lifted themselves to such a place."[43]

Beginning with his book *A Gentleman of the Old Natchez Region: Benjamin L. C. Wailes* (1938), expanding into his *The Development of Southern Sectionalism* (1948), and culminating with his classic work, *American Revolutionaries in the Making: Political Practices in Washington's Virginia* (1952), Sydnor let reign his faith in the uplifting value of a cultured and compassionate elite that shared with its less-favored peers the bounties of a well-ordered society. In the course of gathering materials for his study on slavery, good fortune led him to the Natchez home of Nellie Wailes Brandon, who possessed the extensive papers of her grandfather, Benjamin Leonard Covington Wailes. She generously granted him the "intellectual as well as physical freedom" to explore this massive collection, which included among its numerous documents a thirty-six-volume diary revealing the mind and the exploits of a little-known antebellum planter intent upon civilizing Mississippi's crude frontier.[44]

Sydnor not only found in Wailes a historical figure whose values and life experiences closely mirrored his own, but he also discovered in himself an unaccustomed passion for his subject; he engaged in a project that would become the initial canvas upon which he could express a message close to his soul. Although he would always articulate a modified faith in the scientific method of historiography insisting that the historian remain a neutral observer of the past, this book marked his transition into thesis-oriented history designed as much to influence the future as to illuminate the past. To Sydnor the excesses of Theodore Bilbo's democracy had their roots in fundamental trends commenced a century earlier. The South of the 1830s and 1840s abandoned the sagacious, nationalistic statesmanship of Washington, Jefferson, and Madison—and, on a local level, persons like Wailes—and gave rein to less wise, sectional, and demagogic leaders, and set forth on a destructive course to secession, war, and ruin. However much Sydnor disdained Jacksonian democracy, he blamed its advent on the ideological failures of late antebellum aristocrats. Faced with perceived threats from an aggressive Northern society, they turned inward, protected their narrow class interests, and neglected the welfare of the South as a whole. The tragic results plagued the region well into the twentieth century.

In common with his biographer, Benjamin L. C. Wailes had sprung from the South's privileged classes. Born August 1, 1797, he was the first child of Levin Wailes, the scion of a wealthy Maryland family. A successful frontier speculator in land and slaves, the elder Wailes greatly expanded his inheritance and in 1807 settled at the hamlet of Washington twenty miles east of Natchez, then recently designated Mississippi's territorial capital. For generations the westward-migrating Waileses had "followed rather than led the moving frontier," Sydnor observed. They "stayed close to the frontier but always lived on the civilized side of the line." They were a people as much dedicated to cultivating civilization as to accumulating wealth.[45]

Benjamin L. C. Wailes forsook his ancestors' migrating tradition, focused his attention upon the expansion of his comfortable plantation cushioned by the labor of one hundred fifty slaves, and patronized the intellectual community that flourished throughout the Natchez district. An alumnus of Jefferson College (located in nearby Washington), he served actively as a trustee from 1824 until his death in 1862, became a charter member of and contributed to the Mississippi Historical Society, and developed a national reputation as a geologist who counted among his friends and correspondents John James Audubon and the Mississippi antiquarian J. F. H. Claiborne. Sydnor, enamored with the erudition of Wailes and his circle, explained to the American Historical Association's convention in 1936 that these scholars of the Natchez frontier were dedicated to the "exchanging of ideas, visits and objects of scientific interest" between themselves and like-thinking parties in Philadelphia, New York, Washington, D.C., and elsewhere. "It may not be irrelevant to add that the scholars of old Natchez, who were non-sectional in the intellectual worlds, were likewise non-sectional in politics. In the secession period, they were unionists."[46]

A child of Mississippi's unstable frontier, Wailes distrusted unfettered democracy. He accepted as natural two aspects of government, Sydnor reasoned. One was that the national government must play a vital role, "for its agencies at Washington, especially the fort and land office," were essential to an orderly society. "The other was that government was by men rather than by masses of men. He saw leaders rather than great groups of voters; he saw things accomplished by conference rather than by swaying the populace." Wailes and his close associates stood above the vulgar multitude, created a prosperous and cultured society, and intended to pass its benefits to their progeny.[47]

Democracy, of course, intruded into Mississippi's well-ordered patrician society and in the process disrupted the Natchez district's comfortable life-style. Wailes "distrusted government by universal manhood suffrage," Sydnor wrote. "He believed that government should be by the upper classes, and he was convinced that most of the Democrats were from the lower classes." He "neither understood nor liked the technique of manipulating [the electorate]" and he held in special contempt those members of his own class—among them Jefferson Davis—who exercised undue influence over the masses. Mississippi's stampede out of the Union in 1861 left Wailes bewildered; he lamented its tragic consequences and he blamed its cause upon the "reckless and unprincipled politicians with their secession agitation." The disillusioned aristocrat died the following year, bereaved at his country's melancholy state. "In so far as his happiness depended upon the survival of his civilization," Sydnor concluded, Wailes "had indeed lived too long."[48]

Even as Sydnor penned Wailes's biography, he determined that perhaps he had also lived too long in Mississippi. When in 1936 newly inaugurated Governor Hugh L. White declared war upon the state's higher education establishment, urged the legislature to expand the number of university trustees so that he could make his own appointments, and promised, in Sydnor's words, "to 'fire' the president of the [state college for women] and the president of the State Teachers College for the crime of voting against him," the historian gratefully accepted an offer tendered by Duke University. "Mississippi is incurably politically minded in respect to education," he lamented. "After eleven years of it I am about ready for a change."[49]

Intelligent, cultured, and nonimperious by nature, Sydnor settled with ease into the Duke community. He genuinely liked his colleagues in the Department of History and enjoyed even more his emancipation from Mississippi's restrictive society and from the bureaucratic burdens of his previous employment. Nonetheless, his fellow historians' lack of interest in research and writing mildly disappointed him. In early 1937, Sydnor confided to a friend that there was little in the way of "departmental news" beyond the recent birth of a child to one of its younger members. "Other than this," he sighed, "the department seems at the moment to be relatively unproductive of babies and of books." He remained dedicated to his own scholarship, completing his biography of Wailes in June 1937. Impressed with this carefully researched and well-written book and with the conformity to Southern historical orthodoxy evident in Sydnor's earlier works, Charles W. Ramsdell and Wendell Holmes Stephenson, editors of the recently conceived History of the South series, deemed Sydnor one of the few scholars conversant with the shifting allegiances of the early nineteenth-century South and tendered him an invitation to join their prestigious enterprise.[50]

Jointly sponsored by the Littlefield Fund for the Study of Southern History and Louisiana State University Press, the History of the South series was intended to be a major contribution to Southern apologetic literature, a continuation of neo-Confederate historiography with its characteristic praise of antebellum Southern culture, justification of secession, glorification of the Confederate crusade, and condemnation of Yankee Reconstruction. The project was the legacy of George Washington Littlefield—major in the Confederate Army, wealthy Texas entrepreneur, regent of the University of Texas, and member of the John Bell Hood Camp, United Confederate Veterans. In 1914, Littlefield made his initial donation for the acquiring of primary materials on Southern history and for the publication of a "history of the United States with the plain facts concerning the South . . . fairly stated that the children of the South may be truthfully taught."[51] University of Texas historian Charles W. Ramsdell and Louisiana State University's Wendell Holmes Stephenson, both of whom sympathized with the Confederate partisans' historical assumptions, oversaw the project as coeditors. Following Ramsdell's death in 1942, E. Merton Coulter assumed his duties as coeditor of the History of the South series and took on the additional responsibility of composing a volume on the Confederacy.[52]

Published in 1947, the project's premier volume, Coulter's *The South during Reconstruction, 1865–1877*, proved as satisfying to those scholars sympathetic to the Confederate cause as it was disappointing to historians who hoped for a more balanced interpretation. Among the latter, Columbia University's David Donaldson damned Coulter's work as uninformed by modern revisionist literature and insensitive to evolving Southern social realities. Thoroughly dissatisfied with the author and his work, Donaldson prayed "for a more objective approach in the succeeding volumes of this important series."[53] Sydnor's *The Development of Southern Sectionalism, 1819–1848*, which appeared the following year, constituted an unexpected and significant break with the Confederate partisans' prescriptive interpretations of the past and largely fulfilled the hope for "a more objective approach" toward the South's past.

Neither Ramsdell nor Stephenson anticipated Sydnor's shifting historiographic perspective. Unknown to them, he had not only identified himself with the nationalistic Wailes, but had also come to condemn the excesses of democracy that empowered sectional demagogues to destroy the Natchez planters' cultured world and to lead the South on its ill-omened path to secession and defeat. He saw Southern independence as more the nadir than the zenith of the region's historical experience, a position that would hardly have endeared him to proponents of the "Lost Cause." Sydnor's disdain for the Confederacy and for those who brought about its existence mirrored his contemporary concern that members of his own profession were in the 1930s and 1940s leading the South on a similar course to ruin.

Sydnor saw destructive sectionalism as the fundamental cause of the Civil War. He maintained that chauvinistic Southern politicians shouldered the principal blame for the Union's destruction. When Southern leaders' national influence waned, he wrote in the preface to *The Development of Southern Sectionalism*, "Southerners attempted to invent defenses against what they regarded as northern political ruthlessness. Feelings of fear, desperation, and bitterness possessed them. Their patriotism toward the nation diminished. Their allegiance to their section increased."[54]

Focusing on the critical period from 1819 to 1848, Sydnor chronicled the transformation of the South from a land of national, respected, and progressive leaders—Washington, Jefferson, Madison, Monroe—to a region of lesser demagogues dedicated primarily to the defense of slavery and sectional pride. Early in the nineteenth century, "the South was accepted as a respectable part" of the Union, he reasoned. But "by the 1840s it was regarded by many Northerners as an obstacle to American social and economic progress and as a moral pariah." Unable to bear the North's condescending critiques of the peculiar institution and of those who benefited from it, Southern intellectuals "evolved a remarkable apologia of virtually every aspect of the Southern way of life." These regional champions "claimed that slavery was good, that slavery had a beneficial influence upon Southern life, and that the South like ancient Greece had evolved a noble civilization because the institution of slavery was an integral part of it."[55]

Sydnor concluded that as the decade of the 1840s neared its end, Southern social and political leaders had pledged their faith to a cancerous fiction that proclaimed "their own age was the golden age; and . . . that its foundation was Negro slavery." Having arrived at this "curious, psychopathic condition" they fostered an unhealthy sense of regional ethnocentrism characterized by vitriolic condemnations of the North's venal culture and by "extravagant claims and boastings about the perfect society of the Old South." One thing must be recognized, Sydnor emphasized: "Even though the idealized portrait of the South was false, it was to be a strong and living force in the years ahead. In the long run, the vision of the perfect South was to supply a substantial element in the construction of the romantic legend about the Old South. In the nearer future, it was to give the Confederate soldier something to die for."[56]

Sydnor's *The Development of Southern Sectionalism* marked a milestone in his intellectual sojourn. Almost two decades prior to its publication, he had himself helped strengthen the scholarly underpinnings of the romantic image of the Old South that had for generations kept the region out of step with the nation as a whole. His elementary textbook on Mississippi history together with his monograph on slavery in the state moved in an intellectual current welling from the Southern fire-eaters' antebellum rhetoric. These early works sketched a chimerical image of the Old South that could not withstand critical scrutiny. Theodore S. Bilbo's social radicalism and the historical fanaticism of neo-Confederate historians forced Sydnor through time to reassess his own flawed contemporary South and then to apply the same rigorous discernment in his examination of the region's past—whose image he had helped to construct.

But many leading Southern historians, chief among them Frank L. Owsley, found Sydnor's assessment less than satisfying. Critically analyzing *The Development of Southern Sectionalism* in the *Journal of Southern History*, Owsley doubted the "complete validity" of Sydnor's assertion that "the South's minority status and its defensive attitude toward slavery had the effect by 1848 of closing the minds and eyes of the Southerners to the faults of their society and of bringing them to regard their society as perfect." Paradoxically, however, the review's next sentence helped validate Sydnor's position as Owsley stressed that his own examination of "wills, diaries, private correspondence, and other personal and private expressions of feelings and opinion" revealed a Southern people "deeply troubled by the vicious and indiscriminate attack of their fellow citizens from without—the abolitionists and their political allies—and the presence of a seemingly insoluble race problem within." Suggesting that Sydnor evinced sympathy with "the rule of the majority in the national government" on the Civil War's eve, Owsley reminded his readers that Southern political philosophy had always held to the Lockean faith in the "limited sovereignty" of government and that "in this area . . . the South often denied the right of the majority to have its way." By his own words Owsley made it plain that Southern chauvinism remained a fundamental dogma with many twentieth-century Southern historians, thereby demonstrating the essential legitimacy of Sydnor's argument. Beyond these critiques Owsley judged "Sydnor's tone . . . judicious, unbiased, and modest," a pleasant "contrast with the tone of self-righteous wrath and omnipotence so characteristic of the recent crop of work on this period of American history."[57]

Among Owsley's recent crop of "self-righteous" historians Harvard's Paul H. Buck welcomed *The Development of Southern Sectionalism* as a significant departure from the neo-Confederate tradition of Southern historiography. His effusive essay in the *Mississippi Valley Historical Review* heralded this second addition to the History of the South series as "evidence that Southern historical scholarship [was] . . . in Sydnor's hands, fully matured and uninhibited." With Sydnor's "synthesis" of the period 1819–1848 Buck pronounced that the author deserved to be ranked with two icons of Old South historiography— Ulrich B. Phillips and William Edward Dodd—and of the three, Sydnor was "much the soundest historian." To be "placed in a category with Phillips and Dodd is, of course, the ultimate praise for a Southern historian. Sydnor belongs there because of the competence of his scholarship. It is thorough, judicious, and complete."[58]

When in early December 1948 Sydnor received the North Carolina Historical Society's Mayflower Cup in recognition of his book's significant contribution to Southern studies, one journalist reflected on the obvious parallels between the epoch Sydnor discussed and the region's contemporary political economy. South Carolina governor J. Strom Thurmond and his Dixiecrat party's campaign to insulate the white South from civil rights reforms reflected the antebellum Southerners' resistance to the abolition crusade. Interviewed for the *Raleigh News and Observer,* Sydnor agreed, noting that "we have sectionalism now; we had it then, in the period I have studied. Our aim must be to study it, learn what causes it and how it works."[59]

The Mayflower Cup capped Sydnor's study of Southern sectionalism and its accompanying malevolence. In late December he made public a new area of research emphasis, his intention to understand the political climate that enabled Virginia and the South to nurture successful national statesmen in the waning decades of the eighteenth century. Standing before a joint session of the Southern Historical Association and the American Historical Association to present his paper "Aristocracy and Politics in Revolutionary Virginia," he argued that the colonial Old Dominion was a democratic society free from the taint of demagoguery. Its voters—landholders all—had before them a simple task, the right to choose from among the best of the aristocrats their appropriate leaders. "The cardinal doctrine of the political system that produced such men as Washington, Jefferson, Madison, Mason, and Henry was this emphasis upon the idea that men are not equally fit to hold office, and that a democracy is more likely to flourish if it fills its offices, from the lowest to the highest, with its ablest citizens."[60]

Tormented by nightmarish images of Bilbo, Thurmond, and like-minded rabble-rousers, Sydnor on his historiographical journey had turned to a theme that breathed passion into his historical writings, and he soon gained the opportunity to share it with an international audience. In 1950 Oxford University honored the Duke scholar, appointing him the Harold Vyvyan Harmsworth Professor of American History. The first Southern historian deemed worthy of this esteemed posting, he relished his year among the "dreaming spires" and found in it an opportunity to refine his thoughts while completing his manuscript detailing the virtues of George Washington's Virginia.[61]

"Three propositions . . . are probably well enough accepted to occasion no debate," Sydnor proclaimed in his inaugural lecture before the Oxford dons. "The first of these is that society is fortunate if the offices of government are filled by men of superior intelligence, training, and character rather than by inferior or even average men. The second is that the processes of choosing leadership have an effect upon the kinds of leadership that are chosen. The third proposition is that a group of eighteenth-century Virginians, including George Washington, Thomas Jefferson, Patrick Henry, George Mason, George Wythe, Peyton Randolph, James Madison, and John Marshall, were among the ablest public men to appear at any time in American history." Sydnor put forward the case that eighteenth-century Virginia wove together the best elements of aristocracy and democracy. Blessed with the advantages of wealth, education, and leisure, the colony's patrician class flourished in a cultural environment that taught them to rule well their plantations, that required them to appreciate the fundamental principles of governing their local communities, that advanced the more talented of them to their colonial legislature, and then moved the best of them beyond Virginia to stand as champions of the newly created American nation. The lesson, he emphasized, was that the voters had the uncomplicated privilege of choosing from among its best citizens those worthy of elevation to the higher responsibilities of government. There was "no reason to think that the great generation of Virginians" would have endorsed the modern "faith in the common man," he concluded. That generation mounted "strong protest against mediocrity in leadership. They affirmed that aristocracy and democracy are not mutually exclusive elements in politics; that society needs political processes to discover and place in public office men of superior ability, excellent training, and useful experiences."[62]

Immediately upon Sydnor's return to the United States, he issued his most enduring work, *Gentlemen Freeholders: Political Practices in Washington's Virginia*, which in the eccentric publishing world of the early 1950s was soon brought out in paperback under the more engaging title *American Revolutionaries in the Making*. The latter title, however, was a misnomer. Sydnor's late eighteenth-century Virginians were revolutionaries only in a highly restrictive sense; they were men of fundamental conservative temperament dedicated to the preservation of their distinctively stratified social order. Sydnor both admired and idealized their steady society, seeing in it a judicious mix of democracy and aristocracy. "Statesmen come to the helm of government only if society has ways of discovering men of extraordinary talent, character, and training and of elevating them, rather than their inferiors, to office," he argued in his opening paragraph. "Democracy must do two things and do them well: it must develop men who are fit to govern, and it must select for office these men rather than their less worthy contemporaries."[63]

A master craftsman skilled in the historical discipline, Sydnor had this book move well beyond the limited boundaries of his schooling in "scientific history." In contrast to that school's emphasis upon precisely documented fact and a carefully reconstructed and passionless explication of past events, the argument of *Gentlemen Freeholders* recognized the powerful ties of the past both to the present and to the potentials of the future. Sydnor preached a message he believed critical to the felicity of his own generation. If the present South could but learn from its blighted past, repent of the excessive present-day democracy that bred divisive demagogues, and return to the rational, selfless model of Washington's Virginia, then perhaps its future might be free from hurtful social strife. To be sure, he admitted, many of the political practices of eighteenth-century Virginia would hardly seem democratic to modern Americans. "The secret ballot, universal manhood suffrage, woman suffrage, the direct election of United States senators and other officials previously appointed or indirectly elected . . . have been made in the faith that each would bring democracy closer to perfection." But Sydnor questioned whether "Americans in their intense preoccupation with improving the form of self-government [had] forgotten more important matters." His message to the nation as a whole and to the South in particular was that the only way for democracy to work was for "men of good will to labor incessantly at the job of making it work."[64]

The publication of *Gentlemen Freeholders* raised Sydnor to the pinnacle of his profession. In his mid-fifties and possessed of intellect, talent, and mission, he looked eagerly to future writing projects and to other opportunities to place his message before appreciative audiences. With that in mind, he gratefully accepted offers to present papers before two prestigious gatherings in February and March 1954, first at the annual Claiborne Lectures at the University of Mississippi and followed a few days later by the Walter Lynwood Fleming Lectures at Louisiana State University.[65]

Sydnor and his wife happily anticipated these affairs, seeing in them a long-needed vacation, combining agreeable professional responsibilities with visits to old friends. His schedule called for him to deliver a series of three papers at the University of Mississippi on February 22, 23, and 24, after which he would travel to Biloxi for a luncheon address before the Mississippi Historical Society; he would then move on to his presentations at Baton Rouge. But these events proved far more fateful than Sydnor had imagined.

On February 26 Sydnor addressed the noon gathering of the Mississippi Historical Society, reading his paper "Historical Comments on American Democracy." A former graduate student looked on with concern as Dr. Sydnor delivered his paper. He recalled "a man sorely disturbed over a host of undemocratic trends of these times, both in America and in the world. Here were the troubles that mattered; and with a voice rarely raised to sound alarm, Sydnor spoke with a depth of feeling and what . . . might be termed a prophetic wrath." Distraught by a South dominated by politicians in the inflammatory lineage of Theodore S. Bilbo and a nation rent by the Communist-baiting rhetoric of Joseph McCarthy, Sydnor pled with his audience to forsake the leadership of inferior men "who usurp functions that do not properly belong to them." Americans, he affirmed, have the high duty of selecting only worthy men, those able to make decisions with "wisdom, character and courage." It was his valedictory. Struck by a massive heart attack the following morning, he died on the second of March 1954.[66]

Insofar as Sydnor's happiness depended upon his quest for a suitable South, he did not live long enough. Dedicated to the historian's task, he had been a transitional figure who both departed from the neo-Confederate interpretations of his well-indoctrinated contemporaries and broke with the limited ideological assumptions of his scientific training to embrace a more dynamic form of history, one that allowed him to present lessons relevant to his own time. Tragically, however, for years after his death the mainstream of Southern historiography continued to course along lines charted by academicians sympathetic to their Confederate birthright. Their writings reinforced inflamed memories of the Civil War and nurtured a political climate antagonistic to positive social reform. Arkansas's Orville Faubus, Mississippi's Ross Barnett, Alabama's George Wallace, and Georgia's Lester Maddox crusaded against civil rights for African-Americans, boasting of their rebel heritage.

Months before his passing Sydnor looked with disdain upon the current "fad for displaying Confederate caps and flags" and condemned the reality that "any person in the South trying to accomplish nearly anything can make profitable use of the ancient shibboleths of states' rights, of race, and of Southern traditions." In writing "the history of the South as in writing the history of other places, man cannot entirely free himself from his involvement with the present," he reflected. "But he should not compel the past into the patterns and prejudices of today. Rather, he should use the events of earlier human experiences for clues as to the right directions for man to take today and tomorrow." Intended as the concluding remarks of his Walter Lynwood Fleming Lecture, these words were never delivered. Death had already stilled his plea for moderation.[67]

The author expresses his sincere appreciation to Catherine Pollari and John L. Brinkley of Hampden-Sydney College for helping flesh out Sydnor's undergraduate experiences and to his colleague John L. Robinson for reviewing the manuscript and making numerous recommendations.

W. J. Cash

A Native Son Confronts the Past

BRUCE CLAYTON

Was W. J. Cash a bona fide historian? He completed a few history courses as a college undergraduate, but never did any graduate work in history. He never studied under a well-connected academic mentor, or even audited an advanced seminar in any part of history. Nor did Cash, an obscure journalist most of his life, ever hold an academic appointment of any sort as a historian, or ever write a researched monograph or publish a scholarly article. He never read a paper at a professional convention, or attended a scholarly conference. He never published as much as a book review in a scholarly journal. Needless to say, he had no academic disciples and no group of devoted students to publish a festschrift to honor his work, which consisted of one highly personal, impressionistic book with neither footnotes nor a bibliography. But what a book it was! Few works in history can rival the stunning insights and influence of Cash's single achievement, *The Mind of the South*.[1]

Sixty years have elapsed since Wilbur Joseph Cash published *The Mind of the South* in 1941, but his book continues to provoke argument, agreement, and dissent, and not just from historians. This is no small achievement for the one-book author, a chain-smoking, reclusive North Carolina newspaperman who had amounted to little in life, and who would tragically end his days by his own hand just months after his book appeared to rave reviews. Never out of print, the book is history on the grand scale: a passionate, audacious, sweeping quest for the essence of the Southern experience. It is a brilliantly written personal report from the home front containing the disturbing message that the past, far from being dead, maintains a fateful grip on the present. That Southerners were imprisoned in history was the lamentable message at the core of Cash's profound probing of the tragedy of Southern history. No historian since has had the courage or inclination—some would say foolhardiness—even to try what Cash did. He tried because he was, in his soul, an artist, an intellectual, a writer who claimed the whole of Southern history as his province. Cash's book was a native son's wrenching cry from the heart, a book, as Nietzsche would say, "written in blood."

Joseph Wilbur Cash (who would later reverse the order of his first two names and come to identify himself as W. J. Cash) was born on May 2, 1900, in the rough, growing textile-mill town of Gaffney, South Carolina. His folks were hardworking devout Baptists of modest means and very narrow traditional views. His parents called their first-born son Wilbur; his childhood friends nicknamed him "Sleepy," probably because of the way he squinted his eyes when reading or making a point in conversation in his thick Southern drawl. His earliest education came at a local private academy and then a Baptist high school in Boiling Springs, North Carolina, just north of Gaffney, where his parents made a new home. After that, he did an unrewarding year at nearby Wofford College, a small Christian denominational school, and an excruciatingly lonely semester at Valparaiso University in Indiana. At the first opportunity, Cash eagerly escaped the harshness of Northern winters and returned to North Carolina and enrolled at Wake Forest College, though at first he feared it was just another "preacher's school." He was wrong. There, stimulating teachers, including the historian C. Chilton Pearson, and the dynamic president, William Louis Poteat, an embattled champion of intellectual freedom and the teaching of evolution, introduced Cash to the writings of Charles Darwin, Joseph Conrad, James Branch Cabell, and the South-baiting, acerbic Baltimore journalist H. L. Mencken. From youth onward, Cash was a voracious reader with weak eyes—perhaps the source of his squinting—and he plunged headfirst into the liberating authors his Wake Forest teachers recommended. Mainly, however, the Jazz Age of the 1920s was a period of drift for young Jack Cash, as his new friends now called him. He seemed to have no recognizable or realistic goals, though he tried his hand several times at writing a novel. Cash did a year of law school at Wake Forest (1922–1923) but found the work boring beyond belief. After that he held two uninspiring one-year teaching positions in his home state, the first at a small college, the second at the high school in Hendersonville. While teaching (which he considered drudgery) Cash suffered through a period of unrequited love with a young college girl who was a bit younger than he was but far more sophisticated than the awkward, ill-at-ease rustic boy from the country. Defeated in love, he worked off and on for various local newspapers, and threw himself into the writing of several novels in the mode of Dostoevsky, Conrad, and Theodore Dreiser, writers he admired deeply. Briefly in the fall of 1928, Cash edited a country newspaper in his home county, the *Cleveland Press*. As an editor he opposed Prohibition, championed public education, and lashed out at religious and racial intolerance. Cash was an outspoken "yellow dog Democrat" (he would have voted for a yellow dog had the party nominated one) and gave Al

Smith, the party's presidential candidate, his full support. He sensed (correctly) that much of the local and vitriolic opposition to Smith, a "wet" on the liquor question, a Roman Catholic, and a New Yorker whose Irish brogue gave away his parents' status as immigrants, was thinly disguised nativism cum racism. The presidential campaign was fierce and ugly in North Carolina and the rest of the South as nativists and "drys" railed against Smith.[2]

During the 1920s Cash suffered several nervous breakdowns (the reasons for which are unclear) and he appears to have had a manic-depressive or bipolar mood disorder all his life. In search of help he tried rest and recuperative travel in Europe and he read Sigmund Freud passionately. Still an omnivorous reader, he saturated himself in a host of classical writers from Shakespeare and Cervantes to Nietzsche and Spengler, whose masterpiece, *The Decline of the West* (1918–1922) deeply disturbed Cash and many intellectuals. Along with the Bible, each writer, particularly Freud and Nietzsche, influenced Cash's mind and subtly contributed to the substance, form, and style of *The Mind of the South*.[3]

The inspiration for writing *Mind* came to Cash in 1929 after publishing an article with that title in Mencken's *American Mercury*, in which Cash, an admirer of Mencken's slash-and-burn style, had published several iconoclastic pieces on Southern life. (Actually, as early as his Wake Forest years Cash, as editor of the college newspaper, had been thinking about something he once editorially called "the Mind of the South.") Mencken, flattered by Cash's obvious imitation of his style and point of view, as well as Cash's boldness of thought and literary facility, mentioned Cash's name to the prestigious publisher Alfred A. Knopf. Knopf immediately suggested that the young Carolinian consider expanding his article into a book. Elated, Cash said yes and announced that he was eager to get down to work. But his neuroses rendered him a procrastinator and perfectionist, and he would not finish his book until 1940. The Great Depression had laid its cruel hand on the Piedmont, leaving Cash's parents nearly destitute. Cash returned to journalism to make ends meet for himself and his family. From 1935 on, he worked full time at the *Charlotte News*, home to several top-flight writers and widely and highly regarded as a "writer's" paper. At the *News* he sharpened his writing skills and gained valuable information about the contemporary South, which helped him focus his critical and literary perspective on the region. His passion for creative literature intensified as he read his contemporaries, William Faulkner, Thomas Wolfe, and Erskine Caldwell, and reread his college favorites Cabell and Conrad. The young journalist, reviewing a host of novels and books good and bad but few history books of any sort, tried to buckle down and work on *Mind*. But the writing went slowly, partly because he remained in the thrall of fashioning a novel from the same materials Faulkner and the other writers of the Southern Renaissance were using with such success.[4]

As a result, Cash read very little "history." Still, *Mind* reflects the obvious influence of William Garrott Brown, William E. Dodd, and G. W. Dyer on the Old South and William A. Dunning and Walter Fleming on Reconstruction. Cash was particularly indebted to Broadus Mitchell's highly praised book *The Rise of the Cotton Mills in the South* (1921) and uncritically sympathetic to Mitchell's assumptions about the paternalism of the textile-mill founders. For the post-1865 South's reconciliation with the North, Cash relied upon Paul Buck's scholarly work, *The Road to Reunion* (1935). The early sections of *Mind* make effective use of such standard primary sources as Frederick Law Olmstead, Hinton Rowen Helper, Joseph Glover Baldwin, and Daniel R. Hundley. Cash's later sections draw heavily on his own experiences as a child of the mill culture of the Carolina Piedmont and on his critical reading of the influential sociologists at the University of North Carolina: Howard W. Odum and Rupert Vance on the South as a region with distinct social structure. In addition, Cash had familiarized himself with Arthur Raper's documentation of lynchings and his demolition of the myth that such barbarities were almost always the result of the rape of a white woman by a black, and with Harriet Herring's careful but shocking study of child labor in the cotton mills. Along the way, Cash had thoroughly studied Franz Boas and Melville Herskovits's strictures against racial stereotyping. Cash departed from most Southern historians and read various black writers from W. E. B. Du Bois, namely his *The Souls of Black Folk* (1903), to Langston Hughes and his poetry, and other writers of the Harlem Renaissance. There is no evidence, however, that he parted company with his white contemporaries and took seriously Du Bois's pioneering work, *Black Reconstruction* (1935). It is also clear that Cash did not read C. Vann Woodward's revisionist biography, *Tom Watson: Agrarian Radical* (1938).[5]

The governing fact is that *Mind* rests squarely on Cash's serious and imaginative reading of a few sources and primarily, as he told Knopf at one point, "on the authority of my imagination." His book is full of daring insights, intuitive leaps, and a firm, imaginative grasp of irony and paradox. He boldly coins expressions such as "savage ideal" (to characterize the region's intolerance of dissent) and "proto-Dorian convention" (to summarize the racial bonding of whites, a psychological bonding that transcended class). All of these stylistic innovations flowed from an intellect tempered by wide learning and his personal emancipation from the Piedmont's religiously narrow and anti-intellectual culture. Some have fumed that Cash hated the South and wrote in bitterness. Such is not the case. He loved the South, somewhat in the manner of a jealous lover who cares too passionately and critically about the object of his affection. Unlike many avowedly conservative lovers of Dixie, Cash would never leave the South permanently or for any lengthy period of time. He had a deep ambivalence toward the South, a lover's ambivalence that revealed itself in his criticisms and his inescapable compulsion to write its history in the hope that he might inform and awaken and thus liberate his countrymen from the past. Escaping the past lay at the center of his passionate soul, a "psyche" as he might say, that needed to identify and excoriate the South's human shortcomings and scream the truth at the top of his lungs.[6]

On the surface, *Mind* glides along on the crest of a newspaperman's informal style, a subtle blending of the folksy and slangy with erudite language enveloped in a compelling narrative of nearly unrelenting seriousness. Deep feelings born of intimate knowledge of his subject often emerge dramatically causing the reader to stop and gasp at what Cash is saying. To diminish the intensity, and create something of a good old boy rapport with his reader, he speaks personally, often casually, admitting in frequent asides that "I go too fast" or "I labor the case." Colloquialisms like "cracker," "redneck," "white trash," "bust-head" (bootleg whiskey), and "throat-slitting" abound, standing shoulder to shoulder with high-toned words and expressions like "seraglios," the "proto-Dorian convention," and "Cloud-Cuckoo Land," the latter silently borrowed from Aristophanes by way of James Branch Cabell. In a seemingly casual manner, Cash cites his own experiences to prove points, particularly a horrific fact or one serious readers might tend to doubt: "I have myself known university-bred men who confessed proudly to having helped roast a Negro." At its worst, Cash's style is maddeningly convoluted, rhetorical, and extravagant. But at its best his book is, in the words of Richard King, "a masterpiece of discursive prose, stylistically one of the most sophisticated works in American historiography."[7]

Cash's opus starts boldly, contending that the South is fundamentally different from the rest of the nation and has been characterized, from its beginning and through its history, by a rigid, unbroken intellectual conformity maintained by an unsleeping public opinion and, when necessary, by violence or threats of violence. These twin arguments of unity and continuity inform every page of *Mind* and today provoke rough criticism from historians. Cash begins with a hurried look at the colonial and revolutionary South, barely acknowledging Thomas Jefferson and the Founding Fathers, whom most Southern historians and liberal social critics of Cash's day continued to insist were the "true" Southerners. By page twelve Cash is exploring the story of the Great South of 1820, now the land of cotton and slavery and the plantations' steady westward advance beyond the Appalachians. Along the way Cash attacks the popular, lingering myth of the Virginia Cavalier, saying that the state's celebrated First Families were themselves a one-generation product of the frontier, having sprung from the same common clay as the crackers. To Cash, comfortably at home with Frederick Jackson Turner's famous "Frontier Thesis," the frontier was both a great historical fact and a convenient metaphor to explain why the Southerner was a "hell of a fellow" (and proud of it), ever driven by a simple but intense individualism, a deluded romanticism, a reckless hedonism, and, paradoxically, a simple Puritanism. During Reconstruction, says Cash, faithfully following the prevailing scholarship and thereby succumbing to myths of his day (myths Du Bois's *Black Reconstruction* had exploded), grasping Yankees had humiliated the South and hurled the region back into a devil-take-the-hindmost frontier condition. There followed the emergence, in the 1880s and 1890s, of the textile industry, paternalistic in origins if not in practice, and the New South's attempt to impose alien Yankee values. This had the unwanted and unexpected effect of again turning the South into a renewed version of the frontier that revivified the ancient pattern of unrestrained individualism now further sanctified by the allure of emulating the successful Yankee captains of industry, all the while maintaining Southern disdain for mere "commercialism." But Cash the veteran newspaperman refuses, as he proudly but silently makes clear, to be taken in completely by the rhetoric of the New South Creed. By nature pessimistic and chronically depressed, Cash graphically detailed the horror of mill village squalor and terrible working conditions. Cash was sure that he could detect behind the bragging and boasting of New South boosters "the gallop of Jeb Stewart's cavalrymen." As a result, he contended in a rhetorical flourish, the real, everyday Southerner had no more use for factories and urban skyscrapers "than a hog has for a morning coat."[8]

Using such stylistic pyrotechnics (the sort of writing that makes most academic historians cringe, in anger or perhaps in envy) Cash obviously hoped to grab his reader's lapels. He had a serious argument to make and he wanted his reader's attention. Style aside, one must remember the more important fact that Cash did not share his generation's academic notion of "mind." Cash lived during the era when Perry Miller, a Northern scholar of immense achievement and distinction, helped define "intellectual history" as the probing of the thought of an era's intellectual elite who were assumed to be outlining and probing the assumptions of the people at large. Cash never for a moment considered following Miller's lead set forth so magnificently in *The New England Mind* (1939). Miller's approach, while yielding brilliant insights into the clerical elite of Puritanism, was alien, even irrelevant, to Cash's desires. He was convinced that the everyday Southerner was daily acting out a controlling "mental pattern," "a complex of established relationships and habits of thought." As such, the Southern mind was essentially that of a folk "temperament," a folk mind with deeply embedded fantasies and fears, most of them racial and many sexual and all of them enmeshed in the individual and collective ego. Cash, who had devoured Freud, knew what he was doing when he used psychological terms like *ego* and *psyche*. Cash had a typology of mind as "psyche" that included the working of the unconscious every bit as much as the rational conclusions that Miller's elite intellectuals assumed to be the sum and substance of their thought. Cash's definition of "mind," when fused with a novelist's desire to uncover the mysteries of why people act and "think" as they do, allowed him to concentrate on and thus take seriously the common Southerner's culture, particularly the "feelings" and darker impulses of both the master class and the white masses.[9]

"Strictly," said Cash, borrowing the words directly from Henry Adams, "the Southerner had no mind: he had temperament." At bottom, the Southerner "felt" but did not "think." This conception of mind as temperament is infuriating to Cash's most trenchant critics, led by C. Vann Woodward, who caustically argued that Cash might have quite reasonably entitled his book "The Mindlessness of the South." But lesser minds than Woodward's might easily miss how desperately Cash was trying to get to the bottom of history and therefore explain why his white countrymen acted as they did. First white Southerners condoned slavery, then praised it as a "positive good," and later brutalized African-Americans by lynchings and race riots and through such storm-trooper organizations as the Ku Klux Klan—the analogy to the Nazi thugs is Cash's. His conception of mind as temperament is the view of a modernist intellectual who believes that the values, ideas, feelings, and irrationality of the masses, and of the master class as well (those university-bred men who boasted of helping lynch blacks), are the real stuff of history. It must never be forgotten that Cash was a writer, an intellectual, and most of all a nonacademic and one like William Faulkner, who valued imagination above all, and as such adopted an artist's approach, admittedly impressionistic and flamboyant.[10]

Having put on the full armor of modernist ideas, particularly Freud and Nietzsche, Cash added elements of an economic argument with overtones of Marx and Charles Beard, Cash's contemporary. In his exploration of the social structure of the Old South, Cash concentrates on the competitive scramble involved in settling the frontier that resulted in the triumph of a small "ruling class" of masters. But they were too close to their rugged, no-holds-barred origins to be completely comfortable or confident as aristocrats. Hence their big talk, says Cash, and their tendency to unreality were at bottom Freudian defense mechanisms created and hurled back at the North to protect their ego against Yankee slurs. But with society divided into "Little Men and Big Men," the latter ruled and were clearly and disproportionally in control of the South.

Viewed objectively, Cash announces, the Old South was a society built on class and empowered, for the most part, along class lines. And yet white Southerners, whether Delta master or Piedmont cracker, never understood any of that clearly or consciously. The white Southerner surveyed his world "with essentially naïve, direct and personal eyes." Because his "primary approach to his world was not through the idea of class" there was no corresponding class-consciousness of any importance. Anyway, because the antebellum South was never completely settled and was still a frontier in the making as late as 1861, it was oblivious to class lines in much of its day-to-day life. The thought of belonging to a class was not even in the planter's "subconscious," says Cash. Nor did the poor whites have any "genuine class feeling."[11]

In an attempt to explain this paradox (in which class ruled but few knew it) Cash coined the intriguing phrase "proto-Dorian convention" to describe the intense shared racial consciousness in whites, the profound tacit bonding between masters and the white masses. In harping on white supremacy and Negro inferiority, the common white was blinded to his "real [economic] interests" and was thus dominated by a class system. But "come what may, he would always be a white man. And before that vast and capacious distinction, all others were foreshortened, dwarfed, and all but obliterated," wrote Cash. To explain the paradox of how during secession, war, and Reconstruction the common white man could identify with his masters (and thereby lose sight of his "real interests") Cash argues that the white man at the bottom romantically identified his "ego" with something grander: the idea of the gallant South. His captain's orders at Shiloh or Gettysburg—or anywhere else during the war—became associated, in the psyche of the common man, not with "any diminution of his individuality," but with "great expansion for his ego" and the fullest "development and expression of his individuality." Had Cash never written another word after his explanation of how the white masses could find their "freedom" by surrendering their "individuality" to their white masters (who did in fact have "real interests" in secession and war) he still would have addressed one of the central questions about the South.[12]

Unfortunately, in his treatment of Reconstruction Cash repeats the prevailing myths of Yankee domination and explains the ferocity of the white South's violent response. Reconstruction was rape to the offended whites—and to Cash who proceeds to argue that the rape of the South pushed the proto-Dorian bond even deeper into the white psyche, further obscuring the white South's understanding of its situation. The white South turned inward, embraced ancient totems and taboos, and made African-Americans the object of proto-Dorian frustration and bitter anger. Thus Cash explains the racial violence, the race riots, and the bestial lynchings of the 1880s and 1890s. Once again, Cash believed, race had triumphed over class consciousness, resulting in a "suppression of class feeling that went beyond anything that even the Old South had known."[13]

Such also explains the causes and consequences of Populism's failure. Cash's understanding of the causes of agrarian unrest, resentment, and rebellion slavishly followed the prevailing scholarly view that Southern Populism was the work of misguided white farmers and was little more than a part of the national agrarian unrest and hostility toward Wall Street. Although he had missed Woodward's ground-breaking biography of Tom Watson and was therefore ignorant of the radical role Watson played in bringing black and white Populists together, Cash could certainly see that the Democrats saw in Populism the potential for white farmers to form the "bitterest class consciousness." The danger of class conflict was there, but it was trumped once again by the greater psychological power of the proto-Dorian convention. As Cash saw, and historians would one day document, the frightened, angry Democrats played the race card, conjuring up all sorts of wild mythic and racist images of "black domination" during Reconstruction and thus vanquishing their one-gallus opponents by invoking the ancient racist bond.[14]

In taking his story down through the 1930s, the decade just before his death, Cash describes the rise of the mills, mill village culture, the failure of unionization, the persistence of racism and violence, the continued role of political demagogues, and the growth of urban slums, disease, crime, and murder. His knowledge of the latter-day urban problems came directly from his observations as a journalist in Charlotte. Yet Cash also detected signs of hope. He pointed to black economic progress. He noted with obvious pleasure the rise of a new critical spirit in the South's colleges and universities and among such writers as Howard W. Odum, Lillian Smith, Julia Peterkin, and DuBose Heyward as they tried to view blacks objectively. An aspiring novelist himself, Cash was impressed with the realism of Faulkner, Wolfe, and Caldwell, although he saw traces of the region's rhetorical and regressive romanticism clinging to the work of many of his contemporaries. Still, they had replaced the racist-sentimentalists of his youth, the Rev. Thomas W. Dixon and Thomas Nelson Page. Somewhat surprisingly given Cash's detestation of nostalgia and sentimentality, his treatment of Allen Tate and the Fugitive-Agrarians is restrained and balanced.[15]

Blacks, women, Native Americans, and minorities receive scant attention in Cash's book. While few of his era had written more scathingly of slavery and lynchings, or looked as sympathetically on blacks in the modern-day South, only a few blacks receive as much as a mention in *Mind*. Moreover, in his attempt to sound the dominant Southern white voice, there are slight traces of his generation's casual tolerance for racist language and imagery.[16] Much the same is true of his treatment of women, who are portrayed abstractly and inadequately.[17] Yet Cash's understanding of the working of what has come to be called gender rules and roles is bold and impressive. Southern Indians simply fell outside Cash's scheme and intent to capture the dominant folk mind.

Mind received instant and almost universal approval from general reviewers and from scholars, North and South. Young historians of coming prominence like Woodward, Henry Nash Smith, and Clement Eaton greeted Cash's book warmly, though each had minor reservations. So great was the book's prestige during the 1940s and down through the 1960s that historians routinely borrowed Cash's key ideas, such as the myth of the Cavalier, the South as a frontier, the centrality of race and so-called chivalric violence, the irrelevance of politicians, and the lack of a critical mind. To this day, anthologies of Southern writing invariably include a selection from Cash. Moreover, quoting Cash with his vivid style remains a sure-fire way to enliven a scholarly work or to clinch an argument. In a highly successful textbook on Southern history, published originally in 1947, Francis Butler Simkins gave wide currency to many of Cash's major points, including his notions about the absence of class consciousness. Many of Cash's conceptions, notably of mind and Southern culture, find an echo in William R. Taylor's sophisticated work *Cavalier and Yankee: The Old South and American National Character* (1961). And as late as 1961 the African-American historian Earl E. Thorpe found that Cash's overall view of "the southern mind," while mainly about whites, applied equally to blacks, a contention heatedly denounced recently by Nell Irvin Painter and other black scholars.[18]

It was not until 1971, a full thirty years after *Mind* appeared, that the book received a major critical reassessment by C. Vann Woodward, who rejected virtually every major thesis advanced by Cash. Cash's aim was a noble one, Woodward acknowledged, but time and again Cash had fallen victim to his own flamboyance, exaggeration, and determinism. The South was never of one mind, Woodward argued with passion; the South's past has always been one of diversity and the possibility that events might have taken a different course. That being true, to talk of continuity, of "One South" through time, and to make the case for a single mind is to distort the South's past radically. Indirectly defending his own major works, Woodward reiterated that the South's history has been one of major changes and shifts. Cash's greatest offense, according to Woodward, is that his book's most daring and flamboyant assertions betray "a want of feeling for the seriousness of human strivings, for the tragic theme in history." To Woodward, usually a master of restrained judgment and style, Cash "sometimes reminds one of those who scribble facetious graffiti on Roman ruins."[19]

But in spite of Woodward's brilliant attempt to destroy Cash's reputation, the jury is still out. Cash continues to have his admirers and defenders. In *Place Over Time: The Continuity of Southern Distinctiveness* (1977) Carl Degler extended Cash's twin arguments about unity and continuity down through the post-1945 South. Few historians have taken Cash's arguments more seriously and put them to better use than Bertram Wyatt-Brown in his magisterial work, *Southern Honor: Ethics and Behavior in the Old South* (1982). He gives added weight and dimension to several of Cash's major arguments about honor, violence, and the psychological underpinnings of the white South's veneration of women. In the related fields of sociology and literary history, John Shelton Reed and Fred Hobson have written major works reflecting Cash's influence. After investigations of Southern attitudes, beliefs, and patterns of popular culture, Reed concluded that the South remains distinctive, or in Cash's words, "not quite a nation within a nation, but the next best thing to it." Such also are the contentions advanced by fifteen Southerners in *Why the South Will Survive* (1981). Like Reed, they chart the "persistence" of Southern "distinctiveness"—reincarnations, as it were, of Cash's twin theses of unity and continuity.[20]

Some twenty years after Woodward's critique, which itself was fiercely challenged, Bruce Clayton published a critical but generally favorable biography of Cash and defended him against several of Woodward's major charges. In that year, 1991, two major Southern universities celebrated the fiftieth anniversary of the publication of *Mind* by devoting entire conferences to debating Cash's book. In general, the participants found reasons, major and minor, to quarrel with Cash's ideas, but scholars as distinguished as Richard King, Bertram Wyatt-Brown, and others defended Cash or reasoned that his writing must be put in the context of his time.[21]

Was W. J. Cash a bona fide historian? Given the enormous influence and controversy his book has generated, the answer is a resounding yes.

Defining "The South's Number One Problem"

V. O. Key, Jr., and the Study of

Twentieth-Century Southern Politics

KARI FREDERICKSON

Practically all analyses of twentieth-century Southern politics published in the past fifty years have been significantly influenced by political scientist V. O. Key's 1949 landmark study *Southern Politics in State and Nation.* Although Key produced a prodigious amount of work throughout his relatively brief academic career, this single volume stands as his seminal work, an imposing synthesis that spawned countless studies of Southern politics and today survives virtually unchallenged as the major primer on Southern politics of the 1920s to the 1940s.

Vladimer Orlando Key, Jr., was born March 13, 1908, in Lamesa, Texas, a small town in the western part of the state. His father, a lawyer and farmer, dabbled in local politics. Key later recalled that his interest in modern politics, as well as his keen insight into the peculiarities of the Southern variety, sprang from his personal experiences in the one-party state, particularly from observations made while whiling away the hours around the courthouse square.[1] Key attended McMurray College in Abilene for two years, but eventually transferred to the University of Texas at Austin, where he received his bachelor of arts degree in 1929 and his master of arts in 1930. From there, he journeyed to the University of Chicago to pursue his doctorate in political science. The 1930s was an exciting and transformative decade in the development of the discipline, and the University of Chicago boasted several innovators in the practice of empirical social science methods, including Stuart Rice, L. L. Thurstone, and Harold Gosnell. The "Chicago School," as it came to be known, pioneered new techniques for studying political and administrative behavior, including statistics, field methods, and the study of the role of psychology in politics. Most significantly, the practitioners at the University of Chicago advanced a realistic approach to political science that emphasized power relations. While there, Key came under the tutelage of "that most influential of prewar Americanists," Charles Edward Merriam, the preeminent figure in the Chicago School of political science.[2] Political scientist William Havard has noted that although Merriam was a prolific writer with broad research interests, "[i]n many ways [he] was one of those academicians whose influence on his profession came more through his stimulation of others and his promotion of the discipline than from the seminal nature of his published work."[3] Eventually, student surpassed teacher.

After his training at the University of Chicago, Key went on to become a recognized "leader of the postwar 'behavioral revolution' in American political science,"[4] though Key may never have referred to himself as a "behavioralist." As Havard has stated, Key would "note on occasion that he was *describing political behavior.*"[5] Key received his doctorate in 1934, and his dissertation, *The Techniques of Political Graft in the United States*, was published by the University of Chicago Libraries in 1936.[6]

After a brief teaching stint at the University of California at Los Angeles, Key moved on to Washington, D.C., in 1936, the height of the New Deal, to take successive positions with the Social Science Research Council and, later, the National Resources Planning Board. In 1938, Key accepted a position in the political science department at The Johns Hopkins University, where he remained until 1949. During World War II, Key worked for the U.S. Bureau of the Budget. Key left Johns Hopkins for good in 1949 and joined the faculty at Yale University, where he became the Alfred Cowles Professor of Government and head of the political science department. But Yale could not hold Key for long, and he moved to Harvard University in 1951. At Harvard, Key served as the Jonathan Trumbull Professor of American History and Government, an endowed chair he held until his untimely death on October 4, 1963. Key held a number of important posts throughout his career. During the 1950s, he was an influential member of the Committee on Political Behavior of the Social Science Research Council, and in 1958 he was elected president of the American Political Science Association.[7]

A physically unimposing and, by some accounts, frail man, Key was a prolific scholar. He authored a number of pioneering texts and articles throughout his career, often with the assistance of his wife, Luella Gettys Key, a fellow political scientist who likewise earned a doctorate at the University of Chicago. And while his work represents a wide range of scholarly interests, generally he confined himself to the study of political parties, elections, and public opinion. Key was specifically interested in combining empirical research with political theory and in the creative use of methodology. While always adhering to rigorous scholarly standards, Key likewise understood the importance of writing for the larger American public and frequently wrote for such popular magazines and journals as the *New Republic, New York Times Magazine,* and the *Christian Science Monitor.* In 1942, he published his first major, influential book, *Politics, Parties, and Pressure Groups*, which goes beyond the traditional analysis of party histories to focus on the role of interest groups in the American party system and in the political process in general, as well as on the significance of sectionalism. Key's *A Primer of Statistics for Political Scientists*, published in 1954, emphasized the use of statistics and quantitative methods in the study of political science well before such analytical tools had become common in the discipline. In 1956, he published *American State Politics*, a study that uses aggregate election data to examine the two-party states outside the South. Key's last major work published during his lifetime was *Public Opinion and American Democracy*, which appeared in 1961. In this book, Key examined American political culture, the process of opinion formation, and the relationship between mass opinions and the workings of government. Key's final work, *The Responsible Electorate*, in which he argued for rationality in voting, was published posthumously in 1966.[8]

V. O. Key built his early professional career during years of upheaval for the nation, and, in particular, a pivotal turning point in Southern economic and political development. For decades following the Civil War, the Southern economy had existed in relative isolation, cut off from the national economic mainstream, free from threats to low local wages and labor discipline. New Deal programs initiated transformations that challenged the economic hegemony and control of the planter elites. Eager to feed from the rich trough of federal agricultural programs, planters were unwittingly complicit in the breakdown of the plantation system. Planters often refused to distribute crop reduction payments to sharecroppers and share tenants, thus effectively dislodging them from the plantation system and turning them, to borrow historian Gavin C. Wright's phrase, into "footloose wage laborers."[9] The war, in turn, created new economic opportunities for these workers no longer tied to the land. Labor shortages in agriculture during the war and into the late 1940s were acute. In addition, war also stirred a new race consciousness among Southern blacks that frightened many Southern whites.[10]

The Great Depression and the New Deal likewise inspired a small cadre of white and black reformers in the South dedicated to winning economic and political justice for the region's downtrodden. Through organizations such as the Southern Conference for Human Welfare, these reformers sought to foster an alliance of working-class whites and blacks, and they poured their energies into fighting Southern state suffrage barriers such as the poll tax. Southern institutions also came under more intense scrutiny and attack from bodies outside the region. In 1938, the Roosevelt administration released the *Report on Economic Conditions of the South*, which vividly described the South's colonial relationship to Northern industry, the devastating conditions of its agricultural economy, and the negative effects of its reactionary politics on the region's development. While virtually all Southern leaders endorsed some of the report's specific proposals, most responded angrily and defensively, denouncing it as a slur on the entire region.[11] In 1944, Swedish social economist Gunnar Myrdal published *An American Dilemma*, a searing indictment of segregation and racism.[12] Also in 1944 the Supreme Court, in its decision in *Smith v. Allwright*, declared the Texas Democratic party's white primary unconstitutional, thus toppling one of the most effective suffrage barriers erected by white Southerners and opening the door just a crack to potential black voters. Despite the best efforts of these states to keep them from the polls, blacks registered in impressive numbers. In the wake of a 1946 federal district court decision that opened the Georgia Democratic primary to black voters, approximately one hundred thousand black Georgians registered to vote.[13] Likewise South Carolina's Democratic primary was opened to black voters in 1947; subsequently blacks began enrolling in record numbers for the 1948 election. By 1950, civil rights activists could claim 73,000 registered black voters in South Carolina.[14] A wave of racial violence rolled across the nation during the war years, making national accommodation to Southern sensibilities increasingly difficult. By the time Key had finished *Southern Politics*, President Harry S Truman had publicly declared his support for civil rights, and four Deep South states had bolted the national Democratic party in favor of the States' Rights Democrats or "Dixiecrats" in the 1948 presidential election.

In the midst of this maelstrom, the Bureau of Public Administration at the University of Alabama, which had published a number of studies on the problems of public administration, decided to turn its attentions to the South. Roscoe C. Martin, one of Key's former instructors at the University of Texas and now chairman of the political science department at the University of Alabama and director of the Bureau, originally wished to confine the Bureau's study to the poll tax. But this project quickly mushroomed into a comprehensive analysis of Southern politics. The Bureau received a grant in 1946 from the Rockefeller Foundation to fund a study of Southern electoral processes, and Martin asked the thirty-eight-year-old Key, then at Johns Hopkins University, to direct the research. Key was hesitant, but Martin was relentless in pursuit of his former student. Key repeatedly demurred, citing professional obligations. Martin would not give in. Martin finally prevailed upon Key, although it took a personal letter from no less than President Truman to convince Key to sign on.[15]

The offices of the project opened September 1, 1946, on the campus of the University of Alabama at Tuscaloosa. Key compiled a thirty-two-page outline that included some 240 topics related to the study of Southern politics.[16] Key's staff of research assistants then set about assembling a massive database of election statistics, legal statutes, state constitutions, party rules, and court decisions. They also culled local newspapers and periodicals for data on the workings of Southern politics. But statistics and documents would not tell the entire story. From his childhood spent hanging around the courthouse, Key knew that to truly understand the electoral process, the "day to day practice of politics," one had to learn it from the horse's mouth. Key signed on two field investigators: Alexander Heard, a recent graduate of the University of North Carolina, and Donald S. Strong, a former political science instructor from the University of Texas. Heard conducted interviews and field work in nine states, Strong in two.[17] Key put a significant emphasis on field work, which consumed one-third of the senior staff's time and forty percent of the budget.[18]

Between November 1946 and February 1948, Heard and Strong interviewed 538 Southerners, the majority of them active or retired politicians; election officials; newspaper editors, publishers, and reporters; labor organizers; reformers; black leaders; farm bureau officers; and farmers, both large and small.[19] Only three persons approached by Heard refused to grant interviews. The interviewers criss-crossed the South, spending an average of six weeks in each state. The nature of the project at hand demanded that they remain extremely flexible. Although Heard and Strong used personal and professional contacts and prearranged interviews wherever and whenever possible, almost half of all contacts were made in person, unannounced, and the interview was held immediately. This approach worked well: because the interviewer would be in town only shortly, his request for an interview seemed rather urgent and was granted forthwith. And by avoiding advance appointments the interviewer remained flexible and able to construct his interview to suit circumstances.[20]

In his introduction to the 1984 reprint of *Southern Politics*, Heard recalled how he and Donald Strong enjoyed none of the modern accoutrements of the modern interviewer but instead had to rely upon their powers of observation and memorization. The interviewers did not work from a list of prepared questions, which is not to say they conducted their interviews off the cuff. Rather, they drew their questions from the 240 topics enumerated in Key's original research outline.[21] In preparation for their interviews, Strong and Heard read state histories and newspaper clippings, and they studied party rules and the major political races since 1920: "By showing his familiarity with local conditions, [the interviewer] tried to convince his informant that he was worthy of a man-to-man talk."[22] Eventually, the interviewers secured information on 199 of the 240 topics.[23]

Strong and Heard tried, as much as possible, to fashion their interviews into folksy conversations. To this end, the interviewers also took no notes. Additionally, interviews were granted on the condition that the person interviewed not be quoted.[24] Heard noted that "[i]n those years of a racially sensitive, one-party South, [Key] felt that informal talk might breed trust, and trust might breed candor, and candor might lead to subjects seldom discussed—and never discussed for attribution."[25] Instilling confidence in the person interviewed was of the utmost importance, and the interviewers encountered difficulties even in towns where they had connections. Despite his personal contacts in one Black Belt town, Heard recalled that he "had to assure more than one person that he was not a 'communist' and had not come as an agent of meddling Yankees."[26] In approaching their subjects, the interviewers emphasized their Southern backgrounds and "the indigenous nature of the study": Southerners studying Southern politics. They often adopted local colloquialisms and dress habits. Heard found that "some 'liberal' groups" seemed to be reassured by the fact that he had graduated from the University of North Carolina.[27] Heard was often surprised at the candor of some of the individuals he interviewed. One campaign manager of "perhaps the South's most notorious demagogue" revealed his campaign strategy and proudly displayed his campaign material. He even invited Heard back for a second interview.[28]

Southern Politics is V. O. Key's mid-century assessment of the state of Southern politics as it had existed since the turn of the century. Presented with a large canvass, Key deftly complemented his broad analytical strokes with numerous fine, distinguishing touches—superbly integrated—that have made it difficult for historians to overturn his synthesis. Indeed, it is a tribute to Key that the analysis of what he referred to as "the south's number one problem" today remains relatively unchallenged, although historians have begun to take potshots at the periphery. The work also has served as a model for numerous studies on the development of Southern politics since World War II.

Key identified and studied in great detail those characteristics and institutions unique to the South that contributed to the stunted regional political development: the one-party system, intraparty factionalism, malapportioned state legislatures, and a tiny electorate, as well as the poll tax and other barriers to suffrage. According to Key, these institutions were designed (but ultimately failed) to handle the region's problems, the most significant being "the position of the Negro." He argued that the emergence of a two-party system was crucial for mature political debate and for the integration of African-Americans into the system.

The "hard-core of the political South" was the Black Belt, those counties that contained the region's rich agricultural lands and large-scale plantation agriculture, the heart of the antebellum plantation South and home to the opponents of Populism. Moreover, in these Black Belt counties, blacks outnumbered whites. Not surprisingly, maintenance of white supremacy was the area's primary concern. Following the defeat of the Populists, the Black Belt factions within state governments succeeded in disfranchising black voters, suffocating political dissent from poor whites, and enforcing the region's attachment to the Democratic party. Two-party competition was anathema to Black Belt whites; it would have meant an appeal to black voters and possibly, as some feared, black rule. The ability of Black Belt whites to enforce regional conformity on the race issue in national politics became the South's best protection against federal interference in racial matters. Key evinced a begrudging admiration for the political skills of Black Belt whites, for although they were a minority, "their unity and their political skill have enabled them to run a shoestring into decisive power at critical junctures in Southern political history."[29]

The hegemony of Black Belt whites was felt most keenly in national politics, where Black Belt whites formed the core of Democratic party strength. Under the one-party system, Southern senators and representatives were continually reelected, ensuring their seniority in Congress and hence their ability to prevent federal interference in racial issues. Race remained the basis for Southern unity in national politics. Southern solidarity was threatened when other questions began to carry more weight than the race question, and according to Key, "elements of diversity within the changing South . . . are driving wedges into its unity."[30] In an analysis of voting roll calls, however, Key found that Southern solidarity was most consistent on racial issues and that in the House, for example, other factors, such as urbanization, prompted variations in voting.[31]

Key demonstrated how "consistent and unquestioning attachment . . . to the Democratic party nationally has meant that the politics within Southern states . . . has had to be conducted without benefit of political parties." Instead, "the political battle has to be carried on by transient and amorphous political factions within the Democratic party, which are ill-designed to meet the necessities of self-government."[32] Although the one-party system was, according to Key, the region's major handicap, it did not operate the same way in any two states. Key is at his analytical best in his descriptions of the political systems of each of the eleven states of the Confederacy. By illustrating the diversity of political organizations and varying degrees of political competition, he helped dispel basic misconceptions about Southern politics that tended to treat state politics the same. "Despite common inheritances of war and reconstruction," Key wrote, "each Southern state possesses characteristics that combine into a unique personality."[33]

Key created a spectrum of Southern political activity. On one end stood Virginia, a "political museum piece" run by the Byrd political machine that faced no organized political opposition, and Tennessee, with its rough bifactionalism held together by opposition to Boss Crump; at the opposite end of the pole stood hyper-factionalized Florida. In Georgia and Louisiana, relatively cohesive political blocs coalesced in support of, or in opposition to, the states' most enduring personalities, Eugene Talmadge and Huey Long. The remaining states sported a more fractious politics. Race as a political issue was acutely prevalent in South Carolina, where political power rested almost entirely with the legislature. Mississippi, whose preoccupation with race was equal to that of South Carolina, boasted a moderately factionalized politics organized loosely around competing hill and Delta regions, although decreasingly so. Arkansas represented "pure one-party politics" and politics "devoid of issues other than that of the moment."[34] Key noted a growing division in Texas among economic liberals and conservatives. Alabama evinced a sectionalism that belied a nascent liberal-conservative cleavage—the "branch heads" versus the "Big Mules"—but generally voters organized themselves around candidates and no enduring factions persisted. The "best Southern state," in Key's political index, was North Carolina, whose political leadership was virtually devoid of "the mountebank and clown."[35] Key attributed the state's political health in part to a strong, albeit small, Republican party, whose presence has determined that the dominant faction of the Democratic party possess a cohesiveness and sense of responsibility.[36]

Southern Republicans did, of course, exist during the period in which Key wrote. However, they offered little challenge to the supremacy of the Democrats. Republican enclaves in the South, Key wrote, "scarcely [deserve] the name of a party. [The party] wavers somewhat between an esoteric cult on the order of a lodge and a conspiracy for plunder."[37] Only in North Carolina, Virginia, and Tennessee did the Republicans resemble a real political party. The South had its share of presidential Republicans. Most prevalent in Texas, Arkansas, and Florida, these voters were locally Democrats but voted Republican in national elections. Black Republicans had generally been deserting the party of Lincoln for the party of Roosevelt. Mountain Republicans, present from southwestern Virginia to northern Alabama and the Arkansas Ozarks, "controlled local governments, elected a few state legislators and an occasional Congressman, and sometimes even made the Democrats fearful lest they lose control of their states."[38] Most prevalent in Virginia, western North Carolina, and eastern Tennessee, Key evinced little hope that these mountain Republicans would become more influential, for their radicalism contrasted sharply with regional and national Republican party leadership. Key did not conceal his contempt for Southern Republican leadership, which "might be called palace or bureaucratic politicians, since their chief preoccupation is not with voters but with maneuvers to gain and keep control of the state party machinery."[39] Key noted that the old-time spoils politician no longer existed (for the simple fact that there were no spoils) and that the Southern Republican chieftains were "more typically a business leadership." "These party officials often have only the foggiest notion where the Republican voters in the state live and who they are. Most of them are overwhelmed by the futility of it all, but they keep the faith in the quiet spirit of dedication not unlike that of the Britisher who, although living in the jungle surrounded by heathen, dresses for dinner."[40]

Disfranchisement was, of course, crucial to the decimation of the Southern electorate and the maintenance of the one-party system, although Key stated that it could plausibly be argued that "formal disfranchisement measures did not lie at the bottom of the decimation of the Southern electorate. They, rather, recorded a *fait accompli* brought about . . . by more fundamental political processes."[41] Using Texas as an example, he argued that political opposition had already been removed by the time the poll tax was effected. "Before their formal disfranchisement Negroes had, in most states, ceased to be of much political significance and the whites had won control of state governments," he wrote.[42] Regarding small Southern electorates, Key stated that "suffrage limitations alone do not account for Southern disinterest in voting" and that "[i]n some states at least, and perhaps in all, the formal limitation of the suffrage was the roof rather than the foundation of a system of political power."[43] Consequently, the importance of suffrage barriers had been exaggerated—"more impressive in theory than in practice"—and black disfranchisement had been brought about by informal rather than legal means.[44] Contrary to popular opinion, then, the poll tax was not the "chief villain" conspiring to keep black voters off the registration books: "It is simply one, and not the most important one, of a battery of disfranchising devices."[45] Furthermore, Key contended, whites more so than blacks had been kept from voting by the poll tax. "Negro disfranchisement has been accomplished by extralegal restraints and by the white primary," Key held.[46]

The limitations of and the damage inflicted by the one-party system were significant. The South remained politically isolated from the other national parties, and its politics was issueless. The absence of parties and the proliferation of factions thwarted political expression of the economically disadvantaged—the "have-nots"—and prevented the alliance of working-class and poor whites and blacks. "[O]ver the long run," Key wrote, "the have-nots lose in a disorganized politics."[47]

Key closed his book on a relatively optimistic note. In addition to chronicling and examining the history and status of Southern politics as it stood in the late 1940s, he also predicted future developments that would herald a more democratic South, including increased urbanization, black outmigration, a strong labor movement, and the creation of a viable Republican party. Key argued there were growing doubts about the future course of Southern politics. The New Deal had sharpened class lines in the region's politics, the traditional system of plantation agriculture had been dealt a severe blow by the Great Depression, swelling the stream of black migrants north, and the war had greatly stimulated and diversified the Southern economy. Even more important, in the short run, was the emergence of civil rights as an issue in national politics, the identification of the Democratic party with that issue, and the Dixiecrat revolt of 1948. While Key stressed the importance of the presence of blacks in the South on the development of Southern politics, he argued that certain socioeconomic trends would "probably . . . further free [the region] from the effects of the Negro in its politics." Key predicted the formation of a coalition between Southern blacks and white Southern liberals that would lead to the gradual assimilation of blacks into political life and the eventual triumph over Southern conservatism. According to Key and other contemporary chroniclers, the forces of racial reaction were on the defensive. The Dixiecrat movement had failed to raise the race issue in a "compelling manner" and this failure signified the end of racism as a potent regional political weapon.[48]

Following the publication of *Southern Politics*, Key offered semiregular political commentary on Southern politics and national political realignment in national periodicals. In articles in the *Virginia Quarterly Review*, Key guessed that despite differences among Southern legislators, most Southern voters supported the Democratic party's New Deal and Fair Deal policies, and he predicted that "with increasing industrialization and with growing popular participation in politics, those Southern elements [the working classes and blacks] most predisposed to support the new Democratic amalgam will increase in number," although the Republican party could expect gains in Florida and Texas.[49] To persuade Southerners to vote for a Republican candidate, according to Key, "would require a rabble-rousing campaign of race hatred."[50] He believed that any forward movement on the race issue "will have to be undertaken . . . by Southern state and local governments, under some degree of Federal prodding."[51] He encouraged the national Democratic party to give assistance to those white Southerners "in and out of political life" working for the betterment of blacks.

Following General Dwight Eisenhower's victories in the presidential campaigns of 1952 and 1956, Key noted in articles in the *New Republic* and the *Virginia Quarterly Review* that while "no firmly based new Republican party has been established in any Southern state," internal cleavages within the Democratic party in the South would continue to deepen, sectionalism would decline, and the "kindred interests in South and North" would become more closely aligned.[52] Key was impressed not so much with the General's vote in the former Dixiecrat states as with the ability of state Democratic leaders "to hold their states even against the charisma of the General."[53] Those who stayed with the Democratic party, he noted, were New Deal Democrats, which indicated that the Democratic party in the South was assuming more of the character of the party nationally.[54] Key continued to have faith that a burgeoning middle class in Southern cities and a strong and expanding white working class boded well for the creation of a two-party South. He cautiously observed that "a two-party South is already upon us,"[55] although further political change would be "spasmodic" and would probably occur primarily in the rim Southern states.[56]

Despite these developments toward a two-party system organized along economic lines, Key kept a wary eye on the race issue. Respectful of the power of this issue to subsume any other, Key rightfully noted that "the seer who proposes to sketch out the probable evolution of this issue in detail must possess in large measure either courage or foolhardiness."[57] Unfortunately, Key would not live to witness the fruition of the civil rights movement and the realization of the two-party South, a political transformation brought about, not by the economic alliances he predicted, but by the racial politics he feared.

C. Vann Woodward,
Southern Historian

JOHN HERBERT ROPER

In the South in any era, there have always been those among our historians who commit themselves to a lifetime of research and writing, of detached artistry, of nonpartisan service to the muse of Clio. David Morris Potter (1910–1971) speaks best for himself and for this kind of service, asking rhetorically, *what has a historian to do with hope?* Also in the South in any era, there have always been those among our historians who commit themselves to a lifetime of applied research, of a history written on behalf of specific reforms, that is, a *usable past.* John Hope Franklin (born 1915) speaks best for himself and for this kind of service, insisting that research be on behalf of public policy; Franklin speaks so in many places, but especially in a memorable address given at the University of Chicago during a time of profound social turmoil in that city.[1]

Yet one figure, C. Vann Woodward (1908–1999), has succeeded in playing both the role of the activist and the role of the scholar from the days of the Second New Deal to the very end of the twentieth century. In so doing he was significant as well because his youthful scholarship—his first academic jobs, his first publications—took place during the birth of the Southern Historical Association in 1935 so that his professional birth, development, and maturity came right along with the birth, development, and maturity of Clio's major professional organization in the South.[2] He was then both a son and a father of Southern history, and the life he lived as well as the history he wrote and taught are tasks for the past master of irony. None has ever mastered that art form more thoroughly or lived it out more richly than Woodward. Nor did he suffer very much abuse in that long career—and never anything approaching neglect.

I

His very name *Comer Vann Woodward* was a harbinger of what was to come. Likely, the portentous naming on his birth date of November 13, 1908, was deliberate on the parts of his parents Hugh Allison (Jack) and Bess Vann Woodward. The surname Woodward describes the warder of the king's woods and suggests an aristocratic status based on responsibility for valuable land with the privilege of considerable personal landholdings as part of the arrangement. The young Woodward collected some evidence that ancestors—albeit wrong sheet side—were so entitled, with a claim on the estate of no less than Sir Walter Scott, the romantic novelist himself. This Old World claim was never pursued by the Arkansas Woodwards, and the lack of ardor on Jack's part in this claim angered the youth.

All the same, the extended family laid undisputed claim to rich cotton fields on the Arkansas side of the Mississippi River Valley thanks to his mother Bess, whose people had left good land in Tennessee in favor of even better land west of the "Father of Waters." The *Vann* in Woodward's name came from the maternal side; Bess Vann's family had actually founded the town of Vanndale in which he was born and spent the first few years of his life. *Comer* in the baby's name honored Jack Woodward's brother. Comer and Jack Woodward were both leaders in Southern Methodist circles, and each man was an important administrator in church-affiliated colleges sponsored by their denomination. However, Comer Woodward was a step ahead of his brother Jack in these things, and so the boy Woodward "sainted" his uncle in best Protestant fashion. Even when C. Vann Woodward became a mature academic in his own right, and even after he had abandoned the Methodist church so dear to his uncle, he retained the *C.* in his signature to recognize his hero Uncle Comer who led educational reform—and the mildest and most moderate of civil rights reform—in Arkansas and Georgia.

His youth, like his entire career, was marked by the kind of contradictions that as an English professor at Georgia Tech he called *situational ironies.* So too were his youth and his entire career marked by a generous amount of chance. It was fortuitous more than fortunate, since both good and bad luck arrived at crucial moments, or turning points if you will, in his development. Jack Woodward's appointment as dean at a Georgia junior college enabled Vann Woodward to reconsider student life at Henderson Brown College in Arkadelphia in 1928 at the midpoint of his studies—and also in the middle of a campus crisis largely created by young Vann Woodward and his student allies who were protesting the policies of the college president. At the same time, Uncle Comer was secure enough in his own new role as dean of students at the suddenly rich Emory University at its new campus in Atlanta to urge that his nephew Vann Woodward study there. Still more chance occurrences came: he studied under philosopher LeRoy Loemker, an activist scholar very new to Emory; and he studied alongside dissident Atlanta natives Glenn Weddington Rainey and Ernest Hartsock, the latter a major force in the Georgia phase of the Southern Literary Renaissance that Vann Woodward would study—and defend—in future years.

In 1930 Emory University awarded him the degree Ph.B. in philosophy, but he planned a career as a novelist, or at least a literature critic and professor of English, and he "hung out" with Atlanta's Renaissance figures, not only Hartsock but also multitalented activist J. Saunders Redding, in "his first equal black friendship." He taught English at Georgia Tech, and in order to earn his bona fides as a professor was packed off in 1931 by family friend and benefactor the great liberal Will W. Alexander to earn a graduate degree at Columbia University. These studies were all paid for by a major fellowship provided by the Social Science Research Council. In New York, he roomed with an Arkansas friend and academic Charles Pipkin (later prominent at Louisiana State University), who showed him much of The City and what he could learn of life there. Among other things the graduate student appeared as the one white performer in a Harlem show featuring a dance revue even though the onetime football center was not then or at any time noted for fancy footwork. What he did not do in New York was study very seriously at Morningside Heights, and he passed through a "miscarriage of majors" in sociology, anthropology, and political science before finally writing a forgettable thesis in 1932 concerning the career of Alabama demagogue J. Thomas Heflin.

Returning to Atlanta and to Georgia Tech, he continued to teach English and to review books for local newspapers, and occasionally he wrote travel pieces describing some of his 1930s chance trips abroad. He went to Soviet Russia, where he rode the freight trains with devout Communist peasants and with counterrevolutionary Cossacks, and these experiences made him a youthful sympathizer with and sometime "fellow traveler" alongside American Communists. He went to Hitler's Germany, where he stayed with a Jewish family of professionals who assured him that the Nazis had no political prospects, but he saw enough to hate the brownshirts at once. And in Paris he lived on the left bank of the Seine, bringing home a much-prized stiletto and the Black Sun edition of James Joyce's *Ulysses*, both things illegal to import into the United States of that day. He liked Atlanta and the literary scene there showcased in *Bozart*, the witty journal of his friend Hartsock, and he might well have stayed in the Georgia capital forever. However, in 1932 he fell into leadership of a civil rights campaign on behalf of the black Communist Angelo Herndon in circumstances less situationally ironic than comic. In the course of that controversy, he was quoted in the Communist party political organ *The Daily Worker* with harsh criticism of his benefactor and family friend Will Alexander. Soon angered by the New York Communist party tactics and frustrated by the bizarre trial, he eventually left this campaign and made things up with Alexander.

Fired from the English job at Georgia Tech partly because of his political activities but mostly because of Depression-era finances, in 1934 he served for a time as a sociological investigator for the Works Progress Administration in the countryside near Macon, Georgia. There he encountered a kind of scratch-ankle and dirt-poor desperation that his aristocratic family had shielded him from, and he was all but shocked into activism on behalf of major economic reforms. Relying again on Will Alexander, Uncle Comer, and Jack Woodward's onetime Oxford, Georgia, neighbor Howard W. Odum for a major scholarship, a Rockefeller Fellowship, he went off to study at the University of North Carolina between 1934 and 1937.

Odum was large on the Chapel Hill scene and he tried hard to monitor the graduate student's activities, which likely inspired still more dissidence and rebellion, especially on behalf of textile workers striking in the series of Piedmont labor disputes collectively known as the Burlington Strike. At the moment when Vann Woodward was most rebellious about Odum's warnings to avoid social controversy and most rebellious against the traditionalist history faculty's approach to things, he met the newly arrived Howard Kennedy Beale, an economic determinist and neo-abolitionist who safely guided him through a dissertation that, essentially unrevised, became *Tom Watson: Agrarian Rebel* (1938), one of the most significant biographies in regional studies. Nor did fortuity end there, for the very traditionalists at Chapel Hill against whom he rebelled arranged a teaching job at the University of Florida, where he met his dissident friends Manning Dauer and William Carleton, whose activities on behalf of civil rights would have appalled the very traditionalists who arranged for the young historian to go to Gainesville. Many more chance developments came, but perhaps the point is established: whether it was hiring or firing, moving up or moving out, the career of C. Vann Woodward constantly involved Fortuna and her wheel.

For all the role that luck played on his stage, he very consciously made commitments that actually drove his career, and he made them early. Throughout his youth, and throughout his long years, he spoke of a search, a commitment to The Subject, that is, the South; and often he changed his mind what discipline was best for the pursuit of the subject, as he changed his mind what methodologies were best even when he settled on the discipline of history. Eventually he decided that The Subject was not exactly the South, but the *search for* the South, and he decided that Truth itself is elusive, an abstraction that perhaps does not exist at all, but that the *efforts* to find the facts on the trail of that elusive Truth were concrete and particular and real—and thus themselves truthful. If done honestly, the quest itself is ennobling, especially if you deal fully and fairly with those who disagree with you. Indeed, as his literary friends Robert Penn Warren and Cleanth Brooks put into words the insight he already had, you must respect your critics, for they are actually the wind that supports your kite—and without the critics and the controversies, your kite crashes to the ground. And this fellow had no intentions whatever of letting his kite drop from the skies.

II

The Woodward scholarly career after this strange start divided itself into two parts, and the two parts in combination give the study of Southern history five major new directions. In the first part, between 1935 and 1951, Woodward was a tireless research scholar, ferreting out primary documents at the Southern Historical Collection, at the National Archives, at the manuscript division of the Library of Congress, and also in the attics and in the memories of people not yet accustomed to turning over "family papers" to such repositories. His major publications of this period, including two official studies for the United States Navy and one very popular military history, are all research monographs on the German model and grounded in such meticulous research that even those who disagree with his conclusions confidently rely on them for their facts. These studies are the biography *Tom Watson* (1938); the restricted-distribution studies *Bougainville Landing and the Battle of Empress Augusta Bay* (1947) and *Kolombangara and Vella Lavella* (1947); *The Battle for Leyte Gulf* (1947); *Reunion and Reaction: The Compromise of 1877 and the End of Reconstruction* (1951; rev. 1956); and *Origins of the New South, 1877–1913* (1951; rev. 1971). The latter book, once called "The Old Testament" by erstwhile and somewhat resentful graduate students, capped off this first part of his career.[3]

After 1951 and continuing to the very end of the century, he sustained an even longer career as an essay stylist much influenced by Michel de Montaigne. In his own era at least in certain professional and lay circles his essays became almost as influential as those of his model the Frenchman. In this period he emphasized the scholar's duties to society and to the subject, trying hard to find an honorable position between the poles established by his friends and coworkers David Morris Potter and John Hope Franklin. Most prominent of these publications are the seminal essays collected as *The Burden of Southern History* (1960; rev. eds. 1968, 1993), *The Strange Career of Jim Crow* (1955; rev. eds. 1957, 1966, 1974), *American Counterpoint* (1971; rev. 1983), *The Old World's New World* (1992), and his memoirs *Thinking Back* (1986). Some archival research continued, most notably in his directorship of two very large projects, *Responses of Presidents to Charges of Misconduct* (1974) and the Pulitzer-winning *Mary Chesnut's Civil War* (1981);[4] but in these projects he was less the research "mole" and more the field general guiding a veritable army of "moles." Of course it is during this second period that he gained most notice because of his wildly successful *Strange Career of Jim Crow* and because of his superb graduate students trained at The Johns Hopkins University between 1947 and 1960 and at Yale University between 1961 and 1979. These students in their own time have become most prominent scholars, oftentimes themselves serving as the friendliest of critics—and thus also part of the wind for his kite. The full list of his students in the endnotes includes three winners of the Pulitzer Prize, presidents of the three major national historical associations, university presidents and deans, a director of the National Endowment for the Humanities—and generally damned good historians.[5]

Whether actively searching the primary sources or writing essays based on reflection or directing graduate students or sitting on review boards for university presses and for funds-granting foundations or otherwise advising other scholars, Woodward has emphasized five broad themes about the South:

1. The period between 1877 (the end of Reconstruction) and 1890 (the stirrings of agrarian radical protest, especially in the Populist party) deserves study in its own right and not as a mere interregnum. He describes the 1880s as a time of significant developments in economics, in politics, and above all in race relations; and he demonstrates the year 1889 as the critical "turn year" when more "fluid" race relations began to disappear, to be replaced by the violent Negrophobia of the 1890s and the first years of the twentieth century.

2. Southern dissidents in all eras, but especially in the postbellum decades, have been not only fascinating but oftentimes profoundly influential, establishing in their work strong regional traditions of dissent as noteworthy, if not quite as pervasive, as the more obvious and more often studied traditions of conservatism.

3. Discontinuity has been as prevalent a theme as continuity in Southern institutions, ideas, practices, and personalities. Woodward finds the discontinuity to be especially important in the South that emerged after the Civil War; in contrast with the Old South, he describes a New South more bourgeois, more self-consciously urban, weaker economically and politically on the national stages, and marked by tragic consciousness of defeat in war and guilt over slavery.

4. Distinctive Southern traits grounded in concrete and particular experiences having to do with the institution of slavery and the loss of the Civil War create a region where, to paraphrase Arnold H. Toynbee, *history has happened.*[6] This time-worn identity is in stark contrast with the rest of the United States where prosperity and military successes create an identity of innocence and invincibility in the timeless claim that *history happens in other places.*

5. The origins of *de jure* racial segregation, or Jim Crow, are judged by Woodward to be relatively recent, with practices inconsistently applied and with shallow roots. The "strange career" of these Jim Crow laws is in some

ways antithetical to much longer-lived and much more powerful integrationist traditions among Southern liberals and radicals, and even among conservatives.

Each theme has attracted its own adherents and its own detractors; and each is, in the words of educational critic Mortimer J. Adler, "an impertinent first question" that sets scholars down a new path of inquiry.[7] Each of the five themes in its turn merits some discussion.

III

When Woodward came to Chapel Hill in 1934 and when he attended his first professional meetings, few historians were spending much time or energy on the period between Reconstruction and the rise of the Populists. The romanticizers and other overly zealous apologists whom he detested were focused on other eras, and they were content with celebrating the self-proclaimed Redeemers who used strong-arm tactics and bribery and other fraud to throw out the Republican officeholders—and most of their African-American supporters and co-workers—between 1875 and 1877. Such romanticizers then skipped the next years and focused themselves on the period 1896–1898 as a moment when reasonable men, sometimes the same men, more often men with blood ties to the Redeemers, withstood challenges from various coalitions of African-Americans and poor white farmers. Such coalitions were called by different names, and the biracial composition varied by state: Readjusters in Virginia, Fusionists in North Carolina, elsewhere Alliance men and Populists. Whatever their labels, the romanticizers made quite a celebration of the defeat of the challengers to the Redeemer, or Bourbon, Democrats. Strangely, the romanticizers wrote very little specifically about the actual rule of the Redeemers or Bourbons in their unchallenged sway during the 1880s, except to say that it was traditional, and therefore good.

There were of course some reformists in the South of the 1930s, and Woodward gravitated to them at once, whether he found them in New York, Atlanta, Chapel Hill, or Gainesville. These reformists generally agreed with the romanticizers' assessment that little happened in the 1880s; but they said of the period that it was traditional, and therefore bad. Both the romanticizers of figures such as Wade Hampton, Alfred Colquitt, Joseph Brown, and Lucius Quintus Cincinnatus Lamar and their detractors agreed that nothing really happened in the 1880s. Whether celebrating some kind of "masterly inactivity" or complaining about "do-nothingism," neither group devoted real study to the historian's era, and the books about the 1880s available to Woodward in the 1930s—"left, right, and center," as he put it once—were remarkably underresearched and over-opinionated.

Woodward plunged into such records at once in looking at the career of Tom Watson as he wrote his dissertation. During a brief period at the University of Virginia and again while on leave from an appointment at Scripps College, he was able to work intensively in the manuscripts at the Library of Congress and at the National Archives, where he placed special emphasis on the papers of William Chandler, a prominent Northern businessman and investor in the New South and no less a prominent political player behind the scenes in national politics. The result of all of this was an insistence that the 1880s were a period marked by experimentation in society and economics, with "forgotten alternatives" in race relations and a great deal of grass-roots organizing, often biracial and sometimes interracial, among farmers and others all but overwhelmed by the national transition from a farming to an industrial political economy. Although he never called the 1880s a "golden age"—as some of his own overly enthusiastic supporters and critics have claimed—he did agree with the fine phrase of his good friend and colleague George Brown Tindall, who spoke of "fluidity" in race relations.[8] Woodward extended the concept of fluidity and experimentation to all things in New South society in the 1880s, as he described a people struggling to adjust to new economic and new political worlds. This redating of the important era, or "turn time," was in many ways the most significant thing that Woodward did for professional historians, though of course it seems a small thing to the lay person.

In subsequent years, critics have looked more and more closely at each state —and at each region of each state—for the period of the 1880s, and Woodward's generalizations in *Origins of the New South* have been challenged at every level. In addition to the disagreement from the many specialized studies, Woodward's "Old Testament" has been largely discarded by competing new texts, especially *The Promise of the New South* by Edward L. Ayers.[9] It appears that virtually nothing that he said about why the era is so important will survive his critics, but it also remains the case that even his sharpest critics agree that the era *is* vitally important.

IV

As a youthful dissident himself, Woodward went out and found rebels in all the regions of the 1920s and 1930s South; and as a scholar, he has found and brought to the attention of the profession dissidents who lived and worked during virtually every era of Southern history. In the words of his admiring critic Joel Williamson, Woodward has always "played with wind and fire" in his own dissent from the conservatism generally considered the norm in his native southern Arkansas, in the Georgia Piedmont where he matured, and in the North Carolina Piedmont where he studied. Williamson's point should not be lost in the praise for the historian's courage: he, like M. E. Bradford,

John Shelton Reed, and Eugene D. Genovese, has always criticized Woodward for undervaluing the power and influence of Southern conservatism. It is courageous to battle wind and fire, but it is also futile for they are natural elements that cannot be resisted.[10]

To a large extent, Woodward's critics are correct on this score, and indeed Woodward himself has noted the rather convoluted irony that Southern conservatism was itself a kind of dissidence in eras of national consensus liberalism such as the 1950s. Thus, this regional conservatism on occasion blends with other distinctive Southern cultural traits to make the entire South a "counterpoint" to the main theme of American assumptions of progress, prosperity, invincibility, and self-conscious innocence.[11] Yet he more typically emphasizes the rebel who cries for change—young Thomas Jefferson, young Tom Watson, young Louis Harvie Blair, the Rev. Martin Luther King, Jr., George Washington Cable, Paul Eliot Green ("playwright of the New South"), novelists Erskine Caldwell and Lillian Smith, University of North Carolina president Frank Porter Graham, even to some extent Mary Boykin Chesnut, who in the least likely circumstances as confidante to the Confederate First Lady Varina Davis protests the patriarchy of slavery.

In some cases, solid scholarship has come to question the sincerity of the dissent in some of Woodward's dissenters, whether Tom Watson, Thomas Jefferson, or Mary Boykin Chesnut. That is the verdict pounded home in the studies by Charles Crowe, Barton C. Shaw, and Carl N. Degler.[12] In other cases, scholars accept the Woodward assessment of a rebel's sincerity and note simply that the rebellion fails utterly. Of course, by the end of the twentieth century, the entire national culture had grown so conservative that Woodward's Southern dissidents are in his own words "doubly alienated."

What remains after all the critical shelling on this point is tragic and yet in some ways the most ennobling of all the things in Woodward's life and career. His dissidents appear now lonely and virtually preordained to defeat and ridicule, yet they speak so poignantly that the thinking Southerner cannot dismiss them, even if critics are finally right to say that the dissidents are in fact only a projection in which a brave historian wills himself to see his own courage in others.

V

Woodward started one discussion that exercises professional historians and somewhat frustrates the intelligent lay persons interested in Southern history. This discussion revolves around his insistence on discontinuity, with the "Second American Revolution" of the Civil War effecting a major break in Southern history by dividing it into an Old South (colonial era to outbreak of the Civil War) and a New South. He gained the insight, and the term, from

Charles Austin Beard and Mary Ritter Beard in their major textbook.[13] The Beards were speaking mainly of economic change for the entire nation, and Woodward, especially in *Origins of the New South,* accepts their economic model. However, he takes their concept of economic discontinuity and extends it broadly into questions about the nature of the people in charge, into cultural identity, and even into something that might be called *regional character.*

It is worth remembering the situation that Woodward found when he began serious studies at Chapel Hill. The many reformists in that community and the larger number of traditionalists were in agreement on one thing, viz., the South had not changed much. The disturbing implication was well put by Woodward's fellow Georgian David Potter, who said that one might "denature" himself by trying to change the South. Many of the reformists were more than willing so to denature themselves if the nature of the South was itself evil. After all, the distinguished pioneer historian Ulrich Bonnell Phillips had celebrated continuing and unbroken racism as "the central theme" distinguishing Southern identity from American identity.[14]

Yet in looking around himself at the Chapel Hillians playwright Paul Green, president Frank Graham, and editor William Terry Couch, Woodward saw people who were all but saturated in Southernism and yet they were not racist and were fighting hard for economic and social justice in the Carolina Piedmont. So too were Georgia and Arkansas friends for their own regions. His dissertation director Howard Beale assured him that it was the South, and North Carolina in particular, that was the most promising site of fundamental change in the United States in the period 1936–1940. As for ideological differences between the self-consciously "Yankee immigrant" Beale and the homegrown easterner Doc Graham, Woodward has said, "Beale was not left of Graham; Graham was *south* of Beale," that is, only the manners were different, not the vision and not the substance of their reformism.

Simmering in such a stew, Woodward declared that the South had a history, that some things had a starting point and also an ending point, that "The South" was not an unbroken homogeneous thing stretching from Chesapeake Bay to the Gulf of Mexico and from the Carolina rice fields to the Texas oil fields; nor was The South of William Byrd III really the same as The South of Harry Flood Byrd, although it was certainly the contention of the latter that his "Virginia museum of politics" was vouchsafed by a virtual laying-on of hands in apostolic succession from seventeenth-century figures. Instead, Woodward emphasized variety and complexity, with challenges and changes occurring often. Not all of the changes were an improvement by any means, but if change had come before, it could certainly come again. There was thus without doubt an ideological impulse in his efforts to show a South that changed over time.

As noted, he was talking about much more than were the Beards, and their economic model has shown itself to be a faltering engine. Nevertheless, the Beardian model of economic discontinuity remains the drive wheel for Woodward's concept of cultural and political discontinuity. While he has not written extensively about the antebellum South, he has encouraged the view of Eugene Genovese that Old South leadership was precapitalist, even anticapitalist, more affined to tradition than to innovation, unsure how to use money and markets, and dedicated to a political economy based on land and slaves, with a heavily paternalistic structure of extended families and concentrated local control of communities.[15]

This is the society that Woodward saw collapsing in the Civil War when, as Karl Marx had it, a tide of managerial bourgeoisie who valued impersonal and contractual relationships and innovation with risk-rewards in international markets took hold of the northeastern urban centers of commerce and manufacturing and then overwhelmed the landed elite on the battlefield. Following that line, Woodward says that Southern leaders bowed, made their peace with the victors, and went to the business of making money in a New South. Wade Hampton left his plantations and moved to Columbia to manage railroads and textile factories and L. Q. C. Lamar left his plantations to move to Jackson and Oxford to manage railroads and banks. Sometimes utterly new men, like James Buchanan "Buck" Duke in Durham or Henry W. Grady in Atlanta, came onto the urban scene; and sometimes Northerners controlled things from afar in a "colonial" relationship, as seen in the investment figures and entrepreneurs (and paternalist benefactors) Cornelius Vanderbilt, William Chandler, and Collis Potter Huntington. Woodward did not especially *like* either Old South or New South, since each was marked by class oppression (some of which his family had been party to, however benevolently) and racism (which he saw firsthand as a bug-eyed boy watching Ku Klux Klan members in full battle dress march into his family church to make an offering eagerly accepted by the presiding minister). Always, however, there were the dissidents whom he thought he saw, and sometimes he saw them changing things. With the powerful weapons of irony, he ruthlessly "stripped away the delusions" of apologists for class oppression and racism and poverty; and with something of the earnestness and fervor of the evangelical at a protracted camp meeting, he celebrated the lonely fighters who tried to bring change.

What has happened in the last half of the twentieth century is that scholars have been much inspired by Woodward, especially by *Origins,* to test the hypothesis of discontinuity. Under such extensive testing, the hypothesis is not holding up well, especially in Virginia, South Carolina, and regions of Alabama. Indeed, someone has challenged discontinuity in every Southern state.

Particularly upsetting to him has been the fact that radicals and liberals have attacked his idea. Leftists who have the same desire for change and who harbor the same ideological intentionalities as did the young Woodward are saying that the South is not much changed by the Civil War. The mainstream liberal Carl Degler delivered a Fleming Lecture, recently reprinted, to say much the same thing. Woodward expected that a relatively conservative scholar, such as James Tice Moore studying Virginia in Virginia, would find continuity, but he was nonplussed when people well left of Moore came to say the same kind of things.[16]

The verdict rendered memorably by Sheldon Hackney in 1972, that the pyramid of *Origins* still stands, is simply no longer the case at the beginning of this century. Too long and too subtle to be read by today's undergraduates even as a starting point for discussion, it is largely supplanted by a variety of other texts, although not even Edward Ayers's influential *Promise of the New South* has attained the kind of acceptance that *Origins* once enjoyed.[17] Borrowing Hackney's image, *Origins* with its interpretation of discontinuity is the most visible ruin on the historiographical landscape, albeit one so imposing even as a ruin that serious scholars of all ages and in all stages will continue to pick through the remains looking for—and finding—still-valuable gems.

VI

When Woodward started graduate school, there was little disputing the assertion that his region was distinctive from the rest of America. President Franklin Roosevelt had recently declared the South to be the nation's number-one economic problem and countless reformists regarded the former Confederacy as benighted, if not hopeless. What many reformists—especially Chapel Hill Regionalists working for economic transformation and more leftist Chapel Hill reformists working for social justice—wanted was to make the South more like the rest of the country, and thus less distinctive. When Southern distinctiveness was gone and the regions were truly *American*, then this would be a good land to live in. Those seeking such economic and social change, whether ameliorist Regionalists or much more radical folk, were immediately attractive to Woodward.

On the other hand, the Agrarian tradition, once focused on the Fugitives at Vanderbilt University in 1930, saw plenty of injustice in bourgeois America; and Agrarians could be quite eloquent in decrying the way that something lovely was being destroyed by industrial capitalism, which itself then collapsed in the Great Depression. Woodward was attracted to the Agrarian critique too, and in time he became close friends with Robert Penn Warren and Cleanth Brooks, two onetime Fugitives with whom he taught for many years at Yale.

Woodward wrote most of his heavily researched monographs, between 1935 and 1951, from a Regionalist point of view on economics with a sharply leftist call for social justice. In the next phase of his career, after 1951, he began to meld Agrarianism with Regionalism, putting Chapel Hill reformism together with Nashville poetry in a way equaled by no one at either school. As it was proclaimed at the end of his teaching career, he had restored a sense of tragedy to the study of the South and indeed of America.

In the essays entitled *The Burden of Southern History,* and to a lesser extent in the essays entitled *American Counterpoint,* Woodward notes how certain peculiar experiences—the evil of slavery, the loss of the Civil War, the fact of military occupation and federally directed Reconstruction, the poverty of the postbellum countryside, the painful slowness of industrialization—have made Southerners very different from the rest of the country. He has insisted that a sensibility has emerged from these experiences, and he says that Southerners attuned to such a regional past understand the sins of their antebellum fathers to be arrogance, with concomitant expectations of invincibility. Chickens came home to roost on the fields of Gettysburg and Vicksburg, and on the farms and in the cities not long thereafter; and now Southerners can attest to our own past sins as a warning to the entire nation when it grows arrogant and begins to make assumptions of invincibility based on innocence.

Richard H. King has remarked that Woodward has two kinds of Southern distinctiveness in mind: there is the fact of Southerners learning lessons from our mistakes and then teaching others, and there is the hope that Southerners will learn such lessons and provide such teaching. Michael O'Brien and Gaines Foster and King himself have pretty thoroughly discredited any claim that Southerners have learned any such lessons as suggested in the first part of Woodward's concept of distinctiveness. Indeed, John Shelton Reed's many opinion polls show modern Southerners to be quite immodest about war, wealth, economic speculation, the limits of knowledge and technology, or anything else. O'Brien goes farther in his criticism, completely rejecting the very idea of any hope that Southerners may draw on such lessons for learning or for teaching. He sees no potential of any sort at all, and insists instead that once Woodward starts talking about potential and hope, then the argument had slipped away from him entirely.[18]

Moreover, Woodward's personal revolt against the Methodist piety of his father and of his family may have caused him to miss the thing most enduringly distinctive about the South, that is, the fervent Protestantism of the region. In recent decades, Samuel S. Hill, John B. Boles, Eugene Genovese, and Donald Gene Mathews have led a wave of scholarship that bids fair to establish Protestantism, and especially the strains of fundamentalism and evangelicalism, as the true hallmarks of Southernism.[19] Again, Reed's sophisticated and thorough polling indicates that modern Southerners are much more likely than the rest of Americans to attend church, to take religious teaching seriously, to interpret the Bible as literal truth, and to base important decisions on religious teachings.[20] Indeed, the absence of much discussion of the churches is one of the few things that seems a "wrong fact" in *Origins*.

Despite the frayed nature of Woodward's explanation of Southern distinctiveness, one thing seems to be enduring. He consistently says that racism and poverty and other aspects of injustice can disappear and still there will be a South distinctive from the rest of the nation. It will be up to other historians to tell us exactly what it is that will constitute positive and redeeming aspects of this Southern distinctiveness.

VII

Vann Woodward's life and career not only have had dramatic touches afforded by the sudden turn of luck, but there has also been heroism when he boldly took a stand. On some occasions, one can question his wisdom and judgment, as when he took the offensive to keep the prominent Communist Herbert Aptheker from teaching a special, one-time, and limited-credit course as a visitor at Yale University. On other occasions, as in his joining the march from Selma to Montgomery, his judgment is fully vindicated by history's own results. Of course in that case he was joined by so many people that the individual nature of his heroism there disappears under the sheer collective weight of the Movement itself.

On one occasion, however, he was unambiguously courageous, he was early, and he was alone. This was when he took the moment afforded by the Richard Lecture at the University of Virginia in 1954 right after the U.S. Supreme Court had issued its ruling in *Brown v. Board of Education*. In fact Woodward, with his Florida friends Dauer and Carleton and more prominently with John Hope Franklin, had done some of the research for NAACP counsel Thurgood Marshall as the plaintiff attorney prepared his briefs in the cases leading to the successful Supreme Court appearance. At Mr. Jefferson's University, speaking before an audience of white and black academics and educators, Woodward offered his boldest thesis and set off a firestorm of debates with other scholars.

He demonstrated that the Jim Crow laws themselves were placed on the statute books relatively recently, between 1898 and 1908—in his own infancy; and he offered evidence that these laws varied considerably state to state, with enforcement erratically applied even inside the same state. More to the point, he showed that *de jure* segregation was far from a Southern creation, but in fact had its origins in Northern cities. These facts led to his most striking pronouncement, that the *de facto* practices, or folkways, of Jim Crow had come *after* the laws rather than before. Thus, he concluded, Southern segregation had a "strange" career, Northern in origins, inconsistent, erratic, and above all short-lived.

He offered evidence that Southern political traditions of conservatism, radicalism, and liberalism—personified in the figures of Wade Hampton, Tom Watson, and Louis Harvie Blair—included practices of integration that predated the Jim Crow laws. Segregation, in other words, had a history. It had a starting point; and if it had a starting point, it could also have an ending point, perhaps the shoreline of which had been sighted by Chief Justice Earl Warren and his associates. The effect of his thesis cannot be underestimated for liberal Southerners who wanted to fight for integration without, in Potter's words, *denaturing* ourselves; or put another way, the South could be as integrated as the rest of the United States without losing its distinctiveness. This message was seized on by no less than the Rev. Martin Luther King, Jr., who told liberal white followers on the Montgomery march that Woodward had written "the Bible of the civil rights movement."

None of his works so captivated readers, but over time none has given him such trouble. People with an agenda, "innocent of history" as Potter put it, seized on the thesis and oversimplified it, taking the 1880s as a "golden age" instead of one that was merely "fluid." Too, some people confounded racism, which Woodward knew to be ancient and powerful, with *de jure* racist law. By the end of the decade of the 1950s Woodward found that some of these new friends were not really friendly to his scholarly career. By the middle of the 1960s, scholars began the grinding and fitful processes of testing his hypothesis, inevitably disproving much of it. In fact, his irreverent onetime seminar student David Hackett Fischer wrote:

> Through two revisions, the author has held his ground with a tenacity worthy of a better cause. The result is another fallacy—the overwhelming exception. . . . We are now told that the interpretation applies to all Southern institutions *except* churches, schools, militia, hotels, restaurants, public buildings, jails, hospitals, asylums, gardens, railroads in several states, and the New Orleans Opera House. It applies to all Negroes but freedmen, hired slaves, urban Negroes, South Carolina Negroes, and in some respects Negro field hands.[21]

Beyond the issues of right facts and wrong facts and the issues of logical presentation, Woodward by the 1970s became embarrassed by the concessions he had made to usable history. In his own mind he had swung too far away from his friend David Potter and the ideal of disinterested professionalism. He began to resent his own creation, although he still criticized his critics, and for a time in the 1970s (a decade marked by personal tragedy as he lost his son Peter Vincent, his friends Potter, Richard Hofstadter, and Alexander Bickel to cancer, and as his wife Glenn was diagnosed with a terminal cancer that took her life in 1982) he was out of character, "chalky" in the words of onetime student William McFeely, "not really himself" in the words of Joel Williamson.

Yet he recovered to lead the team of researchers writing *Responses of Presidents to Charges of Misconduct* and to thoroughly captivate congressmen Peter Rodino and Don Edwards during appearances before committee hearings concerned with Richard Nixon's possible impeachment (1972–1974) and the question of extending the Voting Rights Act (1982). Then he won the Pulitzer Prize in 1982 for his editorial leadership of the monumental *Mary Chesnut's Civil War.* And he recovered his sense of humor about his own foibles in *Strange Career,* while not missing any foibles by his critics in their own interpretations. He wrote with wit, and zap too, about all of this and much more in his memoirs *Thinking Back* in 1986. He made peace with himself and with his critics, which meant that he expected to be attacked. His kite was still high up in the skies.

VIII

In trying to assess Woodward's achievements at the end of his century, one could be dismissive, for many of the component parts of his scholarship have had to be discarded. By the most generous judgments, he offered women's history little more than half a loaf; and there was no loaf at all for the vital field of Southern religious studies. His hard work on behalf of integration excluded serious consideration of black separatism; his modernist assumptions about ironies and style have become dated in a world of postmodernism, without being useful to those who reject both modernism and postmodernism. His most famous work on Jim Crow has come to seem most fatally flawed, and his most substantial research work has been largely supplanted.

If, however, the students of history return to the history teacher's greatest lesson, then we find a grand achievement. It is Woodward himself who instructs that historians' Truths do not last, that the nature of the profession is to confront and question, the children eating their parents. No Truth, he tells us in richest modernist tone, can last out a generation; and critic Michael O'Brien wryly observes that Woodward outlived a number of his own observed Truths as well as outliving generations of historians. Yet if the student of history pauses before the insight itself and then looks at this career, an insight emerges whole and clear. It is that historians are searching for facts and a way to organize those facts meaningfully, and this search can only be conducted through the most rigorous questioning of each other, one generation's answers inevitably giving way to those of the next. A tragic view of the nature of knowledge, yes, but a grandly tragic view and not one cutely ironic or harmfully consumed with its own futility.

Woodward was not talking about something either organic or mechanical, two widely used metaphors that have confounded rather than clarified. Nor was he talking about something *evolving into* or *revolting against,* two more phrases that confound. Rather, Woodward was talking about a process that involved all things but above all involved engagement. The historian must search, in so doing recognizing the critics as a necessary part of the process. We can and must change our minds as new research leads not so much to new answers as it leads to entirely new questions. To accept that fact, the final irrelevance of one's dearest insights, was the very hardest thing that Woodward did. The encouragement he gave his critics, although rooted in the upbringing of the Southern aristocrats, was even more rooted in this understanding about knowledge itself.

The result was a life of dignified confrontation and committed detachment, and that life itself, mindful of his magnificent irrelevance, was the achievement of C. Vann Woodward.

John Hope Franklin

Southern History in Black and White

JOHN WHITE

The reputation and work of John Hope Franklin contain at least one irony that would delight his close friend (and supreme Southern ironist) C. Vann Woodward. The most esteemed and celebrated African-American scholar, Franklin has always considered himself a historian of the South, and his concerns "the two great racial groups, black and white, the principal actors in the drama of Southern history."[1] Yet he is best known for a comprehensive and compelling survey of African-American history. First published in 1947, *From Slavery to Freedom: A History of Negro Americans* is currently in its seventh edition, with over three million copies in print.[2]

In successive revisions, *From Slavery to Freedom* (now coauthored by Alfred A. Moss, Jr., handsomely illustrated, and subtitled *A History of African Americans*) has maintained its preeminence as the benchmark text—incorporating new scholarship, and devoting increasing attention to the roles of African-American women, popular culture, and the correction of factual errors in earlier editions.

As two distinguished white contributors to African-American historiography have observed of its first appearance:

> *From Slavery to Freedom,* written from the perspective of integrating Afro-American history into the broader stream of American history, authoritatively summarizing past research and laying out the main contours of the field, was a milestone in the history of Afro-American history. For those teaching Negro history courses in the black colleges, it was a breath of fresh air, the first really systematic survey based upon a thorough mastery of the relevant literature; to the growing numbers of whites who were becoming sensitive to the issue of race, it was the kind of synthesis that provided recognition and legitimacy for this hitherto neglected field.[3]

Franklin's next major publication in the area of African-American history was his biography of George Washington Williams (1849–1891), the peripatetic minister, soldier, journalist, politician, acerbic critic of Belgian rule in the Congo, and author of the two-volume *A History of the Negro Race in America from 1619 to 1880: Negroes as Slaves, as Soldiers, and as Citizens* (1882).[4] In 1945, Franklin read a paper before the Association for the Study of Negro Life and History entitled "George Washington Williams, Historian," and the following year it was published in the *Journal of Negro History*.

Forty years later, Franklin—who had eventually discovered Williams's unmarked grave in Blackpool, England—produced a judicious and meticulously researched life of an engaging but flawed individual whose temperament made him "erratic, restless, controversial, overambitious, faithless, and capable of misrepresentation if not downright falsehood." Often denounced by his contemporaries and largely ignored by posterity, Williams had gained "the full stature of a nineteenth-century American by the time of his death."[5]

W. E. B. Du Bois had recognized Williams as "the greatest historian of the Race"; Franklin believed that in his attention to the roles of blacks in the American Revolution and the antislavery movement, Williams was "essentially a revisionist." By the age of thirty-three and without formal training, Williams had accomplished "what no other Afro-American had achieved and indeed what no other person had achieved . . . a sustained, coherent account of the experiences of the Negro people."[6] *From Slavery to Freedom,* through all its revisions, similarly merits this accolade. Like Williams, Franklin has "revised" our understanding of crucial aspects of the African-American experience.

In a career spanning more than fifty years, Franklin has also made seminal and perceptive contributions to Southern historiography. Most notably, he reexamined the vexed issue of the nature of the several phases of Reconstruction in the post–Civil War South—largely ignored by Williams, since these episodes were barely over when he wrote. Yet, as George M. Fredrickson has observed, Franklin's writings on Reconstruction have "not visibly influenced other scholars in the field as much as his eminence might have led one to expect"—partly, perhaps, because of a careful avoidance of making "explicit moral and ideological judgments in his work."[7]

But by any measure Franklin's stature is enormous, recognized by the historical profession, the American establishment, and the general public. His *curriculum vitae* is simply dazzling—if not daunting. The subject of newspaper articles, radio and TV documentaries, and recipient of over one hundred honorary degrees, Franklin has also been awarded the National Association for the Advancement of Colored People's (NAACP) Spingarn Medal (1955) and the Presidential Medal of Freedom (1995).

Franklin, as he relates in "A Life of Learning," "could not have avoided being a social activist even if I had wanted to."[8] He was an expert witness for the African-American plaintiff in *Lyman Johnson v. The University of Kentucky* (1949), who had been refused admission to the University of Kentucky's graduate program in history. Four years later, he assisted in the preparation of the NAACP Legal and Educational Defense Fund brief in response to the Supreme Court order setting down the school desegregation cases for reargument, which culminated in the epochal *Brown v. Board of Education* decision of 1954.

During his tenure as Pitt Professor of American History and Institutions at Cambridge University, Franklin also commented for BBC viewers—"with what I suspect was a bit of advocacy even in the tone of my voice"—on James Meredith's dramatic attempt to desegregate the University of Mississippi in 1962 and on the historic 1963 March on Washington, D.C.

An admirer of Martin Luther King, Jr., Franklin joined the Selma to Montgomery March of 1965, the climax of the classic phase of the Southern civil rights movement, proud to be in the company of "more than thirty historians who came from all parts of the country to register their objection to racial bigotry in the United States." In 1987, he opposed the Senate confirmation of Robert H. Bork as associate justice of the United States Supreme Court, having informed the Senate Judiciary Committee that there was "no indication— in his writings, his teaching, or his rulings—that this nominee has any deeply held commitment to the eradication of the problem of race or even of its mitigation."[9]

A decade later (at the age of 82 and as the James B. Duke Professor Emeritus at Duke University), he was appointed by President Bill Clinton chairman of a blue-ribbon advisory board on race relations. Franklin made it clear that he favored a formal national apology for slavery, and that the commission would pursue this objective. His commission was successful.[10]

In his chosen discipline, Franklin became the first black president of the Southern Historical Association (SHA) (1970–1971), the Organization of American Historians (1974–1975), and the American Historical Association (1979). Not least, he is held in deep respect and affection by generations of undergraduate and graduate students, academic colleagues, and friends from all walks of life—in the United States and across the world. Through his prolific writings, professional and civic memberships, public offices and activities, Franklin—to adapt the title of Ralph Ellison's famous novel—became an increasingly "Visible Man" in the historical profession.

The thrust of his oeuvre has been to teach non-Southerners more about the South, and Southerners more about themselves. These singular achievements, and his passionate commitment to both scholarly objectivity and racial justice—a *New York Times* writer once called him "The Last Integrationist"—need to be set in brief biographical context.[11]

John Hope Franklin was born in 1915 in the all-black community of Rentiesville in Oklahoma. His background, one commentator has remarked, "embodies the ethnic and racial complexities of the South: his family was part Cherokee, and some of its members served as slaves to the Cherokees in the antebellum decades."[12] Buck Franklin, his father (a graduate of Morehouse College), was a lawyer who had moved to Rentiesville after being informed by a white judge that a black attorney would never represent anyone in his court. "My father," Franklin relates, "resolved that he would resign from the world dominated by white people and try to make it among his own people."[13]

His mother, an elementary school teacher, introduced John Hope and his sister (an older sister and brother were attending a private school in Tennessee) to the writings of Paul Dunbar and James Weldon Johnson, while his father, a student of ancient Greece and Rome, was given to quoting Plato, Socrates, and Pericles to his young son. Less happily, in travels to nearby towns, Franklin experienced the indignities of racial discrimination. On one occasion he and his sister were ignominiously ejected from a train when their mother refused to move from a coach designated for whites only.

Despairing of making a living in Rentiesville, Buck Franklin moved his law practice to Tulsa, intending to send for his young family six months later. But his law offices were destroyed in the race riot of 1921, forcing him to set up in a tent for several months and delaying the family's move to Tulsa by four years.[14] During his secondary school education (at Booker T. Washington High School) in Tulsa, Franklin—an ardent music lover—attended concerts and recitals at Convention Hall, unaccompanied by his parents who refused to accept the segregated seating arrangements strictly enforced in the city's public places.[15] It was also at Convention Hall that Franklin, at age eleven, first saw and heard the outstanding African-American intellectual of his generation, and for whom he would develop an awe-struck respect: W. E. B. Du Bois.[16]

Banned by segregation laws from entering the University of Oklahoma, Franklin's academic career began at Fisk University in Nashville in 1931. At Fisk, he soon gave up thoughts of studying law (and joining his father's practice) after being encouraged to consider a career in history by a white professor, Theodore Currier, who taught him "how to write a research paper" and also partly financed Franklin's graduate work at Harvard University with a loan of five hundred dollars. At Harvard, which he entered in 1935, Franklin roomed with an African-American family in Cambridge and was supervised by Arthur M. Schlesinger, Sr., with whom he felt "very much at ease." Within nine months, Franklin received his master's degree and scholarship funds sufficient to complete the doctoral requirements. His dissertation topic on free blacks in North Carolina was supervised by a white historian of the South, Paul Buck (author of *The Road to Reunion*), with whom he developed a warm friendship and who helped direct him toward the field of Southern history. Franklin recalls that early on in his graduate years, "I had decided I was going to be an historian without regard to race, and that I was going to remove the tag of Negro from any consideration of my work, whether teaching or writing"—a possibly ingenuous resolve that (fortunately) he was unable to sustain.[17]

The years at Harvard were less than inspiring for Franklin. Despite (or because of) the fact that there were few African-American students at the university, he encountered little racial prejudice, but was shocked by the anti-Semitism expressed by fellow graduate students in the Henry Adams Club and the crassly elitist attitudes displayed by some of the history faculty. Resolved to complete his dissertation in absentia, Franklin left Harvard early in 1939, and already "committed to the study, teaching, and writing of history" accepted a position at St. Augustine's College.[18]

When the United States entered World War II in 1941, Franklin was summarily rejected by the U.S. Navy as a clerical worker—despite his possession of a Harvard Ph.D., shorthand skills, and "three gold medals in typing"—solely because of his color. He then turned to the War Department and applied for a position as a military historian, but his application went unanswered. After being subjected to decidedly second-class treatment by a draft board physician when he was required to get a blood test, Franklin decided that "the United States did not need me and did not deserve me," and he passed "the remainder of the war years [at North Carolina College for Negroes] successfully and with malice aforethought outwitting my draft board and the entire Selective Service establishment."[19]

Franklin has also recounted a surreal incident that occurred in June 1945 as he was returning from Greensboro to Durham by train. The black passengers were crowded into the half coach next to the baggage car, and several were forced to sit on their bags or stand in the aisles. "The unusual aspect of this traditional arrangement," he said, "was that in the full coach adjoining the Negro half coach there were no more than six white men." When Franklin asked the conductor why black and white passengers could not reverse places, he was informed that the six white men "were German prisoners of war and could not be moved." To add further insult to palpable injury, the captives "seemed to enjoy our discomfort."[20]

Throughout his academic career Franklin encountered and overcame incidents of racial discrimination. At the end of the war, while researching *The*

Militant South (his third book) in the state archives at Baton Rouge, he was only allowed entry by the librarian when the facility closed for a week as part of the victory celebrations.[21] In his essay "The Dilemma of the Negro Scholar," Franklin asks readers to "imagine the plight of a Negro historian trying to do research in the archives of the South operated by people who cannot conceive that a Negro has the capacity to use the materials there." On a visit to the North Carolina State Department of Archives and History, he was informed by the archivist (a Yale Ph.D.) that the architect had not anticipated such a contingency, while the female head of the Alabama State archives in Montgomery "was shocked to discover despite the fact that I was a 'Harvard nigger' I had somehow retained the capacity to be courteous to a Southern lady."[22]

Moving from Howard University in 1956 to become chairman of the history department at Brooklyn College (an appointment that received front-page coverage in the *New York Times*), Franklin had great difficulty in obtaining a loan from his mortgage company "because the house I wanted was several blocks beyond where blacks should live." Only after a year of "hassles" was he able to purchase a house, and he reflected that "I could have written a long article, perhaps even a small book, in the time expended on the search for housing."[23] Such experiences may partly explain Franklin's decision to return to the South in 1980 (after spending sixteen years at the University of Chicago, during three of which he served as the chair of the Department of History); two years later, he joined the faculty at Duke University as James B. Duke Professor of History.

As he explained to the readers of *Southern Living* magazine, although segregation had been dealt some body blows in the 1960s, *racism* persisted, but "it's not partial to the South, as many people would have you believe. That's one reason I came back to North Carolina . . . I feel more comfortable walking the streets of Durham than those of New York or Chicago."[24]

Franklin (like all African-Americans) still encounters incidents of casual racism. Staying at the Cosmos Club in Washington, D.C. (he has been a member since 1962) prior to receiving the Medal of Freedom, he was accosted by a woman member in the lobby who asked him to fetch her coat. At the St. Moritz Hotel in New York, some months later, another woman handed him her trash and asked him to dispose of it, and shortly after, at the Waterford Hotel in Oklahoma City, a man handed him some car keys and said: "Here, boy, go and get my car."[25]

Early in his academic career, Franklin faced the virtual exclusion of black scholars from the professional historical organizations of which he was a member. After seeing the program of the SHA for its 1946 convention, he wrote to Luther Porter Jackson (author of *Free Negro Labor and Property Hold-ing in Virginia, 1830–1860* [1942]): "An entire session is being devoted to the Free Negro. Too bad the great white fathers in the South couldn't bring them-selves to invite you, [E. Horace] Fitchett or myself to participate."[26]

Through his friendships with leading Southern white historians—most notably, C. Vann Woodward—Franklin campaigned to integrate their premier organization.[27] For the 1949 SHA convention at the College of William and Mary in Williamsburg, Woodward and Bell Irvin Wiley chose Franklin to read a paper. Introduced by the late Henry Steele Commager, Franklin deliv-ered a synopsis of his forthcoming book, *The Militant South,* to an appreciative audience and later dined with his fellow historians at the Williamsburg Inn.[28] Two years later, Franklin also participated in the program of the Mississippi Valley Historical Association. Both physically and metaphorically, the engag-ing and extroverted Franklin was beginning to make his presence (and that of his fellow African-American colleagues) felt within the historical profession. But there were formidable obstacles still to be overcome.

At the 1952 convention of the SHA, in Knoxville, Vann Woodward, as president of the Association, together with program chair LeRoy Graf and SHA secretary Bennett H. Wall, cancelled the annual dinner that was to have been held at the segregated Farragut Hotel because Franklin and fellow black historians, including Clarence Bacote, Elsie Lewis Mitchell, and Sherman Savage, would have been unable to hear Woodward's presidential address. The proceedings were moved to a nearby clubhouse restaurant, which was inte-grated. Woodward reflects that,

> In all this, as in weightier collaborations such as the NAACP brief for the Supreme Court, or in later years related scholarly problems and professional crises, John Hope invariably combined perfect intellectual and moral poise with inexhaustible good humor and a big laugh that banished any inclina-tion to heroic posturing. I naturally appealed to him for help in preparing the lectures on segregation [*The Strange Career of Jim Crow*] and owe him much for the criticism his reading of the manuscript produced.[29]

By the mid-1950s, then, Franklin had made significant forays into the white-dominated world of historical scholarship. His research and publica-tions already suggested that he was a rising star in the firmaments of Southern and African-American historiography.

His first book, *The Free Negro in North Carolina, 1790–1860* (1943), met with a generally favorable critical reception—but one that implicitly acknowledged the racial identity of its author. Writing in the *Journal of Negro History,* its founder, Carter G. Woodson, commended "one of the recent efforts to rewrite the history of the Negro" and adopted a deliberately disingenuous tone in summarizing its contents:

> We were surprised to learn that Free Negroes and whites were intermarrying in North Carolina up to 1715, that the Negroes meeting the qualifications voted there until 1835, and that the outstanding preparatory school for the most distinguished whites of the state prior to the Civil War was conducted by a Negro, John Chavis.

The young author was warmly commended both for the quantity and quality of his research, conveyed in a "succinct and clear style."[30] Woodson was subsequently to encourage Franklin to contribute reviews and articles to the *Journal of Negro History*.

Blanche Henry Clark, reviewer for the *Journal of Southern History*, welcomed the appearance of Franklin's study "at a time when the necessity of understanding racial minorities is of paramount importance," but wondered if its depictions of "an unwanted people" were not too bleak, since custom rather than statute determined antebellum race relations, while "police records and local newspapers" might "frequently reveal a joy of living which even a statute could not quell."[31]

The concerns and contentions of Franklin's next venture into antebellum Southern history, *The Militant South, 1800–1861* (1956), were summarized in his article "Slavery and the Martial South" (1952). Enlarging on the perceptions of Tocqueville, Jefferson, and Fanny Kemble that slavery had produced an aggressive belligerency among white Southerners of all ranks, Franklin argued that not only had the section been dominated by the fear of slave revolts, but also in formulating their proslavery arguments "white Southerners were . . . among the first people of the world to develop a militant race superiority."[32]

This contention had earlier been the subtext of an essay, "Whither Reconstruction Historiography?" (1948), a searching critique of E. Merton Coulter's *The South during Reconstruction, 1865–1877* (1947), a volume in the prestigious History of the South series. Coulter had memorably characterized the period of Congressional or "Radical" Reconstruction as representing "the blackout of honest government," during which an unholy alliance of Northern carpetbaggers, degraded Southern scalawags, and ludicrously inept blacks subjected the prostrate South to an orgy of corruption, misrule, and humiliation.

Franklin questioned not only Coulter's scholarship but also his objectivity in endorsing William Archibald Dunning's description of life in the South under Radical Republican rule as "a social and political system in which all the forces that made for civilization were dominated by a mass of barbarous freed-men."[33] Coulter had asserted that "there can be no sensible departure from the well-known facts of the Reconstruction program as it was applied to the South. No amount of revision can write away the grievous mistakes made in this abnormal period of American history." Given the disparate accounts of Reconstruction by such scholars as Howard K. Beale, Francis B. Simkins, Vernon Wharton, and W. E. B. Du Bois, Franklin asked simply: "What are the well-known facts of Reconstruction?"[34]

He returned to this point in his 1979 presidential address to the American Historical Association: "In the post-Reconstruction years a continuing argu-ment raged, not merely over how the victors did treat the vanquished but over what actually happened." Surveying the peaks (and troughs) of Reconstruction historiography, Franklin forecast that it would be "a happy day" if and when scholars and ideologues "could view the era of Reconstruction without either attempting to use the events of that era to support some current policy or seeking analogies that are at best strained." He suggested that "we would do well to cease using Reconstruction as a mirror of ourselves and begin studying it because it very much needs studying."[35]

In "Whither Reconstruction Historiography?" Franklin had also rejected melodramatic and unhistorical interpretations of the era, including Coulter's suggestion that Radical Reconstruction bore a "glimmering resemblance to the later cults of Fascism and Nazism." In fact, Franklin argued tartly, the Old South rather than the (imagined) South of the Reconstruction era had pos-sessed much more of a resemblance to these totalitarian "cults": "an oppressed race; the great and continuing drive for *Lebensraum;* the annihilation of almost every vestige of free thought and free speech; and the enthusiastic glorification of the martial spirit."[36]

Franklin also found Coulter guilty of making unsupported generalizations, and ignoring the testimony of black officeholders and the records and pro-ceedings of black conventions. Instead, he had made a "rather systematic ef-fort to discredit the Negro in almost all phases of his life during Reconstruc-tion," and implicitly endorsed negative stereotypes of the African-American character.[37]

Having effectively reduced (if not actually demolished) Coulter's reputa-tion, Franklin's fourth book, *Reconstruction after the Civil War* (1961)—dedi-cated to "Theodore S. Currier: Great Teacher and Friend"—was a masterly synthesis of ongoing revisionist scholarship and a discrete contribution to the subject.

Two of his former students note that Franklin's contributions to Recon-struction historiography have been "so vast that paradoxically, they risk being underrated." Quickly accepted and amplified by other historians, his findings have not been sufficiently recognized as ground breaking. Yet his work "offered the first comprehensive response to William Archibald Dunning's American Nation series volume *Reconstruction: Political and Economic* (1907), or at least the first one scholars were willing to hear."[38]

In Franklin's retelling, those traditional villains of the peace—carpetbaggers and scalawags—appear as heterogeneous groupings. Some carpetbaggers may have been political opportunists, but (like other internal migrants in American history) the majority were seeking business opportunities, secured by sound government—which they associated with the Republican party—in a region ripe for redevelopment.

For their part, the much-maligned Southern scalawags had been largely excluded from political and economic opportunities under the rule of the planter class in the Old South, and now looked for incorporation into the new body politic. By no stretch of the historical imagination had they been friends of the freedman. Also and significantly, in no former Confederate state had there been "Negro rule" during Congressional Reconstruction. Yet black leaders themselves had displayed no animus toward whites, and they had not sought any revolution in race relations, preferring instead to engineer an economic basis for black communities in the South.

If the new Republican state constitutions, drafted in 1868, did not contain radical economic (land reform) or educational (integrated schools) provisions, "they did have considerable merit as satisfactory instruments of state government." Indeed, Franklin suggested, "the fact that for a generation no serious constitution-making was undertaken in the South is the best proof of this fact."[39]

Why, then, did Reconstruction fail? Franklin's interpretation is both subtle and provocative. The ingrained racism of Southern whites was certainly a factor, but so were the socioeconomic policies of the "reconstructionists" themselves. Internal squabbles and divisions diverted Republican energies from the necessary task of building the party's strength in the South, and the failure to effect a redistribution of Southern land meant that the putative Republican constituency of blacks and disillusioned whites began to desert the party—even before the Democratic counterattack on Radical regimes. "It was," Franklin concluded, "the absence of effective machinery for sustaining the political organization and for developing some economic independence that served to bring about the eventual downfall of the Republican party and, consequently, of the new governments in the South."[40]

Former Confederates, utilizing a devastating combination of "political pressure, economic sanctions, *and* violence . . . brought Radical reconstruction crashing down almost before it began."[41] Implicit in Franklin's analysis is the belief that white Southerners, in the immediate aftermath of the end of the

Civil War, brought on their own heads the alleged "horrors" of Congressional Reconstruction. The point is made forcibly and deserves quotation:

> At this juncture the former Confederates had complete control of their own states. White manhood suffrage was the basis of the franchise; violence against the Freedmen's Bureau, the philanthropists from the North, the United States Army, and the former slaves was rampant. And, except for representation in Congress, the former Confederates had the destiny of their section in their own hands. A failure to give consideration to the effect of such a state of affairs and to the consequences that resulted from it conveys, consciously or unconsciously, a misrepresentation of the early postwar years that makes impossible any clear understanding of what followed."[42]

Quite appropriately, *Reconstruction after the Civil War* was praised in the *Journal of Negro History* as a "judicious assessment of the controversial Reconstruction era" and as "the best summary available, especially in fitting Southern developments into proper perspective with national issues."

Franklin was commended for offering a counterview to persisting "Reconstruction myths"—which had been recently resurrected by Senator Olin D. Johnston's article "The Good Side of the South" in *Time* magazine (September 3, 1961). Johnston had portrayed "a supine South treating freedmen and Unionists kindly, only to have dictatorial Radical conspirators trample President [Andrew] Johnson and the Constitution while using federal bayonets and illiterate black voters to impose a debauchery of corruption, by venal Carpetbaggers, degenerate Scalawags and ludicrous Negroes, finally forcing helpless Southerners to resort in desperation to violence and fraud to regain their freedom."

Reconstruction after the Civil War had exposed these myths for what they were by showing that comparatively few Union troops remained in the South after the Confederacy's surrender, that many black officeholders were capable and well educated, that extravagance and corruption marked postbellum state governments before and after the imposition of Radical rule, and that Southern violence against blacks commenced even before they obtained and exercised the vote, and continued after they had been effectively disenfranchised.

Yet Franklin had not overstated his revisionist case as was evident in his concession that the Republicans did not lay a solid foundation for black civil, political, and economic progress. The reviewer concluded by recommending the book to all teachers "if they wish their lectures on Reconstruction to avoid outmoded myths."[43]

Not all the notices of Franklin's *Reconstruction* were commendatory. The decidedly "unreconstructed" Southern white historian Avery O. Craven was singularly unimpressed by Franklin's monograph. Without actually naming its author, or referring directly to the book, Craven launched an intemperate—one is tempted to say "craven"—attack on Reconstruction revisionism.

> The emphasis, one sincerely regrets to find, is always on how the Negro fared in this or that situation. White Southerners (a term used interchangeably with ex-Confederates) were as strongly attached to their old way of life as ever and their great purpose was to deny rights to the Negro. The fact that Southerners turned again to their old leaders is viewed not as a perfectly natural step but as an act of intentional defiance.

Such an approach was "based on abstract values" and discounted "all the realities which resulted from a bitter civil war." With an oblique reference to Franklin (then chairman of the Department of History at Brooklyn College), Craven asserted that "scholars sitting in Northern libraries reading the official documents are not reconstructing Reconstruction in a very realistic way. They need to read a few of the letters written by men and women on the scene to understand the mopping up after a civil war." This judgment—which also violated the canon of Southern courtesy—was as ungracious as it was unjust. Craven's remarks can be fruitfully compared with those of Daniel J. Boorstin in his preface to Franklin's book (a volume in the Chicago History of American Civilization series):

> Mr. Franklin cuts his way through a mass of controversial scholarship, resting his conclusions on his own intimate knowledge of the documents. He offers us a balanced account of American life in a time of great challenge, of unfamiliar problems, and of uncertain leadership. *The South after the Civil War* is a chronicle of how Americans bore defeat. While the story is not entirely inspiring, it is by no means as dispiriting as our textbooks have long told us it was. Mr. Franklin reminds us that neither North nor South, neither Yankee nor Rebel, neither White nor Negro, had a monopoly on virtue, ignorance, vice, greed, or courage. And he shows us the kind of compassionate understanding which the historian at his best can give us, and which is especially needed if the era of "Reconstruction" is ever to end.[44]

Shortly after the appearance of Franklin's book, another scholar, "sitting in [his] Northern librar[y]," produced an equally impressive synthesis of revisionist findings on Reconstruction that differed from Franklin's only in stressing racism as the root cause of its failure.

Kenneth M. Stampp's *The Era of Reconstruction, 1865–1877* (1965) remains the best introduction to the subject, and was recognized and endorsed as such by Franklin himself. In an enthusiastic review, he approvingly paraphrased Stampp's "almost classic" statement of the "Dunning thesis" on Reconstruction:

> Motivated by hatred of the South . . . the Vindictives or Radicals sought to defeat President Lincoln's generous and lenient program. President Andrew Johnson carried forward the program of the martyred president, but the Radicals, with their own sinister purposes, proceeded to wreck the new President's efforts and to discredit him, even to the point of impeachment. Then, riding roughshod over presidential vetoes and federal courts, the radicals "put the South under military occupation, gave the ballot to the Negroes, and formed new Southern state governments dominated by base and corrupt men, black and white." Finally, decent Southern white Democrats organized to drive out the Negroes, carpetbaggers, and scalawags from power, "peacefully if possible, forcibly if necessary." Thus one by one the Southern states were redeemed, honesty and virtue triumphed, and the South's natural leaders returned to power.

Stampp, Franklin believed, had offered a "significant repudiation" of this thesis. In many respects, the phrase "Radical Reconstruction" was a misnomer, since "the radical program was not only not very radical, but, in its moderation, was as much the work of the middle-of-the-road members of Congress as the work of true radicals." But whatever its provenance, Congressional Reconstruction had "created the best governments the South ever had and, in the process, introduced practices and institutions that the South had not previously known." Stampp had earned "a prominent place among those who have undertaken to provide a more accurate account of what actually took place in the decade following the Civil War."[45]

To mark the centennial of a signal event of the American Civil War, Franklin published *The Emancipation Proclamation* (1963), a factual (rather than sentimentalized), brief account of the genesis, reception, and consequences of Lincoln's most dramatic acts—there were *two* Proclamations. The Proclamation of January 1, 1863, for all its legal terminology and justification as a necessary war measure was, Franklin asserted, a "great American document of freedom [that] has been greatly neglected." It made Union war aims (more) intelligible to Europeans, forestalled possible British intervention on the side of the Confederacy, and was welcomed by blacks "as a document of freedom" since "they made no clear distinction between the areas affected by the Proclamation and those not affected by it."[46]

A Southern Odyssey: Travelers in the Antebellum North (winner of the Jules F. Landry Award for 1975) was further evidence of Franklin's continuing pre-occupation with the years of the Civil War and Reconstruction. It is a graceful and imaginative collective portrait of the experiences of the thousands of white Southerners who, for a variety of reasons—economic, medical, educational, and cultural—embarked on "grand tours" of the Northern states between the 1820s and the 1860s.

The most revealing chapter, "Crusaders Among Infidels," charts the experiences and adventures of such champions of the Southern Way of Life as George Fitzhugh, Robert Toombs, R. M. T. Hunter, William Lowndes Yancey, and William Gilmore Simms when they crossed the Mason-Dixon line. None were well received. Following his ill-fated lecture tour of 1856, during which he was roundly criticized in the Northern press (and largely ignored by the general public) for his pronounced proslavery views, Simms went back to the South "a hurt and broken crusader [who had] utterly failed to conquer the infidels." Whether they found more to praise than to condemn in the free society of the North, Southerners, hypersensitive to any questionings of their region's peculiar institution, were unwilling (or unable) to "surrender any of the South's self-esteem or its confidence in its own future."[47]

Like his contemporary and confidant C. Vann Woodward, Franklin has always been intrigued by the place that history (as well as race) holds in Southern culture. Like Woodward also, he has been concerned to correct the distortions and exaggerations that for so long marked the "cult of history" in Southern discourse. In an essay published in 1960, Franklin identified both the reasons for and the consequences of the white South's obsession with its past.

> Having failed to establish a separate nation and having gone down to defeat on the field of battle, Southerners in the period after the Civil War turned their attention to their own past with a concentration so great that the cult of history became a permanent and important ingredient of the Southern culture. . . . the writing of history became an act of sectional allegiance and devotion. . . . from its history the South derived an image of itself that has in large measure governed its reactions to successive changes and challenges. If the South has often reacted churlishly and shortsightedly, the fault does not lie with history itself, but with a distorted historical tradition of which even the South's historians have been victims, but which only they can correct.[48]

In his 1971 presidential address to the SHA titled "The Great Confrontation: The South and the Problem of Change," Franklin offered the trenchant comment that

It was in the context of the sectional controversy that white Southerners sharpened their conception of the perfect society; and by the time they defined it they discovered that they had achieved it. In the North the Transcendentalists advanced the idea of the perfectibility of man. In the South there was rather general agreement on the depravity of man, but the real emphasis was on how perfect the social order was.[49]

During his own intellectual "Southern Odyssey"—compounded of heuristic observation and a dedication to "a life of learning"—John Hope Franklin, as much as any historian of the South, has offered seminal "corrections" to our understanding of that section, its inhabitants (white and black), their delusions and discoveries, trials and tribulations.

That he has also been a consummate recorder of the larger African-American experience is also to our mutual advantage and great good fortune. His scholarship, at once humane and objective, refined and accessible—in the face of *de facto* and *de jure* discrimination—is an uplifting and salutary story in its own right. As Drew Gilpin Faust has aptly commented:

> In an era when many scholars in the humanities and social sciences are questioning whether it is possible to identify any foundations for truth or scholarly objectivity, John Hope Franklin offers a compelling case for continuing to struggle toward these goals. Both his life and his work represent a commitment to learning as an important way to "bear witness" in a society that he, perhaps better than any American scholar alive today, knows to be far from perfect. His faith and his achievement cannot but serve as witness and inspiration to all of us privileged to be engaged with him in the historical enterprise.[50]

Faust's encomium gains additional weight when Franklin's most recent monograph is scaled into his oeuvre. *Runaway Slaves: Rebels on the Plantation* (1999), coauthored with Loren Schweninger, is a notable addition to slavery historiography. Utilizing an impressive array of sources—plantation records, petitions to state legislatures, and newspaper advertisements—Franklin and Schweninger show more conclusively than have previous commentators that African-American slaves resisted their bondage in various ways. Slaves (and those free blacks who had been kidnapped by "slave catchers") became runaways and truants and remained at large for days and months, before either returning voluntarily to their owners or being recaptured—and savagely punished. "The scars on the backs of runaways and the severe whippings for repeat offenders bore witness to the emotion, frustration, and anger of owners who could not control intractable slaves."[51] Slave masters employed the full panoply of their considerable powers and influence—local, state, and federal officials, slave patrols, dogs, and law enforcement officers—to repossess their "property."

That many, if not all, of the contentions and conclusions of *Runaway Slaves* will already be familiar to most students of Southern slavery should not detract from or diminish its significance. Aware that recent historiography celebrates African-American adaptability, resilience, and culture, Franklin and Schweninger are properly concerned to demolish romanticized depictions of the Old South's peculiar institution—whatever their ideological provenance. "The vast majority of slaveholders," they report, "considered themselves kind, God-fearing, humane masters. . . . Invariably owners looked upon themselves as decent, compassionate, and well-meaning men and women."[52] For their part, the South's slaves resented and resisted the constraints of slavery, whether imposed by compassionate or cruel masters and mistresses. *Runaway Slaves* is, by turns, depressing and exhilarating, horrifying and inspirational. Above all, it is a work of dispassionate description, inquiry, and exhaustive scholarship.

In his "reconstructions" of the Southern—and the African-American—experience and his vision of a just and humane American social order, John Hope Franklin, throughout his illustrious career, has always been engaged in something more profound and accomplished than simply "Whistlin' Dixie."

A. Elizabeth Taylor

Searching for Southern Suffragists

JUDITH N. MCARTHUR

Antoinette Elizabeth Taylor was born in the west-central Georgia town of Columbus, on the Alabama border, on June 10, 1917, and educated in the public schools there. Her father was a partner in a shoe company and her mother a graduate of Valdosta State College; consequently Taylor grew up expecting to go to college, the Depression's grip on the Southern economy notwithstanding. For a young woman of her class, the predictable life trajectory would have been a few years of teaching secondary school before leaving the work force to marry and raise a family. Taylor, however, harbored a private ambition: at a time when women earned only eighteen percent of the doctorates awarded in history, she aspired to an advanced degree and "something special."[1]

After graduating Phi Beta Kappa from the University of Georgia in 1938, Taylor entered the master's program at the University of North Carolina at Chapel Hill to study Southern history under Fletcher M. Green. Women were tolerated in graduate school, but the faculty made plain their preference for men as students and in job placement. (Mary Elizabeth Massey, who arrived at Chapel Hill a year after Taylor, remembered being told that women were not actually unwelcome there: "It's just that we don't do anything for them.") Following Fletcher Green's suggestion, Taylor wrote her thesis on the convict lease system in Georgia and in 1940, master's degree in hand, took a job at Judson College, an institution for women in Marion, Alabama.[2]

There, as a twenty-three-year-old assistant professor, she stumbled upon the subject that would become her life's work. In the college library she came upon the *History of Woman Suffrage,* the six-volume documentary edited by the leaders of the movement, Susan B. Anthony, Elizabeth Cady Stanton, Matilda Joslyn Gage, and Ida Husted Harper. Knowing "almost nothing about women" and nothing at all about the suffrage movement, she spent an afternoon engrossed in the fat volumes, caught up in the drama of American women's seventy-two-year struggle for the vote. With a research agenda clearly in mind, she finished the academic year at Judson and left to begin work on a doctorate at Vanderbilt University in 1941.

When Taylor proposed woman suffrage as a dissertation topic, her fellow students were frankly skeptical: "How can you write a dissertation on a subject like that?" she recalled being asked. After some hesitation her dissertation committee consented; Daniel M. Robison, Vanderbilt's twentieth-century specialist, supported her choice and served as director. As a practical matter, an unconventional dissertation would make little difference to the already limited job prospects that she faced as a woman. Taylor was the only woman offered a fellowship in history at Vanderbilt that year—and probably the first ever— but the reasons had as much to do with pragmatism as with her own qualifications and promise. Europe was at war and the peacetime draft had reduced the number of male applicants.[3]

Female role models to whom Taylor might have looked were few. The first historians of Southern women, a handful of scholars who had begun pioneering research in the 1920s and 1930s, were, as Anne Firor Scott has written, "unheard voices." Julia Cherry Spruill's path-breaking *Women's Life and Work in the Southern Colonies* (1938) had been well reviewed and then disappeared from sight—as did Spruill herself into the social responsibilities of a dean's wife. Virginia Gearhart Gray, Marjorie Mendenhall, and Guion Griffis Johnson had published their research on aspects of Southern women's history in the nineteenth century, and Eleanor Boatright's article on the political and civil status of Georgia women before 1860 had just appeared. None of the five was able to make a career in university teaching, and their work remained unappreciated for decades, until women's history emerged as a field in its own right in the late 1960s.[4]

Taylor was the first member of the second generation of historians of Southern women, the generation trained during and after World War II, when women found more, albeit still limited, opportunities within the academy. Although their male colleagues took scant notice of their work, the second generation did not comprise unheard voices. Taylor's contribution was to invent the field of Southern suffrage history. Between 1943 and 1980 she published twelve articles and her dissertation, defining the outlines of a field that did not exist when she began doctoral study in 1941.[5]

"The Woman Suffrage Movement in Tennessee," which Taylor completed in 1943, was the first dissertation written on woman suffrage in the United States.[6] She began with the intention of investigating the national movement but quickly discovered that wartime travel difficulties and widely dispersed primary sources would require scaling back to a more modest and manageable topic. There was as yet no scholarly literature on woman suffrage: Eleanor Flexner's seminal history, *Century of Struggle: The Woman's Rights Movement in the United States,* and Aileen Kraditor's *The Ideas of the Woman Suffrage Movement, 1890–1920* would not appear until 1959 and 1965, respectively. With only the participant accounts in the *History of Woman Suffrage* and *Woman Suffrage and Politics* (1923), by National American Woman Suffrage Association (NAWSA) leaders Carrie Chapman Catt and Nettie Rogers Schuler, to serve as guides, Taylor had to map her own territory.

Although by contemporary standards the dissertation is not long, the bibliography and footnotes reveal meticulous research. Using NAWSA's *Proceedings,* nine Tennessee newspapers, the journals of the state legislature, and the official organs of NAWSA, the National Woman's Party, and the National Association Opposed to Woman Suffrage, Taylor pieced together a chronology and identified the leading suffragists and their opponents. She had access to only a handful of manuscript collections and the minutes of one local suffrage league (Nashville's), but she was able to interview Anne Dallas Dudley, a former president of the Tennessee Equal Suffrage Association, and Josephine Pearson, the most prominent antisuffragist.

Taylor articulated no thesis in "The Woman Suffrage Movement in Tennessee" beyond observing that suffragism came late to the South and had little impact before the twentieth century. After a swift four-and-a-half-page survey of the legal and political subjection of women in the nineteenth century, she plunged directly into the Tennessee story. The initial chapters construct the periodization now accepted as standard for the South as a whole: a few instances of bold women petitioning the legislature in the 1870s and 1880s, followed by a short-lived organization in the 1890s; decline and gradual rebirth of a permanent organization in the first decade of the twentieth century; significant growth and activity after 1912. Individual chapters documented the appearance of local leagues, the antisuffragist response, the effort to win municipal and presidential suffrage, and the bitter struggle by which Tennessee in 1920 became the crucial thirty-sixth state to ratify the Nineteenth Amendment.

Working without secondary sources, Taylor had no interpretations to challenge and offered none of her own. "The Woman Suffrage Movement in Tennessee" reflects the approach to history that she had learned under Fletcher Green at Chapel Hill: assembling the facts, structuring an "objective" narrative, and quoting rather than analyzing. Numerous themes that later historians of suffrage would develop into seminal hypotheses are visible in embryo in Taylor's research. Her extensive quotations reveal the shift in suffrage arguments from equal justice in the 1890s to the municipal housekeeping in the 1910s that Aileen Kraditor would elaborate on twenty years later. Taylor noted the presence of Woman's Christian Temperance Union activists among the first generation of suffragists and the endorsement by various women's clubs in the 1910s; Anne Firor Scott in *The Southern Lady* (1970) would explicitly link support for suffrage to previous involvement in the temperance and women's club movements.

When Taylor condensed her dissertation into an article, it was summarily rejected by "a regionally based journal with a national readership." The board of editors informed her that the subject did not merit space in a scholarly journal and suggested that she submit the piece to the American Association of University Women or the League of Women Voters. The newly established *Tennessee Historical Quarterly,* probably in need of manuscripts, proved more receptive, and "A Short History of the Woman Suffrage Movement in Tennessee" appeared in the fall of 1943. By then, Taylor had secured a teaching job, once again at a women's college—and because a male professor had left for the armed forces. Due to wartime travel restrictions, she joined the faculty at Texas State College for Women (now Texas Woman's University) in the small town of Denton, near Fort Worth, without an interview. She remained for nearly four decades.[7]

Taylor began her career at a time when the male-dominated profession expected little from the small number of women in the field, as a study of doctoral degree holders in history that was published while she was completing her dissertation made abundantly clear. Conceding that "taken as a whole, women taught in smaller and poorer schools, held fewer responsible positions, and, presumably carried heavier teaching loads for leaner salaries" (an exact description of Taylor's own situation), the two male authors went on to blame women themselves for being only half as productive as male scholars. Rather grudgingly, they admitted that the output for women degreed during the previous decade was rising—thirty percent were writing articles and thirty-six percent were writing books—before concluding superciliously that "the list of distinguished women scholars is not long."[8]

Taylor's early productivity foretold her eventual place on the list. She broke into print in 1941 with a short piece on the Judson Female Institute in the antebellum period, and in 1942 compressed her master's thesis into a two-part article for the *Georgia Historical Quarterly.*[9] By the spring of 1944 she had published her second suffrage article. During her dissertation research Taylor had discovered that Georgia's woman suffrage movement had begun in Columbus, her hometown, and interviewed the eighty-one-year-old sister of the movement's founder, who still lived there. Based largely on a small collection of papers that the sister had saved, and supplemented with newspaper accounts and NAWSA *Proceedings,* "The Origins of the Woman Suffrage Movement in Georgia," appeared in the *Georgia Historical Quarterly* in 1944.

All of Taylor's subsequent work followed the paradigm she established in 1943–1944. Delimiting suffragism as the formal activity of women working through equal rights associations, she produced state-by-state organizational histories published in regional quarterlies and the *Journal of Southern History*. Each painstakingly researched piece followed an archival trail that led through newspapers, legislative journals, interviews with surviving suffragists, and a smattering of manuscript collections. In the 1940s and 1950s the obstacles to gathering such material were formidable. Manuscript collections were scattered and often in private hands, newspapers and journals had not been microfilmed, and photocopiers did not exist. When she needed copies of entire documents Taylor photographed them and developed the prints herself.[10]

From the isolation of Denton, even researching the Texas movement was a challenge, especially during the war years when she had no car. The nearest research library was at Southern Methodist University, which meant a trip to Dallas via the interurban railway and a further bus journey to campus. Reading the *Dallas Morning News* necessitated weekend excursions to the newspaper's office, where Taylor went through the unindexed bound volumes page by page. Examining the records of the Texas Equal Suffrage Association, which filled several filing cabinets in the home of one of the leaders, required periodic trips to Austin, two hundred miles away, with an extra suitcase. Each time, Taylor took a load of papers back to Denton to work through, returning to exchange them for a new lot.[11] In her most productive decade, the 1950s, she published five articles: those on Texas, Arkansas, and Florida, and the last two parts of her three-part history of Georgia.

Ultimately, Taylor recovered the suffrage histories of eight Southern states in meticulous detail, assembling bone by bone the skeleton to which later historians would add flesh. Each article followed a consistent format, documenting the life cycle of the suffrage associations, the legislative histories of their (usually unsuccessful) bills, speeches by the leadership, membership figures, and organizational activities such as meetings and demonstrations. Collectively, they tell a disheartening story of a movement that began late, faced nearly insurmountable opposition from Southern politicians, and accomplished few of its stated goals. In the 1890s and early 1900s its leaders struggled without success to keep their fragile organizations viable. Stability was finally achieved in the 1910s, but none of the Southern equal rights associations was able to secure full enfranchisement for women.

Taylor did not consider herself to be writing women's history, which did not yet exist as a field; she wrote about a Progressive-era political movement focused on female actors. Decades later, a rising generation of women's historians would redefine politics to include the social reform activism of a vast network of female voluntary associations, through which some middle-class women gradually developed suffrage convictions. Lacking such a context, Taylor asked no questions about the identity of Southern suffragists, how they came to espouse the cause, or what influenced the timing of their movement in a region hostile to feminism.

Consequently, her approach is from the top down and her analysis spare. Her focus is the small number of elite women who guided the state associations and articulated a deeply felt sense of injustice at being deprived of equal citizenship. Nothing in her work suggests that they are "new women of the New South," a generation shaped by economic change, rising levels of education for women, and a female public culture emerging via church societies and secular clubs. Taylor's suffragists appear to descend instead from the ideological lineage of Elizabeth Cady Stanton, Susan B. Anthony, and other Northern antebellum feminists. Most commonly, she quotes Southern women demanding the ballot as a natural right; seldom are they heard speaking of a social or political agenda to which they might apply it.

Focusing tightly on organizational development and ideology, Taylor also left out practical politics, taking a Whiggish view of the progress of suffrage. Since no Southern suffragist chose to reveal herself in print as a successful tactician and lobbyist, Taylor did not explore the reasons behind their few victories. She does not present these Southern ladies as political strategists or ask why they managed to win primary suffrage in Arkansas (1917) and Texas (1918) and municipal and presidential suffrage in Tennessee (1919). The unstated assumption is that suffrage associations were simply stronger in these states, although in the case of Texas, at least, subsequent research has revealed that party factionalism enabled the suffragists to triumph.[12]

Taylor has been directly challenged for undervaluing the National Woman's Party in the South, the more ironically because she was herself an NWP member and president of the Texas chapter for a time in the 1940s. When the Ladies' Home Journal published Dr. Alice Hamilton's "Why I Am against the Equal Rights Amendment" in 1945, Taylor wrote a letter of protest to the editor, explaining in detail the legal inequalities that the ERA would remedy. She convinced the Denton chapter of the American Association of University Women, to which she also belonged, to endorse the ERA, even though the national AAUW actively opposed it.[13]

When Taylor began her research, the NWP papers were not yet available to scholars. Relying on the organization's own reports in The Suffragist, and on abundant quotations from Southern women decrying the NWP's militant demonstrations in Washington, she concluded that NAWSA's rival had little appeal in Dixie. Her later work, produced after the papers had been deposited in the Library of Congress, includes few citations to them. Undoubtedly her focus on formal organization and numerical growth influenced her relative neglect of the NWP; she correctly points out that membership numbers in

Southern branches were very small and organizational strength weak. Sidney Bland, however, has contended that numbers alone do not tell the story, arguing that the NWP's strong leaders and innovative campaign techniques did more to change minds than Taylor conceded.[14]

Living and working in the Jim Crow South, Taylor was predictably inattentive to the racial dimensions of her suffrage stories. Catherine Kenny's account in the *History of Woman Suffrage* of the remarkable cooperation between white and black women to elect a reform slate in Nashville in 1919 led Taylor, during her dissertation research, to Dr. Mattie Coleman, one of the African-American leaders. She did not find the real story; Coleman, for whatever reasons, chose to de-emphasize her own involvement. Based on the interview, Taylor concluded that while suffrage was often discussed at "Negro" meetings, such women did no organized work for the cause; research published more than half a century later tells a different tale.[15] When she turned her attention to Texas, Taylor did not mention the membership inquiry from an African-American women's club in the Equal Suffrage Association records, or the worried exchanges among the white leadership over how to handle it. Not even in passing did she ever note that Southern suffrage associations excluded black women; that would have been obvious and unremarkable to most of her generation.

As a careful historian, Taylor recorded the efforts of the 1890s suffrage generation to persuade their state constitutional conventions, which disfranchised African-Americans, to grant women the ballot as a means of ensuring white supremacy. But racial arguments, either for or against woman suffrage, are quoted thereafter as just one type among many. Even in the articles published after Aileen Kraditor indicted Southern suffragists for racism in *The Ideas of the Woman Suffrage Movement* (1965) Taylor offered no thesis about race, and she never addressed Kraditor's argument. It is impossible to tell from her detached and unanalytical narratives whether she considered Southern suffragists to be racially motivated or simply reacting defensively to antisuffragist race-baiting, as a number of scholars now argue.[16]

Taylor did much of her research and writing at a time when the profession had little regard for the history of women. It was 1951 before she managed to get a conference paper accepted, one of the first on suffrage to be read at the Organization of American Historians. Her dissertation languished, unpublished, for years, while both university and commercial presses informed her that it had no sales potential. She finally had it printed by Bookman Associates of New York in 1957. (In 1978 *The Woman Suffrage Movement in Tennessee* was reissued by Farrar, Strauss, and Giroux as part of its Octagon Books series of scholarly out-of-print works for which there is a continuing demand.) Southern historiography ignored women as a subject; in 1965 Taylor's two decades of scholarship were relegated to part of a footnote in Arthur S. Link and Rembert W. Patrick's *Writing Southern History.*[17]

She produced this body of work without sabbaticals, for which the Texas state university system makes no provision, and while teaching four courses per semester. Privately, she shared her frustration over the heavy workload of a small college with Mary Elizabeth Massey, who was similarly situated in South Carolina: "I'd like to see some of the big university boys, like [Allan] Nevins, stand up under the routine of such institutions as T.W.U. or Winthrop. They'd learn what it means to use the last ounce of energy to finish an article or even do a little research." Only the bequest of an aunt enabled her finally to take a year's leave of absence in 1974–1975. Her periodic efforts to relocate were frustrated by the limited opportunities for women in academia. The history chairman who responded that his department already *had* a woman professor summed up the obstacles that women of Taylor's generation faced.[18]

Despite the difficulties she encountered in a male-dominated profession and her strong support for women's rights, Taylor watched the rebirth of feminism in the 1960s and 1970s with mixed feelings. Stridency and confrontation were at odds with her upbringing as a Southern lady and incompatible with the cordiality she enjoyed with male colleagues. "I guess I like being a voice in the wilderness," she admitted to a close friend. "When feminism became fashionable, I ceased to be an activist." Taylor was not among the founders of the Caucus of Women in History (renamed the Southern Association for Women Historians in 1977) formed within the Southern Historical Association in 1970, but she contributed financial support at a time when few were willing to help. She presided at the first SAWH session to appear on the SHA program—a session accepted because she was willing to chair it.[19]

Taylor capped a long record of service to the SHA, including two terms on the executive council and chairing the Sydnor and Ramsdell Award committees, by heading the first Ad Hoc Committee on the Status of Women. The committee's 1982 report analyzed the existing data on female employment and graduate school admissions and concluded that the situation in the South was not uniquely difficult: women historians were universally disadvantaged. They were less likely to be hired into tenure-track jobs, more likely to hold part-time positions, and less well paid than male faculty.[20]

Although she was asked to continue as chair of the Ad Hoc Committee, Taylor declined a second term. She had retired from Texas Woman's University in 1981, after a thirty-eight-year career during which she received the university's Cornaro Award for teaching and scholarship and was named one of the state's Minnie Stevens Piper Professors. She subsequently moved back to Georgia, where she had always spent part of every summer, intending to concentrate full time on finishing her state suffrage studies. Alabama, Louisiana, Virginia, and Kentucky were still undone, and Taylor hoped ultimately to produce a regional synthesis. "If I live to be 100," she half joked, "I might make it."[21] She lived to be seventy-six, and did not.

The University Press of Mississippi offered her a contract in its Twentieth-Century America series for a volume that would bring together Taylor's previously published articles and the four yet to be written. As planned with series editor Dewey Grantham, the book was to include an introduction discussing the development of the suffrage movement in the United States and the South and a conclusion that summarized Southern state and regional patterns within the national context. Not wanting a deadline, Taylor declined to sign a contract, but she resolved to produce the manuscript.[22]

Although she had researched the remaining states and had a substantial draft for Louisiana, Taylor found it impossible in retirement to bring together the "magnus [sic] opus," as she invariably referred to the book. "Forty years ago I would have pushed right ahead and done it," she confided to a correspondent, lamenting that she seemed perpetually distracted by household maintenance and social obligations. With typical honesty she added, "but the chief culprit is me." She worried that the volume might not be well received, that "my style of research and writing (old-fashioned history) will be a mark against me." Proud that her articles were "solid history—informative and factual," she was defensively aware that the noninterpretive, untheoretical approach to historical writing that she had learned in graduate school was at odds with newer norms.[23]

While she struggled unsuccessfully with the "magnus opus," Taylor contributed to projects inspired by her scholarship. At the invitation of a publisher in Austin, Texas, she wrote a short retrospective of her career entitled "A Lifelong Interest." It became the introduction to *Citizens at Last: The Woman Suffrage Movement in Texas,* which reprinted Taylor's 1951 article together with a collection of primary documents. When the University Press of Kentucky reissued Paul Fuller's *Laura Clay and the Woman's Rights Movement in Kentucky* in 1992, Taylor wrote the foreword. She had helped nurture the book from its beginnings as a dissertation a quarter of a century earlier, urging Fuller to see it through and volunteering as a reader when the manuscript was being considered for publication. She followed and encouraged the progress of Marjorie Spruill Wheeler's dissertation, published in 1993 as *New Women of the New South: The Leaders of the Woman Suffrage Movement in the Southern States.*[24]

At the same time, she took satisfaction in the advances women had made in the historical profession. The Julia Cherry Spruill Professorship established at the University of North Carolina at Chapel Hill ("How the world has changed since my graduate school days!") and the growth and vitality of the

Southern Association for Women Historians were especially gratifying. In 1989 the SAWH honored Taylor's pioneering scholarship by establishing the A. Elizabeth Taylor Prize for the best article published in women's history; the first Taylor Prize was awarded in 1992.[25]

In 1990 Taylor was one of six scholars invited to speak at a symposium sponsored by the Tennessee Historical Society commemorating the seventieth anniversary of the Nineteenth Amendment and Tennessee's crucial role as the final ratifying state. The symposium papers became part of *Votes for Women! The Woman Suffrage Movement in Tennessee, the South, and the Nation*, edited by Marjorie Spruill Wheeler. Taylor finished the revisions on her essay, "Tennessee: The Thirty-Sixth State," a subject she had first investigated half a century earlier, shortly before her death on October 10, 1993. Dedicating *Votes for Women!* to Taylor's memory, Marjorie Wheeler summarized her importance to women's history and Southern history: "She was the first to focus attention upon the suffrage movement in the region; she continued to labor alone in this neglected field, state by state, article by article, until she published a body of scholarship that has served as a virtual encyclopedia for those . . . who have attempted to follow in her footsteps."[26]

David M. Potter

Lincoln, Abundance, and Sectional Crisis

DAVID S. HEIDLER AND JEANNE T. HEIDLER

David M. Potter dedicated his life to writing about and teaching history, doing so with such elegant style and penetrating understanding that by the time he died at age sixty-one many contemporaries regarded him as possibly the greatest historian to have lived in the twentieth century. It was an extraordinary accolade for a Georgia boy who in 1910 had been born in Augusta, a sleepy town on the Savannah River. Potter was a Southerner by nativity and by chance came of age in a place that persisted in calling the tumult of 1861 to 1865 "the War," with no need for elaboration. All other wars would need distinguishing names. "The War" did not; it marked the great Before and After for everything Southern and every Southerner, white or black, rich or poor, schooled or ignorant. When Potter took rank with the educated by graduating from Emory University in 1932, he had spent over two decades in a land that still felt itself shaped by a contest more than a half century past and many of whose white population still framed their days with murmured might-have-beens.

Perhaps that was why David Potter would eventually claim that he was no longer a Southerner. Instead he detached himself from his native region to write searching and objective works that explained the past—especially the past that embraced "the War"—with commendable objectivity nonetheless tempered by sharp perception. By the time he died in 1971, he had wandered far from the place itself to live a continent away, and to die there, on the Pacific Coast, as far from the South geographically as, by then, his South had moved psychologically from its defining moment, the one he understood so well.

He never said, at least in a public forum, when he ceased to be a Southerner.[1] "I lived," he wrote in 1968, "in the long backwash of the war in a land that remembered the past very vividly and somewhat inaccurately, because the present had nothing exciting to offer, and accuracy about either the past or the present was psychologically not very rewarding." His departure from the

South—after Emory he went to New Haven, Connecticut, to study under Ulrich B. Phillips, the celebrated historian who was then at Yale—placed him in a world removed from it and its habit of vivid but inaccurate memory.[2] Potter completed his master of arts degree at Yale and began his doctoral studies, during the course of which he taught at the University of Mississippi and then in 1938 at Rice Institute (now Rice University). He was a transient at both Oxford and Houston, however, and after he earned his doctorate in 1940, he was soon bound for other places. In 1942, he returned to Yale, this time as a member of the faculty. With the exception of a brief visiting professorship in 1969 at Stetson University in DeLand, Florida, he would never live in the South again. He would note three years before his death that he had "lived longer outside of the South than in it, and hopefully [had] learned to view it with detachment, though not without fondness."[3] The fondness would make the South a permanent fixture of his scholarly inquiry and the detachment would make that scholarship uniquely invaluable.

Potter spent nineteen years on the faculty at Yale. While there he would publish two of the three major books that established his reputation as one of the most important historians in the country. The first was a revision of his dissertation. *Lincoln and His Party in the Secession Crisis* set the tone for most of Potter's later work. Evident here was his belief that hindsight clouded an understanding of the past as much as unfounded speculation or prejudice did. So his analysis empathized with the perceptions of participants and observers. Only then, he thought, could one grasp the motives of those people who had lived through and made American history. Such was the key to his comprehension of why things happened the way they did.

Only thirty-two when he published *Lincoln and His Party in the Secession Crisis*, Potter nevertheless revealed remarkable maturity in his scholarship and analysis. The book examined the months between the election of Lincoln and the firing on Fort Sumter, concluding that there was no reason to blame those engulfed by the secession crisis for not avoiding the war. Historians from their vantage could see it all precisely because they knew how it had all turned out. Lincoln and fellow Republicans certainly knew after the fact that their failure to placate the South had led to war—though they doubtless would have put it differently. Yet the Republican party could not have anticipated that turn of events. This was a way of viewing the past from which Potter would never waiver. The important players in the sectional drama simply had chosen their paths based on what they knew at the time.

Potter provided more than a simple narrative that merely would have retold the actions of Lincoln and his party. He analyzed the complex, often overlapping, motives that moved these men into uncharted and perilous political territory. True enough, Lincoln's foremost desire was to preserve the Union, but

Potter repeatedly shows that Lincoln ultimately had no idea how to do so short of war. An elaborate analysis of the inner workings of the Republican party helped explain why. Potter reminded readers that the Republicans were a minority party that had never held power. Republicans could agree on anti-slavery, but they agreed on little else. Lacking a comprehensive and coherent policy, they were frustrated in their attempts to formulate one by numerous internal factions, each viewing the postelection crisis differently.

Most Republicans, however, did agree that secessionists were only bluffing. Southerners had been making the same threats for years and had never acted on them. Potter noted how most Northerners, Republicans included, believed that secessionist threats were nothing more than a design to extort concessions on slavery in the territories. Lincoln quietly assumed the leadership of his party by urging congressional Republicans to oppose any compromises that might expand slavery into the territories. In addition to violating the Republican Platform, such compromises would only tempt Southerners to lodge additional demands. Further, Lincoln believed treating with radical secessionists would strengthen them at the expense of Southern unionists. His strategy, developed after the election, was to act in such way as to invigorate Southern moderates so they could thwart the plans of the radicals.

Lincoln and his supporters persisted in this hope for Southern moderation even after seven states in the Deep South seceded. Because he really believed that most Southerners did not want disunion and that Southern unionists ultimately would prevail over extremists, rejecting compromises that might dull the desire to preserve union seemed altogether reasonable. In fact, Republicans did not think their choice was exclusively between compromise or conflict. Potter observed Lincoln consistently acting on the notion that supporting Southern unionism would preserve the nation without war.

On the whole, critics praised *Lincoln and His Party in the Secession Crisis.* One 1942 critic even expressed surprise that a Georgian could be unbiased in his treatment of Lincoln and the Republicans.[4] Yet some found fault, especially criticizing Potter for emphasizing Lincoln's peaceful intentions. Was it wise to reject the possibility that by April 1861 the president believed war was the only way to save the Union?[5] In his preface to the 1962 edition of the book, Potter answered the criticism with one of his own. Twenty years of reflection had not moved him from his original conclusion, and he remarked upon the subtle though essential difference between Lincoln believing that war was possible and Lincoln resigned to it as inevitable. Lincoln certainly had to accept by April 1861 that war was likely, so he had worked to position the Union as advantageously as he could for its survival. But that was a long way from his deliberately provoking the Confederacy into firing a shot that would start a war.[6]

Potter insisted that the compelling evidence was Lincoln's offer to evacuate Fort Sumter for a promise that the border states would not follow their Deep South neighbors. Such an offer, said Potter, belied any Lincoln plan to provoke a war with the Sumter crisis. Instead, the persistent belief in Southern unionism guided the president's actions and encouraged his counselors. Lincoln and William H. Seward could count: eight of the fifteen slave states remained in the Union after the inauguration. Unionism, in short, had prevailed so far in most of the South and who could say it would not eventually recover control of the seven seceded states when, as Lincoln had said, it was touched again by the better angels of everybody's nature.

Of course, the peace policy miscarried, but that did not indict it as a complete failure. Potter observed that Lincoln's primary goal—the preservation of the Union—left him with diminishing alternatives. Finally, his decision to resupply the fort was dictated by the need to face down Southern radicals, not a wish to animate them. The war came, according to Potter, as a consequence of Lincoln's action, but not necessarily because he had premeditated it.

Potter's first book established him as an important new voice in American historical studies. Yet this careful scholar would wait twelve years before publishing another book-length study of a single subject. Other activities mortgaged his time. In addition to his teaching duties at Yale, he delivered a prodigious number of speeches and lectures at scholarly meetings. He became a prolific writer of essays, journal articles, and book reviews. These shorter pieces gave seed time to many of his later ideas, but they also immediately produced discussion and controversy. Historians, inspired by Potter, began to employ new methods to explore a whole new range of historical issues.

The potential for such new methods of historical inquiry became evident in Potter's next major work. In 1954, he published *People of Plenty: Economic Abundance and the American Character*. Taken from the Walgreen Lectures he had delivered at the University of Chicago four years earlier, *People of Plenty* took an old idea and boldly illuminated it with a new kind of light. The exercise created a stir in the academic community.

Potter said nothing original when he posited that Americans were different from everybody else because of their uninterrupted enjoyment of material abundance. The bountiful natural resources of North America had played a part in shaping American character, but Potter concluded that the American experience with and relationship to those resources had inspired Americans to produce economic growth in other areas.

The theory itself had long had many detractors, and Potter's revival of it alone produced controversy. But his method of inquiry excited even more argument. Some historians doubted the existence of a unique American character, and others who acknowledged it could not agree about its origins. Historical inquiry had failed to provide answers, so Potter turned to the methods of social scientists. Those methods could first reveal the actuality of group character and then explain how it had formed. In a historical setting social science could establish with strict rules of evidence whether a unique American character existed. And if it did exist, social science could tell us why.

The social sciences, said Potter, could bring a singularly pertinent perspective to the questions surrounding national character and thereby complement the unsatisfactory inquiries of history. Precisely because anthropology, sociology, and psychology provided the tools to explain the phenomenon of group character, these disciplines should be better utilized by the historian when examining social history. The anthropologist could contribute a greater understanding of human culture, the sociologist a broader knowledge of group behavior, and the psychologist a better sense of character formation.

Some reviewers saw Potter's work as a ground-breaking effort at interdisciplinary studies that would "rank high among the significant books that have influenced historical interpretation in the United States."[7] Yet others castigated Potter's approach as a lazy way of doing history. Fred A. Shannon in the *Mississippi Valley Historical Review* not only doubted the existence of a single American character but also questioned the abundance that Potter identified as its shaping force. Shannon concluded his caustic review by stating that the book hardly constituted a historical work.[8] In spite of these criticisms, it remained undisputed that Potter's contribution to a more interdisciplinary approach to history and his careful analysis of the American experience made a substantial contribution to the American historiographical debate. He roused historians and social scientists to discuss the validity of his conclusions, but he also shook the complacent from their preconceived notions of historical method.

Potter began *People of Plenty* by examining the historical scholarship on American character and the debate regarding the existence of such a thing as a national character and surveying the work of those historians who did accept its existence. Having so far pursued his subject down an orthodox path of inquiry, he broke away from standard method with a will. Following his survey of the historical literature was an analysis of the development of the social sciences, especially in the twentieth century, and how these disciplines approached the issue of character in individuals as well as in groups. He then argued persuasively for the incorporation of these disciplines into historical studies particularly when those studies dealt with group behavior.

Having established this argument as his framework, Potter began part two of his study with his view of the nature of American abundance, how that abundance affected the perception of mobility in American society, the development of democratic government in the United States, and America's seeming mission to spread that democracy to other parts of the world. These reasonably cohesive arguments gave way to a digressive chapter on the relationship between his theory of abundance and Frederick Jackson Turner's "Frontier Thesis." Also he included a chapter relating how American abundance had contributed to the development of the American advertising industry and how that industry, in turn, affected American abundance. Potter brought the subject to a congruous close, though, with the final chapter on how abundance in America had shaped character in this country both for the individual and the nation.

Because it was such a new way of investigating an old subject, Potter's *People of Plenty* warrants some parsing. His systematic survey of American historiography on the subject of a national character and his description of the evolution of the social sciences were themselves notable contributions to the literature. Yet, it was in the second part of his study—really the heart of the book—that Potter achieved his best stride by relating several highly conceptual premises with admirable clarity. Beginning with his interpretation of the nature of American abundance, he explained that even during the days when the first American colonies struggled for survival, Europeans viewed North America as a virtual promised land flowing with milk and honey. It was an image so persistent that it endured from the colonial to the early national period and remained a force of considerable power in modern times.

Potter argued, however, that a continuing American abundance was the result of actions that went beyond the mere availability of natural resources in North America. It was how Americans used those resources that produced the tremendous abundance of the twentieth century. Ineffable qualities of hard work, individualism, and ingenuity contributed as much to the American enjoyment of plenty as did material well-being.

According to Potter, American society encouraged these laudable traits in part because of its extraordinary social mobility. Social mobility was inextricably tied to the American concept of equality, and consequently Americans never viewed themselves as finished products. Individuals never regarded themselves as part of a particular class because they never felt permanently fixed in their current situation.

This attitude bolstered a dedication to the equality of opportunity, allowing individuals to rise to however high their talents and hard work would take them. The opportunity for mobility itself produced a dynamic incentive for improvement. It became an obligation to better one's status. Failure to do so revealed deficiencies in the individual, not society. Thus the perception of America as a classless society conceived a fundamental belief that every individual could prosper if diligent and resolved.

As he was concluding his research in the 1950s, Potter saw profound changes permeating the culture of plenty. An American class system was not only being actualized, it was becoming increasingly rigid. An enduring belief in social mobility without its realization would frustrate large numbers of Americans, and the unhappy result would be a peculiar kind of class conflict. Because Americans never had felt they belonged to a particular group, when mired in one they were more likely to suffer alienation because of a lack of status. Not belonging in American society, Potter argued, produced the greatest anxieties of all. And it was the modern manifestations of abundance that promised to change things in other aspects of American life as well, and not always for the good. He believed the new plenty was responsible for the growth of the aggressive advertising industry. To create a demand proportionate to the profusion of goods, the United States paid out more per household on advertising than it did on education.

Yet in sum *People of Plenty* was an optimistic work, for Potter still believed the cornerstone of American society and government rested on the possibility of individual improvement. In fact, more than anything else abundance was responsible for American democracy. Potter asserted that abundance produced the best breeding ground for a democratic system. "Economic abundance," he declared, "is conducive to political democracy."[9]

The observation was key to understanding why the American mission to export democracy had so often failed. Countries lacking abundance also lacked the context of plenty, so that they seldom grasped the larger meaning of affluence. In essence, they remained basically poor countries with a lot of material things. Americans believed erroneously that American manufactures would inspire emulation of American political habits, but Potter concluded that nothing more had happened than the export of goods unaccompanied by any shred of the ethos that made those goods abundantly available.

Potter saw modern forms of American abundance as only the latest American bounty, but that did not disguise the fact that it had all started with the land. From that vantage, he saw merit in Frederick Jackson Turner's "Frontier Thesis," viewing it as an early articulation of the role of abundance in American history. He correctly interpreted Turner's theory as an explanation of all of American history rather than only that of the West, but he argued that "American development and the American character are too complex to be explained by any single factor."[10]

Potter concluded *People of Plenty* by closing the circle, returning to the social sciences to analyze how abundance in American life had shaped the character of individual Americans. He believed that the same factors that shaped the United States had shaped the American family and hence the way American children were reared in that society. American children were fed more, lived in homes with central heating and indoor plumbing apart from an extended family, and were more comfortably clothed than children anywhere else in the world. And just as these aspects of an American child's environment were a result of abundance, from the upbringing of a single individual to the development of the entire nation, Potter saw abundance as America's defining characteristic.

Following the publication of *People of Plenty*, Potter continued a habit of high activity in his profession and immersion in his studies. His devotion to work had already taken a personal toll. His marriage to Ethelyn E. Henry had lasted only six years, ending in divorce in 1945. Even after remarrying in 1948, he commenced a taxing schedule of visiting professorships and lecture presentations that had him gathering honors and accolades as he traveled extensively. In 1947–1948, he was the Harmsworth Professor of American History at Queen's College, Oxford, from which post his inaugural lecture, "The Lincoln Theme and American National Historiography," would be published in 1948. He became the Coe Professor of American History at Yale in 1951 and was a visiting professor at Connecticut College in 1947 and at the University of Wyoming in 1952 and again in 1955, sandwiching in a visiting stint at the University of Delaware in 1954. Preceding his move to Stanford in 1961, also as the Coe Professor of American History, he visited that institution in 1957 and 1958 and was a visitor on the faculty at Stetson University in DeLand, Florida, in 1959. Along the way, he had picked up honorary degrees from the University of Wyoming (1955) and from his Atlanta alma mater, Emory University (1957).

His scholarly activity also increased in the form of lectures, papers at scholarly meetings, journal articles, and book reviews. Many of these shorter pieces amounted to trial balloons of the ideas that would later emerge in his masterwork, *The Impending Crisis*. Others would appear later in the collections published as books before and after his death.

In *The South and the Sectional Conflict* (1968), Potter brought together a collection of essays, most previously published, that addressed general topics and specific areas to which he would return later. The first three essays examined the nature of the South and how the nature of "Southernness" fit into historians' use of and definition of nationalism. The next three analyzed the entire literature on the South and the sectional conflict, a job for which no one in the 1960s was better equipped than David Potter.

The book's final section consisting of five essays addressed diverse aspects of that sectional conflict and the Civil War it spawned. In "John Brown and the Paradox of Leadership among American Negroes," Potter concluded that Brown had failed in his climactic attempt to incite slave rebellion at Harpers Ferry because he was deaf to those people he wanted to lead. In the essay entitled "Horace Greeley and Peaceable Secession," Potter argued that Greeley's oft-quoted statement in his November 9, 1860, *New York Tribune* editorial that "we insist on letting them [the slave states] go in peace" had been misinterpreted to mean that Greeley willingly accepted the dissolution of the Union.[11] By examining the qualifiers Greeley placed on this statement and parsing earlier and later editorials and letters, Potter resolved that Greeley never really accepted the validity of peaceful separation.

"Why the Republicans Rejected Both Compromise and Secession" was a reprise of Potter's first book, *Lincoln and His Party in the Secession Crisis,* but the essay "Jefferson Davis and the Political Factors in Confederate Defeat" explored new territory, moving beyond the sectional conflict to examine the policies of Jefferson Davis as president of the Confederacy.

The most masterful performance, however, was the final essay in the collection, "The Civil War in the History of the Modern World: A Comparative View." With this probing and insightful analysis Potter could rightly lay claim to the assessment by some contemporaries that he was one of the greatest American historians of his generation. Foreshadowing the work of the comparative historians of the 1990s, Potter addressed the parochialism of many colleagues by placing the American Civil War in a global context. "The War" was an important event in the history of the world, not just the United States.

Critics lauded the collection. In fact, according to Chase C. Mooney, *The South and the Sectional Conflict* placed Potter in the "first rank of American historians."[12] And it was true that Potter's research and analysis that addressed such a wide range of topics clearly signaled the tremendous insights that would make his next and last major project his greatest work.

People of Plenty was to be the last book-length study David Potter would complete, although in 1954 he began work on what became his magnum opus. When he died in 1971, Potter had completed in draft form all but the last two chapters of this new work. Don E. Fehrenbacher, a friend and colleague at Stanford, edited the manuscript and completed the final two chapters so that the book was ready for publication five years after Potter's death. When the long-awaited *Impending Crisis* appeared in 1976, it was hailed as a masterpiece of analysis and interpretation.

Potter in this work again insisted that no one could understand participants' motivations in the tragic trace toward war without abandoning the wisdom of hindsight. As he had stated in *Lincoln and His Party in the Secession Crisis,* Potter repeated in *The Impending Crisis* that the major actors in the sectional drama neither wanted nor foresaw war. In that recapitulation, *Impending Crisis* provided an appropriate conclusion to Potter's scholarly career. At the start of his studies, Potter had argued that the Republican rejection of compromise after the election of 1860 did not necessarily mean a choice for war; in this last major work, Potter presented compelling evidence that during the tumultuous years spanning 1848 to 1861, the country's leadership dealt with major issues

from this safe, comfortable albeit illusory perspective. Nothing they did necessarily anticipated that their decisions would lead to a civil war.

Clearly the territory gained from the Mexican-American War revived the
slavery question and brought on the national crisis of 1850. The Compromise
of 1850 temporarily calmed tempers, but the territorial issue that emerged in
1848 would remain a barely scabbed sore all through the remaining years of
peace. Potter agreed, but he repeatedly insisted that nobody could have fore-
seen these results. He showed that a significant number of the senators who
voted to ratify the Treaty of Guadalupe Hidalgo did so to end a war they
opposed, not to acquire more territory. They were the last to anticipate the
crisis of 1850, let alone the one a decade later.

Potter used this fundamental finding to interpret the real meaning of the
crucial period. When the organization of the Mexican Cession caused a tumult in 1848, neither proslavery forces nor Free Soilers were prepared for it,
and neither could fathom the vehemence of their opponents. The next two
years proved for Potter that there was neither a Northern nor a Southern conspiracy, but he could also see how the charged atmosphere made it seem so.
Southerners regarded Northern solidarity in Congress on issues such as the
Wilmot Proviso and the slave trade in Washington, D.C., as a clear indication
of the growing influence of the abolitionists. At the same time, Northern congressmen were alarmed by John C. Calhoun's efforts to form a Southern party.
Calhoun's initiative failed, but not for want of trying. Southerners frequently
had met, darkly discussed solidarity, and by consequence appeared to be con-
cocting a Southern conspiracy.[13] When radical Southerners succeeded in calling a Southern convention, Northerners were confirmed in their suspicions.
Throughout his analysis of the controversy in 1850, Potter iterated this theme
of perceptions governing behavior. Reality had ceased to matter. Southerners
saw a growing Northern conspiracy to destroy their way of life and promulgate
race war. Northerners saw a Southern attempt to bypass the democratic system by foisting a slave system on an unwilling people. The belief in the conspiratorial impulse of their opponents, rather than real events, led to the crisis
threatening the union in 1850.

Southern disunion, however, frightened moderates, and President Zachary
Taylor's refusal to concede to Southern demands raised the specter of civil war.
Potter argued that reasonable men rushed to the middle ground of compromise from an exaggerated fear of Southern unity. Yet, it seemed the conspiratorial forces were in full flower—whether Northern or Southern depended on
one's point of view—when Northerners and Southerners working separately
defeated Henry Clay's Omnibus Bill. Stephen Douglas's shrewd legislative
plan to separate the Omnibus Bill into components and secure their individual
passage with shifting majorities appeared to be a design to thwart the "con-

spiracies," a triumph of moderation over extremism. Neither moderates nor extremists on both sides could know, said Potter, that they had only postponed the crisis.

To the men who had made it, there was a finality to the compromise. When other issues arose that threatened sectional accord, such as the route for a transcontinental railroad, most people saw them as less serious than the divisive arguments resolved in 1850. Potter insisted that the 1850s did not move inexorably toward a climax. Instead, the country debated issues, such as the railroad, without underlying motives regarding slavery. Consequently, Stephen Douglas should not be vilified for pushing through the Kansas-Nebraska Act that repealed the Missouri Compromise, for he could not have predicted the mess that would result from a political deal traditionally brokered and sealed.

Per Potter, the victory enjoyed by Franklin Pierce in 1852 was so seemingly national that it lulled both parties into a deadly complacency. They ignored the courtship by Northern Democrats and Whigs of Free Soilers; they did not see the alliance made between Southern Democrats and Whigs and radical proslavery interests. Initially, Whigs suffered most from these sectional divisions, partially because Southern Whigs regarded Zachary Taylor's posture in 1850 as rank apostasy. The slow death of the Whig party, accelerated to consummation by the Kansas-Nebraska Act, led to the formation of the Republican party and created the illusion of unity within the Democrats, if only because it was the only national party remaining.

Just how illusory that unity was became increasingly apparent after the election of 1856, but Potter again warned that the disintegration of the Democracy was more apparent to modern observers than it was to those who experienced it. As "Bleeding Kansas," the *Dred Scott* decision, and finally Brown's raid at Harpers Ferry drove deeper wedges into the brittle party, most Democrats believed that moderates would prevail and wounds would heal. Potter observed that other divisive issues preoccupied the nation and often provoked the same alarm as the sectional discord over slavery. We know that the Panic of 1857 and the growing tide of nativism did not bring on the upheaval that the slavery controversy eventually did, but to the people of the 1850s, these controversies were as important as any arguments over slavery.

When the Democrats split at the Charleston and Baltimore conventions in 1860, thus all but guaranteeing a Republican victory in November, most people still did not believe disunion was inevitable. Returning to themes developed in *Lincoln and His Party in the Secession Crisis,* Potter explained that even after Lincoln's election, moderates on both sides expected a compromise to defuse the crisis. Republicans, however, had heard Southern threats of disunion for so long they did not feel compromise was necessary to preserve the union.

The Impending Crisis closed, as Potter had done three decades earlier, arguing that Abraham Lincoln did not start the Civil War by resupplying Fort Sumter. The president knew that war was a possibility, but he neither tricked the Confederacy into firing the first shot nor backed away from the potential consequences of his actions. Like everyone else in this grand drama, Lincoln weighed the hazards and acted. Only time revealed the results.

Critics enthusiastically received this extraordinary work. Maurice G. Baxter was representative in his praise of Potter for the "thorough presentation of evidence" and "the sophisticated interpretation of its meaning."[14] And when *The Impending Crisis* received the Pulitzer Prize for history in 1977, the triumph sustained what many had already embraced as inescapable truth: the author had been dead for over half a decade, but his extraordinary perspicacity and unparalleled gift for cogent analysis yet endured.

Just as Fehrenbacher had labored to midwife this last of Potter's great contributions to historical interpretation, he and other colleagues worked to collect and publish several collections of Potter's essays, both those previously published as articles or book reviews and the manuscripts from presentations delivered at conferences. *History and American Society*, edited by Fehrenbacher, appeared in 1973.[15] The volume, which had been in the planning stages before Potter's death, demonstrated the striking diversity of his historical interests. Loosely organized around the two themes of history as a profession and America as a society, essays covered topics that ranged from historical research to profiles of specific historians to speculations on the role of national character in history. In one ground-breaking essay, first published in 1962, Potter addressed the importance of women in any discussion about national character. Specifically, Potter questioned traditional methods of determining national attitudes by examining exclusively male perspectives and then projecting them as representative of the entire population. Urbanization and the advent of machines had obviously changed the role of women in modern society, but Potter concluded that notions of female subordination still impeded strides toward equality. Such notions either were strangely persistent in some cases or had been invigorated by the transformation of women from processors to consumers of goods. In any case, Potter resolved that the place of women in the American historical experience was not merely a subject for special inquiry by specialized historians. It should be taken "as a coordinate major part of the overall, comprehensive study of the American character as a whole."[16]

Two other collections published after Potter's death gave wider voice to his sparkling lecture presentations. Potter's Walter Lynwood Fleming Lectures, delivered in 1968 and published in 1972, appeared under the title *The South and the Concurrent Majority*.[17] In the carefully argued manner that had become his trademark, Potter explained the idea of John C. Calhoun's concurrent majority and how it failed. Yet, Potter showed how the "Solid South" with its reflexive allegiance to the Democratic party had combined with the congressional seniority system and adopted careful use of the filibuster to dominate national legislation until the New Deal. Potter concluded that the expansion of the Democratic party during the New Deal had spelled the end of Southern dominance. The region's representatives were consequently unable to block the civil rights legislation of the 1960s.

Finally in 1976 a collection entitled *Freedom and Its Limitations in American Life* was drawn from Potter's 1963 Commonwealth Fund Lectures at University College, London.[18] He had returned to many of the themes of *People of Plenty,* arguing that a lack of status in American society obliged people to conform to prevent their alienation. This compelling need to conform, he wryly noted, could only but fetter freedom. With its appearance in this final collection of his work the observation, rendered almost as a warning, gave fitting close to a career in scholarship that had never succumbed to the ordinary and had never parroted the tenets of mere consensus.

David Potter never sought popular acclaim. Instead, he aimed his brilliant analytical observations at influencing the scholarly community. His vivid prose style and his sense for the drama of history, however, saw him read perhaps more widely than one would think by a public that enjoyed the deft talent of an accomplished stylist. When cancer finally killed him in 1971, he closed a life occasionally marked by stunning tragedy—his second wife, Dilys Mary Roberts, committed suicide in 1969—but one that was also inscribed with a ceaseless devotion to truth in scholarship and the avoidance of pretense in professorship. His students at all the institutions he graced with his presence revered him, marking him as mentor and friend, both a wise counselor and an unassuming advocate. His colleagues lavished such praise that one so modest as Potter must have found it vaguely embarrassing. When he died, he was the president of both the American Historical Association and the Organization of American Historians, posts reserved for the most honored and most honorable of the profession.

By the end of his life, Potter claimed that his youthful ties to the South were so vestigial that he did not regard himself as a Southerner anymore. And it was true that after his undergraduate days at Emory, he was in residence in the South only briefly afterward. In spite of being so long from the place where he grew up, however, Potter would insist that he was "not yet completely denatured."[19] And he would explain that "as a student of the South, I have sometimes tried to explain aspects of the Southern experience to myself by writing about them."[20]

Not being completely denatured, though, meant more than just a perennial fascination with a place or occasionally musing in print as a path to revelation about that place. It meant the lyric of the place, the gentle congeniality of its rhythms, the imbued sense of words as great messengers, and the past as not only vivid but worth remembering, accurately and wholly. Emerging from "the long backwash of the war," David Potter understood that history was not the stuff of faceless forces and disembodied trends, and he wrote about the past with the unwavering resolve to commend it to his and future generations with its uncertainties intact and its humanity real. It was a noble goal, one worthy of the gentleman who so gracefully pursued it.

David Herbert Donald

Southerner as Historian of the Nation

JEAN H. BAKER

In 1976 David Herbert Donald contributed an unusual op-ed piece to the *New York Times* entitled "The Southernization of America." By this bicentennial year, it was rare that a scholar ever left the ivory tower to write for a newspaper. For decades the general audience American historians claimed in the nineteenth century had dwindled with the disappearance of exciting multivolume narratives of broad scope and dramatic writing. Instead, contemporary historians studded their monographs with complex statistics and learned methodologies in volumes that gathered dust on the bookshelves of other authorities and their students.

Unlike his colleagues, Donald rarely wrote such history. While it was unusual for historians to seek a wider audience and to consider the South as the trailblazing part of the United States, Donald had never limited himself to a single scholarly format, ranging instead from articles, biographies, monographs, textbooks, reviews, and essays to pictorial histories of the Civil War. By 1976 his bibliography also included several new editions of overlooked or out-of-print diaries and compilations of letters to which he added graceful introductions. Thus for him to publish a revised version of a commencement address on the editorial pages of the *New York Times* was hardly unusual. Rather, it was his argument that was exceptional.

Wrote Donald: "[A] century after the Civil War and Reconstruction, the United States has finally decided to rejoin the South. . . . In every aspect of American life Southern influences have become dominant."[1] Using evidence from historiography, literature, the economy, and (in a presidential-election year when Georgian Jimmy Carter won the presidency) politics, Donald defined two Souths. One was the violence-prone, racist region below the Mason-Dixon line where Theodore Bilbo and Bull Connor held court; the other "a real South of goodness and decency whose inhabitants, black as well as white, have a deep sense of attachment to place, a strong feeling of kinship and a profound belief in their God. . . . We must make sure that the future histori-ans can write that when the United States finally rejoined the South in 1976, it was in order to affiliate with this nation's humanity, its sense of community and its deep dependence upon the Almighty."

Donald's argument was classically iconoclastic. For years he had been ap-preciated as the foremost contrarian of his time—a scholar with the insightful brilliance and profound understanding of the evidence to turn the conven-tional wisdoms of the academy on their head. Never was his historical imagi-nation stunted by what Harold Bloom once called "the anxiety of influence," and he left to others the task of historical landfill, that is, accumulating evi-dence for existing arguments. As an interpretation of contemporary society, what was unusual about the "Southernization of America" was Donald's sum-mary view of a process that others had previously noted only in fragments such as discussions of the growth and maturity of Southern cities.

But there was another unfamiliar feature of his essay. In terms of Donald's personal world what surprised was his identification with his roots. In "The Southernization of America," he wrote of "*we* Southerners," "*my* Northern-born friends," and jokingly "*our* Confederate money," as he offered "*our* erring sisters of the North" an invitation to rejoin *his* South.

In fact, David Donald has spent a lifetime with his back to the South, heading northward from Mississippi. After twenty-five years spent teaching at primarily Columbia, Princeton, and Johns Hopkins Universities, in 1973 he settled professionally at that most Yankee institution of higher learning, Har-vard University, living nearby in Lincoln, Massachusetts. Donald's work re-flects his migration. Although his field is the Civil War and Reconstruction, rarely has he concentrated on the staples of Southern historians, that is, con-tinuity and change and that region's similarity to, or divergence from, the rest of the nation. Nor has he focused on race. Twice a Pulitzer winner in biogra-phy, he has never written the life story of a Southerner of the Civil War period. In fact, Donald seems to have identified with William Herndon, the subject of his first biography. Herndon once told a friend: "I am a Southerner—born on Southern soil, reared by Southern parents, but I have always turned New England–wards for my ideas, my sentiments, my education."[2]

Even a casual content analysis of Donald's work suggests that Southern-only topics represent less than fifteen percent of his historical writing. Instead, from the beginning of a long publishing career that now spans fifty-five years, he has emphasized the importance of national topics, seeking to integrate into an American framework those issues and time periods such as Reconstruction that have become the staples of historical versions of "Reading Southern His-tory." In Donald's approach to history as well as his personal life his sec-tional roots are implanted in national dispositions and instincts. "I am pretty rootless," he declared recently, "a hothouse plant that adapts to pretty much any climate as long as it is academic."[3] But if Donald's Mississippi roots do not define his subject matter in the way that similar antecedents do other Southern-born historians, they certainly provided a background for the way he thinks about the American past.

David Herbert Donald was born in Goodman, Mississippi, in 1920 on a large farm just beyond the margins of the famous Mississippi Delta where the richest plantations of the South were located and the loamy soil produced as much as a bale of cotton an acre. Never so prosperous, eastern Holmes County, the rural county where he was born near the Big Black River, was too far from the Yazoo River to benefit from the rich, sediment-filled soil deposited during its periodic floodings. In 1920 sixty percent of the 24,831 residents of the county were white; forty percent were black. Few of the latter owned land, and whites, almost all of whom were engaged in agriculture, owned farms between twenty and forty acres in size.

Donald's paternal grandfather was a dirt farmer who had started with a small holding that guaranteed for his family no more than a hardscrabble life on the margins of poverty. Donald's father, benefiting from hard work, effective economic management, and high prices during World War I, amassed substantial holdings of over 1,500 acres to which he added another farm of 1,000 acres in nearby Attala County when Donald was a young boy. Here he raised cotton and corn, using mules, not machines, for tilling and plowing. The corn fed the mules, and the cotton, which Donald can remember stacked in bales in his backyard, was the cash crop. The land was rented to black share-croppers who lived in rough cabins on his place. It was a classic Southern setting, and it afforded the Donald family a middle-class rural status that survived the boll weevil, the introduction of the cotton picker, the migration of Mississippi blacks north, and the fluctuation of cotton prices.[4]

It also permitted sufficient affluence for the Donalds to send their son to Millsaps College in Jackson, Mississippi; in fact, Donald's mother encouraged higher education for all her children. It was she who diluted the implacable Southern culture of a childhood spent in what Mississippians proudly call "the most Southern place on earth."[5] The daughter of a Union cavalry lieutenant in the First Vermont Regiment who had settled in Acona, Mississippi, after the Civil War with the purpose of teaching school, Sue Ella Belford attended Mississippi State College for Women in Columbus. At a time when women were "feminizing" American education, she found a job as a teacher at Goodman High School. In Goodman, a town of less than a thousand, she met Ira Unger Donald, who had never gone to high school, instead completing his book learning with the eight grades of elementary and middle school. Their romance survived the comments of his relatives that "her daddy was a Yankee."[6] Besides lessons in the importance of education, this mother's legacy to her son was that of a mixed sectional heritage and a duality of perspective that is apparent in Donald's approach to historical themes.

Arguably, there was no better place in the United States than Mississippi from which to observe contrast and ambiguity. A state where, in 1920, stately plantations existed next door to primitive shacks and where frequently neither had indoor plumbing, the Mississippi of Donald's youth was a land of disparities that served as an observation tower onto national paradoxes. The high proportion of blacks to whites in a community that applied white supremacy in a nation seeking, on paper, racial equality; the variation in the state's landscape from fertile fields of cotton in the west to sandy soil and piney woods in the east; the unremitting dedication of state officials to the Democrats in a supposedly competitive two-party system; the denial of the constitutionally guaranteed vote to black males; and even the survival of the rhetoric of states' rights doctrines during the New Deal—all were part of a landscape of contradiction and irony. "Humankind cannot bear very much reality," David Donald once said, quoting T. S. Eliot, and growing up in Mississippi had taught him that lesson.[7]

From such a background Donald fashioned his own paradoxes. He is a historian who crafts the kind of brilliant prose usually associated with novelists; he is a Southerner who chooses national themes; he is a son of the South who kept moving north until he reached New England; he is an ambitious scholar whose youth was spent in a state rarely associated with the ethic of hard work; he is married to Aida DiPace, a New Yorker with a doctorate from the University of Rochester. He has made significant contributions to both the techniques and practices of the historical profession, even as he has experimented with different approaches and fashioned sometimes contradictory interpretations intended as much to intrigue as to convince.

A courtly gentleman of impeccable manners who sent his future wife roses weekly during their courtship, he proved a stern dissertation adviser to his worshipful graduate students. Their egos were often shattered by his devastating criticisms of their work. But unlike all the king's men of Humpty Dumpty folklore, David Donald always set his students up again, restoring their confidence and serving, along with his role as an intellectual counselor, as their agent and promoter. At a time when university professors seemed more interested in their own publications than their students' seminar papers, Donald provided prompt—and searching—commentary, even while he became one of the most productive American historians of the twentieth century.

Donald graduated from Millsaps College, a small Methodist, liberal arts institution, in 1941. Majoring in history, he studied there with Vernon Wharton, who was also a Millsaps graduate as well as a historian of the first rank.

During Donald's years in college Wharton was writing a history of blacks in Mississippi. It was Wharton who turned Donald's attention to the then neglected field of the Civil War and Reconstruction, and it was also Wharton who encouraged further graduate training for his exceptional undergraduate.

Beginning a lifelong pattern, twenty-one-year-old Donald went north to Urbana, Illinois, following the line of the Illinois Central Railroad, which ran through Goodman, the whistle of its trains ever a reminder of other places and other things. Years later, rereading Thomas Wolfe, Donald was touched by Wolfe's "magnificent recreation of locomotives snaking their way north."[8] Except for visits, like Wolfe, David Donald would not go home again.

At the University of Illinois, Donald entered a respected program in American history, completing his doctorate in 1946. It was the age of apprenticing when earnest young men sat at the feet of their professors, gratefully checking the footnotes of these heroes, compiling their bibliographies, and tracking down historical clues for their books. Donald served his assistantship with one of the great Civil War historians of the twentieth century, James G. Randall, who had grown up in the border state of Indiana. As Wharton had introduced Donald to the historian's natural habitat of revisionism through his study *The Negro in Mississippi, 1865–1890,* so Randall, who was writing the first volumes of *Lincoln the President,* led Donald to an understanding of a form both men mastered: the biography. Years later, accepting the Lincoln Prize in 1996, Donald paid tribute to Randall: "he quite unconsciously taught me most of what I know about how a historian works and thinks."[9]

The influence of Wharton, Randall, and graduate courses at the University of Illinois in statistics and sociology were apparent in Donald's early publications. The famous sociologist Florian Znaniecki was then teaching at the University of Illinois, and his detailed data collection about, and analyses of, Polish peasants based on their life histories provided a model for the kind of empirical evidence and prosopography that Donald would apply to historical topics. In a profession that sometimes consigns its practitioners to long pauses before (and after) their first publications, David Donald was a fast starter. As it turned out, he would also be a long-distance runner of durability and stamina with an influential array of publications on diverse subjects produced over a long career.

Published in the prestigious *Journal of Southern History* two years before Donald received his doctorate, "The Scalawag in Mississippi Reconstruction" revised the standard interpretation of the "renegade white men . . . who were the veritable Esaus of the Caucasian race." At least in Mississippi—and Donald's methodology and conclusions were duplicated elsewhere—scalawags who cooperated with the new governments were former Whigs, not unprincipled traitors to their race and section. In many cases they had been wealthy, reputable citizens in their antebellum communities, like James Alcorn, and were anti-Democratic as much as pro-Republican. Only distortion could fashion them into native Simon Legrees raised to prominence by the chaos of the Civil War, as Southern myth had done.[10]

Donald's interpretation of policies known as the Mississippi Plan was less enduring. As he saw it in 1944, these efforts to disenfranchise blacks had been simplified, in some history books, into an attempt to intimidate blacks. Donald believed this conclusion simplified the intent of the legislature. In his view, the Mississippi Plan was intended to create a coalition of all Southern whites within one party—a political union of the whites who had been divided during the postwar period.[11]

In "The Scalawag in Mississippi Reconstruction" and three later articles on solely Southern topics, Donald focused on an essential question of Southern history, the degree to which the South changed or stayed the same after the Civil War. From his now-Northern perspective he found continuity and persistence in everything from politics to economics. The views in an article on Confederate soldiers as "fighting men" written in 1959 when Donald was teaching at Columbia University ran counter to the heroic images held by twentieth-century Southerners of their revered "rebels." Instead, Donald's deromanticized Southern soldiers resembled fighting men everywhere at any time, from Caesar's legionnaires to Billy Yank, their adversary on the battlefields of the Civil War. By no means unique, Confederate fighting men were no more courageous nor cowardly than "all soldiers in all wars."[12]

In his 1965 inaugural address as Harmsworth Professor at England's Oxford University, Donald dealt with the same theme of continuities before and after the war, along with the other unavoidable chestnut of Southern history, the section's similarity to or dissimilarity from the North. Like his mentor Allan Nevins, whom he encountered as a respected colleague during his decade at Columbia University, Donald believed that history was a series of problems. Never hesitant about addressing important issues, Donald asked why the South had lost the war.

His answer, "Died of Democracy," turned previous explanations upside down, for most historical interpretations gave the North, not the South, credit for upholding American values during the Civil War. Running against the historiographical tide and the civil rights movement of the 1960s when the South was a national pariah, Donald concluded that the Confederacy's devotion to democracy (itself an aspect of historical continuity) hampered the discipline of its soldiers who insisted on electing their officers and then defying these officers in displays of individualism ill-suited to wartime. Moreover, this same allegiance to democratic individualism marked the South's political and economic life during the war. Wrote Donald: "The collapse of the Confederacy . . . came not from deficient economic resources, insufficient man-power, defective strategy, or weak political leadership . . . The real weakness of the Confederacy was that the Southern people insisted upon retaining their democratic liberties in wartime . . . we should write on the tombstone of the Confederacy: Died of Democracy."[13]

Unlike much of his work, his judgments on the democratic nature of the Confederacy have not survived recent investigations, especially in the comparative analysis of the Confederate and Union governments as administrative states undertaken by Richard Bensel.[14] Still, Donald's argument advanced his efforts to break down the differences between the two sections of the country, and to argue for national similarity rather than difference. This same theme reemerged in *Liberty and Union,* in which he wrote that "as a nationalist, I am not much impressed by the importance of sectional, or ethnic, or racial, or religious differences in the United States."[15]

In 1971 Donald returned to the theme of Southern similarity to the rest of the Union. In his presidential address to the Southern Historical Association —an occasion requiring a sectional topic—he reconsidered the proslavery argument of antebellum Southern intellectuals. Donald believed the defense of its peculiar institution the South's sole claim to any philosophical tradition. But the proslavery argument was not only a uniquely sectional endeavor in a region about which it was said, as Donald quoted, "Alas for the South—Her books have grown fewer / She never was much given to literature." Amid the increasing democratization making the prewar South more like the rest of the nation, it was also an internal effort to return to a nostalgic illusion of unity, grace, and patriarchal authority and to resist the modernization that Southern conservatives associated with the North.[16] Implicitly, when slavery ended, so too did any Southern intellectual tradition.

Established as a historian of the Civil War by the 1950s, David Donald turned to Reconstruction in the 1960s. By this time he had moved to Johns Hopkins University, where he completed, in 1969, another revision of James G. Randall's and now, given his extensive revisions and expanded bibliography, his own *Civil War and Reconstruction.* Wryly noting that there would be no enthusiastic contemporary remembrance of the dismal period of postwar Reconstruction, he acknowledged the influence on him of the now politically incorrect Dunning School of Reconstruction historians. The connection was, of course, not that school's unenlightened treatment of blacks, but rather, in the Donald leitmotiv, the way that the Dunning School viewed the postwar period as not just important in Southern history but as having "great meaning . . . in our national history."[17]

In his classic pedagogical style Donald enumerated three transforming changes: economic, social, and political. He chose to work on the latter. In a revised version of the Walter Fleming Lectures delivered at Louisiana State University in 1965 entitled *The Politics of Reconstruction, 1863–1867*, Donald systematically investigated the voting behavior of the so-called Radical Republicans. Unhappy with the "stalemate" in Reconstruction historiography, he offered a new strategy of careful analysis of voting behavior. Again, such empirical research harvested counterintuitive results. For, as Donald argued, not only did the Radical Republicans of the Dunning School myth tend to vote with conservative Republicans on many Congressional roll calls, but those Radicals who did vote for significant social changes in legislation such as the Civil Rights and Military Reconstruction Acts of the 1870s tended to come from safe districts in which they controlled large voting majorities.

Moreover, the legislative history of the 1867 Reconstruction Act—the quintessential expression of radicalism—appeared as a series of compromises, as what Donald described as a "pendulum" of legislation that moved back and forth, finally coming to rest at the equilibrium point required for acceptance by a majority. *The Politics of Reconstruction* was a bravura performance of both historical technique and interpretation, as Donald effectively destroyed another stereotype of the Old South, that of Radical Reconstruction. Donald decided not to write the Harper New American Nation series book on Reconstruction, a task eventually completed by Eric Foner, because he felt that Reconstruction—unlike the Civil War—was impossible to synthesize due to the fact that enough ground had been prepared in social history.[18]

To be sure, as one of the few historians of the twentieth century with a national reputation outside the academy and its classrooms, David Donald is best known for his biographies. Few Americans know his textbooks or his monographs or his shibboleth-shaking arguments. He began his career writing about individuals as a graduate student at the University of Illinois, when, at Professor Randall's suggestion, he chose as his dissertation topic Lincoln's friend and law partner William Herndon. In 1948 Alfred A. Knopf published the twenty-eight-year-old Donald's *Lincoln's Herndon.* In his introduction Carl Sandburg acknowledged the wonder that "a young man born and raised in the State of Mississippi, on a plantation of thousands of acres, with more than a score of Negro field hands, should migrate to Illinois and in the course of his scholarship write a comprehensive and vivid study of a striding and vehement Republican agitator against slavery extension—this is an American phenomenon."[19]

It was also an American phenomenon that a Mississippi-born historian could provide such an even-handed account of a man who, by the 1850s, believed that the South was dragging the United States into a Civil War. But for a fledgling historian and future biographer of Lincoln, writing about Lincoln's biographer William Herndon was an exercise in the techniques of biography, in the creditability of witnesses, and in sorting through issues of factual and interpretative accuracy. Herndon had published his biography *Herndon's Lincoln* in 1889, and it had become one of the standard accounts of Lincoln's life. In Donald's account of Herndon, this biography of Lincoln appears as a historical character. In Donald's index only the entries to his two central characters, Abraham Lincoln and William Herndon, are longer than those to *Herndon's Lincoln*. Thus the process by which Herndon wrote his biography of Lincoln became the central theme—a play within a play—of Donald's biography of Herndon.

Tangentially enmeshed in the Herndon story at first, in time Lincoln became a lifelong preoccupation for Donald. The life and death of the sixteenth president seemed to capture the essential themes of the coming of the war as well as its importance. In Donald's view, through Lincoln one encountered the growing sectionalism represented by the Republican party, the tactics of wartime leadership, the social history of the period as it was revealed in the marriage of Abraham and Mary Lincoln, the politics of the period as indicated by Lincoln's leadership of the Republican party, the relationship of the president with congressional Republicans, the process of emancipation, and even the meaning of the war. All these became the contents of what Donald christened, eponymously, the Age of Lincoln.

But he did not rush into writing a biography of Lincoln and instead published in 1956 *Lincoln Reconsidered,* a series of short, provocative articles on the sixteenth president.[20] In this volume Donald reconsidered topics ranging from Lincoln's relation with his cabinet, the American people, his wife Mary Todd Lincoln, and especially the so-called Radical Republicans to the historical reputation of Lincoln. All the hallmarks of Donald's written history were on parade in this book of essays: good writing, the challenge to familiar interpretations, and the ability to evoke character and thesis through style and avoid, through precise language, any slackness of argument.

Lincoln Reconsidered appeared at a time when Donald had already begun what would eventually become a two-volume biography of Charles Sumner. Certainly Charles Sumner, the Massachusetts senator during the Civil War and Reconstruction, deserved a biographer of Donald's caliber, and it had been fifty years since any full-scale study. Earlier treatments of Sumner's life either condemned or praised a man who was undeniably at the heart of every significant cause and movement in mid–nineteenth-century America. Still Donald and Sumner were an unlikely match—the reform-minded peace and antislavery zealot who insulted Southerners in his 1856 speech on the floor of the Senate and the newly announced "Christian and conservative" historian from Mississippi. But in his first volume Donald explained the rules for biography that regulated all his history writing and that removed him from any subservience to expected interpretations or timely recreations of historical figures. A biographer must not engage in judgments and intrude. The purpose of history is to recreate the past, which could never be accomplished by tailoring the record to present styles.

Based on prodigious research in a massive archive of Sumner letters and related primary sources, *Charles Sumner and the Coming of the Civil War* won the 1961 Pulitzer Prize in biography. The book displayed Donald's technical virtuosity as a historian whose integration of suggestive quotations was matched by his use of scenes that, as in good theater, conveyed broader meaning. Donald let Sumner tell his own story. He refused to speculate on the motivations of a man who considered himself an embodiment of principle, but who was also, as Donald showed, an astute politician adept at turning principled stands to his own advantage. And in historical terms, Donald recast Sumner's sometimes despised radicalism within the more realistic framework of the emergence of the Republican party in the late 1850s. Still, there were a few complaints that Donald had too much defended "the most objectionable man in American history."[21]

In 1970 Donald completed the second volume of his Charles Sumner biography, professing that he knew more about this perplexing reformer and self-proclaimed moralist than his subject did about himself. As in the first volume, Donald presented quotations and scenes that might lead readers to speculate about Sumner's intentions and mentality, even as he avoided what he believed would deaden the book—any explicit Freudian psychoanalysis of his subject. "I think of myself as a portrait painter, not a photographer," he later acknowledged.[22]

If the second Sumner volume could not be challenged for its psychology, Donald was nonetheless criticized for his view of a subject who, in the hands of another writer, might have been promoted into the pantheon of American heroes of civil rights. Such criticism was, after a decade of the civil rights movement, unavoidable, as the dominant views of the time shifted to the possibility of a Sumner resurrected, untarnished, as a problack champion.

Then in 1980 in a surprising but ultimately successful choice of subject, Donald looked below the Mason-Dixon line for the story of a Southern novelist he had first encountered reading *Look Homeward Angel* when he was a young boy in Goodman, Mississippi. Like Donald himself, Thomas Wolfe had gone north from North Carolina as a young man, returning only for brief visits as he churned out his massive and usually autobiographical novels that— and this point was one of Donald's important contributions to understanding Wolfe's work—Wolfe's editors shaped and significantly rewrote.

But any emphasis on the connection between the life stories of the Southern historian and the novelist is superficial and inaccurate, although both flourished in the North. Both also understood the torment that Southerners experienced in the North's cold climate and that region's supercilious attitudes about the South. In Wolfe's posthumously published *You Can't Go Home Again,* the hero must constantly choose irretrievably between opposites. And such was, for both Wolfe and Donald, their choice of the North. As Wolfe wrote, "the process of discovery" is that you can't go home again. A man could not go "back home to one's family, back home to one's childhood, back home to the father one has lost, back home to romantic love . . . back home to the escapes of Time and Memory."[23] Perhaps only a historian born in the South could have crafted such a perceptive reading of a novelist of the South, and *Look Homeward: A Life of Thomas Wolfe* won Donald his second Pulitzer Prize in Biography.

Finally, in 1988, it was time for work on Lincoln, and Donald began a full-scale retelling of a story parts of which he already knew well. Determined to let Lincoln tell his own life story and anxious to avoid the judgments that infected other biographies (and surely Herndon's *Herndon's Lincoln* was an offender), Donald quoted extensively. His central characters spoke in their own words to the reader. Again Donald's biography lacked villains or heroes, and to the chagrin of many readers, Donald's Lincoln was not the apotheosis of virtue and magnanimity. Nor did this American hero take control of affairs as he is sometimes supposed, in myth, to have done. Lincoln's famous comment that he had not controlled events, but that events had controlled him summarized Donald's view of Lincoln's passiveness.

In Donald's hands the President resembled a sharp-witted ambitious country lawyer of partisan instinct and behavior who, while no one can properly call the ill-starred President lucky, nonetheless gained from certain fortuitous accidents—such as his election to the presidency in an almost unheard of four-way election, his handling of the Sumter crisis, and even his reelection in 1864. Donald wrote that his book "suggests how often chance, or accident, played a determining role in shaping his life," though chance and passiveness sometimes seemed in conflict with Donald's rendering of Lincoln's ambition.[24]

Acclaimed as a biography, *Lincoln* was an immensely popular book, staying on the best-seller lists for months in the fall of 1995. Appropriately, Donald's most successful book focused on the national topic of the Union president during a period of American history in which the rest of the country nationalized the South. As Donald would have it, the region of his birth would be seen reversing influences that in Donald's mind had never been entirely separated.

Kenneth Stampp's Peculiar Reputation

JAMES OAKES

When Kenneth Stampp was a young boy his parents drove him to a rally for Daniel W. Hone, the socialist mayor of Milwaukee. On the way, while his father stopped to fill the car with gas, his mother turned to the young boy and said, "Kenneth, when you grow up I want you to be a good socialist lawyer." If Stampp decided not to take his mother's career advice, he did cling to his parents' political convictions. As a student at the University of Wisconsin during the 1930s, Stampp was attracted to Charles Beard's vision of American history as a continuing struggle between the haves and the have-nots. Outside the classroom Stampp's radicalism was reinforced at the socialist and communist party meetings that were held openly at the Student Union. He briefly joined the Socialist party but not the CP, although, as he later recalled, "I might as well have."[1]

The assumptions Stampp carried with him from his youth later shaped the central theme of his classic 1956 study of antebellum Southern slavery, *The Peculiar Institution.*[2] It was a familiar trajectory for many historians of Stampp's generation. His friends Richard Hofstadter and C. Vann Woodward had both come from similarly radical backgrounds, and like Stampp each went on to produce scholarly landmarks that bore the powerful imprint of youthful convictions. But just as Hofstadter's profound radicalism became all but invisible to a later generation of historians, so too was *The Peculiar Institution* retroactively pressed into service as the quintessential "liberal" interpretation of the 1950s.

This misreading began with the publication in 1960 of *Slavery* by Stanley Elkins, a book that really can be profitably read as a product of postwar liberalism. Elkins claimed that historians of slavery were stuck in an unproductive debate that continually recapitulated the nineteenth-century struggle between the abolitionists and slavery's defenders. Thus U. B. Phillips, the greatest student of slavery in the first half of the twentieth century, merely reproduced the defense of the Southern way of life that had been worked out before the Civil War. Stampp by extension was the premier neo-abolitionist: William Lloyd Garrison with footnotes. Indeed Elkins complained that the entire structure of *The Peculiar Institution* was determined by Phillips. Stampp had allegedly produced a chapter-by-chapter refutation of Phillips's earlier classic, *American Negro Slavery* (1918).[3] This is clearly false. In his emphasis on the profitability of slavery, for example, Stampp openly dissociated himself from the abolitionist critique of the Southern economy. Those same abolitionists had emphasized the passivity of the slave population, a theme Elkins himself would adopt. But Stampp pointedly rejected this reading, arguing that the slaves resented and frequently resisted their masters' authority.

Stampp's distance from the orthodoxies of postwar America was evident even in the introduction, where he explicitly rejected "race" as a meaningful category of analysis. Here Stampp was no doubt disputing Phillips's claim that race was the central theme of Southern history. But *The Peculiar Institution* went well beyond the obvious fact that Phillips's assumptions about racial inferiority were wrong. Stampp was disputing the very idea of "race" as a productive category of analysis. To be sure, Stampp recognized that slavery superimposed a caste system onto an underlying class structure. But the absurdity of caste, as Stampp saw it, lay not in its assumption that blacks were inferior to whites, but in its assumption that "race" had any meaning whatsoever. Race itself, according to Stampp, was a piece of "mythology"; *The Peculiar Institution* would assume "the basic irrelevance of race." Elkins actually took Stampp to task for this and in so doing demonstrated that it was the critic rather than the author who expressed the assumptions of postwar liberalism.[4]

Stampp's relentless emphasis on slavery's intrinsic tensions cannot be reduced to a mere inversion of U. B. Phillips. Nor was it the more or less mindless regurgitation of the old abolitionist critique dressed up in the pieties of post–World War II liberalism. Nevertheless Elkins's charge stuck. Long after the scholarly community had cast its doubts on most aspects of the "Elkins thesis," Elkins's claim that *The Peculiar Institution* was a neo-abolitionist inversion of Phillips held its ground. As a result, Stampp's central argument has gone all but unnoticed by later generations.[5]

Indeed, in the larger context of Stampp's published work, *The Peculiar Institution* is anomalous in its focus on Southern society. If there is a center of gravity in his scholarship, it is not Southern social history but Northern and national political history during the era of the Civil War. Northern politics are the focus of his first two books, *Indiana Politics during the Civil War* (1949) and *And the War Came* (1950), the latter a major study of the Northern political response to the secession crisis. In *The Era of Reconstruction* (1965), Stampp focused on the political conflicts centered in the nation's capital rather than on the social transformations underway in the postbellum South. Stampp's collected essays, *The Imperiled Union* (1980), and his most recent book, *America in 1857* (1990), range more widely, but still reveal Stampp's overriding interest in political history.[6]

Nevertheless, *The Peculiar Institution* is not simply an inexplicable outlier in Stampp's work. For, even as a political historian, Stampp has always insisted on the centrality of slavery. *And the War Came* assumes that the abolitionists were right, that the secession crisis was first and foremost about slavery. If there are heroes to be found in Stampp's history of Reconstruction, they are the Radical Republicans who similarly insisted that national policy should be geared to the protection of the former slaves. Even *America in 1857* takes as its underlying theme the question of when the Civil War became "irrepressible" because the slavery controversy could no longer be avoided.

By the mid-1950s Stampp had already established himself as a significant student of the Civil War era, and his later work would cement that reputation. But only in *The Peculiar Institution* did Stampp lay out his essentially tragic vision of the antebellum South. For Stampp the tragedy had two sources, both resting on the progressive and socialist assumptions of his youth. First of all there was the conflict, wrenching, unending conflict—social, economic, intellectual, and psychological—to which slavery subjected virtually all antebellum Southerners. And to what end? The perpetuation of an anachronistic institution that the progressive forces of the nineteenth century were leaving behind. Here was the second element of the tragedy: for Stampp the antebellum South really was stuck holding a tiger by the tail, unable to let go of slavery yet fully aware that slavery was making the South into a pariah throughout much of the world.

Stampp spelled out the central thesis of *The Peculiar Institution* on the very first page of the very first chapter: slavery's "spiritual stresses and unremitting social tensions became an inescapable part of life in the Old South."[7] This dialectical approach immediately distinguished Stampp from a generation of scholars more often remembered for stressing the relative absence of fundamental conflict in American history. For Stampp the primary tension within slavery was the powerful class antagonism that pitted master and slave against one another. Pervasive class conflict created a fundamental problem of "control" for the slaveholders, and in their attempts to address the problem the master class revealed still other internal tensions. The law of slavery, for example, was split by the intrinsically contradictory status of slaves as both persons and property. Slave life itself stood "between two cultures," the African one that had been lost and the American one from which the slaves were excluded. Even the masters' own psyches were torn between the liberal and

Christian precepts of fundamental human equality and the cruelty and inequity built into the structure of slavery.

After an opening chapter summarizing the limited scholarship then available on the origins of slavery in colonial America, *The Peculiar Institution* turns to a lengthy examination of the circumstances under which Southern slaves worked. Indeed, Stampp's claim that "slavery was above all a labor system" became one of the most widely quoted lines. Stampp showed that working conditions varied so widely—between size of farms, crops, masters, regions, styles of management—that no single generalization could capture their essence. There is no particular emphasis on the cruelty of overwork in this pivotal chapter. Yet his fundamental claim about Southern slavery—that it was above all a system of labor—laid the groundwork for Stampp's famed examination of violence and cruelty in subsequent chapters.[8]

At the core of the slave labor system, Stampp argued, lay an irreconcilable conflict between the master and the slave. On the one hand, "masters desired a steady and efficient performance of the work assigned each day." But "they could not expect much cooperation from their slaves," for the simple reason that the slaves "had little reason to care how much was produced." As a result the labor process on slave farms and plantations involved protracted negotiations in which "often neither side was a clear victor." Thus the slave labor system was built upon a fundamental social conflict. And it was to that conflict that Stampp turned in the third and fourth chapters.[9]

Stampp entitled chapter three "A Troublesome Property," a reference to the frustrations so many masters expressed regarding the behavior of their slaves. There was nothing startlingly new in the claim that the slaves resisted their condition. Raymond and Alice Bauer had already published an important essay entitled "Day to Day Resistance to Slavery," and Herbert Aptheker had recently produced a book-length compendium of slave revolts.[10] But Stampp put slave resistance within the framework of his overarching thesis. "Slaves apparently thought of the South's peculiar institution chiefly as a system of labor exploitation," he began. "If discontented with their bondage, they could be expected to direct their protests principally against the master's claim to their work." With that, Stampp launched into more than fifty pages detailing the various devices by which slaves resisted the masters' demands on their labor. Here *The Peculiar Institution* shifts into the heroic mode. "The record of slave resistance," Stampp wrote, "forms a chapter in the story of the endless struggle to give dignity to human life."[11]

Though the history of Southern bondage reveals that men can be enslaved under certain conditions, it also demonstrates that their love of freedom is hard to crush. The subtle expressions of this spirit, no less than the daring thrusts for liberty, comprise one of the richest gifts the slaves have left to posterity. In making themselves "troublesome property," they provide reassuring evidence that slaves seldom wear their shackles lightly.

At this point—having outlined the various claims masters made to the slaves' labor and the equally various methods by which the slave resisted those demands—Stampp at last turned to the peculiarly repressive nature of the slave regime. The violence of slavery is the theme for which *The Peculiar Institution* is most often remembered. Yet in retrospect Stampp was studiously evenhanded on the matter, arguing at one point that "the great majority" of masters "preferred to use as little violence as possible."[12]

What gives chapter four, "To Make Them Stand in Fear," its chilling edge is its claim that violence was intrinsic to the system regardless of the preferences of individual masters. The chapter is thus strategically placed to advance a carefully constructed argument. The slaves did not resist because they were repressed. On the contrary, masters employed a host of repressive mechanisms *because the slaves resisted.* Violence was the product not of sadistic slave owners, of which there were few, but of the intrinsic problem of control, which was pervasive. "One of the inherent tragedies of slavery," Stampp concluded, "was that a humane master's impulse to be kind to his slaves was severely circumscribed by the inescapable problem of control."[13]

Controlling slaves was a problem for the state as well, and so Stampp introduced the second major tension intrinsic to slavery. On the one hand the slaves were property, *chattels personal,* and were legally defined as such. Southern lawmakers established the rules for the distribution of slaves whose masters died intestate, or whose slaves were forfeited in bankruptcy. Beyond the bounds of the master's control, most of the "law of slavery" was therefore located in property law. On the other hand, the slaves were a distinctive "species of property," which is to say they were human beings, and the law could not help but recognize them as such. Southern legislatures thus established minimum standards of treatment for slaves, for example. If a master subjected a slave to a murderous assault or if a slave committed a crime the law similarly recognized the slaves as humans who could be either protected or held responsible for their actions. The tensions between slaves as humans and slaves as property, Stampp argued, were not always easy for masters to control.[14]

The problem of "control" is thus profoundly complicated in *The Peculiar Institution.* By the time readers are halfway through the book, Stampp introduces them to a startling theme: the slave system controlled the masters as much as the masters controlled the slaves. He closed his chapter on the law of slavery with an intriguing quotation suggesting that for a minority of masters reconciling slavery's "inescapable" tensions was all but impossible. A North Carolina master explained in his will why, upon his death, he was freeing his slaves:[15]

> Reason the first. Agreeably to the rights of man, every human being, be his or her colour what it may, is entitled to freedom. . . . Reason the second. My conscience, the great criterion, condemns me for keeping them in slavery. Reason the third. The golden rule directs us to do unto every human creature, as we would wish to be done unto; and sure I am, that there is not one of us would agree to be kept in slavery during a long life. Reason the fourth and last. I wish to die with a clear conscience, that I may not be ashamed to appear before my master in a future World. . . . I wish every human creature to deliberate on my reasons.

Stampp made no comment whatsoever on this extraordinary passage. Yet through it he introduced another theme, another of slavery's intrinsic tensions, the psychological and emotional turmoil it created for many masters. Here were the "spiritual stresses" to which he referred at the book's opening. But before Stampp took up that theme directly, he jacked up the stakes in the discussion by introducing the explosive topic of "slavemongering."

Chapter six explores the dynamics of slave trading in the Old South. The right to buy and sell slaves, Stampp began, "was a fundamental attribute of chattel slavery." Indeed, it would be hard to imagine Southern slavery without the internal slave trade. The profitability of slavery in the upper South rested on sales of "surplus" slaves to the lower South. Conversely, the growth of the cotton belt—actually, the entire westward expansion of slavery—depended on a well-established market in slaves. Yet slave traders had a bad reputation in the Old South, even among those who came to view slavery itself as a "positive good." Why? If slavery was morally justified, and if the slaveholders themselves constantly utilized the services of the slave traders, then why was the slave trade so disreputable? Here too, Stampp suggested, was evidence of bad conscience. And once again he made the suggestion by means of another lengthy quotation, this time from a Maryland planter who had sold a slave "down the river" to Louisiana, thereby breaking up the slave's family. One of his slaves, Eliza, had begged the master to sell her together with her daughter, Jennie. The slaveholder wrote:

> As to letting Jennie go to live with you . . . I can hardly make up my mind what to say. I would be reluctant to part with her. . . . However I profess to

be a Christian and have the happy and comforting assurance that I am . . .
what I profess to be. . . . Be assured that I greatly regret the occasion that
resulted in the separation of you from your child.

Stampp argued that although there was a great deal of self-serving "cant" in
the master's reply, the "necessity" of breaking up slave families was intrinsic to
the peculiar institution. Like the widespread disdain for slave trading, the fact
that almost all masters spoke of the breakup of slave families as a painful "necessity" suggested to Stampp that at some level the master class felt uneasy
about itself. It also suggested that the masters' imperfect control of their system was both objectively true and subjectively felt.[16]

Still more evidence of unease was reflected, as Stampp saw it, in the way
proslavery writers defended the material conditions in which the slaves lived.
Throughout *The Peculiar Institution,* but especially in chapter seven, "Maintenance, Morbidity, Mortality," Stampp used proslavery writings as a foil for his
own analysis. He was nearly contemptuous of the frequent claim that Africans
were uniquely suited to slavery, that blacks could withstand backbreaking work
in heat and the swamps that would otherwise have sickened or killed whites.
But Stampp also took aim at the more intriguing claims of conservative proslavery authors, especially the claim that the master-slave relationship protected slaves from the ravages of industrial wage labor. In the light of subsequent scholarship Stampp's conclusions would require more nuance, but
they would not necessarily be overturned. The cliometric revolution has dramatically enhanced our understanding of the homes and diets of Southern
slaves. Yet most of this technical scholarship sustains Stampp's basic claim that
the slave diet was adequate in calories but in crucial respects lacking in nutrients. Similarly, while many scholars have treated the intellectual defense of
slavery far more seriously than did Stampp, not everyone agrees that there is
much that remains useful in the more sophisticated musings of proslavery re-
actionaries.[17]

Like the chapter on the slaves' material well being, Stampp's discussion of
slave culture has been overtaken by subsequent scholarship. "Between Two
Cultures" reads like a crucial first step in the direction slavery studies would
move in the late 1960s and early 1970s. Maintaining the theme of intrinsic tension, Stampp argued that Southern slaves were trapped in subjective "chaos"
somewhere between the African culture—much of which they had lost—
and the mainstream American culture from which they were excluded. Here
Stampp equated "culture" with literacy and education, the works of art and
literature that constitute the most exalted achievements of Western civilization. Elsewhere in the same chapter, however, Stampp assumed an ethno-
graphic definition of culture more characteristic of recent scholarship. Thus

"Between Two Cultures" sympathetically explores the folklore, the songs, and the religious practices of the slaves in ways that stand up even today. "The tales of Br'er Rabbit, in all their variations, made virtues of such qualities as wit, strategy, and deceit," Stampp wrote. Such tales, he added, were "the weapons of the weak in their battles with the strong." The two themes of the chapter did not always make for smooth synthesis. Having argued, for example, that the slaves "lived in a kind of cultural chaos," Stampp went on to demonstrate the importance of the slaves' folk culture and religious practices. Chapter eight is best viewed as a historiographical turning point: a rejection of the racist condescension of earlier scholarship, a serious attempt to recover the subjective experience of the slaves themselves, but an incomplete formulation of an adequate alternative.[18]

More successful was Stampp's attempt to reverse the long tradition that saw slavery as an unprofitable enterprise. Here Stampp was up against a powerful orthodoxy that was accepted by both abolitionist critics and proslavery defenders. Yet Stampp's once-controversial claim—that slavery was profitable—has been so thoroughly vindicated that nowadays it is hard to fathom the conventional wisdom against which he wrote. A powerful phalanx of sophisticated econometricians separates us from the historiographical universe of the 1950s. Certainly there are still disagreements about such crucial questions as whether slavery inhibited Southern industrial development. But no one any longer disputes the profitability of slavery, and the voices questioning slavery's economic "viability" are likewise diminishing. If Stampp reached his conclusion by methods that now seem primitive, that only makes his achievement all the more impressive.[19]

That said, there remains a sophisticated layer of analysis in Stampp's chapter "Profit and Loss." It would be incorrect to claim, for example, that Stampp viewed slave labor as indistinguishable from other forms of capitalist exploitation. On the contrary, he clearly understood that the political economy of slavery differed in crucial ways from the political economy of wage labor. *The Peculiar Institution* openly explores the distinctively weak incentive structure of slavery. Unlike wage earners, slaves could not be motivated by raises, promotions, the long-term prospects of upward mobility, or the threat of unemployment. But slaveholders compensated for this by managing their plantations efficiently, by putting women and children to work more often than was true of free laborers, and by the constant threat of sheer physical coercion. Thus a political economy that slaveholders and abolitionists—indeed, that all of classical economics—agreed could not sustain its profitability nevertheless did so. After a veritable revolution in the study of the slave economy, Stampp's basic argument stands largely undamaged.[20]

Yet for Stampp slavery's profitability only enhanced the historical tragedy, for it fastened the South's allegiance to a system that made money but was no longer socially or politically viable. Here is the final and perhaps most significant tension that shapes *The Peculiar Institution*. Slavery's profits committed the master class to the defense of a labor system that was out of step with the tendencies of the nineteenth century and so was held in rising contempt by the rest of the world. What is more, the masters knew this and if Stampp is right the more thoughtful among them found the strain unbearable. The slaveholders "were disturbed to have the world against them," Stampp wrote, "and what disturbed them even more (their denials notwithstanding) was the suspicion that the world might be right."[21]

Stampp was not the first person to claim that the slaveholders, or at least some of them, felt "guilty" about their peculiar institution. But it was Stampp's claim that raised the most vocal objections. Critics detected the outbreak of a new disease, "guiltomania," among otherwise levelheaded scholars. In a book that generally awes its readers with its profuse documentation, the claim that slaveholders felt guilty allegedly stands naked, stripped of all supporting evidence.[22] This is not quite correct. When Stampp cited the master who freed his slaves so that he could "die with a clear conscience," it was hard to dispute such straightforward evidence. But there was not much of it. More important, the empirical question remains entangled in a more complicated analytical problem: What *would* constitute evidence of "guilt" outside of rare expressions like the one cited above?

For Stampp the slaveholder's misgivings were inseparable from the intractable tensions of the system itself. Few masters openly confessed to feelings of "guilt," and Stampp never even used that word. But many masters insisted, over and over again, that they loved their slaves, that their slaves were content, that they traded slaves and broke up families only when necessary. At some basic level it was all true. Some masters really did love their slaves; some slaves actually were content; and most masters disliked having to break up slave families. But this only made matters worse. For masters who loved their slaves still had to force their slaves to work and thus faced the inescapable problem of control. Some slaves may have been content, but plenty were not and the masters were quite aware of it. All were trapped in a system that treated human beings as property, that destroyed families by "necessity," and that required a level of violence that brutalized the slaves and in so doing offended the sensibilities of many masters. So when masters protested their kindness, their affection, and their good will, Stampp argued that perhaps they did protest too much. Maybe they did and maybe they didn't. But critics of the "guilt thesis" have latched onto a distraction. Slavery's "spiritual stresses" were but one manifestation of the social, economic, and intellectual tensions intrinsic to the peculiar institution. The tension, not the guilt, was Stampp's primary concern.

No doubt Stampp's emphasis on conflict was the logical outcome of his radical origins and progressive intellectual lineage. But it has resulted in a curious inversion of historiographical orthodoxy. In slavery studies, the major work of the 1950s stressed conflict rather than consensus. It was the later, post-sixties scholarship that rejected this emphasis and focused on various claims to a more or less unified Southern culture: an all-pervasive planter hegemony, a powerful cult of honor, a world that masters and slaves "made together."[23]

But conflict was not the only distinguishing hallmark of *The Peculiar Institution*. "When freedom came," Stampp concluded, "the Negro, in literal truth, lost nothing but his chains." Here was the fundamental, and perhaps the most enduring, achievement of the book: it was the first comprehensive history of slavery to sympathetically reconstruct the experience of the slaves themselves. For this reason, if no other, *The Peculiar Institution* still stands as a monument to scholarship that is at once rigorously professional, fiercely passionate, and profoundly humane. Readers can only be grateful that, in a small but significant act of resistance, Stampp chose to become a good social historian instead of a good socialist lawyer.[24]

Continuity and Change

George Brown Tindall and
the Post–Reconstruction South

SUSAN YOUNGBLOOD ASHMORE

In a 1991 interview with three of his former students, George Brown Tindall stated clearly his view of the post-Reconstruction South. "I would say I have a tendency to come down on the side of both continuity *and* change," he explained, "because I think that's the way it is." "I don't believe there's any revolution in human history that has involved total change and total destruction of the old," he elaborated, "except for maybe where there has been total genocide. . . . But short of that there's going to be continuity." Spanning a productive career of over forty years of teaching and conducting research, Tindall produced fifty books, articles, and essays that convey this theme of tension between Southern endurance and transformation.[1]

Aware of the inaccuracies created by historians committed to specific convictions, most notably those associated with the Dunning School of Reconstruction history, Tindall communicated his thesis without the taint of an ideological agenda. Using historical evidence and borrowing liberally from the humanities and social sciences, he expanded the historical view of the region after Reconstruction. The South Tindall depicted is populated with black and white people who participate together in making the area distinct. He told a comprehensive story that includes race, class, religion, politics, literature, labor, and agriculture. A master story-teller who perfected the use of metaphor and the turn of a phrase, Tindall rooted his work deeply in the archival evidence, which has stood the test of time.[2]

The post-Reconstruction period on which Tindall focused coincides with his own life. He was born in up-country South Carolina in the early 1920s; his parents and grandparents grew up in the Reconstruction era, and as a child he was exposed to the contradictions of Southern racial mores. Tindall remembered his fourth-grade teacher on one occasion lecturing her class after her white students had gotten involved in a sidewalk shoving match with some black children. Laura Butler informed Tindall's classmates that they did not have special privileges on that public thoroughfare and should learn to share the space because black parents paid taxes and therefore owned the sidewalk too. This early lesson in race relations left its mark on Tindall. "That stuck in my mind," he recalled, "and it's still stuck there." Reared in the Baptist church, Tindall also acknowledged the Social Gospel and "some influences from the interracial movement" affecting his attitudes about racial bigotry.[3]

After earning his bachelor of arts degree from Furman University in 1942 with a double major in English and history, the young graduate entered military service. He received another lesson in the changing South while serving in Truman's desegregated armed forces. In officer candidate school in Montgomery, Alabama, Tindall had his first experience with token integration. One black officer candidate, Cecil Poole, attended classes and ate meals with his fellow white classmates throughout their training, although he was not allowed to share sleeping quarters with any of them.[4]

Upon completing his tour of duty, Tindall tucked these experiences away to be recalled later and entered graduate school in the spring of 1946 at the University of North Carolina at Chapel Hill. It was during this period of his life that he began to connect his personal experiences to a broader understanding of the South. Intending to study English, the young scholar grew restless with his course work and transferred to Southern history after a friend from Furman introduced him to Professor Fletcher M. Green. Tindall had not taken any courses in recent American or Southern history as an undergraduate but realized that his penchant for current events—he described himself as a "newspaper junkie"—would serve him well in his new pursuit.[5]

As a budding Southern historian, Tindall received the best the South had to offer at Chapel Hill. With Green as his major professor, Tindall worked with "the dominant figure in the training of Southern historians in the years before and after the Second World War." He also entered graduate school at a time when the history of the post-Reconstruction period was undergoing significant change. Historians began to challenge the distorted image created by the Dunning School interpretation of Reconstruction as well as the "Negro advancement" monographs that promoted racial pride to undermine the white supremacist belief in black inferiority. Starting with Carter G. Woodson in 1916, the work produced by black scholars began to reach a critical mass in the 1930s. Influenced by the Great Migration, the "New Negro" movement, and the recent impact of African-Americans on national politics, this new scholarship broke the static image of the period. "It was only with the development of an increasing fluidity and militancy in Negro life," Tindall would later explain, "that the temper of the times began to adjust historical perspectives into new focus." In 1948, two years after Tindall entered North Carolina, John Hope Franklin published *From Slavery to Freedom*, which Tindall described as "the best overall survey of American Negro history."[6]

In addition to Green and the revitalized historiography, the strong presence of the sociology department at the University of North Carolina also shaped Tindall's basic understanding of the South. Howard W. Odum came to Chapel Hill in 1920 to lead the sociology department and proceeded to transform it into "the Wisconsin of the South." Odum launched the *Journal of Social Forces* and founded the Institute for Research in Social Science, the first university institute of its kind in the country. His efforts brought prestige to the campus and helped to make the University of North Carolina an academically viable university. During the 1930s, Odum pushed forward his idea of "regionalism" in an effort to calm the troubled waters of sectional tension that divided the South from the rest of the country. Odum's regionalism promoted the integration of the South into the nation but without losing its distinctive character. "Regionalism is a means of synthesis of all the social sciences and to some extent, of the humanities," Tindall explained in an article honoring Odum after his death in 1954. "It is the method whereby one can study society and see it whole, not in bits and snatches from the viewpoint of some narrow specialty." Although Odum never got the chance to see his ideas implemented fully—he thought the New Deal's focus on the South as the nation's "number-one economic problem" plunged the country deeper into sectionalism—the concept continued to have value and influenced scholars beyond the sociology department. Odum's and Rupert B. Vance's Regional approach, unlike the Agrarianism so prevalent at Vanderbilt University, acknowledged that the South had serious problems, yet insisted on regional solutions that would take into account Southern sensibilities, Southern predilections, and Southern history. Tindall recalled that Chapel Hill was "sort of in the twilight years of the Southern Regionalist movement" when he was a graduate student. He knew Odum and had audited sociologist Gordon Blackwell's "Southern Regions" course as a graduate student. Tindall's body of work reflected this broad approach to the study of Southern history using other fields of the social sciences and the humanities to create a more complete understanding of the region.[7]

Because he was shaped by the contradictory experiences of race in his own life—growing up in the Jim Crow South and witnessing cracks in the foundation of white supremacy—it is not surprising that George Tindall concentrated on the post-Reconstruction period. "With the best of intentions the historian cannot completely transcend the human limitations imposed by the temper of his times, his regional identification, his race, or causes that arouse his sympathies," Tindall wrote perceptively in 1965. "His view of historical reality, the very selection of the facts with which he is concerned, inevitably will be shaped and distorted by the perspective in which he views them." Tindall's first published article dealt with the tensions of continuity and change that he had witnessed in his own life. It originated as a paper in Fletcher Green's seminar and eventually became the topic of his master's thesis.

Tindall had heard J. Mauldin Lesesne, a doctoral candidate at the University of South Carolina, describe a discussion about "how you define *Negro*" that had taken place during the Palmetto State's constitutional convention in 1895. George Tillman, the older brother of the famous Populist governor, Benjamin "Pitchfork Ben" Tillman, had balked at the proposition of using the "one-drop rule" to define the racial status of South Carolina citizens. Tindall distinctly remembered hearing George Tillman say that "this would embarrass some respectable families who were respected and accepted in the white community." "Moreover," Tindall recalled, "he [Tillman] even made the radical statement that there was probably not a single pureblooded Caucasian on the floor of that convention." The young historian had not realized the shifting nature of the concept of race. "I'd never heard anything like this," he later told some of his students, "and that lodged in my mind and it was still there when I decided to switch to history, and so I decided I'd look into that convention of 1895." Published in 1949 in the *Journal of Southern History,* "The Campaign for the Disfranchisement of Negroes in South Carolina" introduced Tindall's thesis to a wider audience.[8]

As he worked on his master's thesis, a fellow student of Fletcher Green, Vernon Lane Wharton, published his dissertation, *The Negro in Mississippi, 1865–1890,* which significantly influenced the direction of Tindall's career. Wharton moved beyond political history to uncover a comprehensive understanding of the African-American experience in the Magnolia State. "Its central theme," Tindall assessed, "was the evolution of white supremacy's new *modus vivendi* in the years after the destruction of slavery." Through Wharton's monograph, and in his own research on South Carolina's constitutional convention, Tindall understood that segregation had not been established fully and immediately after the Civil War and Reconstruction. In fact, the relationship between white and black Southerners had been rather fluid and flexible until the 1890s when racial lines hardened and Jim Crow made his home in the region.[9]

Following the path Wharton had cut in Mississippi, Tindall broadened his work on South Carolina for his dissertation topic. Published in 1952, Tindall's *South Carolina Negroes 1877–1900* confirmed the pattern that Wharton had found in Mississippi, debunking the image of African-Americans created by "Lost Cause" mythology. "[T]he eight year period of Republican control, long denounced by partisan historians as an era of unparalleled corruption and abuse," Tindall stated early in the book, "has in the third and fourth decades of the twentieth century been subjected to re-examination . . . and found to have been also a period not only of constructive social and economic progress, but also of substantial governmental achievement." Hoping to provide a "usable past," he traced the African-American experience in the Palmetto State, exploring political activism and disfranchisement, agriculture and other forms of labor, migration, religion, education, racial violence, crime and convict leasing, the care of orphans and the mentally ill, social life, and the establishment of the color line. While the various experiences of South Carolina's black citizens remained the focus of this study, the role white members of the state's society play in relation to their minority neighbors was the subtext of Tindall's history.[10]

With this monograph Tindall took up his theme of continuity *and* change supported by his commitment to revealing the actions of black and white Southerners that created the distinctiveness of the region. The first third of the book features the racial politics of the state from Reconstruction through the 1895 constitutional convention; the remaining two-thirds concentrate on the activities of the African-American community, some of which led the Tillman forces to push for their eventual disfranchisement. Although the monograph is filled with tragedy and missed opportunities, none of the participants are portrayed as passive victims who willingly accepted their changing circumstances and contracting freedoms.

That the war and its aftermath had changed the political landscape of South Carolina was clear in the state's choice for governor in 1876. Conservative Democrat Wade Hampton, a Confederate hero, won the tightly contested race. One year later, as the Democratic party took back the reins of government in the regular session of the legislature, the new governor planned to reconcile the breach left by civil war and federal rule using tactics based on moderation and reform. As a result, the road to redemption in the Palmetto State took an unexpected left turn toward interracialism before the hardening of the color line in the 1890s straightened out its path. Hampton made room for "the talented and trained Negro," appointing several African-Americans to minor state offices.

Yet, despite this evidence of limited political integration, the legacy of white supremacy endured. Hampton's attempt to establish interracial goodwill faltered when African-Americans began to join the Democratic party and win elected office in 1878. This new political reality caused concern for those who viewed the party as a place reserved for white men. Hampton abandoned state politics at this crucial point to fill the U.S. Senate seat vacated by John Patterson. Although the Democratic governors who followed Hampton continued the pattern of limited interracialism throughout the 1880s, their party kept African-Americans from accessing the Democratic election machinery across the state. Throughout the decade it also became more difficult for black men to cast their votes as the legislature modified registration and election laws to hamper African-American political successes. The new legislation gave voting registrars the power to strike names on the voter list who were thought to have moved, and in 1882 the "eight box law" passed, requiring voters to place their ballots in the correct ballot box labeled for each office. "In practice," Tindall pointed out, "it would be simple for election managers to help those illiterates who would vote 'right' and let others void their ballots through ignorance." Although black politicians protested these and other adjustments, by 1889 the minority vote ceased to carry the clout it once had in state politics. This cleared the way for the ascendancy of Ben Tillman and his movement, especially after he won the governor's race in 1890.[11]

Tindall attributed the failure of shared power, even on this modest level, to several factors. Wade Hampton's program relied on the governor's prestige and the goodwill of white people. When both evaporated—with Hampton moving to Washington, the weakening of African-American political power, and the increased influence of racist rhetoric—the state was left with men who rallied around Tillman's movement of agrarian discontent and Negrophobia. With Tillman in the governor's chair, the removal of black South Carolinians from the political scene followed in short order. After the Tillman movement picked up more seats in the election of 1892, the governor had enough sway over the state legislature to pass a referendum convening a constitutional convention to disfranchise black voters without violating the United States Constitution. Tillman succeeded in controlling the convention, which led to one-party rule in South Carolina. "The great fear of the Negro vote palsied those who had liberal or progressive tendencies," Tindall contended, "and white Democrats were frequently elected by direct appeals to racial prejudice." This retooled version of the Old South, modified to withstand the scrutiny of the United States Supreme Court, would hold the state captive for the next seventy years.[12]

In addition to explaining how the Tillman forces pulled their agenda through the convention, Tindall stressed the other side of the story to decipher these racist actions. He described how African-Americans worked to gain a place within the larger community throughout the eighteen years from 1877 to 1895. Black men held seats in the state legislature and gained federal Republican patronage jobs in such positions as postmaster and inspector of customs. Three African-American Republicans had been elected to Congress after Reconstruction—Robert Smalls, Thomas Ezekiel Miller, and George Washington Murray—and each represented his district well. Smalls secured appropriations for the improvement of Georgetown harbor and Winyah Bay, located a naval station at Parris Island, and procured funds for storehouses and docks. Miller held his congressional seat in Washington for two terms beginning in 1888. Returning home in 1892, he ran for state office and left public service four years later to serve as the first president of the state college for African-Americans in Orangeburg. Taking Smalls's seat in the House of Representatives in 1892, George Washington Murray became the last black man to represent South Carolina in Congress until after the modern civil rights movement of the twentieth century. Miller and Smalls attended the constitutional convention in 1895 along with four other African-American delegates. Murray campaigned throughout South Carolina against the disfranchisement movement to "educate and arouse our people up to a realization of the situation and what they can do to help themselves."[13]

Black churches also rose up against Tillman's moves, choosing a state executive committee "to organize Negroes all the way down to ward and precinct levels." Tindall's research showed the assertive stance taken by the black delegates during the convention. With regard to the suffrage article James Whigg "bluntly attacked the doctrine of white supremacy with the argument that it was sheer fallacy" and Robert Smalls said the suffrage plan "might fool the 'crackers' but no one else as to its essentially fraudulent nature." Public education also became an issue during the convention, and the African-American delegates exploited the pull toward a segregated society to at least secure a separate state college for black people. They also took this opportunity to bring the problem of lynching to the attention of the convention. And, when the issue of interracial marriage came to the floor, Robert Smalls introduced an amendment that "any white person guilty of cohabiting with a Negro should be barred from holding office and further that the child of such a relationship should bear the name of its father and inherit property the same as if legitimate." These assertions made by the African-American delegates underscored how much had changed since the end of Reconstruction in 1877.[14]

In the face of this testimony, which implied "social equality," Tillman's forces rallied around old shibboleths. Tindall reported that the governor told the Senate after the convention, "We of the South have never recognized the right of the negro [sic] to govern white men, and we never will." And, although the new constitution accelerated the restriction to voting, Tindall made it plain that old forms of intimidation, violence, and fraud continued to be the main instruments for enforcing disfranchisement after 1895. "The fear of violence is a basic context in which the history of South Carolina Negroes during the period must be studied to be clearly understood," Tindall concluded. Yet, the Democrats did not hesitate to use a more "civilized" avenue to make their point. Three years after the drafting of a new state constitution, the first law segregating public accommodations appeared on the books. It required divided first-class coaches, "separated by a substantial partition," for passengers

on all railroads more than forty miles in length. By 1900, Tindall argued, segregation had "rapidly bec[o]me an established and unquestioned fact in all the
institutions and relationships of the two races." At the turn of the century,
after nearly twenty years of flexible race relations, slavery had been finally replaced by a racial caste system. Change begot continuity.[15]

The Tindall thesis of endurance and transformation can also be found
beyond the political stage, which clarifies why the Tillman forces gathered
strength enough to reassert the power of white supremacy after 1895. In the
dawn of the post-Reconstruction period, African-Americans in South Carolina did not fade from the scene. Tindall discussed how the tenant farm system
evolved and showcased the variety of experiences this new farming method
harvested. A handful of black farmers became quite successful, and Tindall
highlighted fifteen thousand who had moved through the tenant system to
become landowners. Yet, the vast majority suffered great injustices trapped in
debt peonage as a result of the crop lien. Off the farm, African-American
laborers fared somewhat better. Although most worked in domestic and personal services, others entered better paying jobs in transportation, manufacturing, and professional services. Some united with their white counterparts in
labor unions. From 1869 until the 1890s, black and white longshoremen in
Charleston organized into the Longshoremen's Protective Union Association.
Tindall discovered that skilled carpenters and bricklayers also maintained
effective unions in the coastal city. The editor of an African-American newspaper reported on the curious phenomenon the integrated union created during a parade in 1886. "It is a fact that black and white men can dwell together
in peace, even in South Carolina," he stated. "The order presented a very fine
appearance, and the sight will not be soon forgotten." Beyond the working
classes, Tindall found evidence of a burgeoning black middle class, centered in
Charleston, that owned businesses, saved money, and bought homes. Nevertheless, no black controlled a bank or credit facility, and most professionals—
teachers, preachers, lawyers, doctors, and journalists—served their own race.[16]

Although the period after 1877 appeared to be a time of interracial flexibility,
Tindall discovered important parts of South Carolina society where the color
line had established itself during and immediately after Reconstruction. In this
regard the continuity and change thesis finds another form. The church stands
out as an example of racial segregation that benefited African-Americans. In
this sacred world, blacks found cultural space that they could control completely. Tindall held that "for the great numbers of the race, especially in the
rural areas, the center of social activity was in the church, the most universal
and highly organized of Negro institutions." Black churches played an important role in the movement for education and offered members the opportunity
to develop skills in organization, management, finance, self-government, and

self-reliance. The Baptist denomination attracted the most members because of its evangelical fervor and congregational form of organization. The African Methodist Episcopal church followed as the second most popular faith. As significant as this example of racial separation would be for the black community, Tindall still managed to locate vestiges of the old pattern of biracial worship in the Episcopal and Presbyterian churches but, like everything else regarding integration in the 1890s, this evaporated as the century drew to a close.[17]

Tindall identified the black clergy as an important nucleus of leadership for their community. The variety of responses he uncovered also underscored the fact that the black community was not a monolithic entity. "[Some] Negro ministers figured prominently in political conventions, others urged their flocks to eschew politics," he explained. "Some were important agents of conciliation with the whites, whole others bitterly denounced them." Tindall also rejected the opportunity to write a hagiography and instead offered a balanced picture of the leaders that filled the pulpits of South Carolina's black churches. Some were incompetent, others profited from the ignorance of their flocks, and many served their parishioners well. Jacob Wilson sold a paper to his congregation purported to be a letter from Jesus Christ. "But for men of sincerity and ability, interested in advancing the cause of their people," Tindall iterated, "the ministry offered the most promising field of service and the most effective medium of propaganda." He found many individuals who fought their way "up from slavery through poverty to become responsible leaders."[18]

As the Republican party became a less effective means for political expression—especially after it became more difficult for black men to cast their votes—the church stood out as a beacon for the community. Here African-Americans found a source of strength and a refuge from the constrictions of daily life in South Carolina, as well as a place to voice their discontent with the larger society. For example, in the aftermath of a close-range shooting of "Democrat" Riley, a prominent African-American in Charleston, blacks gathered at the Morris Brown Church to urge their ministers "to prepare and publish 'an address to the races' on the subject of interracial violence."[19]

The declaration drafted by the black ministers revealed their distinct understanding of the root cause of interracial violence. They pointed out that, although they had lived among white people for 250 years, "they were still completely unknown and misunderstood by their white brethren." The address stated that white South Carolinians believed "the Negro was not a man, but a higher order of beast" and that "the Negro was dying out without the fostering care of slavery." Worse than these misconceptions were the assumptions that "the Negro was improvident, without a conscience, a born thief, liar, and sensualist, and that female chastity did not exist."[20]

To counter these stereotypes the ministers recounted the progress that had been made in their community since emancipation: "Colored lawyers, editors, clergymen, physicians, teachers, merchants, and artists show what the race has accomplished in every department of mental activity." They highlighted the institutions supported by the black community including schools, "churches, parsonages, [and] . . . benevolent societies," which proved that their community respected and venerated "morality and religion." Their clear-eyed reasoning exposed the fallacy of white supremacy and speculated darkly about what could happen if blacks continued to be oppressed. After pointing out that they were deprived of the standard American rights "to the protection of life, liberty, and property," the ministers warned that "it may not be long before the revolutions of St. Domingo in the times of Toussaint L'Ouverture will be repeated in the South." They closed their address with "hope for the reassertion of a sense of justice among the whites." This statement proved that the flexibility in race relations since Reconstruction had provided some room for African-Americans to assert their rights and, as a result, pushed those in the white community to support the Tillman faction when the forces of moderation began to fade in the 1890s.[21]

Unlike the black church that served the interests of the African-American community, there were other aspects of a rigid color line that surfaced immediately after Reconstruction that foreshadowed what was to come after 1895. Public education for both races developed in South Carolina as an element of Reconstruction, but integrated schools were never part of the plan. State leaders harbored the long-standing belief that "to educate a Negro is to spoil a laborer and train up a candidate for the Penitentiary." As a result South Carolina, like other Southern states, established a dual school system with unequal funding that forced black schools to struggle along with inadequate facilities and unprepared, underpaid teachers. The convict-lease system that developed in the 1870s also followed the path of segregation. Tindall's research revealed that "the few whites who were sentenced to the state penitentiary were generally charged with serious crimes, for which they were kept within the walls of the penitentiary." Although South Carolina reformed this abusive system two years after its inauguration, the 1895 constitution "provided that leased convicts should remain under officers appointed by the penitentiary."[22]

With the publication of *South Carolina Negroes*, Tindall contributed significantly to shifting the construct of post-Reconstruction historiography. He demonstrated that South Carolina experienced a period of interracial flexibility and fluidity that lasted almost twenty years in which African-American activities were not circumscribed completely. Some blacks had been able to succeed and hold respected positions of power within their own community and in the larger society. Nevertheless, vestiges of the Old South remained—

222 / Susan Youngblood Ashmore

in education, racial violence, criminal justice, and economic control—that kept the door of the past cracked for the post-1895 era. As a result of African-American successes, and white political divisions, a backlash ensued that etched the color line into the state and made a place for Jim Crow for the next seventy years. In the third edition of his best-selling history of racial segregation in the South, *The Strange Career of Jim Crow* (1974), C. Vann Woodward acknowledged the pioneering work of Tindall and Vernon L. Wharton in conceiving of a time of fluid race relations in the South. A further state study of Virginia paralleled Tindall and Wharton and confirmed Woodward's thesis that Southern "segregation developed gradually out of circumstances in the late nineteenth century." Tindall found satisfaction in the fact that his monograph had some relevancy for the present. "[I]t was also kind of gratifying," he reminisced, "that I'd done something that had to do with live issues, it wasn't just the dead past."[23]

George Tindall continued his work throughout the 1950s and 1960s writing essays and giving lectures that laid the groundwork for his seminal 1967 book, *The Emergence of the New South*. In these essays, Tindall honed his thesis of continuity and change while maintaining that the South would preserve its distinct character within the nation. In the 1960 essay "The Central Theme Revisited," Tindall offered a response to Ulrich Bonnell Phillips's famous 1928 statement that preservation of white supremacy was the central theme of Southern history. Agreeing that Southerners have been preoccupied with issues of race, Tindall disagreed with Phillips's contention that there had been a unanimous response to these matters. Tindall argued that when the South makes peace with its racist past it will still continue to be different from the rest of the country.[24]

After tracing the origins of segregation to the 1890s and reiterating that it was a twentieth-century phenomenon, Tindall untied the Gordian knot of the new peculiar institution in an effort to explain that the South was more than a sanctuary for white supremacists. He found continuity between the antebellum South and the post-Reconstruction South in the resurrection of proslavery justifications found in the religious world through the Scriptures and in the business world through the need for "mudsill" labor. Both the proslavery faction and the prosegregationists supported their views claiming an interest in social stability. New grounds for segregation developed, too. "As the races drew apart and as opportunities for personal acquaintance, even in a paternalistic setting, diminished," Tindall wrote, "the antebellum argument that the Negro was biologically distinct from and inferior to the white man gained an acceptance which had been prohibited during the slavery regime by the opposition of churchmen and by the more intimate knowledge of Negroes." Newer strands got braided into the knot, including the cult of the

"Lost Cause" from such classics as D. W. Griffith's film adaptation of the Reverend Thomas W. Dixon's "Birth of a Nation," and the promotion of "innate racial instincts" and "folkways of the South" from newer schools of sociology. As the new century progressed, "influenced by dynamic forces of social Darwinism and imperialism," Tindall argued, the white South felt less compelled to justify itself to the rest of the nation.[25]

Clearly written before the racial tumult of the 1960s—before the desegregation of the University of Mississippi, and the Birmingham, Selma, and Northern urban riots—Tindall's reexamination of "the central theme" claimed that although the system of segregation found a place in the South, it was never in the same league as slavery, and therefore it was not long before people began attacking its foundations. Geneticists and anthropologists could not find conclusive evidence for biological racial inferiority. Literate Southerners grew less sure of Scriptural interpretations for the subjugation of black people. Mechanization in agriculture and manufacturing reduced the need for an unskilled labor force. And racial violence did not erupt in places where African-Americans had regained the vote.[26]

In addition to clarifying these flaws in Phillips's argument, Tindall pinpointed outside pressures as well as forces from within that restrained "the most extreme expressions of racism, and have thereby contributed importantly to the erosion of the Southern credo." The South's celebrated acknowledgment of the American Creed—as personified by Thomas Jefferson, Andrew Jackson, and agrarian individualism—was one external influence. Tindall also saw Christianity and the Social Gospel as providing "ideologies and conditioning attitudes" that did not harmonize well with Jim Crow's tune—a point on which perhaps Tindall is at his weakest. A much stronger rejoinder to Phillips's theme, however, was that "the Negro has been a Southerner." Tindall argued that without the presence of African-Americans the South would not be the South. "In shaping patterns of speech, of folklore, of music, of literature, and in the manifold products of their labor," he wrote, "Negro Southerners have everlastingly influenced and enriched the culture of their region. To overlook this contribution would be to neglect much that has made the South distinctive."[27]

Not to appear as a paean to the Southern liberal, Tindall indicated that the South of 1950 was not the South of 1850. The massive resistance that roared through parts of the region after the 1954 *Brown v. Board* Supreme Court decision, he felt, was a rear-guard action of defense, "seeking only to hold the ground already occupied, or even to retreat to the line of separate but equal." In contrast, the slave owners of the 1850s were on the offensive trying to expand into new parts of the country. A century later, the solid front of white intransigence had weakened, yet distinctive characteristics remained. Throughout the mid-twentieth century Southerners could be found voicing different opinions from their fellow Americans on subjects beyond race—which, Tindall felt, disproved Phillips's thesis—including the Southern education movement, the campaign against freight-rate discrimination, the Agrarian manifesto of 1930, and Howard Odum's Southern regionalism. Tindall argued that the South's experience with defeat and poverty; the climate and physical effects on life, tempo, emotion, and character; the presence of African-Americans; the religious nature and the awareness of good and evil; and the rural culture all combined to make the region what it is. Ending on a hopeful note Tindall closed his essay by reporting that "the Southern way of life has involved infinitely more than a system of segregation and proscription. And more and more frequently, as time passes, he [the Southerner] can report that a consciousness of loyalty to the South may even take the form of opposition to the old Southern credo." Although Tindall may have rephrased some of his opinions in light of the events of the modern civil rights movement after 1960, the basic argument of "The Central Theme Revisited" still stands. The South has maintained a distinctive character that transcends its racist past and is sustained by both black and white Southerners.[28]

In 1964 Tindall penned an essay that logically followed the 1960 piece, "Mythology: A New Frontier in Southern History." In it he called for Southern historians to use literature and poetry as a way of understanding the myths of the South that bound the inhabitants of the region to each other. Tindall's willingness to go beyond the traditional boundaries of historical research is one of the primary characteristics of his interpretation of Southern history. What was important for Tindall was that "the South . . . has been the seedbed for a proliferation of paradoxical myths, all of which have some basis in empirical fact and all of which doubtlessly have, or have had, their true believers."[29]

Tindall wrote the essay in response to fellow historians C. Vann Woodward and David Potter. Woodward had claimed that the crux of Southern identity was to be found in its "failure and defeat in a land that glorifies success; sin and guilt amid the legend of American innocence; and a sense of place and belonging among a people given to abstractions." Potter, meanwhile, asserted that Southern folk culture was the key to understanding "the enigma of the South." Instead of looking for the answer in the past, not surprisingly, Tindall found it in the present—and in his old academic discipline of English literature. For him, it was change and the South's reaction to change that ultimately defined the region.

Tindall looked to literature to provide an understanding to that response. "As far back as the twenties," he wrote, "it was the consciousness of change that quickened the imaginations of a cultivated and sensitive minority, giving us the Southern Renaissance in literature." Ellen Glasgow, William Faulkner, Thomas Wolfe, Erskine Caldwell, and the Fugitive-Agrarian poets were all suspended between two worlds, "a double focus looking both backward and forward," in an effort to understand the anxiety that resulted in living in a region surrounded by change. "Can it be that the historians have been looking in the wrong places, that they have failed to seek the key to the enigma where the poets have so readily found it?" Tindall asked. For him, Southern myths— the proslavery South, the Confederate South, the demagogic South, the states' rights South, the fighting South, the lazy South, the folklore South, the South of jazz and blues, the booster South, the rapacious South running away with northern industries, the liberal South of the interracial movement, the white supremacy South, the Anglo-Saxon (or Scotch-Irish) South, the patriotic South, and the internationalist South—shaped the character, unified the society, developed a sense of community, and made the region aware of its distinctiveness.[30]

These two essays revealed the manner in which Tindall was addressing his next venture, the tenth volume in Louisiana State University Press's prestigious History of the South series. Originally assigned to Rupert Vance, "the eminent Chapel Hill sociologist-historian," the commission went to Tindall after 1956 when Vance withdrew from the project. Apart from inheriting a preliminary bibliography that had been prepared for Vance in the early 1940s, Tindall had to conduct massive basic research in manuscript collections for the thirty-two-year period before World War I and through the end of World War II.

The book is almost overwhelming in its comprehensive coverage of the South in this period as it addresses the changing region politically, socially, and culturally. "Chapter after chapter amounted to minimonographs," Dan Carter has noted. "Chapter after chapter broke ground in research, analysis, and interpretation, challenging a new generation of scholars." The South witnessed dramatic transformations during the years that this volume spanned. In 1913, cotton still dominated the region and Jim Crow maintained his grip on Southern manners. By 1945, Dixie had begun to shed some of its most familiar characteristics and stood poised to reconcile its long separation, politically and culturally, from the rest of the country. "Tindall's achievement in mastering the materials and structuring the developments of these three decades is Herculean," David Potter wrote in his review of the book, "and it reflects what must have been tireless and sustained concentration over a period of many years." Published in 1967, *The Emergence of the New South, 1913–1945* told the story of the South's journey toward modernity and established George Tindall as one of the preeminent scholars of twentieth-century Southern history.[31]

Tindall's work on the post-Reconstruction period in South Carolina provided him with important context for venturing beyond 1900. Patterns that he found in his research for *South Carolina Negroes* reappear over and over in *The Emergence of the New South*. Continuity and change are prevalent throughout the book as are the actions of both black and white Southerners in making the region distinct. Tindall followed his own advice by incorporating a variety of disciplinary approaches to make sense of the South in this period, including history, literature, political science, and sociology. And he tied all of these perspectives together by using the overarching theme of "emergence" for the period. "In national life under Woodrow Wilson and Franklin D. Roosevelt Southern leaders reached positions of influence unequaled since the Civil War," Tindall explained in his preface. "In regional life the Southern people moved into a far more diversified, pluralistic society." Tindall argued that both the renaissance in literature and an acceptance of critical attitudes about the region inspired a willingness to find answers to the South's problems. During this period as well, the early stirrings of the modern civil rights movement began, which created the conditions for changing race relations that followed quickly on the heels of V-J day.[32]

After three decades, many of the interpretations found in this monograph continue to be relevant for those interested in the twentieth-century South and still serve as the starting point for scholars who study this period. The South began to emerge from its political isolation with the election of Woodrow Wilson in 1912 and, as the region began to rejoin the rest of the country, social and cultural modifications followed. "Wilson's importance to the Democratic party," Tindall explained, "was that he offered it a chance to establish a record of achievement which had not been available since the Civil War." Half of the new president's cabinet came from the South, and Southerners filled leadership positions in both houses of Congress. As a result, the political landscape started to change in the region with the broader acceptance of the state's role in public service. Tindall pointed out that these Southern politicians must have felt right at home with their new leader, especially when the president brought segregation to the capital—encompassing government offices, shops, restrooms, and lunchrooms.[33]

World War I brought a prosperity to the South that increased the revenues of state governments and inspired new economic development. With the affluence came a new reality to the Southern conscience, the inevitability of change; a response to that certainty followed. Tindall located the reaction to this transformation in various places throughout Southern culture. The reemergence of the Ku Klux Klan and the fundamentalist fight against Darwin's theory of evolution and "demon rum" took one avenue. Journalists took another by investigating the problems of Southern society including Klan violence, lynching, public health issues, and child and convict labor practices. The renaissance of Southern literature marked a third route to this new conscious-ness. As Vanderbilt poet Allen Tate said, "After the war the South again knew the world, but it had a memory of another war; with us, entering the world once more meant not the obliteration of the past but a heightened conscious-ness of it; so that we had a double focus, a looking two ways, which gave a special dimension to the writings of our school." Novelist Ellen Glasgow ex-plained this Janus-faced response to the new realities of the South after World War I. "I do not like the twin curses of modern standardization and mass production," she said in 1931. "I do not like filling stations and smoke stacks in place of hedges. Yet I like even less the hookworm and pellagra and lynching of the agrarian scene, the embattled forces of religious prejudice and the snarl-ing feature of our rural dry-nurse prohibition."[34]

During the 1920s, the progressive agenda embraced by Southern politicians during Woodrow Wilson's administration became what Tindall dubbed "busi-ness progressivism." Ignoring social justice issues, instead this new approach focused on business and what it could bring to the region. "The 'progressive' community," Tindall felt, "was one that had good government, great churches, improved schools, industry, business, [and] real estate booms." Arkansas gov-ernor John E. Martineau's slogan, like that of other governors throughout the South, captured the essence: "Better roads and better schools."[35]

The region benefited from this new approach with improved roads, better education, and more effective public health and social welfare programs. The South witnessed an institutionalization and professionalism new to Dixie. Tindall's research demonstrated that the increase in paved road mileage from 69,797 in 1914 to 209,880 in 1930 brought with it profound changes. These roads pierced provincial isolation, made it easier to commute from the farm to the factory, and brought new economic opportunities associated with the automobile: service stations, motels, and tourism. Education received much-needed support under this new governmental activism as well as public health campaigns to combat tuberculosis, hookworm, malaria, pellagra, and syphilis —long the banes of Southern existence.[36]

Tindall noticed this progressive spirit penetrating the 1928 presidential election between Al Smith and Herbert Hoover. Although this is cited as the election that broke the "Solid South," with traditional Democrats voting for Hoover because they could not support a New York Catholic who was the product of Tammany Hall, other issues were also at play. Not everyone who voted for the GOP nominee did so out of disgust for Al Smith. Tin-dall's analysis of election returns disclosed that Hoover had also succeeded in Southern cities that were acutely "progress-conscious" like Houston, Dal-las, Birmingham, Atlanta, Chattanooga, and Richmond. Despite evidence of change in the civic realm, Tindall also made clear that this form of progressivism left many people out of its plans, which emphasizes the continuity of old traditions in Southern politics. "Race relations were assumed to be a settled issue. The economic problems of the underprivileged, farm tenants and factory workers, were not its problems; their remedy would come, if at all, through economic growth." As a result, the South witnessed a change in the concept of government—one that promoted efficiency, professionalism, and an increase in services—while old patterns of paternalism and neglect continued unabated.[37]

With the economic collapse of 1929, the South's problems came to the forefront of the nation. Despite the progress made in some Southern cities, the majority of Southerners still lived in rural areas that had been plagued by falling cotton and tobacco prices. The drought of 1930 made a bad situation worse. "Deliverance," Tindall explained, "came under the familiar banner of the Democracy and in the person of the Dutch squire of the Hudson Valley." Franklin Roosevelt would be an ally of Dixie—he knew the South and was sympathetic to its problems—but his New Deal programs would assist in transforming the South by upsetting long-cherished traditions. As Tindall showed, the New Deal induced "the first real stirring of the Southern 'proletariat'—submerged elements like the sharecropper, the textile worker, and the Negro domestic servant."[38]

The pace of change that began in the years before the First World War accelerated during the New Deal. Southern Democrats supported the increased federal presence in their region because of unprecedented desperation and hopelessness. Tindall's book discussed the legislation passed before 1936 and the Southern politicians associated with the new laws, such as Alabama's Senator John H. Bankhead II, sponsor of the Agricultural Adjustment Act. "The farm program . . . clearly helped the South more than any other region in benefits, prices, and income," Tindall wrote, but he also pointed out the harm caused by this important program. After describing how the AAA hurt tenants and sharecroppers, Tindall explained the reasons behind this: "[T]he farm program was the product of the first New Deal of stabilization and recovery, not the second New Deal of reform and social democracy."[39]

Other New Deal programs found acceptance among impoverished Southerners more than among businessmen and politicians. Although declared unconstitutional in 1935, the National Industrial Recovery Act (NIRA) drastically altered labor standards in the South, bringing the region closer to its Northern neighbors. "The experiment was generally put down as a failure," Tindall wrote, "but it left a permanent mark on the South." The forty-hour work week, the minimum wage, and an end to child labor remained even though the Supreme Court struck down the legislation. In addition to new labor standards, the NIRA "encouraged modernization of machinery." The recognition of collective bargaining found in its critical Section 7(a) dramatically "spurred the rise of the labor movement in the South."[40]

New Deal welfare programs continued to push the South to embrace what the federal government offered and, in the process, modified long-held Southern traditions. The work relief programs sponsored by the Works Progress Administration provided new levels of income for many Southerners, which increased their loyalty to the nation while threatening those who had benefited from the South's low-wage practices. Many Southern states altered the legislation to fit with local conventions. "In Louisiana," Tindall discovered, "regulations stipulated that relief offices should consider sharecroppers for WPA referral only after consultation with the plantation management or the usual source of credit." Tindall uncovered other discrepancies in how New Deal programs operated in the South. Social Security old-age insurance did not benefit agricultural workers and domestic servants. By 1937, he showed, "all Southern states had entered the program but it covered only a third of their labor force compared to a half in other states. . . . Still, the Federal money held out a compelling lure and expenditures for public welfare in the South expanded phenomenally." Beyond offering a safety net, the Social Security Act altered the relationship between the states and the federal government and helped to modernize Southern state governments with budgets, merit systems, and retirement programs.[41]

Social changes brought on by the New Deal precipitated serious changes in Southern society, most notably in the areas of labor practices and race relations. Tindall attributed to these federally sponsored programs the further realization of the emerging New South, which also fostered the disenchantment of many Southern Democrats with the New Deal effort. Before the Supreme Court ruled the NIRA unconstitutional, in *Schenck v. U.S.* (1935), John L. Lewis took the lead in bringing his United Mine Workers of America to the South. Even on the heels of the 1934 failure of the general strike in textile organizing, the South's working classes witnessed transforming possibilities just one year later with the passage of the National Labor Relations Act and the creation of the Congress of Industrial Organizations (CIO). Although the CIO faltered in organizing Southern textile mills, Tindall credited the new industrial unions with setting the stage "from which unionism made further rapid gains during World War II." Finally, Tindall made clear the importance of this legislation. "Under the stimulus of Federal aid all Southern states by 1940 provided for unemployment insurance and public employment services. . . . Between 1935 and 1941 six Southern states established or reorganized labor departments." By reminding his readers of the importance of these changes in labor practices, Tindall brought them back to his essential theme of continuity and change. While he agreed that the New Deal left "a legacy of permanent unionism and minimal standards set by legislation," he concluded that these were not truly revolutionary changes because "unionism involved a minority of workers and the legal standards exempted vast numbers from their application."[42]

Parts of the New Deal also assisted black Southerners in new and varied ways. Tindall claimed that the Great Migration, the "New Negro" movement, the National Association for the Advancement of Colored People, the interracial movement, and new concepts in anthropology began the process of "undermin[ing] the intellectual respectability of racism" before the 1930s. In some cases the New Deal continued the process of cracking the foundation of white supremacy, especially in the Interior and Justice departments, in the National Youth Administration, and in the Social Security Administration. In these bureaus black administrators worked as advisors making sure programs addressed the needs of African-Americans. And, although some legislation hurt more than it helped (such as the AAA that pushed out tenants when crops were limited and the National Recovery Administration that raised wages, displacing black workers for white workers), Tindall's research indicated that "in urban areas, both North and South, the proportion of Negroes on the relief rolls was greater than in the population." As a result of this new federal support, and of their inclusion in the industrial unions of the CIO, African-Americans made an epic shift in 1936 from the party of Lincoln to the party of Roosevelt.[43]

Throughout the 1930s changes were also afoot in the private sector. For the working classes, the CIO tried to keep its unions open to black people and opposed Jim Crow practices in its official policies—although this did not always successfully translate to Southern locals. For the middle classes, NAACP attorneys—under the guidance of Charles Hamilton Houston—began to attack the "separate but equal" doctrine in public education beginning at the graduate and professional school level. These efforts laid the groundwork for the burgeoning civil rights movement that moved forward after World War II. Nevertheless, the repeating Tindall motif of change and stasis reemerged. "New themes appeared in every department of Negro life. But up the back alleys and down the by-paths of the South, Negroes still lived in a world remote from the battlefronts of social and economic issues. . . . [yet] underneath the stagnant surfaces of Negro life new forces stirred, new directions emerged, new expectations quickened."[44]

Throughout the early New Deal, Southern politicians of all stripes supported FDR's programs. Nevertheless, as his administration moved forward, a growing federal presence made enemies for the president. Tindall wrote that "crop limitations antagonized the cotton trade, codes and labor standards annoyed industrialists, relief policies and the NRA raised the issue of wage differentials." More significantly, "all touched on racial discrimination and all threatened existing relationships in the social power structure." As the so-called "second New Deal" stirred into action after 1935, conservative Southern members of Congress realized that "the New Deal jeopardized a power that rested on the control of property, labor, credit, and local government"—not to mention racial control.[45]

Not willing to confront the powerful president outright, these congressmen took the opportunity to put the genie back in the bottle when Roosevelt gave them the opportunity. In 1937 they mobilized to defy FDR's attempt to pack the Supreme Court with justices sympathetic to his cause. The relationship between the president and his fellow Southern Democrats further unraveled when Roosevelt campaigned openly against congressional opponents in the 1938 elections. The New Deal's decline was under way as Southern leaders "cut relief expenditures, eliminated the Federal Theater Project, rejected Roosevelt's appointments, [and] abolished the undistributed profits tax." Many Southerners associated with the power structure were afraid of the New Deal. Not only did it threaten traditional conventions, but it also gave federal aid and comfort to liberals who could now work independently from local and state parties. Dixie's politicians reacted by working to thwart any further progress. Tindall concluded that "Roosevelt, like Wilson, failed in any fundamental way to reshape the amorphous factionalism below the Potomac."[46]

The onset of World War II partially healed the disaffection between the president and the Southern Democrats. Largely through their assistance, Roosevelt was able to offer crucial support to the Allies before the United States entered the war. Tindall explained that Southerners as ideologically diverse as Carter Glass and Claude Pepper backed FDR in these endeavors because of their "internationalism." Without their endorsement, the president "would have lost on neutrality revision in 1939 and 1941, the Lend-Lease Act, draft extension, and authorization for seizing foreign and arming American merchant ships."[47]

With the advancement of the war effort, the South's emergence reached its peak. Tindall explained that the war "intensified established trends: in economic development, race relations, and politics." War industries brought to the South better paying jobs and people from outside of the region and union membership increased. The war put Southern soldiers and sailors into contact with people and places far beyond the Mason-Dixon line in military camps and on Europe's battlefields. A. Philip Randolph's threatened "March on Washington" movement pushed FDR to sign Executive Order 8802 establishing the Committee on Fair Employment Practices, which acknowledged that African-Americans should benefit from the war effort too. During the 1940s the Supreme Court struck down the all-white primary in its *Smith v.*

Allwright decision. Tindall wrote of young blacks challenging segregation at lunch counters and in railroad dining cars. He quoted a black soldier who told his white tormentors, "If I've got to die for democracy, I might as well die for some of it right here and now."[48]

By 1945, the Southern landscape had been dramatically transformed from the days before World War I. To make this clear, Tindall chose the words of Alabama writer Herman Clarence Nixon: "In 1945 the South emerged from the war with fewer sharecroppers but more pipe-fitters and welders, with less plowing and hoeing but more mowing and sowing, with less rural isolation and more urban sophistication, with nearly a million people in the ranks of organized labor and a growing movement for antiunion laws, with veterans returning from new experiences beyond the seven seas, and with a standard of living for the common man that was undreamed of in its prewar philosophy." In the face of this "emergence," old patterns remained. Despite the internationalism of Southern politicians, many refused to embrace true change on the home front. Tindall closed his magnum opus by leaving readers poised on a precipice. "[W]hich would prevail," he asked, "the broader vision or the defensive reaction?"[49]

After publication of *The Emergence of the New South* Tindall continued to write articles, teach undergraduates, mentor graduate students, and deliver lectures until his retirement in the early 1990s. In the 1970s he gave the Mercer University Lamar Memorial Lecture series published as *The Disruption of the Solid South* and the Louisiana State University Fleming Lectures called *The Persistent Tradition in New South Politics*. He found his now-familiar theme of continuity and change in these subjects as well, "reflecting his growing strength as a synthesizer of Southern history," according to his former graduate student Dan Carter. Although one can still argue which part of the pattern dominates—the transforming South or the enduring South—George Tindall offered a provocative way to understand the process by which the region emerged after the post-Reconstruction period. His commitment to incorporate all members of Dixie's society—black, white, and ethnic—and his use of literature and sociology enriched his historical narrative and left a strong foundation for any study of this period in Southern history. In his 1973 presidential address to the Southern Historical Society, "Beyond the Mainstream: The Ethnic Southerners," Tindall reminded his audience of the value in understanding this evolutionary transformation of the South. "Change is manifest and undeniable," he declared. "Yet we learn time and again from the Southern past and the history of others that to change is not necessarily to disappear. And we learn from modern psychology that to change is not necessarily to lose one's identity; to change, sometimes, is to find it."[50]

Anne Firor Scott

Writing Women into Southern History

ANASTATIA SIMS

Anne Firor Scott readily admits that she did not invent Southern women's history. Indeed, she has edited a collection of works by historians who were writing about women in the South decades before she published her first article. However, her predecessors labored outside the mainstream of the historical profession and their work received little recognition. When Scott began her research in the late 1950s, women were, at best, peripheral figures in monographs and textbooks. Most historians ignored women because their experiences seemed irrelevant to the major questions of historical inquiry. As Scott has pointed out, the index to Arthur S. Link and Rembert W. Patrick's 1965 survey of Southern historiography listed only three references to women. In 1967, a collection of essays by historians, sociologists, and other social scientists entitled *Perspectives on the South: Agenda for Research* did not mention women at all, an omission that seems particularly glaring in retrospect, since the volume grew out of a symposium held at Duke University, where Scott taught. Three years later, the publication of *The Southern Lady: From Pedestal to Politics, 1830–1930* heralded the emergence of Southern women's history and established Anne Firor Scott as its preeminent scholar. The book defined the framework for much subsequent research, and it remains the starting point for studies of middle- and upper-class white women in the nineteenth and early twentieth centuries.[1]

Like many of her generation, Anne Scott did not set out to write women's history; in fact, she did not set out to write history at all. Born in 1921 in the south-central Georgia village of Montezuma, she was, she recalled, reared "to be a proper Southern lady in behavior, speech, and manner." But her parents, John William and Mary Moss Firor, never imposed any "intellectual distinctions on the basis of sex" on her or her three younger brothers. Although she majored in history at the University of Georgia, she "dreamed impartially about becoming a medical doctor or the mother of six." After she graduated in 1941, uncertainty about her long-term goals led her to make several false starts. She worked briefly for IBM, served as a Congressional intern, got a master's degree in political science from Northwestern University in 1944, then joined the staff of the League of Women Voters. In June 1947 she married Andrew Mackay Scott. That fall, they moved to Cambridge, Massachusetts, and enrolled in graduate school, he in Harvard's political science department; she in Radcliffe's program in American civilization. By 1950 she had finished course work, passed preliminary examinations for the doctorate, and begun research for a dissertation under the direction of Oscar Handlin. By this time, however, Andrew had completed his degree and was ready to embark on his career. Over the next eight years, the Scotts moved three times and Anne gave birth to three children. In addition, she edited the League of Women Voters' monthly newsletter for two years. Still, she carved out time to finish her dissertation, "Southern Progressives in the National Congress, 1906–1916," and received the doctorate in 1958. She held temporary appointments at Haverford College and the University of North Carolina before joining the faculty at Duke University as a part-time assistant professor in 1961. This job, too, was supposed to be temporary; she was told that she could stay only until the history department hired a "suitable replacement" for a man who had recently resigned. Recounting the circumstances of her initial employment at Duke twenty-two years later, Scott noted wryly, "Presumably the department never found a 'suitable replacement' for the departed colleague, for I am there yet." She was named W. K. Boyd Professor of History in 1980 and remained at Duke until her retirement in 1991.[2]

While teaching at Haverford she began research on the life of Jane Addams; in 1964 she published a new edition of Addams's *Democracy and Social Ethics*. However, the Scotts' move to North Carolina in 1958 quashed her plans to write a biography. Instead, she shifted her gaze southward, and began following leads she had first uncovered while doing research for her doctoral thesis. Histories of Southern Progressivism—including her own dissertation —focused on male reformers, but she had repeatedly encountered women in primary sources. She started searching for more examples of white women's activism in the early twentieth century, and slowly the project evolved, from a seminar presentation to a conference paper to one article, then two, and eventually a monograph that spanned a century.[3]

It took Scott longer than she anticipated to complete the manuscript, but the delay worked to her advantage. *The Southern Lady* could not have appeared at a more propitious time. In 1970 trends in scholarship and politics were converging to establish women as legitimate subjects for historical research. Scholars were redefining social history to emphasize the experiences of groups that previously had been neglected. Simultaneously, activists in a resurgent feminist movement decried historians' omission of women and challenged women to reclaim their collective past. Although it occurred by accident rather than design, Scott's decision to publish when she did demonstrated a flair for timing worthy of her impeccable title character. *The Southern Lady* found a ready audience among professors seeking to revise existing courses in Southern history or develop new ones in women's history, graduate students striving to make their mark in an emerging field, feminists searching for their foremothers, and a reading public possessing a seemingly endless fascination with the Old South in general and Southern womanhood in particular.

Scott was one of the first Southern historians to write about women and one of the first women's historians to write about the South. At the time *The Southern Lady* was published, historians of the Old South were wrestling with questions of class and race—exploring relationships between planters and nonslaveholding whites, revising descriptions of plantation life, and reinterpreting the meaning of slavery for both African-Americans and whites. But they did not factor gender into their analyses or consider the unique experiences of women in their narratives. In addition to providing a window into the plantation household, Scott reminded scholars that while patriarchy encompassed relationships between masters and slaves, it rested on relationships between men and women. Citing proslavery apologist George Fitzhugh, she explained, "Any tendency on the part of any of the members of the system to assert themselves against the master threatened the whole, and therefore slavery itself." Scott introduced an argument that other historians would expand upon: white women must remain in their place so that slaves could be kept in theirs.[4]

New South historians suffered from the same blindness to gender that afflicted their peers who studied the antebellum era. They were preoccupied with political and economic issues, and they assumed that women—who controlled neither votes nor property—played no role in the stories they were trying to tell. The majority of scholars, male and female alike, considered the maxim "woman's place is in the home" an accurate, though perhaps quaint, description of historical reality. This notion was so firmly embedded in historians' minds that they did not see women, even when historical records clearly indicated their presence. But Anne Scott *had* seen them, and her desire to resolve the paradox of discovering women in places where they were not supposed to be sparked the research that developed into *The Southern Lady*. By tracing women's participation in late nineteenth- and early twentieth-century reform movements, she contradicted the conventional wisdom that Southern women had been excluded from politics before they got the vote. Although she accepted the prevailing assumption that Southern Progressivism was "for whites only," she proved conclusively that it was not for men only.[5]

The Southern Lady not only broke new ground in Southern history, it also integrated white Southerners into the nascent literature on American women. Since we now live in an era when publishers boast of their lists in women's history and bookstores display dozens of titles under the category of Women's Studies, it is easy to forget just how sparse the historiography was in 1970. Books and articles about women's history written before 1955 were, for the most part, out of print and forgotten. The available secondary literature consisted of fewer than two dozen books and a scattering of articles in anthologies and journals. Works about white Southern women comprised only a small constellation in this tiny universe. Scott's was the first monograph to describe the experiences of women throughout the South since Julia Cherry Spruill's *Women's Life and Work in the Southern Colonies,* published in 1938.[6]

In 1970 most of the historians who were writing about women were concentrating on the women's rights movement, a subject compatible with conventional political history. But Scott moved beyond the boundaries of traditional historical topics. She was among a small number of scholars who anticipated the question Gerda Lerner posed nine years later: "What would history be like if it were seen through the eyes of women, and ordered by values they define?" Although Scott examined women's participation in politics and reform, she also looked closely at aspects of women's private lives—courtship and marriage, sexuality and reproduction, gender roles and family relationships—subjects that had always been crucial to women and that became a major focus of women's history.[7]

One of the central themes Scott addressed concerned the interplay of image and reality in women's lives, a question that also preoccupied other historians. In the mid-1960s, Barbara Welter combed through nineteenth-century magazines, sermons, and advice books to uncover "the cult of true womanhood"—the celebration of the four cardinal virtues of purity, piety, submissiveness, and domesticity that, she argued, constituted the core of the antebellum feminine ideal. Gerda Lerner also described female role models in a 1969 article entitled "The Lady and the Mill Girl." But Welter and Lerner relied on sources from the industrializing, urbanizing Northeast. While the Southern lady that Scott portrayed possessed many of the same characteristics, she was rooted in the soil of the South, in an economy based on slavery and a society built on the premise that all men were *not* created equal. Northerners and Southerners shared similar notions about feminine nature and appropriate feminine behavior, but true womanhood carried different connotations south of the Mason-Dixon line.[8]

Anne Scott delineated a portrait of the Southern lady and her real-life counterparts that has been incorporated into virtually all subsequent scholarship on white women of the Old South. The idealized Southern lady never complained, never questioned patriarchal authority, always sacrificed her own desires to the needs of others, and maintained an unwavering religious faith that sustained her through sorrow and disappointment. Real women found it difficult to measure up to such an exacting standard although, as Scott discovered when she read their diaries and letters, many tried. Perhaps they wished for forbearance such as Scott's lady had to help them endure the hardships of their own lives for, despite their privileged status, elite Southern women did not fritter away their days painting china, stitching fancy needlework, and practicing their French. Instead, they worked hard to carry out the duties that managing a large household entailed. Although they supervised slaves who performed much of the physical labor, planters' wives bore ultimate responsibility for providing food, clothing, and medical care for everyone on the plantation. As Scott explained, "the mistress was expected to understand not only the skills of spinning, weaving, and sewing but also gardening, care of the poultry, care of the sick, and all aspects of food preparation from the sowing of seed to the appearance of the final product on the table." In addition to these tasks there were the ever-present obligations of motherhood. Because of the lack of effective contraception, women spent most of their adult lives bearing and rearing children. Frequent pregnancies took both a physical and an emotional toll; every time a woman approached childbirth she knew she risked death. Scott debunked the myth of the plantation mistress as a carefree, elegant lady of leisure, and used elite women's own words to provide insights into their feelings about their lives and their assigned role in Southern society.[9]

Slavery was among the topics elite women discussed, and Scott concluded that they secretly despised it. "Most Southern women who expressed themselves on the peculiar institution opposed slavery and were glad when it was ended," she declared. She buttressed her assertion with comments ranging from complaints about laziness and insolence to sentimental reminiscences of beloved personal servants. Furthermore, she connected white women's opposition to slavery with their abhorrence of its by-product, miscegenation. In both *The Southern Lady* and an article published in the *Journal of American History* four years later, she emphasized the humiliation and pain that slaveholders' wives endured when their husbands strayed into the slave quarters, and she deduced that women translated their private anguish into a critique of the institution of slavery.[10]

Like all historians, Scott was limited by the sources she used. Although she cited some contemporaneous manuscripts, she relied heavily on memoirs and diaries—such as Mary Boykin Chesnut's oft-quoted *Diary From Dixie*—that were published decades after the Civil War. White Southern women who promised to share an inside view of the Old South with the reading public revised, embellished, and, perhaps, suffered from selective amnesia. Historians now know (as they did not in 1970) that Chesnut not only edited her journal, she rewrote it several times to increase its appeal to readers. Other authors did the same. As Jean E. Friedman has pointed out, "women made their most damning antislavery statements in their memoirs."[11]

In the years since the publication of *The Southern Lady* scholars have searched for more definitive evidence to support, or refute, Scott's argument. Examination of letters and diaries penned by slaveholding women between 1780 and 1835 led Catherine Clinton to conclude that they held a "soft" position on slavery. "The plantation mistress," she asserted, "saw herself as the conscience of the slave South." Women interceded with their fathers and husbands to protect slaves from harsh punishments and to stop sales that would break up families. However, Clinton stopped short of describing elite women as opponents of slavery. She observed that women's opinions varied according to age. Young wives adjusting to their new responsibilities as household managers were more likely to denounce slavery, while "matrons, many years of experience later, generally groaned over the evils of *slaves* rather than the curse of slavery." In her study of Petersburg, Virginia, Suzanne Lebsock also distinguished between white women's feelings about individuals and their attitudes toward the institution. Comparing the wills of male and female slaveholders, she found that more women than men made special provisions for favorite slaves, in the form of small bequests, restrictions on future sales, or, in a few instances, manumission. Her sample was small, and although she described women as a "subversive influence on chattel slavery," she concluded that their actions stemmed from affection for individuals rather than hatred of the system. Jean Friedman took a different view. She acknowledged that "some black and white women formed extraordinary relationships of affection and mutual respect"; however, she emphasized the factors that separated mistresses from slaves and argued that "slavery divided women." In 1998 Elizabeth Varon added a new dimension to the discussion. Looking at newspapers, journals, broadsides, and legislative petitions, she found that a number of slaveholding women in Virginia were active in the American Colonization Society in the 1830s and the 1840s. Their participation in an organization committed to gradual emancipation and expatriation demonstrated the desire of some Southerners to find a "'middle ground' between the philosophies of radical abolitionism and proslavery ideology." It also reflected the range of opinions among elite white women; some joined because they sympathized with African-Americans; others because they feared them.[12]

Elizabeth Fox-Genovese offered the most direct challenge to Scott in her study of white and African-American women on plantations. She argued that despite their complaints, slaveholding women understood that "slavery, with all its abuses, constituted the fabric of their beloved country—the warp and woof of their social position, their personal relations, their very identities." Thus they accepted the peculiar institution and had no desire to witness its demise. Fox-Genovese grounded her argument in an analysis of the world view of Southern slaveholders, a view predicated on a belief in hierarchy and racial inequality that precluded the development of abolitionist sympathies. Like Clinton and Scott, she looked to women's diaries for evidence. In particular, she closely examined Mary Boykin Chesnut's famous journal, in all of its versions. She insisted that, contrary to opinions expressed in several well-known passages of *A Diary from Dixie,* Chesnut was no advocate of equality for African-Americans or for women. Although Fox-Genovese mentioned neither *The Southern Lady* nor its author by name in her chapter on slaveholding women's attitudes toward slavery, her intensive scrutiny of Chesnut's life and writings suggested that she wrote at least in part in response to Scott, who had used the published diary to support her conclusions.[13]

Scott addressed the modifications and challenges to her interpretation in the afterword to the twenty-fifth anniversary edition of *The Southern Lady.* If she were rewriting the book, she conceded, she would be "more cautious in attributing antislavery views to large numbers of white women because . . . there is as yet no way of quantifying the evidence or knowing how representative were the views I had unearthed." She reiterated, however, that some slaveholding women harbored serious moral reservations about slavery, while others objected to the burdens slave ownership imposed on whites. She called on scholars to mine the primary sources "to give some sturdier underpinnings to the various points of view."[14]

Scott generated still more controversy with her assessment of the Civil War and its impact on white women. The war, she wrote in the first edition of *The Southern Lady,* "speeded social change and opened Pandora's box." She documented the upheaval that occurred when men marched away and left women behind to manage plantations, farms, and businesses, cope with dire shortages of food, clothing, and other necessities, and, on occasion, confront invading armies. The war and the era of Reconstruction that followed tested white Southern women's courage, ingenuity, and perseverance, and most came through with flying colors. Brought up to depend on men for protection and sustenance, they learned when men left that they could fend for themselves and their children.[15]

But how did they interpret those lessons? That question has stimulated an ongoing debate among historians. Scott argued that the war changed forever white women's self-images and expectations. Although the ideal of the lady lingered, the New Woman began to emerge from the ruins of the Confederacy, as women seized new opportunities in employment, education, and politics. According to Scott, the patriarchy was among the casualties of war, and in the years after Appomattox white women, as well as their former slaves, embarked on the road to full emancipation.[16]

Several scholars have disagreed. In the epilogue to *The Free Women of Petersburg* Suzanne Lebsock speculated that the assault on the patriarchy brought about by the end of slavery and Confederate defeat may have retarded progress for white women. Although she admitted that only further research could produce definitive answers, she predicted that historians might discover that "male authority was wounded, and for women this had to be dangerous." LeeAnn Whites, writing about Augusta, Georgia, confirmed that the Civil War was "a crisis in gender" that led white Southern men to turn to "the domestic arena as the one remaining location of legitimate domination." In an essay about refugees, Joan Cashin agreed that the war disrupted the South's system of gender relations and argued that, after the fighting ended, white women "dealt with it by denial." They refused to acknowledge that men had failed to protect them; instead they channeled their energies into rebuilding their households. In his study of Confederate women, George Rable found the postwar changes to be more illusory than real. While the end of the war raised the possibility of a revolution in gender roles, "for most white women, as for Southerners generally, the promise of a 'New South' remained unfulfilled." Jean Friedman reached a similar conclusion. Gaines M. Foster offered an even bleaker assessment of the war's impact on white women in *Ghosts of the Confederacy: Defeat, the Lost Cause, and the Emergence of the New South;* he maintained that "the war and defeat had done little to alter the patriarchy of the Old South." Drew Gilpin Faust, focusing on elite women in a book entitled *Mothers of Invention: Women of the Slaveholding South in the American Civil War,* concluded that the war left an ambiguous legacy. As she explained in a subsequent essay, "After Appomattox dependence seemed dangerous, yet the burdens of independence appeared frightening." During and after the war white Southern women learned lessons about both self-reliance and vulnerability, lessons that caused them to doubt men on the one hand, and to acknowledge their own limitations on the other. Faust argued that these messages shaped women's self-perceptions as they assumed new public roles in the decades after Reconstruction and profoundly influenced the development of a distinctively Southern brand of feminism.[17]

Anne Scott took issue with this interpretation in a review published in the *Journal of Southern History.* She chided Faust for glossing over the variations in slaveholding women's individual responses to the war. "For every one who deplored the necessity of taking new responsibilities," she claimed, "there was another who found such demands satisfying, even exhilarating." Furthermore, Scott disputed Faust's analysis of the impact of war and defeat on women's public activities in the late nineteenth century. Where Faust saw women torn between resolve to be self-sufficient and reluctance to "abandon the possibility of white male power and protection entirely and forever," Scott described female reformers as women who embraced change and shed no tears for the world they had lost. In her review, Scott reiterated points she had made earlier in response to historians who challenged her contention that the Civil War was a watershed for white Southern women. She repudiated any suggestion that the war brought little or no alteration in white women's status and denied the possibility that they might have suffered a setback because of the Confederacy's defeat. She insisted that the war triggered a chain reaction of positive change for women that has continued to the present day. "Each succeeding generation of Southern women, down to this moment," she wrote in 1995, "has had broader opportunities than did their mothers."[18]

That optimistic assessment pervaded the second half of *The Southern Lady*. Scott described the gains women made in employment, education, and public life. She paid particular attention to the proliferation of voluntary associations. Missionary societies, temperance unions, and women's clubs, she argued, provided the bridge that enabled white Southern women to step off the pedestal and into politics. Organizations gave women a public voice long before they got the vote, and Scott emphasized the ways in which women used that voice to denounce the injustices they saw around them. At the same time, participation in voluntary associations transformed demure Southern ladies into poised political activists; according to Scott, elite women traveled a straight line from the parlor to the voting booth. "The biographies of hundreds of women show the same progression: missionary society, temperance society, woman's club," she declared. Clubs, in turn, "created a potential constituency of self-confident women" to lead the fight for suffrage. Changes in behavior brought changes in the prevailing feminine ideal. By the mid-1920s, Scott wrote, the New Woman had replaced the Southern lady. Although the lady's image "lived on as habit or useful protective coloration . . . it had largely lost its force as a blueprint for woman's life."[19]

In the years since 1970 scholars have written numerous books, articles, dissertations, and theses about women's voluntary associations at local, state, and regional levels. These studies have confirmed Scott's discovery that women were key players in Progressive reform and in the creation of the welfare state. Women's organizations founded libraries, established parks and playgrounds, cleaned up schoolhouses, supported reformatories for juvenile offenders, campaigned for prohibition, advocated compulsory education, sought regulations on working conditions for women and children in industry, lobbied for increased state assistance to the indigent, the ill, and the elderly, and undertook numerous other projects in their attempt to solve the social and economic problems of the New South. Before and after suffrage, they developed and promoted a political agenda that centered on what they defined as women's issues: education, health, and public welfare.[20]

At the same time that historians have amplified Scott's analysis of women and Progressivism, they have reassessed the impact of women's public activities on the suffrage movement and the image of the Southern lady. Recent scholarship has emphasized the diversity among women's voluntary associations. While Scott focused on reformist groups such as the Woman's Christian Temperance Union and women's clubs, scholars have now begun to examine organizations committed to preserving tradition, most notably the United Daughters of the Confederacy (UDC). The UDC was one of the largest and most influential voluntary associations for white Southern women. Dedicated to commemorating the Lost Cause and glorifying the Old South, the Daughters shaped Southerners' interpretations of the past and simultaneously promoted a model of womanhood for the present. They celebrated a feminine ideal that combined the gentleness and grace of the antebellum lady with the resourcefulness and strength of Confederate heroines. While they did not call for a return to the days of female subordination and dependence—indeed, they were ardent champions of increased educational opportunities for women—they believed that women could best serve their state and nation by acting as preceptors of patriotism rather than as participants in politics. Many members of the UDC and other patriotic societies opposed woman suffrage and used the skills they had gained in voluntary associations to lead the fight against it. In a comparative analysis of the backgrounds of suffragists and antisuffragists, Elna Green found that while "women's clubs were extremely popular among women on both sides," suffrage opponents were more likely than advocates to be active in patriotic societies, especially the UDC. Just as women reacted in a variety of ways to the independence spawned by the Civil War, so, too, did they draw different lessons from the expanded public roles created by voluntary associations.[21]

The UDC, women's clubs, and the first Southern suffrage organizations developed in the 1890s, the same decade in which white women were incorporated into the political process not as participants, but as symbols. White supremacists used "protection of white womanhood" as their rallying cry. They claimed that emancipation and enfranchisement had produced an epidemic of sexual assaults. To save the virtue of white women, they insisted, they had to deny political rights to African-American men, by law if possible, by force if necessary. Although the white supremacy campaigns were beyond the scope of Scott's study, subsequent historians have scrutinized the consequences of the rhetoric of rape for white Southern women. Just as the South's first New Women were beginning to assert their independence, white men adopted a political strategy that emphasized female vulnerability. Jacquelyn Dowd Hall has suggested that the timing was not coincidental. Politicians instilled fear in white women—an awareness of what one woman called a "nameless horror"—that would continue to have a chilling effect on Southern feminism. Moreover, white supremacists assigned a new and potent political meaning to the image of the Southern lady. Rather than fading into oblivion as a relic of a bygone era, she was revitalized by men like North Carolina's Charles Brantley Aycock, who exhorted voters to approve disfranchisement "in the name of 'the White Goddess of Democracy'—the White Womanhood of the State."[22]

White supremacists linked gender, race, and the right to vote and established the parameters within which women would wage their battle for the ballot. Southern suffragists were compelled to confront the race issue, and for more than three decades historians have debated the nature of their response. Aileen S. Kraditor initiated the discussion in 1965, with the publication of *The Ideas of the Woman Suffrage Movement, 1890–1920*. In a chapter devoted to the "Southern Question," she contended that defense of white supremacy was the cornerstone of the prosuffrage argument in the South. Five years later, Anne Scott disputed this interpretation in *The Southern Lady*. While she acknowledged that some suffragists tried to win support for their cause by promising that white women's votes would offset those of black men, she maintained that such statements were only a minor part of suffragists' strategy. Suzanne Lebsock concurred. In an essay about Virginia suffragists and white supremacy, she blamed antisuffragists for introducing racism into the campaign. She argued that suffragists practiced a "politics of denial"; because they considered race a "bogus issue," they tried to ignore it. Elna Green took the argument one step further. She held that the opposing camps interpreted the term "white supremacy" in different ways: antisuffragists wanted a "white monopoly," which would exclude all African-Americans from the polls, while suffragists endorsed a version of white supremacy that accepted the presence of some blacks in the electorate—and, implicitly, the principle of political equality for African-Americans—as long as whites continued to constitute a majority. Like other scholars, Green recognized a spectrum of opinions on the race issue among suffragists, ranging from virulent racism at one extreme to "remarkable racial egalitarianism" at the other. Overall, however, she conveyed an impression of suffragists as racial liberals who deviated from Southern orthodoxy on white supremacy, minimized the importance of race as a political factor, and consistently refused to play the race card throughout the thirty-year history of the suffrage movement in the South.[23]

Marjorie Spruill Wheeler presented the most comprehensive analysis of Southern suffrage ideology in *New Women of the New South: The Leaders of the Woman Suffrage Movement in the Southern States*. She accepted the premise that woman suffrage and white supremacy were intertwined in Southern politics, but she pointed out that the relationship was complex and changed over time. The early days of the suffrage movement coincided with the first efforts to enact laws disfranchising African-American men. In fact, Wheeler wrote, the predominance of the race issue in Southern politics in the 1890s influenced the timing and tactics of first-generation suffragists. White supremacy campaigns launched a debate over who was qualified to vote, and suffragists seized the opportunity to call for the enfranchisement of women. Frustrated by their failure to convince legislators that women deserved the ballot as a matter of justice, suffragists resorted to appeals to racial solidarity, pointing out that if white women joined white men at the polls, white voters would outnumber blacks. By 1910, however, circumstances had changed. Literacy tests and poll taxes had removed African-American men from politics, and the argument that white women's votes would neutralize those of black men was no longer relevant. From then on, most suffragists referred to race only when necessary to counter their opponents' claims that woman suffrage would destroy white political hegemony. Wheeler's evidence for the period 1910 to 1920 supported the views of Scott and Lebsock that suffragists regarded race as "a 'non-issue' trumped up by their opponents," and she found that during that time leaders made "relatively few attempts to exploit the race issue strategically." Unlike Green, however, she rejected the notion that their defensive stance implied an acceptance of political equality for African-Americans. Instead, suffragists attempted to break the link that white supremacists had forged between race and gender and to divorce their political destiny from that of black men. Wheeler concluded that suffragists' attitudes on race defied simple categorization. Most were relatively enlightened on racial matters when compared to the majority of their contemporaries, but they were, nevertheless, products of their place and time who shared the prevailing view among Progressives that voting was a privilege that should be restricted to the "best classes" of society; therefore, they failed to denounce white supremacy.[24]

Anne Scott revisited the question of white supremacy and woman suffrage in her review of Drew Faust's *Mothers of Invention*, published in 1996. She challenged two of Faust's conclusions: first, that when viewed from a late-twentieth-century perspective, women's postwar public activities represented "an almost inexplicable paradox of progress and reaction," and, second, that race inhibited the development of Southern feminism by leading white women to subordinate gender issues to racial solidarity. Scott argued that there was nothing at all paradoxical about women who "were members in good standing of the United Daughters of the Confederacy while they were trying in dozens of ways to change Southern society," and she dismissed the implication that "the principal motivation of Southern suffragists was countering the black vote." She listed half a dozen suffrage leaders as examples of Southern women who energetically "worked for women's rights and human rights."[25]

Among the women she named was Rebecca Latimer Felton, who seems a curious choice in this context. While Felton was renowned as a prohibitionist, a suffragist, an opponent of the convict-lease system, and the first woman to become a United States senator—an honorary appointment that she held for only one day—she was equally well known for speeches and newspaper columns in which she urged white men to resort to lynching if necessary to protect white women from black rapists. A reformer who simultaneously stoked the fires of racial violence, Felton personified rather than contradicted the paradox Faust identified.[26]

Scott's inclusion of Felton as a champion of human rights illustrates a hallmark of her interpretation of Southern women's history. Throughout *The Southern Lady,* she cast her subjects in a favorable light that minimized or erased their flaws. She told a story of appealing and often admirable women progressing from a subordinate and powerless position to a state of equality and autonomy—a journey she neatly summarized in the book's subtitle, *From Pedestal to Politics.* Scott's tendency to accentuate the positive aspects of women's history and to highlight the words and deeds of women who deplored the ugliest aspects of the South's past has drawn fire from critics. Her optimistic perspective shades every major point on which her work has been challenged or revised—the attitudes of slaveholding women toward slavery, the impact of the Civil War, the influence of white supremacy on Southern feminism. Since 1970, historians have demonstrated that the road from the parlor to public life was circuitous rather than direct, and that while some white women were in the vanguard of feminism and racial reform, others upheld and perpetuated the patriarchy.

In the past three decades scholars have also expanded their vision to include women who made only fleeting appearances in Anne Scott's book. In Southern minds, *lady* was a specific term, not a generic synonym for woman, and Scott focused on the South's most visible ladies: middle- and upper-class whites of "good" families and impeccable behavior. Slaves, wage earners, and the wives and daughters of sharecroppers and tenants were beyond the pale of ladyhood and Scott paid little attention to them. She acknowledged her own historical blindness in her presidential address before the Southern Historical Association in 1989. Calling African-American club women "most invisible of all," she traced the history of black women's voluntary associations and urged historians to "do justice to black women." Subsequently, she encouraged scholars to pay more attention to the lives and work of rural white women as well.[27]

None of the criticisms and revisions of *The Southern Lady* diminish the book's significance—even taken together. In the 1960s and early 1970s, pioneers like Anne Scott labored on the fringes of the historical profession. They fought long and hard to convince mainstream historians that women had a history worthy of serious consideration and to create a respected field within the discipline. Scott explored new terrain in Southern history and charted a path for others to follow; like all trailblazers, however, she saw only a portion of the vast territory she opened.

Anne Scott was nearly fifty years old when *The Southern Lady* appeared. It marked the beginning of the most fruitful phase of her career. She went on to write a history of women's voluntary associations and to edit and coauthor seven additional books as well as essays and speeches. She accumulated awards and honors, and served professional organizations in various capacities, including terms as president of the Organization of American Historians (1983–1984) and the Southern Historical Association (1988–1989). In 1993, fifteen historians honored her with a festschrift entitled *Visible Women: New Essays on American Activism*, a fitting tribute to a woman who devoted her career to bringing women to the foreground of historical scholarship.[28]

Despite her other accomplishments, Anne Scott remains best known for *The Southern Lady*. For more than a generation, her name has been synonymous with Southern women's history. It is not surprising that historians have revised some of her conclusions; that is, after all, what historians do. What is remarkable is that three decades after its initial publication the book is still being read, discussed, and debated; few other monographs have had such a long life span. Scott welcomes the debate. She ended the afterword to the 1995 edition with the hope that the book "will still seem worth arguing with." Since 1970, *The Southern Lady* has stimulated countless discussions and arguments in classes and seminars; at conferences and colloquia; in dissertations, journal articles, and books. It endures as a classic in women's history and Southern history. Anne Firor Scott saw women who had been invisible to most historians and ensured that Southern women would never again be relegated to historical oblivion.[29]

"Ethos Without Ethic"

Samuel S. Hill and Southern Religious History

TED OWNBY

Early in his first book, Samuel S. Hill wrote that most Southerners had written in a mode that was more poetic than analytical. The question for so many great Southern writers, he suggested, concerned "what is it like to be me?" instead of "why are we the way we are, and how might we change?" For Hill, the best and most influential historian of Southern religion, the task was to combine the two.[1]

The son of a preacher and Baptist leader, a preacher himself as a young man, and always an inspired commentator on the need for social change, Samuel Hill has written to understand himself and people like him. But he has also used the tools of social and theological analysis to investigate the place of religion in Southern society. In the tradition of troubled white Southerners who confront the story of their own region, Hill writes with the belief that by coming to a greater understanding of themselves, white Southerners can make significant changes in their visions of community, inclusiveness, and justice. Early in his career, he wrote in the mode of Southern writers who saw the region as backward but with potential to move positively toward "the national norm."[2] Hill has also written in the tradition of a smaller number of writers—most importantly C. Vann Woodward—who hope to show how Southerners might change by drawing on elements within their own culture.

Much of his writing, no matter how scholarly and subtle, ultimately has a sermonic quality. Hill tells readers that he loves Southerners, he understands them, but they have a problem and he wants to help. More than most scholars identified with Southern history, Hill has been willing to spell out exactly how changes might take place. His first scholarly articles in 1963 and 1964 and his first two books, *Southern Churches in Crisis* (1967) and *Religion in the Solid South* (1972), concluded with the idea that the churches of white Southerners needed to change dramatically, especially in their stance on race relations, or they would likely decline in popularity and significance.[3] Unlike so many scholars who conclude with their criticisms, Hill spelled out specific recommendations.

The intellectual background for Hill's work lies more in the Bible and religious studies than academic works in history. Perhaps surprisingly, Hill did not begin his works by attacking a stereotyped image. The images were there in H. L. Mencken's famous depiction of religious white Southerners as degenerate, ignorant, closed-minded, anti-evolutionist snake-handlers and in W. J. Cash's famous suggestion that the white Southerner wanted "a faith as simple and emotional as himself," characterized by "primitive frenzy and blood sacrifice."[4] But Hill, as a sympathetic but critical insider, has tended to work not by disproving false or simplistic images of Southern religion but by building his interpretations step by logical step.

When Samuel Hill first began writing, he made proper references to the work of historians William Brownlow Posey and W. W. Sweet on the frontier and denominational development and to Rufus Spain and Kenneth Bailey on the limits of political activism in Southern religion. But Hill had a great deal of freedom to set his own agenda, since, as John Boles wrote in 1987, "the poverty of the historical imagination with regard to Southern religion was stultifying until the early 1960s."[5] Many of Hill's most important intellectual inspirations were the most respected scholars of American religious history. In different ways, Perry Miller, Sidney Mead, Martin Marty, Winthrop Hudson, and Robert Bellah discussed an American sense of collective mission, the idea of America as a promised land, or denominationalism and the growing acceptance of religious heterogeneity. Hill has often used their ideas as counterpoints from which to say the South does not fit a national model. City on a hill scholarship and perhaps city on a hill thinking gave Hill a foil for making arguments about the less idealistic and less inclusive nature of Southern religion.

One of the most significant intellectual influences is the regional essayist. C. Vann Woodward seems almost the intellectual patron saint of Hill's *The South and the North in American Religion* (1980), with its attention to regional differences and identities within a broader range of shared American experiences. Both Hill and Woodward believe that there is a South to be analyzed, but only if the historian uses great care and subtlety. Hill often uses Woodwardian language of burdens, counterpoint, and irony, and he shares Woodward's belief in the value of comparison. Also Woodward-like is Hill's use of the essay; Hill's work consists of inspired think pieces rather than monographs.

Finally, Hill's work shows the influence of Ernst Troeltsch, the German religious scholar who developed the idea of the tendency of "sects," characterized by separatism, creativity, and devotion to the one true way, to become "churches," which adapted to their society and learned to deal with other religious groups. Countless religious scholars have used Troeltsch's ideas as a basis for arguments about decline from some earlier passion and sense of special mission. Hill more intriguingly has assessed how Southern churches that went from challenging outsiders to comfortable insiders within the South nevertheless have kept their identities as outsiders shunned by other Americans.

As a historian, Hill tends to be a logician, a sociologist, a comparative scholar, and a social critic. He analyzes how theological ideas and behavior fit together logically. Like a sociologist, he frequently discusses the functions of ideas and forms of behavior. His works are full of intellectual models drawn from sociology, especially the center and periphery model developed by Edward Shils. As a comparative scholar, Hill wants to illuminate central themes by comparison to other societies, usually the American North. As a social critic, Hill draws conclusions about the lessons he hopes his books suggest. The very title of his first book implied that he was thinking first of the present—*Southern Churches in Crisis*—before he looked into the past to discover the roots of the problem. What Samuel Hill is *not* is a conventional historian who compiles archival evidence and uses it to tell stories.

Three basic principles have guided Hill's most important works. Beginning with *Southern Churches in Crisis*, Hill strove to show there was a Southern religion. Despite all of the exceptions and complications, there was a central story, and much of Southern religious history involved the changing relationship between that central story and numerous peripheral stories. Evangelical churches—the Baptists and Methodists—stood at the center of the story, and Southern religious history revolved in large part around how these groups came to dominate in numbers and perspective, how they related to other denominations, and how they dealt with theological and moral issues. Second, the conversion experience was the "central theme."[6] Understanding anything for Southern evangelicals began with believing that the state of the soul of each individual was what really mattered. Third, Hill developed numerous consequences of the central theme, letting its power and beauty show but stressing its limits, its flaws, and its increasing irrelevance to the contemporary world.

A possible fourth principle has been an increasing appreciation of diversity within Southern religion. After working so hard to clarify the central theme and its consequences, Hill has been drawn more recently to a vision of Southern religion as a more complex and changing organism, perhaps without a clear center.

I

Regional distinctiveness begins with the traditional significance of the Baptists and the Methodists. Those two groups dominated Southern religion since the antebellum period. Presbyterians were important as well, but after the early 1800s they never had comparable numbers of members. Baptists and Methodists, Hill argues, have had such numerical dominance and such similarities in their theologies, church lives, and views of the world that it seems "legitimate to speak of a transdenominational 'Southern church,' embracing what may be called 'popular Southern Protestantism.'"[7] With such domination by the so-called evangelical groups, Hills sees the South as a "limited-options culture" in church membership and in many aspects of religious life.[8]

Methodist and Baptist dominance did not in itself define regional distinctiveness. Comparing Southern religion to American religious life outside the region, Hill argues that homogeneity has been one of the key features of Southern religion. Summarizing the work of many religious scholars, Hill sees American church history outside the South as the story of the disestablishment of official churches and the growing acceptance of widespread diversity within a denominational norm. To him, the history of American religion outside the South is the story of change, moving through stages of Puritan identity and idealism, to efforts to recover that identity, to the political importance of religion in the American Revolution, then through a long series of "adjustments, reinterpretations and accommodations" over intellectual and demographic changes, to "religious diversity, then religious pluralism, and finally ideological pluralism with secularism in the vanguard."[9]

For Hill, idealism, change, and pluralism were stories significantly absent in the South. The basic story line in Southern religion began with diversity and the relative weakness of church life in the colonial period, followed by the awakenings that led to evangelical dominance, and then to a long, long history of general stasis. The only real change between the 1830s and 1960s was the steady strengthening of evangelical religion within both church life and society. The key to regional distinctiveness, then, began with the limits of change and the limits of difference. Engaging in dramatic hyperbole, Hill suggested, "One wonders if any people in the history of Christendom after the Middle Ages has been so thoroughly indoctrinated with a particular version of the Christian world view."[10] One can imagine that as a young Southern scholar writing in the 1960s, Samuel Hill viewed a monolithic religion much as Woodward and V. O. Key, Jr., viewed monolithic one-party politics: as a tragic obstruction to necessary reform.

Hill clearly recognizes the logical difficulties of claiming there was a central Southern story. The story has too many exceptions; it leaves out too many people and too much complexity. He sees the problem in arguing that some periods were more "Southern" than others; the late 1800s and early 1900s turn out to be the most "Southern" in the strength and intolerance of Baptist and Methodist churches.[11] The tenuous nature of his regionalist claims shows in his intentionally shaky introduction to *Religion in the Southern States:* "The South is an identifiable cultural and social unity—well, mostly, in certain ways, some parts of it."[12] Nonetheless, Hill persevered in arguing that the South is not simply a place but a cultural system with a center and numerous peripheries. By the mid-nineteenth century, the South had a normative tradition in which people either knew they belonged to the center or chose to be outsiders.[13]

II

The central theme was "the salvation of the individual."[14] Many Christians have believed that human beings are sinners, cut off from God, needing a conversion experience to be redeemed from their sinful natures. And many Protestants have conceived of reality as "two units, the eternal, morally perfect and demanding God, and the sinful, punishment-worthy individual."[15] Conflicts in the history of Protestantism often divided groups who stressed communal aspects of religious life and others who emphasized the experience of the individual. In the South, the communal experience lost out every time, and the region's Methodists and Baptists developed a "near-exclusive dedication to the inner dimensions of religious life."[16] Showing extraordinary understanding of the meaning of the conversion experience, Hill wrote that Southern religion "places decisive stress on the memorable, usually emotional, moment of entrance into the Christian life. The remainder of one's life is in effect an appendix to the fact of entrance—or at least so much is made of the initial experience that hearers are likely to conclude that this is so."[17]

Beyond their status as the dominant religious forces in their culture, Southern Methodists and Baptists differ from other evangelicals in their commitment to revivalism and a particular form of fundamentalism. The centrality of conversion makes the revival the crucial time in the year of the church, because it is the point when many congregations expect individuals, especially young people, to have conversion experiences and join churches. All church life points toward converting the unconverted; even when Baptist and Methodist groups campaign to build hospitals and schools, they use the language of revivalism. Hill's understanding of revivalism also helps him explain the differences among fundamentalists. It was once popular among nontheologians to characterize twentieth-century Southern theology as fundamentalist. Hill demonstrates that Southern Baptists and Methodists have a particularly revivalist form of fundamentalist theology. Unlike the course taken by theologians in the Northeast and Midwest who developed the term *fundamentalism* in the early twentieth century as an aggressive rejection of the attempt by theological modernists to reconcile Christianity with contemporary science, Southern theology had a smoother history. Modernism was largely irrelevant and deserved condemnation more than a fully developed intellectual response. Rather than constructing a new intellectual system, Southern evangelicals adopted the term *fundamentalism* with the idea that they had known all along what was most important—the conversion of individuals. Hill argues that Southern Baptist and Methodist sermons tend to draw on a surprisingly few New Testament texts, particularly sections in Paul's letters about the process of individual conversion.

Samuel Hill brought to Southern scholarship an unmatched aesthetic appreciation of the conversion experience. Too many writers prior to Hill wrote of religious experience as mere anti-intellectualism or sheer revivalistic frenzy, and too many have related religious life to Southern power relations without trying to understand the experiential dimension. It is particularly striking how effectively Hill portrays the language and emotion of what is really the heart and soul of evangelical religion.[18] For all that he worried about the tragic consequences of evangelicalism, Hill treats the central experience with great respect and, as befits an old preacher, he can preach. The basic message of the Second Great Awakening, he wrote, was that "every person is lost, without God, without hope, the way, or the truth, and must be told the news." After the conversion experience, the person "lives in sweet and close relationship to the Lord and, especially, with the glorious assurance of everlasting life beyond death."[19] In his conclusion to *Religion in the Southern States*, Hill reiterated that for the converted individual, "everything centered in the proclamation of the biblical message that all had sinned and come short of the glory of God: that Christ had paid the sin-debt for each and every person; that saving grace was immediately available to all who would open their hearts to receive it experientially; and that the person so converted could rely on the Lord's promise of everlasting life in heaven and a constant sweetness of presence every moment of every day."[20] This is the language of the believer, and it helps distinguish Hill from most scholars who would never feel comfortable using terms like *sin-debt, sweetness,* or *glorious assurance.*

The great suspicion in reading Hill's early work is that he very understandably turned his own experience as a Southern Baptist believer and preacher into the basis for interpreting and critiquing history. One wonders whether Hill has written in part to explain the historical roots and limitations of his own experience—an experience that no doubt included giving sermons in which the need for and beauty of conversion was the central theme. One can imagine the young Pastor Hill delivering sermons that called for individuals to come forward to be saved, celebrating or lamenting the successes or failures of that call, and then wondering and worrying whether his sermon might have affected the lives of the church members after they left the church. Part of the power of his work lies in his explanation of the tragic consequences of things he understood so deeply.

III

The most compelling consequence of the extraordinary emphasis on conversion and church-building, Hill's third principle, was the failure of white evangelicals to embrace African-Americans as equals and to use the power of Christianity to combat racism, poverty, and injustice. The civil rights movement was the paramount concern when Hill wrote in the mid-1960s. The Baptist and Methodist churches populated by white Southerners faced the issue of how to respond—to share in the movement and push it forward, to ignore it in favor of other matters, or to oppose it.[21] To Hill, the primary response of whites' churches was to ignore the civil rights movement, not especially out of disdain for African-Americans but more out of a belief that legal and political change was peripheral to their main concerns.

White supremacy, according to Hill, was the defining element of Southern identity, and a primary fact of Southern religion involved its support for that identity. A superficial reading of Hill's work might suggest that his main interest concerned what Southern religion was *not* more than what it *was*. And in fact the failures and blindnesses of white evangelicals are among his primary intellectual and moral passions. Part of Hill's work, especially *The South and the North in American Religion,* lies in an enduring tradition of studying the region by contrasting the "South" to "America." At its best, America had a social conscience, a sense of mission that strove to include all groups, and an ethic that saw justice as a religious ideal. On issues of race, to Hill, the South had none of those things.

Hill was not interested, however, in depicting only what the South lacked. He wanted to show the roots of the failure of evangelicalism to address critical moral questions and he wanted to suggest how it might change. Hill made his ideas about evangelicalism and racial issues particularly clear in "The South's Two Cultures," a powerful essay published in 1972 as part of the collection *Religion and the Solid South.* One might expect that the South's two cultures, as suggested by the Kerner Commission report published four years earlier and still crucial to cultural discussion, would have referred to the South's white and black cultures and the tragic consequences of their separation.[22] Instead, Christianity and white supremacy constituted the two cultural systems. Hill argued that Christianity, with all its room for many theological differences, contained essential beliefs. Central among them were the assumptions that

254 / Ted Ownby

"love is the ultimate power and purpose of reality, and the norm for human behavior" and that "all human groups and individuals are to be judged as human, not as members of a racial or national group, or as accomplished, or as unlettered, or by association with any phenomenal quality."[23] In other words, hatred and racism are unchristian, so something in the South must have gone wrong.

For Samuel Hill, a Christianity that allowed racism and injustice represented more contradiction than hypocrisy, so he tried to explain how people could believe in a religion of love and respect but act in ways that belied their beliefs. He stressed that white Southerners were not essentially heartless or evil. Nor, he wrote, were churches in the region always and essentially apolitical. The reasons Hill offered for the contradiction were functionality and theology. Conservative approaches to political and moral questions functioned to give believers "a formulated, coherent framework of meaning" by reassuring troubled people that God loved them and that they were good and decent people in a good and decent society.[24]

To describe the everyday behavior of white evangelicals, Hill developed the intriguing concept of "ethos without ethic."[25] Perhaps inspired by Max Weber's question of how Protestants act to prove the unprovable question of the state of their own souls, Hill asked how white Southern churchgoers understood their own actions. Christianity demanded action, but Southern Christianity did not demand action to challenge poverty and racial injustice. People who believed they were converted tried hard to adhere to expectations of friendliness and neighborliness, to church practices and beliefs, and to strict community standards on issues of personal morality. Evangelicalism demanded belief in the basic virtues of their society and discouraged questioning of those supposed virtues. White Southerners did not merely dismiss the civil rights movement as irrelevant, they also rejected serious questions about their own actions. They got along, they felt a sense of community with like-minded believers, they assumed that they and the people around them were good enough folks, and they rejected criticism and new ideas.

Early in his career Hill tended to set up dichotomies between political action for social justice and political action on issues of personal morality. The great majority of white Southerners viewed pornography and above all alcohol as the best reasons for religious people to turn to the law. But for most evangelicals, he argued, "there is no time for the church to engage in general civilizing activities when lost souls languish in darkness and despair."[26] Hill modified the rigidity of that dichotomy in response to a series of articles in which Wayne Flynt argued that Southern evangelicals' activism in addressing issues of poverty and working conditions constituted a Southern version of a social gospel. Always generous with citations and always keen on the most recent scholarship, Hill responded that Southern Baptists and Methodists did indeed address those problems, but never as an organized emphasis and certainly never with a sense that overcoming poverty and injustice was a primary religious concern. In his introduction to John Lee Eighmy's *Churches in Cultural Captivity,* Hill emphasized that Baptists tended to see each social concern "as simply one item on a list," while converting the unconverted remained their most important mission. "The Southern Baptists are a people who notice when pain and harm are inflicted on others. But *as church men and women,* they understand their responsibility primarily in other ways. Social ministries seem closer to being a spillover, an after-effect."[27]

As for theology, Hill returned to the central theme. To people single-mindedly concerned with the salvation of souls, pursuing justice for African-Americans, or fighting discrimination, or expanding the circle of community life simply took time and energy that should have gone into more important matters—or, in fact, the only truly important matter. Because the "principal mode of Southern religious sensibilities" involved only the status of being saved or unsaved, it was difficult for evangelicals to identify new goals as being important enough to address. In fact, Hill wrote that many preachers "have declared that the primacy of evangelism is being eroded by undue attention to economic and racial matters."[28]

One of the many tragedies of this rejection of criticism and a desire for certainty has been a refusal to engage in theological experimentation. In *Southern Churches in Crisis, Religion and the Solid South,* and *The South and the North in American Religion,* Hill argues that a defining feature of Southern religion has been a strong tendency toward intellectual rigidity. All forms of Christian fundamentalism uphold a literal interpretation of the Bible, but Hill shows that Southern fundamentalism emphasizes biblical anecdotes, generally unchallenging personal stories, and an unquestioning acceptance of simple maxims.

It was in theology that Hill believed Southern evangelicals might find new inspiration for a broader vision for social action. He called on Christians "to bring the gospel's meaning and power to bear upon all individuals in every society across the entire range of human needs and problems."[29] The emphasis on conversion, he ultimately suggested, was troubling only because it was too limiting. Let us look at entire human beings, he said, not just souls, and let us look at entire societies, not just members of particular churches. This new outlook would combine the moral, the intellectual, and the spiritual; evangelicals should "review Christianity's truth-claims constantly" to see if they could stand tests of both "transcendent revelation and practical relevance."[30] Conversion, he ultimately hoped, could mean something broader than ever. A religion that changed the lives of entire people meant a religion that dealt with "physical, material, economic, political, and social psychic needs—*all seen as funda-*

mentally spiritual."[31] Here the South could draw on the strength and importance of religion. In Hill's terms, one of the South's two cultures—Christianity
—could be the weapon in overcoming its racist culture.

IV

Hill was always troubled by his emphasis on white Baptists and Methodists as
the embodiment of the Southern story. He apologized in his first book and
some of his later works for not discussing Catholics, for de-emphasizing the
religious lives of African-Americans, and for barely stopping to note the
countless exceptions to his rule of evangelical hegemony. One way he has tried
to address the problem is by promoting new varieties of scholarship on Southern religion. For example, he edited two crucial works on the broad topic of
Southern religion. The 878-page *Encyclopedia of Southern Religion* (1984 and
1997) offered a wide range of topics beyond the evangelical center, from abolitionism to Jessie Daniel Ames to Fire Baptized Holiness to Greek Orthodoxy to Daniel Alexander Payne to Salzburgers to Episcopal bishop John
Freeman Young.[32] *Religion in the Southern States: A Historical Study*, edited by
Hill in 1983, consisted of sixteen state studies by different scholars, with Hill
writing the introduction, the conclusion, and the entry on Florida. As a group,
the essays suggest differences within the South, simply because of their divergent emphases. Hill's entry on Florida mentioned that two of the most distinctive features in the state were the strength of Catholicism in the colonial
period and the growing diversity in the twentieth century, marked by the return of a Catholic numerical majority and a growing Jewish population.[33] In a
third edited work, the significantly titled *Varieties of Southern Religious Experience*, Hill and his contributors covered groups and experiences outside the
evangelical mainstream with an expanded array of topics, including essays on
Catholicism, *Sophie's Choice*, people who do not go to church, the electronic
church, and considerable material on African-American religion.[34]

In these works, Hill does not give up the notion that the distinctive features
of Southern religion are the evangelical core and the conversion experience. In
his essay on Florida, for example, Hill used the distinctiveness of the state's
history to argue that Florida "was unmistakably a Southern state, society, and
culture" in the late 1800s and early 1900s but has become more "eccentric"
by the Southern evangelical model since then.[35] "Southern" meant Baptist
and Methodist domination, self-confidence, institution-building, and intolerance toward outsiders and drinkers of alcohol. In his conclusion to *Varieties
of Southern Religious Experience*, when Hill optimistically asserts that "the
study of religion in the South, now such a promising enterprise, must operate
dialectically—back and forth between 'the South' and the numerous parts that

make it up,"[36] he is still identifying the region by referring to the central theme.

Hill has dramatically increased the visibility of African-Americans in his work. The Southern churches that were in crisis in the mid-1960s were clearly the churches of white Southerners, and he included a few remarks about African-American churches that do not conform to the importance we know those institutions played in the civil rights movement.[37] Hill has offered few original arguments about African-American religion, but he has effectively built on the work of scholars such as Albert Raboteau, John Boles, and William Montgomery. Hill argued that the religion of black Southerners "shared much more with the Evangelical Protestantism of the region's whites than it diverged from it."[38] African-Americans belonged to the same denominations as whites and had largely similar theologies, but the differences in music, expressiveness, and "the overall vibrancy of the gathering" became more clear after emancipation.[39] With the chance to form their own denominational churches, African-American Christians began emphasizing a theology of hope and strength more than one of sin and punishment and, most obviously, started to use churches as institutions for political liberation. Samuel Hill has never adopted the Afro-centric approach that emphasizes the West African roots of African-American belief and religious practice. Operating within a framework of Christian universalism, he has suggested that Christianity held potential to create and sustain a sense of community that might build on and surpass the South's best elements in order to overcome the region's worst traditions.

His most recent book, *One Name but Several Faces: Variety in Popular Christian Denominations in Southern History* (1996), is an intricate analysis of the process of religious change among various Baptists, the groups that call themselves Christians, Churches of Christ, and Disciples of Christ, and the Pentecostal groups Hill refers to as the "Of God" churches. African-Americans are crucial to this story of change and challenge, as are people who do not fit neatly into the traditional categories of evangelical religion. Hill works here less as a moralist and regionalist seeking the roots of especially Southern problems and more as a scholar of issues of denominational development. The book sees no central problem, and its central theme concerns diversity and religious innovation.

One Name but Several Faces is fascinating in a study of Hill's development because it stresses discontinuity and variety—two of the things the young Samuel Hill had seen as lacking in the religion of the South. The reader finds no sermons in *One Name;* nor does one find evils to condemn or potential on which to build. One wonders whether if in getting right the story of diversity and change, Hill has moved past part of his original reason for doing religious scholarship. He has discovered another tradition that unites all three groups—the restlessness of earnest evangelicals. "Since nothing 'here on earth below' corresponds to God's perfection, Christians must be vigilant, ever on the alert, to contend with sin in living and with heresy and sloth in the church. Because of their intensity over these concerns, disease, reform, and schism are predict-able courses of behavior."[40]

Hill came closer to writing history with a sermon in his discussions of the religious and political conservatism that began to assert itself so aggressively in the late 1970s and 1980s. The topic was immediately important, given Hill's prediction in 1967 that the churches of white Southerners would lose their importance in Southern culture if they did not change dramatically. Did the Moral Majority movement, the increasing political activism on issues of per-sonal morality, and the popularity of conservative television preachers repre-sent the culmination of the traditions Hill wrote to challenge in the 1960s and 1970s? Were they the end to his hope that Southern religion held the key to the moral transformation of the South?

Hill answered no. In an article published in 1985 and in a book coauthored with colleague Dennis Owen, he argued that the "new religious-political right" differed dramatically in background and emphasis from previous evan-gelicalism. First, a great many of the most important conservative leaders, most obviously Ronald Reagan, were not from the South. Second, one of the South's leading conservatives, Jesse Helms, showed his conservatism more on economic issues than issues of personal morality. Third, the old interests in alcohol and racial segregation gave way to newer concerns over abortion and homosexuality.

Hill concluded that the new political right was not a direct descendant of the traditional evangelicalism. It was only one of several strands of Southern religious traditions alive and important in the 1980s. In fact, he predicted it would not gain in popularity, in part because of the power of a Southern reli-gious tradition that stressed brotherhood and improving the world and led less often to smug self-righteousness.[41]

In his recent work, to conclude, Hill finds far more change and diversity in political approaches, in church life, and in religious thinking than he suggested in *Southern Churches in Crisis*. In fact, he decided in *One Name but Several Faces* that "most of us who studied this subject in the early years of the recovery of Southern religious history—especially a few venerables like me—erred in claiming virtual continuity from the late colonial season to the present."[42] Per-haps rather than concluding simply that Samuel Hill has changed his mind about some important issues, we can see his recent work as dealing with some of the newer concerns of Southern religion. He writes, as all of us in Southern religious history write, at a time when diversity is far more evident than ever before in Southern life, when political right-wingers make special efforts to support a somewhat new agenda, when politicized African-American churches have developed a widely celebrated and much studied reform tradition, when generally apolitical Pentecostals are growing faster than any other religious group, and when ideals of multiculturalism have seriously challenged notions of a single American mission. Just as Hill wrote to explain the South of the 1960s, he writes to explain the South of the 1990s.

It is fair to say that Samuel Hill's intellectual influence has been extraordinary. The most important scholars in Southern cultural life have continued and elaborated on his emphasis on the basic conservatism of the religion of white Southerners. Hill is particularly important because he studies the confluence of religion, conservatism, and intellectual life, all three of which continue to inspire important scholarship. Other scholars who look for the possible cracks in the system look to Hill as well. Studies of nineteenth-century evangelicals who felt they were outsiders and numerous studies of twentieth-century reformers motivated by evangelical commitments share Hill's idea that evangelicalism held revolutionary potential to cut across boundaries and use Christian love to support an inclusive notion of community. A new generation of Southern religious historians writing in the 1990s tend to see more diversity than Hill did in his early books, but they are very much influenced by his study of the relationship between power and religious belief. And they, along with many folklorists and ethnographers, draw strength from Hill's attempt to understand evangelicals on their own terms. At this moment, searching for a central theme is a bit out of style, but Hill's concerns, and his passion for the moral meaning of scholarship, seem likely to inspire discussion for some time.

Notes

Introduction: The Pursuit of Southern History

1. This approach is in keeping with John Shelton Reed and Daniel Joseph Singal's observation, found in their chapter on Rupert Vance in this volume, that a complicated "society like the American South cannot rightfully be vivisected for the convenience of academic departments."

2. Arthur S. Link and Rembert W. Patrick, eds., *Writing Southern History: Essays in Historiography in Honor of Fletcher M. Green* (Baton Rouge: Louisiana State University Press, 1965).

3. John B. Boles and Evelyn Thomas Nolen, eds., *Interpreting Southern History: Historiographical Essays in Honor of Sanford W. Higginbotham* (Baton Rouge: Louisiana State University Press, 1987).

4. Cash quoted in C. Vann Woodward, *American Counterpoint: Slavery and Racism in the North-South Dialogue* (1964; reprint, Boston: Little, Brown, 1971), 272.

5. Ulrich Bonnell Phillips, "The Central Theme of Southern History," *American Historical Review* 34(October 1928): 30–43.

6. Franklin's latest effort clearly fits this mold. See John Hope Franklin and Loren Schweninger, *Runaway Slaves: Rebels on the Plantation* (New York: Oxford University Press, 1999).

7. Some of these sophisticated and less exclusive works are discussed in Glenn Feldman, "Race, Class, and New Directions in Southern Labor History," *Alabama Review* 51(April 1998): 96–106.

8. C. Vann Woodward, "The Elusive Mind of the South," in C. Vann Woodward, *American Counterpoint: Slavery and Racism in the North-South Dialogue*, 282 83.

9. John B. Boles explicated many of these reasons in his keynote address, "The 'New' Old South," at the Annual Meeting of the Alabama Association of Historians, Orange Beach, Alabama, 4 February 2000.

10. Steven F. Lawson, "Freedom Then, Freedom Now: The Historiography of the Civil Rights Movement," *American Historical Review* 96(April 1991): 456–71.

11. Armstead L. Robinson and Patricia Sullivan, eds., *New Directions in Civil Rights Studies* (Charlottesville: University Press of Virginia, 1991); John Dittmer, *Local People: The Struggle for Civil Rights in Mississippi* (Urbana: University of Illinois Press, 1994); Adam Fairclough, *Race and Democracy: The Civil Rights Struggle*

in Louisiana, 1915–1972 (Athens: University of Georgia Press, 1995); John Egerton, *Speak Now Against the Day: The Generation before the Civil Rights Movement in the South* (New York: Alfred A. Knopf, 1994); and Patricia Sullivan, *Days of Hope: Race and Democracy in the New Deal Era* (Chapel Hill: University of North Carolina Press, 1996).

12. This idea of the "two sides of the civil rights coin" first appeared in Glenn Feldman "The Ku Klux Klan in Alabama, 1915–1954" (unpublished Ph.D. diss., first draft, Auburn University, 1996), 682, 741, and later in Glenn Feldman, "Review of Kimberley L. Phillips, *AlabamaNorth: African-American Migrants, Community, and Working-Class Activism in Cleveland, 1915–1945*" *Labor History* 41 (August 2000): 366–67.

13. Thankfully, there are encouraging signs here. Three recent works place great emphasis on the importance of race in the labor movement. See Timothy J. Minchin, *Hiring the Black Worker: The Racial Integration of the Southern Textile Industry, 1960–1980* (Chapel Hill: University of North Carolina Press, 1999), Ernest Obadele-Starks, *Black Unionism in the Industrial South* (College Station: Texas A & M University Press, 2000), and Kimberley L. Phillips, *AlabamaNorth: African-American Migrants, Community, and Working-Class Activism in Cleveland, 1915–45* (Urbana: University of Illinois Press, 1999). A model of scholarship that successfully integrates recent work on gender, households, spheres, memory, public history, private and public spaces, agency, whiteness, identity, and discourse to augment the study of Southern politics and, in fact, provide a treatise on the "new Southern political history" is Jane Dailey, Glenda Elizabeth Gilmore, and Bryant Simon, eds., *Jumpin' Jim Crow: Southern Politics from Civil War to Civil Rights* (Princeton: Princeton University Press, 2000).

14. See, for example, Paul K. Conkin's 1997 presidential address at the sixty-third annual meeting of the Southern Historical Association in Atlanta, "Hot, Humid, and Sad," *Journal of Southern History* 64(February 1998): 3–22.

15. This humanistic conception of history is perhaps most closely associated with R. G. Collingwood's classic *The Idea of History* (Oxford: Clarendon Press, 1946).

16. Charles S. Sydnor, "The Southern Experiment in Writing Social History," *Journal of Southern History* 11(November 1945): 456 (quotation).

17. John Hope Franklin, "As For Our History," reprinted in John Hope Franklin, *Race and History: Selected Essays, 1938–1988* (Baton Rouge: Louisiana State University Press, 1989), 63 and 70 (quotation).

Chapter 1. Ulrich Bonnell Phillips and the Beginnings of Southern History

1. William Shakespeare, *Julius Caesar*, in *The Complete Works of William Shakespeare*, ed. William Harness (New York: Alden and Beardsley, 1855), 664.

2. "Historical News and Comments," *Mississippi Valley Historical Review* 21(June 1934): 139.

3. Merton L. Dillon, *Ulrich Bonnell Phillips: Historian of the Old South* (Baton Rouge: Louisiana State University Press, 1985), 1–4.

4. Eugene D. Genovese, "Foreword: Ulrich Bonnell Phillips and His Critics," in Ulrich B. Phillips, *American Negro Slavery: A Survey of the Supply, Employment, and Control of Negro Labor as Determined by the Plantation Regime* (1918; rev. ed., Baton Rouge: Louisiana State University Press, 1987), vii.

5. Ulrich B. Phillips, "The Central Theme of Southern History," *American Historical Review* 34(October 1928): 30–43.

6. C. Vann Woodward, *The Strange Career of Jim Crow,* 3d rev. ed. (New York: Oxford University Press, 1974), 8.

7. Bruce Collins, *White Society in the Antebellum South* (New York: Longman, 1985), 51–66. See also Ulrich Bonnell Phillips, "The Central Theme of Southern History."

8. Ulrich B. Phillips, "The Plantation Product of Men," *Proceedings of the Second Annual Session of the Georgia Historical Association* (Atlanta: Georgia Historical Association, 1918), 14.

9. Dillon, *Ulrich Bonnell Phillips,* 5.

10. Wendell Holmes Stephenson, *Southern History in the Making: Pioneer Historians of the South* (Baton Rouge: Louisiana State University Press, 1964), 165.

11. Dillon, *Ulrich Bonnell Phillips,* 15.

12. Ibid., 16–17.

13. Ulrich B. Phillips to Carl L. Becker, 13 October 1925, Frederick Jackson Turner Collection Manuscripts, Henry E. Huntington Library, San Marino, California.

14. Mark Smith, "U. B. Phillips," in *Encyclopedia of Southern Culture,* ed. Charles Reagan Wilson and William Ferris (Chapel Hill: University of North Carolina Press, 1989), 297.

15. Dillon, *Ulrich Bonnell Phillips,* 21–22.

16. E. Merton Coulter, "Ulrich Bonnell Phillips," in *Dictionary of American Biography, Supplement I,* vol. 21 (New York: Charles Scribner's Sons, 1944), 597.

17. Dillon, *Ulrich Bonnell Phillips,* 26–31.

18. Michael R. Hill, "Edward Alsworth Ross," in *American National Biography,* vol. 18, ed. John A. Garraty and Mark C. Carnes (New York: Oxford University Press, 1999), 907–08.

19. Keay Davidson, "Franz Boas," in *American National Biography,* vol. 3, 83–86.

20. Ulrich B. Phillips, "Azandeland," *Yale Review* 20(December 1930): 313.

21. Gerald N. Grob and George Athan Billias, *Interpretations of American History: Patterns and Perspectives,* vol. 1 (New York: Free Press, 1982), 321.

22. Dillon, *Ulrich Bonnell Phillips,* 44.

23. John David Smith, "Historiography of Slavery," in *Dictionary of Afro-American Slavery,* ed. Randall M. Miller and John David Smith (Westport, Conn.: Prager Publishers, 1997), 329.

24. Coulter, "Ulrich Bonnell Phillips," 597–98.

25. Richard Hofstadter, "U. B. Phillips and the Plantation Legend," *Journal of Negro History* 29(April 1944): 109–24; Lewis C. Gray, *History of Agriculture in the Southern United States to 1860* (Washington: Carnegie Institution, 1933); Frank Lawrence Owsley, *Plain Folk of the Old South* (Baton Rouge: Louisiana State University Press, 1949).

26. Peter Kolchin, *American Slavery, 1619–1877* (New York: Hill and Wang, 1993), 134–35.

27. Peter J. Parish, *Slavery: History and Historians* (New York: Harper and Row, 1989), 6–7.

28. Phillips, *American Negro Slavery*, 342.

29. Ernst Breisach, *Historiography: Ancient, Medieval, and Modern* (Chicago: University of Chicago Press, 1994), 367.

30. John David Smith, "Ulrich Bonnell Phillips," in *The Historical Encyclopedia of World Slavery*, vol. 2, ed. Junius P. Rodriguez (Santa Barbara: ABC-CLIO, 1997), 507.

31. Phillips, *American Negro Slavery*, 296.

32. Ibid., 327.

33. Eugene D. Genovese, "Race and Class in Southern History: An Appraisal of the Work of Ulrich Bonnell Phillips," *Agricultural History* 41(October 1967): 345–46.

34. Peter Chew, "Black History, or Black Mythology?" *American Heritage* 20 (August 1969): 106.

35. Ulrich B. Phillips, "The Decadence of the Plantation System," *Annals of the American Academy of Political and Social Science* 35(January-June 1910): 37–41.

Chapter 2. Broadus Mitchell: Economic Historian of the South

1. "Autobiography of Broadus Mitchell," p. 55, Broadus Mitchell Papers, Southern Historical Collection, Wilson Library, University of North Carolina, Chapel Hill.

2. Broadus Mitchell, *The Rise of Cotton Mills in the South* (Baltimore: The Johns Hopkins University Press, 1921), vii–viii, 161.

3. Ibid., viii.

4. Broadus Mitchell, "Security and Capitalism," 9 May 1935, Samuel Chiles Mitchell Papers, Southern Historical Collection, Wilson Library, University of North Carolina, Chapel Hill. For a glimpse of Mitchell at the Bryn Mawr Summer School, see the documentary film "Women of Summer."

5. Broadus Mitchell, "Fleshpots in the South," *Virginia Quarterly Review* 3(2 April 1927): 166.

6. Broadus Mitchell to Samuel Chiles Mitchell, 2 March 1933, and "Prof. Broadus Mitchell," newsclipping from *Afro American* [Baltimore], 18 February 1932, Samuel Chiles Mitchell Papers; Broadus Mitchell, *Depression Decade from New Era through New Deal, 1929–1941* (New York: Rinehart and Winston, 1947), 311.

7. Broadus Mitchell interview by Daniel J. Singal, 1972, Oral History Research Office, Columbia University, and the Southern Oral History Program Collection, Southern Historical Collection, Wilson Library, University of North Carolina, Chapel Hill, 119–27; Broadus Mitchell interview by Mary Frederickson, 14–15 August [year not given], Wendell, Massachusetts, Southern Oral History Program Collection, 76–80; "Autobiography of Broadus Mitchell," 170–85.

8. "Autobiography of Broadus Mitchell," 185.

9. Ellen W. Schrecker, *No Ivory Tower: McCarthyism and the Universities* (New York: Oxford University Press, 1986), 171–79.

10. Broadus Mitchell, *Frederick Law Olmstead, A Critic of the Old South* (Baltimore: Johns Hopkins University Press, 1924), *William Gregg, Factory Master of the Old South* (Chapel Hill: University of North Carolina Press, 1928), (with George Sinclair Mitchell), *The Industrial Revolution in the South* (Baltimore: Johns Hopkins University Press, 1930), (with Louise Pearson Mitchell), *American Economic History* (Boston: Houghton Mifflin, 1947), *Depression Decade: From New Era through New Deal* (New York: Rinehart and Winston, 1947), and *Alexander Hamilton*, 2 vols. (New York: Macmillan, 1957, 1962).

11. Mitchell, *Rise of Cotton Mills in the South;* C. Vann Woodward, *Origins of the New South, 1877–1913* (Baton Rouge: Louisiana State University Press, 1951), 133–35, 223–27; David L. Carlton, *Mill and Town in South Carolina, 1880–1920* (Baton Rouge: Louisiana State University Press, 1982), 72; Jacquelyn Dowd Hall et al., *Like a Family: The Making of a Southern Cotton Mill World* (Chapel Hill: University of North Carolina Press, 1987).

12. Daniel J. Singal, *The War Within: From Victorian to Modernist Thought in the South, 1919–1945* (Chapel Hill: University of North Carolina Press, 1982), 81; Broadus Mitchell, "A New Voice in the South," clipping from *The Commonweal*, 30 April 1930, p. 734–35, in Broadus Mitchell Papers, Southern Historical Collection, Wilson Library, University of North Carolina.

13. Broadus Mitchell and George Sinclair Mitchell, *The Industrial Revolution in the South*, 264; Mitchell, "Security and Capitalism."

Chapter 3. E. Merton Coulter and the Political Culture of Southern Historiography

1. E. Merton Coulter, "What the South Has Done about Its History," *Journal of Southern History* 2(February 1936): 3, 18–19 (quotations on pp. 18–19).

2. For discussions of the social values of Owsley and Abernethy see: Fred A. Bailey, "Plain Folk and Apology: Frank L. Owsley's Defense of the South," vol. 4, pp. 101–14 in *Perspectives on the American South: An Annual Review of Society, Politics, and Culture*, ed. James C. Cobb and Charles Reagan Wilson (New York: Gordon and Breach, 1987); Fred A. Bailey, "Thomas Perkins Abernethy: Defender of Aristocratic Virtue," *Alabama Review* 45(April 1992): 83–102.

3. For discussions of the creation of the upper-class historical paradigm see the following, all by Fred A. Bailey: "Free Speech and the 'Lost Cause' in Texas:

A Study of Censorship and Social Control in the New South," *Southwestern Historical Quarterly* 47(January 1994): 453–79; "Free Speech and the 'Lost Cause' in the Old Dominion," *Virginia Magazine of History and Biography* 103(April 1995): 237–66; and "Free Speech and the 'Lost Cause' in Arkansas," *Arkansas Historical Quarterly* 55(December 1996): 143–66.

4. Roger G. Osterweis argues in his *The Myth of the Lost Cause, 1865–1900* (Hamden, Conn.: Archon Books, 1973) that the legend of the "Lost Cause" "persisted into the second half of the twentieth century and beyond." Its "values included a way of life rooted in the land, centered in the family, manifested by the symbols of a traditional aristocracy which somehow represented honor, courage, orthodox religion, respect for women, *noblesse oblige* to inferiors, and white supremacy" (p. 152). More recently, Gaines M. Foster questioned whether the "Lost Cause" myth greatly influenced Southern thought deep into the century. Exploring the importance of the "Lost Cause" mentality in the South from 1865 to 1913, he concluded that the Confederate celebration in books, monuments, and memorial days was less a "revival of rabid sectionalism" and more the championing of common regional values that provided the Southern people stability throughout the trying transition from the Old to the New South. He was struck by the ex-Confederate appeal to national reconciliation and the South's insistence that history must be written "devoid of a northern or Southern slant." See Foster, *Ghosts of the Confederacy: Defeat, the Lost Cause, and the Emergence of the New South, 1865 to 1913* (New York: Oxford University Press, 1987), 8. E. Merton Coulter's intellectual crusade suggests that the "Lost Cause" served fundamental social and political purposes well past the civil rights crusades of the 1950s and 1960s. For discussions of the development of a climate of historical conformity see: Fred A. Bailey, "Free Speech at the University of Florida: The Enoch Marvin Banks Case," *Florida Historical Quarterly* 71(July 1992): 1–17, and "Mildred Lewis Rutherford and the Patrician Cult of the Old South," *Georgia Historical Quarterly* 78(Fall 1994): 509–54.

5. Sallie Yates Faison, "Report of Historical Committee," *Minutes of the Ninth Annual Convention of the United Daughters of the Confederacy, North Carolina Division . . . 1906* (Newton, N.C.: Enterprise Job Print, 1906), 24–25.

6. Horace Montgomery, "A Few Words about E. Merton Coulter," *Georgia Historical Quarterly* 58(Spring 1974): 7; W. E. Wright, "Ellis Merton Coulter," [typescript, 1948], Kenneth Coleman, "Ellis Merton Coulter," [published clipping, no date], E. Merton Coulter, "Coulter, John Ellis," [typescript, 1947], E. Merton Coulter to Mrs. Rufus Powell, 9 March 1957 (first quotation), and E. Merton Coulter to Arthur H. Park, 2 July 1973 (second quotation), E. Merton Coulter Papers, Special Collections, the University of Georgia Library (UGA), Athens; Victor A. Coulter, *The Coulter Family of Catawba County, North Carolina* (n.p., privately published, 1975), 31; E. Merton Coulter, *John Ellis Coulter: Small-Town Businessman of Tarhellia* (n.p.: privately printed, 1962), 7–10. John Ellis Coulter's entrepreneurial activities and civic service fits the model of those North Carolina elites who exercised rigid social control over their communities. See Paul D.

Escott, *Many Excellent People: Power and Privilege in North Carolina, 1850–1900* (Chapel Hill: University of North Carolina Press, 1985), 197–205.

7. E. Merton Coulter to Dan Abrams, 22 May 1969 (quotation), and E. Merton Coulter to Margaret E. Elmore, 16 December 1969, Coulter Papers, UGA. For a discussion of Southern textbook and juvenile literature themes as the nineteenth century merged into the twentieth see: Osterweis, *Myth of the Lost Cause*, 38–55; Fred A. Bailey, "Thomas Nelson Page and the Patrician Cult of the Old South," *International Social Science Review* 72(Fall 1997): 110–21, and "Textbooks of the Lost Cause: Censorship and the Creation of Southern State Histories," *Georgia Historical Quarterly* 75(Fall 1991): 507–33.

8. E. Merton Coulter to W. E. Wright, 8 April 1949, Coulter Papers, UGA; E. Merton Coulter to John Ellis Coulter, 17 September 1910, 2 April, 1 December 1911, 22 February, 7 March 1912 (quotation), John Ellis Coulter Papers, Southern Historical Collection (SHC), University of North Carolina, Chapel Hill.

9. E. Merton Coulter, "Random Observations and a Thought Continuation of the Petty and Personal Reminiscences of the Author," [1916], Coulter Papers, UGA; John Herbert Roper, *C. Vann Woodward, Southerner* (Athens: University of Georgia Press, 1987), 85.

10. Rebecca Cameron to Francis P. Venable, 20, 24 May, 2 June 1911, Francis P. Venable to Rebecca Cameron, 22 May 1911, University of North Carolina Presidential Papers, the University of North Carolina Archives, Chapel Hill, North Carolina; Rebecca Cameron to J. G. de Roulhac Hamilton, 13 June and 4 September 1911, J. G. de Roulhac Hamilton Papers, SHC; R. L. Flowers to Rebecca Cameron, 29 June 1911, William Preston Few Papers, Duke University Archives (DUKE), Durham, North Carolina; *Minutes of the Fifteenth Annual Convention of the United Daughters of the Confederacy, North Carolina Division . . . October 25–27, 1911* (Newton, N.C.: Enterprise Print, 1912), 24–25 (quotation on p. 24).

11. E. Merton Coulter to John Ellis Coulter, 28 April, 3, 11 May, 3 September 1913, 20 April 1914, 15 April 1915, 16 April 1916, 8 October 1917, John Ellis Coulter Papers, SHC; E. Merton Coulter, "Random Observations and a Thought" (quotation); E. Merton Coulter to Annie Laurie McDonald, 14 December 1945, Coulter Papers, UGA; Montgomery, "A Few Words about E. Merton Coulter," 9. Coulter's dissertation was published as *The Civil War and Readjustment in Kentucky* (Chapel Hill: University of North Carolina Press, 1926); for a discussion of this book's importance in Southern historiography see: John David Smith, "E. Merton Coulter, the 'Dunning School,' and *The Civil War and Reconstruction in Kentucky*," *Register of the Kentucky Historical Society* 86(Winter 1988): 52–69.

12. E. Merton Coulter to Patricia Waltington, 2 June 1974, Coulter Papers, UGA; Montgomery, "A Few Words about E. Merton Coulter," 9–10.

13. E. Merton Coulter, *The South during Reconstruction, 1865–1877*, vol. 8, History of the South series, ed. Wendell Holmes Stephenson, Charles Ramsdell, and E. Merton Coulter (10 vols.; Baton Rouge: Louisiana State University Press, 1947–1977).

14. Michael Vaughan Woodward, "E. Merton Coulter and the Art of Biogra-

phy," *Georgia Historical Quarterly* 64(Summer 1980): 159–71, and "Ellis Merton Coulter" (Ph.D. diss., University of Georgia, 1982); J. G. de Roulhac Hamilton to Ulrich B. Phillips, 9 May 1929, Hamilton Papers, SHC.

15. Michael Vaughan Woodward, "The Publications of Ellis Merton Coulter to 1 July 1977," *Georgia Historical Quarterly* 61(Fall 1977): 268–78.

16. E. Merton Coulter, *Georgia: A Short History* [1933] (Chapel Hill: University of North Carolina Press, 1947), 267 (first and second quotations), 274 (third, fourth, and fifth quotations).

17. Coulter, *Georgia,* 305 (first and second quotations), 314 (third quotation).

18. Ibid., 303 (first, second, and third quotations), 337 (fourth quotation), 339–45, 347 (fifth quotation).

19. Ibid., 348 (first quotation), 349 (second and third quotations), 350 (fourth quotation), 355 (fifth quotation). Reviewing *Georgia: A Short History,* Haywood J. Pierce, Jr., of Brenau College, explained that the "attractiveness of the book is certainly not lessened by a certain quiet humor which the author reveals on occasion. As one example, writing of the negro in reconstruction days, [Coulter] says: 'The Negroes . . . flocked into churches . . . with as much the feeling of getting something here as hereafter' (p. 339). A little humor leaveneth the whole, even in historical writing." *Georgia Historical Quarterly* 18(June 1934): 200–1.

20. Coulter, *Georgia,* 371 (first, second, and third quotations), 372 (fourth quotation), 381 (fifth quotation).

21. Montgomery, "A Few Words about E. Merton Coulter," 11.

22. E. Merton Coulter, "Review of *The Tragic Era: The Revolution after Lincoln* by Claude G. Bowers," *Georgia Historical Quarterly* 14(June 1930): 175, and "Review of *The Epic of America* by James Truslow Adams," *Georgia Historical Quarterly* 16(December 1932): 318.

23. E. Merton Coulter, "Review of *Old Massa's People: The Old Slaves Tell Their Story* by Orland Kay Armstrong," *Georgia Historical Quarterly* 17(March 1933), 73 (first quotation), "Review of *Economic Bases of Disunion in South Carolina* by John G. Van Deusen," *Georgia Historical Quarterly* 14(March 1930): 85 (second quotation), "Review of *The Northern Teacher in the South, 1862–1870* by Henry Lee Swint," *Georgia Historical Review* 25(December 1941), 406 (third quotation), and "Review of *Race, Class, and Party: A History of Negro Suffrage and White Politics in the South* by Paul Lewinson," *Georgia Historical Quarterly* 17(September 1933): 241 (fourth quotation).

24. E. Merton Coulter, "Review of *Slave Insurrections in the United States, 1800–1865* by Joseph Cephas Carroll," *Georgia Historical Quarterly* 23(June 1939): 212 (first quotation), "Review of *The Negro in Tennessee, 1865–1880* by Alrutheus Ambush Taylor," *Georgia Historical Quarterly* 25(September 1941): 300 (second quotation), "Review of *The Negro in American Politics* by William F. Nowlin," *Georgia Historical Quarterly* 17(June 1933): 165 (third quotation), and "Review of *The Collapse of the Confederacy* by Charles H. Wesley," *Georgia Historical Quarterly* 23(March 1939): 100 (fourth quotation). Note: Coulter was inconsistent in his policy of capitalization of the word *Negro.*

25. E. Merton Coulter, "Review of *Black Reconstruction: An Essay toward a History of the Part Which Black Folk Played in the Attempt to Reconstruct Democracy in America, 1860–1880* by W. E. Burghardt Du Bois," *Georgia Historical Quarterly* 20(March 1936): 95 (first quotation), and "Review of *Reconstruction: The Battle for Democracy (1865–1877)* by James S. Allen," *Georgia Historical Quarterly* 22(September 1938): 299 (second quotation).

26. E. Merton Coulter, "Review of *The Negro in the Civil War* by Herbert Aptheker," *Georgia Historical Quarterly* 23(December 1939): 401–2 (first quotation), and "Review of *Essays in the History of the American Negro* by Herbert Aptheker," *Georgia Historical Quarterly* 31(December 1947): 328 (third quotation); Herbert Aptheker to E. Merton Coulter, 18 December 1939, 21 June 1940, and E. Merton Coulter to Herbert Aptheker, 24 June 1940 (second quotation), Coulter Papers, UGA.

27. Eugene C. Barker to George W. Littlefield, 5 December 1912, 28 April 1913, 24 March 1914, and George W. Littlefield to Eugene C. Barker, 17 March 1914, Holding Records to the George W. Littlefield Papers, Eugene C. Barker Center, University of Texas, Austin; George W. Littlefield to Clarence Ousley, 24 April 1914, recorded in entry of 28 April 1914, p. 377, Minutes of the Board of Regents, University of Texas, vol. D, December 1909 to June 1916, Board of Regents Office, University of Texas, Austin (quotation); Bailey, "Free Speech and the 'Lost Cause' in Texas," 467. The two textbooks in question were Henry W. Elson, *History of the United States of America* (New York: Macmillan Company, 1904), and Edward Channing, *A Student's History of the United States* (New York: Macmillan Company, 1898).

28. Wendell Holmes Stephenson to E. Merton Coulter, 4 November, 17 December 1937, Eugene C. Barker to E. Merton Coulter, 7 July 1942, Eugene C. Barker to Milton R. Gutch, 16 July 1942, and E. Merton Coulter to Bruce Fant, 23 January 1969, Coulter Papers, UGA; E. Merton Coulter to Fletcher Melvin Green, 1 March 1944, Fletcher Melvin Green Papers, SHC; E. Merton Coulter to Wendell Holmes Stephenson, 7 August 1942, and Wendell Holmes Stephenson to E. Merton Coulter, 21 July 1942, 21 June 1952 (quotation), Wendell Holmes Stephenson Papers, DUKE.

29. David Donaldson, "The Southern Memory," [Roanoke] *New Leader* clipping, 31 July [1947], Stephenson Papers, DUKE.

30. J. G. de Roulhac Hamilton, "Review of *The South during Reconstruction, 1865–1877* by E. Merton Coulter," *Journal of Southern History* 14(February 1948): 135 (first quotation); Frank Lawrence Owsley, "Review of *The South during Reconstruction, 1865–1877* by E. Merton Coulter," *Annals of the American Academy of Political and Social Science* 258(July 1948): 154 (second quotation).

31. E. Merton Coulter, "Review of *From Slavery to Freedom: A History of American Negroes* by John Hope Franklin," *Georgia Historical Quarterly* 33(September 1949): 277 (first quotation); John Hope Franklin, "Wither Reconstruction Historiography?" *Journal of Negro Education* 17(Fall 1948): 446–61 (second quotation on p. 461). For Coulter's response to both John Hope Franklin's and Howard K.

Beale's critiques of this work see: E. Merton Coulter, "To the Editor," *Pacific Historical Review* 23(February 1954): 425–29.

32. E. Merton Coulter to Margaret E. Elmore, 16 December 1969 (first quotation), and E. Merton Coulter to Thomas Perkins Abernethy, 6 April 1958 (second quotation), Coulter Papers, UGA.

33. E. Merton Coulter to H. B. Fant, 29 June 1955 (first quotation), and E. Merton Coulter to Donnie B. Bellamy, 9 October 1968 (second quotation), Coulter Papers, UGA. For other examples of Coulter's resentment toward Franklin see: E. Merton Coulter to Herbert Weaver, 26 February 1955, E. Merton Coulter to Ed Young, 29 March 1955, E. Merton Coulter to James I. Robertson, Jr., October 1961, and E. Merton Coulter to Bell I. Wiley, 18 May 1965, Coulter Papers, UGA; E. Merton Coulter to Wendell Holmes Stephenson, 23 December 1953, 3 April 1954, and Wendell Holmes Stephenson to E. Merton Coulter, 18 March 1954, Stephenson Papers, DUKE.

34. Wendell Holmes Stephenson to Charles Ramsdell, 20 February 1939 (Coulter's comments are abstracted in this letter, first quotation), Stephenson Papers, DUKE; Wendell Holmes Stephenson to E. Merton Coulter, 18 February, 23 February 1939, E. Merton Coulter to J. Fred Rippy, 25 October 1961 (second quotation), and E. Merton Coulter to Randall Kennedy, 11 April 1973, Coulter Papers, UGA.

35. James W. Silver, *Running Scared: Silver in Mississippi* (Jackson: University Press of Mississippi, 1984), 76, and "Mississippi: The Closed Society," *Journal of Southern History* 30 (February 1964): 3 (first quotation), 4 (second quotation), 5 (third quotation). Silver's expanded address became his book *Mississippi: The Closed Society* (New York: Harcourt, Brace and World, 1963).

36. E. Merton Coulter to Bennett H. Wall, 11 November 1963, Coulter Papers, UGA.

37. E. Merton Coulter, untitled manuscript, ca. March 1958, E. Merton Coulter Writings Collection, UGA.

38. *Congressional Record,* 105, pt. 31 (31 August 1959), 17, 368–70 (quotation on p. 17 and p. 369); E. Merton Coulter to J. Fred Rippy, 8 September 1959 (second quotation), Coulter Writings Collection, UGA.

39. E. Merton Coulter, Albert B. Saye, and Spencer B. King, Jr., *History of Georgia* (New York: American Book Company, 1954), 135 (second and third quotations), 159 (first quotation), 184 (fifth quotation), 185, 192 (fourth quotation), 193–96, 290 (sixth and seventh quotations).

40. E. Merton Coulter, "Henry M. Turner: Georgia Negro Preacher-Politician during the Reconstruction Era," *Georgia Historical Quarterly* 48(December 1964): 371–410, "Aaron Alpcoria Bradley: Georgia Negro Politician during Reconstruction Times," part I, *Georgia Historical Quarterly* 51(March 1967): 15–41, part II, 51(March 1967): 154–74, and part III, 51(September 1967): 264–306, "Tunis G. Campbell: Negro Reconstructionist in Georgia," part I, *Georgia Historical Quarterly* 51(December 1967): 401–24, and part II, 52(March 1968): 16–52, and *Negro Legislators in Georgia during the Reconstruction Period* (Athens: *Georgia Historical Quarterly*, 1968), 180 (quotations).

41. E. Merton Coulter to Mr. and Mrs. James Spruill, 12 January 1946, Coulter Papers, UGA.

Chapter 4. Frank L. Owsley's *Plain Folk of the Old South* after Fifty Years

1. Major works of Frank L. Owsley and of the Owsley School include: Frank L. Owsley, *State Rights in the Confederacy* (Chicago: University of Chicago Press, 1925); Owsley, *King Cotton Diplomacy: Foreign Relations of the Confederate States of America* (Chicago: University of Chicago Press, 1931); Owsley, *Plain Folk of the Old South* [1949] (Baton Rouge: Louisiana State University Press, rev. ed. 1982); Owsley and Harriet C. Owsley, "The Economic Basis of Society in the Late Antebellum South," *Journal of Southern History* 6(February 1940): 24–45; Owsley and Owsley, "The Economic Structure of Rural Tennessee, 1850–1860," *Journal of Southern History* 8(May 1942): 161–82; Frank L. Owsley, "The Pattern of Migration and Settlement on the Southern Frontier," *Journal of Southern History* 11(May 1945): 145–76; Blanche Henry Clark, *Tennessee Yeomen, 1840–1860* (Nashville: Vanderbilt University Press, 1942); Herbert Weaver, *Mississippi Farmers, 1850–1860* (Nashville: Vanderbilt University Press, 1945); Harry L. Coles, Jr., "Some Notes on Slaveownership and Landownership in Louisiana, 1850–1860," *Journal of Southern History* 9(August 1943): 381–94; Chase C. Mooney, *Slavery in Tennessee* (Bloomington: Indiana University Press, 1957). Frank L. Owsley's more important essays are contained in Harriet Chappell Owsley, ed., *The South: Old and New Frontiers; Selected Essays of Frank Lawrence Owsley* (Athens: University of Georgia Press, 1969).

2. This essay is intended neither as a thorough analysis of Owsley's scholarly career nor as a comprehensive examination of the historiography on plain folk in the Old South. Rather, the essay focuses on identifying key arguments in *Plain Folk*, on assessing how well these arguments have withstood scrutiny, and on gauging the relevance of *Plain Folk* for current and future work in the field. Overviews or compilations of plain folk historiography include: James C. Bonner, "Plantation and Farm: The Agricultural South," in *Writing Southern History: Essays in Historiography in Honor of Fletcher M. Green*, eds. Arthur S. Link and Rembert W. Patrick (Baton Rouge: Louisiana State University Press, 1965); Harry L. Watson, "Conflict and Collaboration: Yeomen, Slaveholders, and Politics in the Antebellum South," *Social History* 10(October 1985): 273–98; Randolph B. Campbell, "Planters and Plain Folks: The Social Structure of the Antebellum South," in *Interpreting Southern History: Historiographical Essays in Honor of Sanford W. Higginbotham*, eds. John B. Boles and Evelyn Thomas Nolen (Baton Rouge: Louisiana State University Press, 1987); Samuel C. Hyde, Jr., ed., *Plain Folk of the South Revisited* (Baton Rouge: Louisiana State University Press, 1997).

3. Harriet Chappell Owsley, ed., *The South: Old and New Frontiers*, v, 51–107, 177–204; Owsley, "The War of the Sections," *Virginia Quarterly Review* 10(October 1934): 630–35; Fred A. Bailey, "*Plain Folk* and Apology: Frank L. Owsley's Defense of the South," *Perspectives on the American South* 4(1987): 101–14, and

272 / Notes to Pages 51–54

"William E. Dodd: The South's Yeoman Historian," *North Carolina Historical Review* 66(July 1989): 301–20; Twelve Southerners, *I'll Take My Stand: The South and the Agrarian Tradition* (New York: Harper and Brothers, 1930); Paul K. Conkin, *The Southern Agrarians* (Knoxville: University of Tennessee Press, 1988).

4. Owsley, *Plain Folk*, xix–xxi, 1–6.

5. Ibid., 8.

6. Ibid., xix.

7. Ibid., 51.

8. Ibid., 23–50; Forrest McDonald and Grady McWhiney, "The Antebellum Southern Herdsman: A Reinterpretation," *Journal of Southern History* 41(May 1975): 147–66, and "The South from Self-Sufficiency to Peonage: An Interpretation," *American Historical Review* 85(December 1980): 1095–118; Grady McWhiney, *Cracker Culture: Celtic Ways in the Old South* (Tuscaloosa: University of Alabama Press, 1988), 51–79; Terry G. Jordan, *Trail to Texas: Southern Roots of Western Cattle Ranching* (Lincoln: University of Nebraska Press, 1981).

9. Owsley, *Plain Folk*, 52.

10. Ibid., 53–75.

11. Ibid., 76.

12. A detailed and different treatment of the Southern frontier can be found in Thomas D. Clark and John D. W. Guice, *Frontiers in Conflict: The Old Southwest, 1795–1830* (Albuquerque: University of New Mexico Press, 1989).

13. Owsley, *Plain Folk*, 78.

14. Ibid., 79–89.

15. Ibid., 150–229.

16. Ibid., 170–73.

17. Ibid., 174–75 (quotation on p. 175).

18. Ibid., 175.

19. The earliest critique of Owsley's methods and findings appeared before the publication of *Plain Folk*. See Fabian Linden, "Economic Democracy in the Slave South: An Appraisal of Some Recent Views," *Journal of Negro History* 31(April 1946): 140–89.

20. Gavin C. Wright, "'Economic Democracy' and the Concentration of Agricultural Wealth in the Cotton South, 1850–1860," *Agricultural History* 44(January 1970): 63–93.

21. Ibid., 67.

22. Donald L. Winters, "'Plain Folk' of the Old South Reexamined: Economic Democracy in Tennessee," *Journal of Southern History* 53(November 1987): 565–86, quotation on p. 585; Randolph B. Campbell, "Planters and Plain Folk: Harrison County, Texas, as a Test Case," *Journal of Southern History* 40(August 1974): 369–98; Donald Schaefer, "Yeomen Farmers and Economic Democracy: A Study of Wealth and Economic Mobility in the Western Tobacco Region, 1850–1860," *Explorations in Economic History* 15(October 1978): 421–37; Carl H. Moneyhon, "Economic Democracy in Antebellum Arkansas, Phillips County, 1850–1860," *Arkansas Historical Quarterly* 40(Summer 1981): 154–72; S. Charles Bolton,

"Inequality on the Southern Frontier: Arkansas County in the Arkansas Territory," *Arkansas Historical Quarterly* 41(Spring 1982): 51–66.

23. Owsley, *Plain Folk*, 133.

24. Ibid., 134.

25. Ibid., 137.

26. Ibid., 138–45.

27. See the following works by Eugene D. Genovese: *The Political Economy of Slavery: Studies in the Economy and Society of the Slave South* (New York: Pantheon Books, 1965), *The World the Slaveholders Made: Two Essays in Interpretation* (New York: Pantheon Books, 1969), *Roll, Jordan, Roll: The World the Slaves Made* (New York: Pantheon Books, 1974), and "Yeomen Farmers in a Slaveholders' Democracy," in Genovese and Elizabeth Fox-Genovese, *Fruits of Merchant Capital: Slavery and Bourgeois Property in the Rise and Expansion of Capitalism* (New York: Oxford University Press, 1983), 249–64.

28. Steven Hahn, *The Roots of Southern Populism: Yeoman Farmers and the Transformation of the Georgia Upcountry, 1850–1890* (New York: Oxford University Press, 1983); Robert Shalhope, "Republicanism and Early American Historiography," *William and Mary Quarterly*, 3d ser., 39(April 1982): 334–56; Daniel T. Rodgers, "Republicanism: The Career of a Concept," *Journal of American History* 79 (June 1992): 11–38.

29. James Oakes, *The Ruling Race: A History of American Slaveholders* (New York: Alfred A. Knopf, 1982); Lacy K. Ford, Jr., *Origins of Southern Radicalism: The South Carolina Upcountry, 1800–1860* (New York: Oxford University Press, 1988); J. Mills Thornton III, *Politics and Power in a Slave Society: Alabama, 1800–1860* (Baton Rouge: Louisiana State University Press, 1978); J. William Harris, *Plain Folk and Gentry in a Slave Society: White Liberty and Black Slavery in Augusta's Hinterlands* (Middletown, Conn.: Wesleyan University Press, 1985).

30. In addition to the works cited in note 29 see George M. Frederickson, *The Black Image in the White Mind: The Debate on Afro-American Character and Destiny, 1817–1914* (New York: Harper and Row, 1971); William J. Cooper, Jr., *The South and the Politics of Slavery, 1828–1856* (Baton Rouge: Louisiana State University Press, 1978); Anthony Gene Carey, *Parties, Slavery, and the Union in Antebellum Georgia* (Athens: University of Georgia Press, 1997).

31. Owsley, *Plain Folk*, 92–93.

32. Charles B. Dew, "The Slavery Experience," in *Interpreting Southern History*, 120–61; Peter J. Parish, *Slavery, History, and the Historians* (New York: Harper and Row, 1989); Peter Kolchin, *American Slavery, 1619–1877* (New York: Hill and Wang, 1993).

33. Bailey, "*Plain Folk* and Apology," 102–9; Frank L. Owsley, "The Irrepressible Conflict," in *I'll Take My Stand*, 61–91.

34. Ulrich B. Phillips, "The Central Theme of Southern History," *American Historical Review* 34(October 1928): 30–43.

35. Owsley, *Plain Folk*, 90–132.

36. Ibid., 91.

37. Ibid., 117–18. To say the least, later scholars have moved far beyond Owsley's description of Southern culture. See, for example, Bertram Wyatt-Brown, *Southern Honor: Ethics and Behavior in the Old South* (New York: Oxford University Press, 1982).

38. Bill Cecil-Fronsman, *Common Whites: Class and Culture in Antebellum North Carolina* (Lexington: University Press of Kentucky, 1992); Charles C. Bolton, *Poor Whites of the Antebellum South: Tenants and Laborers in Central North Carolina and Northeast Mississippi* (Durham: Duke University Press, 1994); Frederick A. Bode and Donald E. Ginter, *Farm Tenancy and the Census in Antebellum Georgia* (Athens: University of Georgia Press, 1986), 1–146; Stephanie McCurry, "The Two Faces of Republicanism: Gender and Proslavery Politics in Antebellum South Carolina," *Journal of American History* 78(March 1992): 1245–64; McCurry, *Masters of Small Worlds: Yeoman Households, Gender Relations, and the Political Culture of the Antebellum South Carolina Low Country* (New York: Oxford University Press, 1995); Elizabeth Fox-Genovese, *Within the Plantation Household: Black and White Women in the Old South* (Chapel Hill: University of North Carolina Press, 1988); Victoria E. Bynum, *Unruly Women: The Politics of Social and Sexual Control in the Old South* (Chapel Hill: University of North Carolina Press, 1992).

Chapter 5. W. E. B. Du Bois: Ambiguous Journey to the Black Working Class

1. David Levering Lewis, *W. E. B. Du Bois: Biography of a Race, 1868–1919* (New York: Henry Holt, 1993); Michael B. Katz and Thomas J. Sugrue, eds., *W. E. B. Du Bois, Race, and the City: The Philadelphia Negro and Its Legacy* (Philadelphia: University of Pennsylvania Press, 1998); Eric J. Sundquist, ed., *W. E. B. Du Bois: The Oxford Reader* (New York: Oxford University Press, 1996); Elliott Rudwick, *W. E. B. Du Bois: Voice of the Black Protest Movement* (1960; reprint, Urbana: University of Illinois Press, 1982); Bernard W. Bell, Emily Grosholz, and James B. Stewart, eds., *W. E. B. Du Bois on Race and Culture: Philosophy, Politics, and Poetics* (New York: Routledge, 1996); Arnold Rampersad, *The Art and Imagination of W. E. B. Du Bois* (Cambridge: Harvard University Press, 1976); Manning Marable, *W. E. B. Du Bois: Black Radical Democrat* (Boston: Twayne, 1986); Cedric Robinson, *Black Marxism: The Making of the Black Radical Tradition* (New Jersey: Zed Books, 1983); Francille Rusan Wilson, *The Segregated Scholars: Black Social Scientists and the Development of Black Labor Studies, 1895–1950* (Charlottesville: University Press of Virginia, forthcoming); James E. Blackwell and Morris Janowitz, eds., *Black Sociologists: Historical and Contemporary Perspectives* (Chicago: University of Chicago Press, 1974); Dan S. Green and Edwin D. Driver, eds., *W. E. B. Du Bois on Sociology and the Black Community* (Chicago: University of Chicago Press, 1978).

2. W. E. B. Du Bois, *The Suppression of the African Slave-Trade to the United States of America, 1638–1870* (New York: Russell and Russell, 1965); W. E. B. Du Bois, ed., *The Negro Artisan* (Atlanta: Atlanta University Press, Conference

Publications no. 7, 1902); W. E. B. Du Bois and Augustus Dill, eds., *The Negro American Artisan* (Atlanta: Atlanta University Press, Conference Publications no. 14, 1912), citations in text refer to this volume; W. E. B. Du Bois, *The Philadelphia Negro: A Social Study* (1899; reprint, Philadelphia: University of Pennsylvania Press, 1996); W. E. B. Du Bois, *Black Reconstruction in America, 1860–1880* (1935; reprint, New York: Atheneum, 1992). Also see Joe W. Trotter, "African-American Workers: New Directions in U.S. Labor Historiography," *Labor History* 35(Fall 1994): 495–523.

3. W. E. B. Du Bois, *The Autobiography of W. E. B. Du Bois: A Soliloquy on Viewing My Life from the Last Decade of Its First Century* (New York: International Publishers, 1968), 78–79, and *Darkwater: Voices from Within the Veil* (New York: Schocken Books, 1969), 9.

4. Lewis, *W. E. B. Du Bois*, 26–31; W. E. B. Du Bois, *The Souls of Black Folk* (Chicago: A. C. McClurg, 1903), quote in Sundquist, *W. E. B. Du Bois*, 101; Rudwick, *W. E. B. Du Bois*, 15–38; John Henrik Clarke et al., *W. E. B. Du Bois: Black Titan* (Boston: Beacon Press, 1970).

5. Du Bois, *The Autobiography*, 97–100; Green and Driver, *W. E. B. Du Bois*, 3.

6. Du Bois, *The Autobiography*, 121.

7. Ibid., 108–31, quote on p. 108; Lewis, *W. E. B. Du Bois*, 56–82.

8. Lewis, *W. E. B. Du Bois*, 83–116; Du Bois, *The Autobiography*, 132–53.

9. Lewis, *W. E. B. Du Bois*, 117–49, quote on p. 147; Du Bois, *The Autobiography*, 154–82, quote on p. 183.

10. Du Bois, *The Autobiography*, 183–204; Lewis, *W. E. B. Du Bois*, 150–78.

11. Charles H. Wesley, "W. E. B. Du Bois: The Historian," in Clarke et al., *W. E. B. Du Bois*, 82–97, quote on p. 85; Robert Gregg, "Giant Steps: W. E. B. Du Bois and the Historical Enterprise," in Katz and Sugrue, *W. E. B. Du Bois*, 77–100.

12. Lewis, *W. E. B. Du Bois*, 161.

13. For recent assessments of Du Bois's historical and sociological writings, see Thomas C. Holt, "W. E. B. Du Bois's Archaeology of Race: Re-Reading 'The Conservation of Races,'" 61–76; Mia Bay, "'The World Was Thinking Wrong About Race': *The Philadelphia Negro* and Nineteenth-Century Science," 41–60; and Gregg, "Giant Steps," 77–100, all in Katz and Sugrue, *W. E. B. Du Bois*; Robinson, *Black Marxism*, 266–348.

14. Quote in Du Bois, *The Autobiography*, 148.

15. Ibid.

16. Lewis, *W. E. B. Du Bois*, 160.

17. See W. E. B. Du Bois, "Conservation of Races," in Sundquist, *W. E. B. Du Bois*, 38–47, quote on p. 44. For an excellent discussion of effort to pinpoint key consistencies and inconsistencies in Du Bois's thought, see Holt, "W. E. B. Du Bois's Archaeology of Race," 61–76. Also see Bay, "'The World Was Thinking Wrong About Race,'" 41–60.

18. See Antonio McDaniel, "The 'Philadelphia Negro' Then and Now: Implications for Empirical Research," in Katz and Sugrue, *W. E. B. Du Bois*, 155–94;

Elijah Anderson, introduction to the 1966 reprint of *Philadelphia Negro*, ix–xxxv; Du Bois, *Philadelphia Negro*, 1–9.

19. W. E. B. Du Bois, *The Negroes of Farmville, Virginia* (Washington: U.S. Government Printing Office, Bulletin no. 14 of the U.S. Department of Labor, 1898), 1–38, quotes on pp. 22–23. See also J. H. O'Dell, "Du Bois and 'The Social Evolution of the South,'" in Clarke et al., *W. E. B. Du Bois*, 154.

20. See Ernest Kaiser, introduction to *The Atlanta University Publications*, iii–ix, quote on p. iv (Atlanta: Atlanta University).

21. Louis R. Harlan, *Booker T. Washington: The Making of a Black Leader, 1856–1901* (New York: Oxford University Press, 1983); August Meier, *Negro Thought in America, 1880–1915: Racial Ideologies in the Age of Booker T. Washington* (Ann Arbor: University of Michigan Press, 1973).

22. Du Bois, *Souls of Black Folk*, quote in Sundquist, *W. E. B. Du Bois*, 131.

23. Lewis, *W. E. B. Du Bois*, 297–342, 408–65.

24. Jervis A. Anderson, *A. Philip Randolph: A Biographical Portrait* (Berkeley: University of California Press, 1986).

25. Marable, *W. E. B. Du Bois*, 75–165; Tony Martin, *Race First: The Ideological and Organizational Struggles of Marcus Garvey and the Universal Negro Improvement Association* (Westport, Conn.: Greenwood Press, 1976); Judith Stein, *The World of Marcus Garvey: Race and Class in Modern Society* (Baton Rouge: Louisiana State University Press, 1986).

26. See W. E. B. Du Bois, "Returning Soldiers," in Sundquist, *W. E. B. Du Bois*, 380–81.

27. Du Bois, *The Autobiography*, 290; Ferruccio Gambino, "W. E. B. Du Bois and the Black Proletariat in Black Reconstruction," in *American Labor and Immigration History, 1877–1920: Recent European Research*, ed. Dirk Hoerder (Urbana: University of Illinois Press, 1983), 43–60. See also Du Bois, "Reconstruction and Its Benefits," *American Historical Review* 15(July 1910): 781–99; Lewis, *W. E. B. Du Bois*, 383–85.

28. Du Bois, *The Autobiography*, 305.

29. See Eric Foner, *Reconstruction: America's Unfinished Revolution, 1863–1877* (New York: Harper and Row, 1988); David R. Roediger, *The Wages of Whiteness: Race and the Making of the American Working Class* (New York: Verso, 1991); and Trotter, "African-American Workers," 495–523.

30. Tera Hunter, "The 'Brotherly Love' for Which This City Is Proverbial Should Extend to All: The Everyday Lives of Working-Class Women in Philadelphia and Atlanta in the 1890s," in Katz and Sugrue, *W. E. B. Du Bois*, 127–52. See also Jacqueline Jones, "'Lifework' and Its Limits: The Problem of Labor in *The Philadelphia Negro*," also in Katz and Sugrue, *W. E. B. Du Bois*, 103–26.

31. Du Bois, *The Autobiography*, 290–91; Rampersad, *The Art and Imagination of W. E. B. Du Bois*, vii.

32. Paul Gilroy, *The Black Atlantic: Modernity and Double Consciousness* (Cambridge: Harvard University Press, 1993).

Chapter 6. Rupert B. Vance: A Sociologist's View of the South

1. Rupert B. Vance, *Human Geography of the South: A Study in Regional Resources and Human Adequacy* (Chapel Hill: University of North Carolina Press, 1932).

2. Edwin Mims, *The Advancing South: Stories of Progress and Reaction* (Garden City, N.Y.: Doubleday, 1926).

3. Rupert B. Vance, "Region," in *International Encyclopedia of the Social Sciences*, vol. 13, ed. David L. Sills (New York: Crowell, Collier, and Macmillan, 1968), pp. 377–82.

4. Howard W. Odum, *American Social Problems: An Introduction to the Study of the People and Their Dilemmas* (New York: Henry C. Holt, 1945).

5. Vance's major papers and articles on the South have been collected in John Shelton Reed and Daniel Joseph Singal, eds., *Regionalism in the South: Selected Papers of Rupert B. Vance* (Chapel Hill: University of North Carolina Press, 1982).

6. Rupert B. Vance, "A Karl Marx for Hill Billies: Portrait of a Southern Leader," *Social Forces* 9(December 1930): 80–90.

7. H. L. Mencken, "The Sahara of the Bozart," *New York Evening Mail* (13 November 1917). Reprinted in H. L. Mencken, *Prejudices: Second Series* (New York: Alfred A. Knopf, 1920), 136–37, 139, 153.

8. Rupert B. Vance, *Human Factors in Cotton Culture: A Study in the Social Geography of the American South* (Chapel Hill: University of North Carolina Press, 1929).

9. Rupert B. Vance, *Research Memorandum on Population Redistribution within the United States* (New York: Social Science Research Council, 1938).

10. Rupert B. Vance, *All These People: The Nation's Human Resources in the South* (Chapel Hill: University of North Carolina Press, 1945).

11. Rupert B. Vance, "The Old Cotton Belt," in Carter Goodrich et al., eds., *Migration and Economic Opportunity* (Philadelphia: University of Pennsylvania Press, 1936), pp. 124–63.

12. Rupert B. Vance, "The Urban Breakthrough in the South," *Virginia Quarterly Review* 31(Spring 1955): 223–32.

13. Rupert B. Vance and Nicholas Demerath, eds., *The Urban South* (Chapel Hill: University of North Carolina Press, 1954).

14. Howard W. Odum, *Southern Regions of the United States* (Chapel Hill: University of North Carolina Press, 1936).

Chapter 7. Charles S. Sydnor's Quest for a Suitable Past

1. Chester M. Morgan, *Redneck Liberal: Theodore Bilbo and the New Deal* (Baton Rouge: Louisiana State University Press, 1985), 45–46; A. Wigfall Green, *The Man Bilbo* (Westport, Conn.: Greenwood Press, 1963), 73–76; Larry Thomas Balsamo, "Theodore G. Bilbo and Mississippi Politics, 1877–1932" (Ph.D. diss., University of Missouri, Columbia, 1967), 212–14; Bobby W. Saucier, "The Pub-

lic Career of Theodore G. Bilbo" (Ph.D. diss., Tulane University, New Orleans, 1971), 86.

2. Morgan, *Redneck Liberal*, 46; Green, *The Man Bilbo*, 76.

3. Charles S. Sydnor, "The Southern Experiment in Writing Social History," *Journal of Southern History* 11(November 1945): 456 (quotation); Charles S. Sydnor, "The Old South as a Laboratory for Cultural Analysis," [1940], typed ms., Charles S. Sydnor Papers, William R. Perkins Library, Duke University, Durham, North Carolina. Sydnor originally presented this address to the Graduate Studies Program in American Culture and Institutions at the University of Michigan in 1940.

4. For discussions of the cultural origins of Owsley, Abernethy, and Coulter's historiography see the following, all by Fred A. Bailey: "*Plain Folk* and Apology: Frank L. Owsley's Defense of the South," in *Perspectives on the American South, an Annual Review of Society, Politics and Culture, IV,* ed. James C. Cobb and Charles Reagan Wilson (New York: Gordon and Breach, 1987), 101–14; "Thomas Perkins Abernethy: Defender of Aristocratic Virtue," *Alabama Review* 45(April 1992): 83–102; "History in Service to the South: E. Merton Coulter and the Political Culture of Southern Historiography," a paper presented before the Southern Historical Association, Birmingham, Alabama, November 1998.

5. Sydnor, "The Southern Experiment in Writing Social History," 459 (first, second quotations), 460–61 (third, fourth quotations).

6. Epaphroditus Sydnor, Last Will and Testament, 26 December 1782; Confederate Pass granted to G. Sydnor, 2 June 1862; [Charles S. Sydnor to family], December 1952, all in the Sydnor Papers.

7. John K. Bettersworth, "Charles Sackett Sydnor," *Journal of Mississippi* 17(January 1955): 53. For a discussion of the essential characteristics of this "better class" of people see: Louis B. Wright, *Culture on the Moving Frontier* (New York: Harper Torchbooks, 1961), 12, 39, 79–80, 95.

8. Fred A. Bailey, "Mildred Lewis Rutherford and the Patrician Cult of the Old South," *Georgia Historical Quarterly* 78(Fall 1994): 509–54. For discussions of the creation of the neo-Confederate historical paradigm and its impact on Southern education see the following, all by Fred A. Bailey: "Textbooks of the Lost Cause: Censorship and the Creation of Southern State Histories," *Georgia Historical Quarterly* 75(Fall 1991): 507–33; "Free Speech and the 'Lost Cause' in Texas: A Study of Censorship and Social Control in the New South," *Southwestern Historical Quarterly* 47(January 1994): 453–79; "Free Speech and the 'Lost Cause' in the Old Dominion," *Virginia Magazine of History and Biography* 103(April 1995): 237–66; "Free Speech and the 'Lost Cause' in Arkansas," *Arkansas Historical Quarterly* 55(December 1996): 143–66.

9. Sydnor, "The Southern Experiment in Writing Social History," 460.

10. *Raleigh News and Observer* clipping, 28 September 1952, Sydnor Papers; *Directory of American Scholars* (Lancaster, Pa.: Science Press, 1942), 517. McCain left the Darlington School in 1915 to serve first as vice-president and then president of Agnes Scott College, Decatur, Georgia.

11. *Kaleidoscope* (Hampden-Sydney, Va.: Hampden-Sydney College, 1916), 66,

116, 146; *Kaleidoscope* (1917), 58, 60–61 (first quotation), 69, 116–17, 139; *Kaleidoscope* (1918), 12, 47 (second, third, fourth quotations), 48–49, 72, 73, 78, 96–97, 104–5, 117, 119–20, 125, 136.

12. *Kaleidoscope* (1917), 60–61 (quotation); *Kaleidoscope* (1918), 12, 47, 62–63, 97, 105.

13. *Raleigh News and Observer* clipping, 28 September 1952, Sydnor Papers; John Luster Brinkley, *On This Hill: A Narrative History of Hampden-Sydney College, 1774–1994* (Hampden-Sydney, Va.: privately published, 1994), 567.

14. Although Broadus Mitchell, a student of New South industrialism, taught in the Department of History during the period of Sydnor's study at The Johns Hopkins University, the two men do not appear to have had a significant relationship. Daniel Joseph Singal, *The War Within: From Victorian to Modernist Thought in the South, 1919–1945* (Chapel Hill: University of North Carolina Press, 1982), 62.

15. *Raleigh News and Observer* clipping, 28 September 1952 (first quotation), *Raleigh News and Observer*, 5 December 1948 (second, third quotations), Sydnor Papers.

16. *Raleigh News and Observer* clipping, 28 September 1952.

17. Brinkley, *On This Hill*, 542; *Raleigh News and Observer* clipping, 28 September 1952, Sydnor Papers.

18. *Raleigh News and Observer* clipping, 28 September 1952, Sydnor Papers; Brinkley, *On This Hill*, 583; "Dr. Charles Sackett Sydnor," *Record of the Hampden-Sydney Alumni Association* 28(April 1954): 4.

19. Allen Cabaniss, *The University of Mississippi: Its First Hundred Years* (Hattiesburg: University and College Press of Mississippi, 1971 [1949]), 7, 136; Morgan, *Redneck Liberal*, 46.

20. Bailey, "Textbooks of the Lost Cause," 508–9.

21. Franklin L. Riley, *School History of Mississippi* (Richmond: B. F. Johnson, 1915 [1900]), 227–29; Franklin L. Riley, J. A. C. Chandler, J. G. de Roulhac Hamilton, contract, 21 September 1910, Franklin L. Riley to J. G. de Roulhac Hamilton, 24 April, 6, 9 May 1913, J. G. de Roulhac Hamilton to J. A. C. Chandler, 5 February 1914, J. G. de Roulhac Hamilton Papers, Southern History Collection, The University of North Carolina, Chapel Hill; Franklin L. Riley, J. A. C. Chandler, and J. G. de Roulhac Hamilton, *Our Republic: A History of the United States for Grammar Grades* (Richmond: Riley and Chandler, 1910); Eron Rowland to George C. Hurst, 25 September 1914 (quotation), Virginia Fraer Boyle to Eron Rowland, 25 August 1924, Kate Dowdle Davis to Eron Rowland, 2 February 1925, Eron Rowland Papers, Mississippi Department of Archives and History, Jackson, Mississippi.

22. Charles S. Sydnor and Claude Bennett, *Mississippi History* (New York: Rand McNally, 1930); Charles S. Sydnor, *Slavery in Mississippi* (New York: D. Appleton-Century, 1933).

23. Bailey, "Textbooks of the Lost Cause," 521–27, 533.

24. Sydnor and Bennett, *Mississippi History*, vii (first, second quotations), 178 (third, fourth quotations).

25. Ibid., 181.

26. Ibid., 181–82.

27. Ibid., 187.

28. Ibid., 201 (first quotation), 202 (second, third quotations), 206, 207 (fourth quotation), 208 (fifth quotation), 209.

29. Ibid., 211–13, 214 (first quotation), 215 (second, third, and fourth quotations).

30. Ibid., 217 (first and second quotations), 218 (third quotation), 222 (fourth and fifth quotations).

31. Bailey, "Textbooks of the Lost Cause," 533.

32. Sydnor, *Slavery in Mississippi*, viii–ix.

33. Ibid., 252 (first quotation), 253 (second quotation).

34. Charles S. Sydnor to J. Fred Rippy, 5 March 1936, J. Fred Rippy Papers, Southern Historical Collection, Wilson Library, The University of North Carolina, Chapel Hill.

35. Morgan, *Redneck Liberal*, 47–48; Vincent A. Giroux, Jr., "Theodore G. Bilbo: Progressive to Public Racist" (Ph.D. diss., Indiana University, Bloomington, 1984), 1–3.

36. Morgan, *Redneck Liberal*, 44–45; Green, *The Man Bilbo*, 72–74; Saucier, "Public Career of Theodore G. Bilbo," 83; Balsamo, "Bilbo and Mississippi Politics," 208–9; Cabaniss, *The University of Mississippi*, 138.

37. Cabaniss, *The University of Mississippi*, 141–43 (quotation on p. 142).

38. Morgan, *Redneck Liberal*, 45–46; Green, *The Man Bilbo*, 74–76; Saucier, "Public Career of Theodore G. Bilbo," 83–86; Balsamo, "Bilbo and Mississippi Politics," 213–15; Cabaniss, *The University of Mississippi*, 145–46.

39. Green, *The Man Bilbo*, 75; Charles S. Sydnor to J. Fred Rippy, 5 March 1936, Rippy Papers.

40. Sydnor, "The Southern Experiment in Writing Social History," 468.

41. Ibid.

42. Charles S. Sydnor to R. L. Rainwater, 3 November, 17 November 1937, Sydnor Papers.

43. Charles S. Sydnor to Charles Ramsdell, 16 September 1937, Charles S. Sydnor to Guy Stanton Ford, 18 November 1947 (quotation), Sydnor Papers. While researching *Slavery in Mississippi*, Sydnor published "The Free Negro in Mississippi before the Civil War," *American Historical Review* 32(July 1927): 769–88.

44. All of the following by Charles S. Sydnor: *Slavery in Mississippi*, 256–57; *A Gentleman of the Old Natchez Region: Benjamin L. C. Wailes* (Durham, N.C.: Duke University Press, 1938), ix; *The Development of Southern Sectionalism, 1819–1848*, vol. 5, History of the South series, ed. Wendell Holmes Stephenson, Charles Ramsdell, and E. Merton Coulter (10 vols.; Baton Rouge: Louisiana State University Press, 1947–1977); *American Revolutionaries in the Making: Political Practices in Washington's Virginia* (New York: Free Press, 1952).

45. Sydnor, *A Gentleman of the Old Natchez Region*, 34, 36, 37 (quotation).

46. Ibid., 93, 128–30, 133, 136, 204–33, 239–58; Charles S. Sydnor, "Intellectual Activities in the Old Natchez District," a paper presented before the American Historical Association, 1936, [typescript], p. 15 (quotations), Sydnor Papers. In addition to this paper presented before the American Historical Association, Sydnor presented from his research on Wailes a paper entitled "B. L. C. Wailes, Scientist and Historian" before the first meeting of the Southern Historical Association (October 1935) and also published three articles in professional journals. William C. Binkley to Fletcher Green, 14 June 1935, Fletcher Melvin Green Papers, Southern Historical Collection, Wilson Library, The University of North Carolina at Chapel Hill; William C. Binkley, "First Annual Meeting of the Southern Historical Association," *Journal of Southern History* 2(February 1936): 74. All of the following by Charles S. Sydnor: "The Beginning of Printing in Mississippi," *Journal of Southern History* 1(February 1935): 49–55; "Historical Activities in Mississippi in the Nineteenth Century," *Journal of Southern History* 3(May 1937): 139–60; "A Slave Owner and His Overseers," *North Carolina Historical Review* 14(January 1937): 31–38.

47. Sydnor, *A Gentleman of the Old Natchez Region*, 43.

48. Ibid., 293 (first, second, third quotations), 295 (fourth quotation), 306 (fifth quotation).

49. Charles S. Sydnor to J. Fred Rippy, 10 February (second quotation), 5 March (first quotation), 1936, Rippy Papers; "Historical News and Notices," *Journal of Southern History* 2(May 1936): 292. Sydnor also considered a posting to Emory University in Atlanta. Charles S. Sydnor to Fletcher Green, 23 March 1936, Green Papers.

50. Charles S. Sydnor to J. Fred Rippy, 1 February 1937, Rippy Papers. Reviewing the Wailes biography in the *American Historical Review*, Stephenson praised Sydnor for his skill at weaving the life story of this "dynamic ante-bellum Mississippian" into the "history of the evolving civilization in the Natchez region from its frontier days in 1800 to the beginning of the Civil War." He was especially struck by Sydnor's meticulous search of both printed and manuscript sources and his writing style, which he described as "never dull; at times it sparkles with humor." Wendell Holmes Stephenson, "Review of *A Gentleman of the Old Natchez Region: Benjamin L. C. Wailes* by Charles S. Sydnor," *American Historical Review* 44(April 1939): 654–55.

51. Eugene C. Barker to George W. Littlefield, 5 December 1912, 28 April 1913, 24 March 1914, George W. Littlefield to Eugene C. Barker, 17 March 1914, Holding Records to the George W. Littlefield Papers, Eugene C. Barker Center, The University of Texas, Austin; George W. Littlefield to Clarence Ousley, 24 April 1914, recorded in entry of 28 April 1914, p. 377, Minutes of the Board of Regents, The University of Texas, volume D, December 1909 to June 1916, Board of Regents Office, The University of Texas, Austin (quotation); Bailey, "Free Speech and the 'Lost Cause' in Texas," 467–69. Suitable textbooks were Henry W. Elson, *History of the United States of America* (New York: Macmillan, 1904), and Edward Channing, *A Student's History of the United States* (New York: Macmillan, 1898).

52. Wendell Holmes Stephenson to E. Merton Coulter, 4 November, 17 December 1937, Eugene C. Barker to E. Merton Coulter, 7 July 1942, Eugene C. Barker to Milton R. Gutch, 16 July 1942, E. Merton Coulter to Bruce Fant, 23 January 1969, E. Merton Coulter Papers, Special Collections, the University of Georgia Library, Athens, Georgia; E. Merton Coulter to Fletcher Melvin Green, 1 March 1944, Green Papers; E. Merton Coulter to Wendell Holmes Stephenson, 7 August 1942, Wendell Holmes Stephenson to E. Merton Coulter, 21 July 1942, Wendell Holmes Stephenson Papers, Special Collections, William R. Perkins Library, Duke University, Durham, North Carolina.

53. E. Merton Coulter, *The South during Reconstruction, 1865–1877*, vol. 8, History of the South series, ed. Wendell Holmes Stephenson, Charles Ramsdell, and E. Merton Coulter (10 vols.; Baton Rouge: Louisiana State University Press, 1947–1977); David Donaldson, "The Southern Memory," [Roanoke] *New Leader* clipping, 31 July [1947] (quotation), Stephenson Papers. For examples of positive reviews of Coulter's Reconstruction volume see: J. G. de Roulhac Hamilton, "Review of *The South during Reconstruction, 1865–1877* by E. Merton Coulter," *Journal of Southern History* 14(February 1948): 135; Frank Lawrence Owsley, "Review of *The South during Reconstruction, 1865–1877* by E. Merton Coulter," *Annals of the American Academy of Political and Social Science* 258(July 1948): 154.

54. Sydnor, *Development of Southern Sectionalism*, ix.

55. Ibid., 332 (first quotation), 336 (second quotation).

56. Ibid., 339.

57. Frank L. Owsley, "Review of *The Development of Southern Sectionalism* by Charles S. Sydnor," *Journal of Southern History* 15(February 1949): 108–10. Angered by his belief that most American history textbooks had been "written by Yankees," Owsley announced to his friend Allen Tate in 1932 that the "purpose of my life will be to undermine by 'careful and detached,' 'well documented,' 'objective' writing, the entire Northern myth from 1820 to 1876." His books would "not interest the general reader. Only the historians will read them, but it is the historians who teach history classes and write text books and they will gradually and without their own knowledge be forced into our position." Quoted in Harriet Chappell Owsley, *Frank Lawrence Owsley: Historian of the Old South* (Nashville: Vanderbilt University Press, 1990), 79. For samples of Owsley's neo-Confederate writings see the following: "The Irrepressible Conflict," in Twelve Southerners, *I'll Take My Stand: The South and the Agrarian Tradition* (New York: Harper and Brothers, 1930); "The Fundamental Cause of the Civil War: Egocentric Sectionalism," *Journal of Southern History* 7(February 1941): 3–18.

58. Paul H. Buck, "Review of *The Development of Southern Sectionalism* by Charles S. Sydnor," *Mississippi Valley Historical Review* 34(December 1949): 514–16 (quotations on p. 515).

59. *Raleigh News and Observer* clipping, 5 December 1948, Sydnor Papers.

60. Charles S. Sydnor, "Aristocracy and Politics in Revolutionary Virginia," a paper delivered before a joint session of the Southern Historical Association and the American Historical Association, December 1948, pp. 13–14, Sydnor Papers. Participating in a panel discussion at the November 1947 meeting of the Southern

Historical Association, Sydnor hinted at his developing interest in the economic and political history of the colonial South. T. Harry Williams, "The Thirteenth Annual Meeting of the Southern Historical Association," *Journal of Southern History* 14(February 1948): 98–99.

61. *Durham Herald* clipping, 8 May 1950, Sydnor Papers.

62. Charles S. Sydnor, *Political Leadership in Eighteenth-Century Virginia* (Oxford: Clarendon Press, 1951), 3 (first quotation), 19 (second quotation).

63. Charles S. Sydnor, *Gentlemen Freeholders: Political Practices in Washington's Virginia* (Chapel Hill: University of North Carolina Press, 1952) and *American Revolutionaries in the Making*, 13 (quotation).

64. Charles S. Sydnor, *American Revolutionaries in the Making*, 117–18.

65. Bettersworth, "Charles Sackett Sydnor," 54; untitled newspaper clipping, 1954, Sydnor Papers.

66. Ibid. (first quotation); untitled newspaper clipping, 1954 (second quotation), Sydnor Papers.

67. Charles S. Sydnor, "Walter Lynwood Fleming Lectures," [typescript], 1954, Sydnor Papers.

Chapter 8. W. J. Cash: A Native Son Confronts the Past

1. For an overview and comment on Cash's life and book, see Joseph L. Morrison, *W. J. Cash, Southern Prophet: A Biography and Reader* (New York: Alfred A. Knopf, 1967), and Bruce Clayton, *W. J. Cash: A Life* (Baton Rouge: Louisiana State University Press, 1991).

2. Clayton, *W. J. Cash*, 61–78.

3. Bruce Clayton, "W. J. Cash and the Creative Impulse," *Southern Review* 24(1988): 777–90; Richard H. King, *A Southern Renaissance: The Cultural Awakening of the American South, 1930–1955* (New York: Oxford University Press, 1980), 146–72.

4. W. J. Cash, "Jehovah of the Tar-Heels," *American Mercury* 17(1929): 310–18; "The Mind of the South," *American Mercury* 17(1929): 185–92; "The War in the South," *American Mercury* 19(1930): 163–69.

5. Bruce Clayton, "No Ordinary History: W. J. Cash's *The Mind of the South*," 3–22, in *The Mind of the South Fifty Years Later*, ed. Charles W. Eagles (Jackson: University Press of Mississippi, 1992); Fred C. Hobson, Jr., *Serpent in Eden: H. L. Mencken and the South* (1974; reprint, Baton Rouge: Louisiana State University Press, 1978), 12–13, 16–20; C. Vann Woodward, *Tom Watson: Agrarian Rebel* (New York: Macmillan, 1938).

6. Clayton, *W. J. Cash*, 107–29; King, *A Southern Renaissance*, 146–55.

7. King, *A Southern Renaissance*, 149.

8. W. J. Cash, *The Mind of the South* (1941; reprint, New York: Alfred A. Knopf, 1969), 203–4, 218, 224–25, 229.

9. Ibid., 102.

10. C. Vann Woodward, "The Elusive Mind of the South," in *American Counterpoint: Slavery and Racism in the North-South Dialogue* (Boston: Little, Brown and Company, 1971), 265, 266–83.

11. Cash, *The Mind of the South*, 35–37.

12. Ibid., 40–44, 109–14.

13. Ibid., 173–74.

14. Ibid., 161–75.

15. Ibid., 389–94.

16. Ibid., 51–53, 87, 321–22, 333.

17. Ibid., 87–89. For a commentary on Cash's treatment of women, see Elizabeth Jacoway, "The South's Palladium: The Southern Woman and the Cash Construct," 112–33, in *W. J. Cash and the Minds of the South*, ed. Paul D. Escott (Baton Rouge: Louisiana State University Press, 1992).

18. Francis Butler Simkins, *The South, Old and New: A History, 1820–1947* (New York: Alfred A. Knopf, 1947); William R. Taylor, *Cavalier and Yankee: The Old South and American National Character* (New York: George Braziller, 1961); Earl E. Thorpe, *The Mind of the Negro: An Intellectual History of Afro-Americans* (Baton Rouge: Louisiana State University Press, 1961), xi, xx; Nell Irvin Painter, "Race, Gender, and Class in *The Mind of the South*," 88–111, and C. Eric Lincoln, "Mind and Countermind: A Personal Perspective on W. J. Cash's *The Mind of the South*," 226–42, both in Escott, ed., *W. J. Cash and the Minds of the South*.

19. Woodward, "The Elusive Mind of the South," 280–81.

20. Carl N. Degler, *Place Over Time: The Continuity of Southern Distinctiveness* (Baton Rouge: Louisiana State University Press, 1977); John Shelton Reed, *The Enduring South: Subcultural Persistence in Mass Society* (Chapel Hill: University of North Carolina Press, 1972), and *One South: An Ethnic Approach to Regional Culture* (Baton Rouge: Louisiana State University Press, 1982); Fred Hobson, *Tell About the South: The Southern Rage to Explain* (Baton Rouge: Louisiana State University Press, 1983), 244–73; Fifteen Southerners, *Why the South Will Survive: Fifteen Southerners Look at Their Region a Half Century after "I'll Take My Stand"* (Athens: University of Georgia Press, 1981), with an afterword by Andrew Lytle. It should be noted that Woodward, in one of his most celebrated essays, "The Search for Southern Identity," found distinctiveness and persistence in the South's uniquely un-American history of poverty, defeat, persistent sense of guilt, and a consuming sense of place, which made up a large part of the "burden" of Southern history. See C. Vann Woodward, *The Burden of Southern History* (1960; rev. ed., Baton Rouge: Louisiana State University Press, 1968), 18–23.

21. King, *A Southern Renaissance*, 146–73; Bertram Wyatt-Brown, *Southern Honor: Honor, Ethics and Behavior in the Old South* (New York: Oxford University Press, 1982), and *Yankee Saints and Southern Sinners* (Baton Rouge: Louisiana State University Press, 1985), 131–54.

Chapter 9. Defining "The South's Number One Problem": V. O. Key, Jr., and the Study of Twentieth-Century Southern Politics

1. Alexander Heard, "Introduction," in V. O. Key, Jr., *Southern Politics in State and Nation* (New York: Alfred A. Knopf, 1949; reprint, Knoxville: University of

Tennessee Press, 1984), xxii. All references herein to *Southern Politics* are to the reprint version, unless otherwise noted.

2. For Key's early years, see Walter Dean Burnham, "V. O. Key, Jr., and the Study of Political Parties," in *V. O. Key, Jr. and the Study of American Politics,* ed. Milton C. Cummings, Jr. (Washington: American Political Science Association, 1988), 3–4; Milton C. Cummings, Jr., "V. O. Key, Jr.," in *American Political Scientists: A Dictionary,* ed. Glenn H. Utter and Charles Lockhart (Westport, Conn.: Greenwood Press, 1993), 156–60; and Richard C. Clark, "V. O. Key, Jr.," in the *Encyclopedia of World Biography,* vol. 6 (New York: McGraw Hill, 1973), 182–83.

3. William C. Havard, "V. O. Key, Jr.: A Brief Profile," in Key, *Southern Politics,* xxix.

4. Burnham, "V. O. Key, Jr., and the Study of Political Parties," 4.

5. Havard, "A Brief Profile," xxxiv.

6. Burnham, "V. O. Key, Jr., and the Study of Political Parties," 3.

7. Cummings, "V. O. Key, Jr.," 156–57.

8. All of the following by V. O. Key, Jr.: *The Techniques of Political Graft in the United States* (Chicago: University of Chicago Libraries, lithoprinted, 1936), *Politics, Parties, and Pressure Groups,* 1st ed. (New York: Thomas Y. Crowell, 1942), *A Primer of Statistics for Political Scientists* (New York: Thomas Y. Crowell, 1954), *American State Politics: An Introduction* (New York: Alfred A. Knopf, 1956), *Public Opinion and American Democracy* (New York: Alfred A. Knopf, 1961), and with Milton Cummings, Jr., *The Responsible Electorate: Rationality in Presidential Voting, 1936–1960* (Cambridge: Harvard University Press, 1966).

9. See Gavin C. Wright, *Old South, New South: Revolutions in the Southern Economy since the Civil War* (New York: Basic Books, 1986), 199, 260 (quotation).

10. Wright, *Old South, New South,* 241.

11. Alan Brinkley, "The New Deal and Southern Politics," in *The New Deal and the South,* ed. James C. Cobb and Michael V. Namorato (Jackson: University Press of Mississippi, 1984), 107.

12. Gunnar Myrdal, *An American Dilemma: The Negro Problem and Modern Democracy* (2 vols., New York: Harper and Brothers, 1944).

13. Numan V. Bartley, *The Creation of Modern Georgia,* 2d ed. (Athens: University of Georgia Press, 1990), 201.

14. *The State* (Columbia, S.C.), 27 June 1950.

15. Heard, "Introduction," xxiii–xxiv.

16. Alexander Heard, "Interviewing Southern Politicians," *American Political Science Review* 44(December 1950): 887–88, 893–94.

17. Roscoe C. Martin, "Foreword," in Key, *Southern Politics* (1949 edition), vi; also see Heard, "Interviewing Southern Politicians," 886; and John Egerton, *Speak Now Against the Day: The Generation before the Civil Rights Movement in the South* (New York: Alfred A. Knopf, 1994), 522.

18. Heard, "Introduction," xxii, and "Interviewing Southern Politicians," 886.

19. Key, *Southern Politics,* vi.

20. Heard, "Interviewing Southern Politicians," 890–91, 893.

21. Heard, "Introduction," xxi, and "Interviewing Southern Politicians," 887–88.

22. Heard, "Interviewing Southern Politicians," 887, 892.

23. Ibid., 893–94.

24. Key, *Southern Politics*, vi.

25. Heard, "Introduction," xxi.

26. Heard, "Interviewing Southern Politicians," 889.

27. Ibid., 891.

28. Ibid., 892.

29. Key, *Southern Politics*, 6.

30. Ibid., 316.

31. See V. O. Key, Jr., "The Future of the Democratic Party," *Virginia Quarterly Review* 28(Spring 1952): 171.

32. Key, *Southern Politics*, 11.

33. Ibid., 205.

34. Ibid., 184.

35. Ibid., 228.

36. Ibid., 223.

37. Ibid., 277.

38. Ibid., 280.

39. Ibid., 292.

40. Ibid., 293.

41. Ibid., 533.

42. Ibid., 535.

43. Ibid., 551, 553.

44. Ibid., 555.

45. Ibid., 579.

46. Ibid., 618.

47. Ibid., 307.

48. Ibid., 671.

49. Key, "The Future of the Democratic Party," 172.

50. Ibid., 173.

51. Ibid.

52. V. O. Key, Jr., "Solid South: Cracked or Broken," *New Republic* (1 December 1952), 9, and "The Erosion of Sectionalism," *Virginia Quarterly Review* 31(Spring 1955): 162. See Jane Dailey, Glenda Elizabeth Gilmore, and Bryant Simon, eds., *Jumpin' Jim Crow: Southern Politics from Civil War to Civil Rights* (Princeton: Princeton University Press, 2000).

53. Key, "Solid South," 10.

54. Ibid.

55. Key, "The Erosion of Sectionalism," 163, 165.

56. Ibid., 166–67. Historians and political scientists have supported Key's assessment of 1950s Southern politics. See, for example, Numan V. Bartley and Hugh Davis Graham, *Southern Politics and the Second Reconstruction* (Baltimore:

Johns Hopkins University Press, 1975), 185–87; Alexander P. Lamis, *The Two-Party South* (New York: Oxford University Press, 1984), 25–27.

57. Key, "The Erosion of Sectionalism," 169.

Chapter 10. C. Vann Woodward, Southern Historian

1. For full biographical details, see John Herbert Roper, *C. Vann Woodward, Southerner* (Athens: University of Georgia Press, 1987); unless otherwise noted, biographical details are from this book. For critical analyses of Woodward's work on Southern topics, see idem, ed., *C. Vann Woodward: A Southern Historian and His Critics* (Athens: University of Georgia Press, 1997), hereinafter cited as *Woodward*. See also Glenn Feldman, "C. Vann Woodward: Liberalism, Iconoclasm, Irony, and *Belles-Lettres* in Southern History," *Southern Humanities Review* 29(Spring 1995): 127–44. Potter quoted in Roper, *C. Vann Woodward, Southerner*, 194; see also interviews: Woodward, 18 and 19 July 1978, 12 October 1980, 21 March 1983, and on Franklin, interview: John Hope and Aurelia Franklin, 10 November 1978, John Herbert Roper Papers of the Southern Historical Collection at the Library of the University of North Carolina at Chapel Hill. See Franklin, *The Historian and Public Policy*, Nora and Edward Ryerson Lectures, No. 23 (Chicago: University of Chicago Press, 1974).

2. Indeed, the program committee of the 1997 Southern Historical Association arranged that the 1998 meeting in Birmingham be a sixty-year anniversary celebration for the organization's meeting in that city and a ninety-year birthday celebration for that historian. In the year of the SHA's inception, he attended as a scholar holding a major fellowship and as one who had already published book reviews—and as one who had already been in trouble with an academic dean over a matter of public policy and the professorial role. "News and Notes," *Journal of Southern History* 64(August 1998): 602; Program of the Southern Historical Association, Birmingham, 11–14 November 1998.

3. C. Vann Woodward, *Tom Watson: Agrarian Rebel* (New York: Macmillan, 1938); *Bougainville Landing and the Battle of Empress Augusta Bay* (restricted distribution; Washington: Government Printing Office, n.d. [ca. 1947]); *Kolombangara and Vella Lavella* (restricted distribution; Washington: Government Printing Office, n.d. [ca. 1947]); *The Battle for Leyte Gulf* (1947; reprint, New York: W. W. Norton, 1965); *Reunion and Reaction: The Compromise of 1877 and the End of Reconstruction* (1951; rev. ed., Garden City, N.Y.: Doubleday, 1956); *Origins of the New South, 1877–1913*, History of the South series, ed. E. Merton Coulter and Wendell Holmes Stephenson (1951; rev. ed. with bibliographic essay by Charles B. Dew, Baton Rouge: Louisiana State University Press, 1971).

4. Idem, ed., *Responses of Presidents to Charges of Misconduct* (New York: Delacorte, 1974); idem, ed., *Mary Chesnut's Civil War* (New Haven: Yale University Press, 1981).

5. Alphabetical list of doctoral students from The Johns Hopkins University: Daniel H. Calhoun, 1956; Suzanne Carson (Lowitt), 1952; Vincent De Santis, 1952;

Charles B. Dew, 1964; Tilden G. Edelstein, 1961; Louis R. Harlan, 1955; Warren W. Hassler, Jr., 1954; Ludwell H. Johnson III, 1955; Charles F. Kellogg, 1965; James M. McPherson, 1962; Otto H. Olsen, 1959; Willie Lee Nichols Rose, 1961; Robert B. Sharkey, 1957; Gustavus G. Williamson, 1954; and Bertram Wyatt-Brown, 1962. Alphabetical list of doctoral students from Yale University: John Blassingame, 1971; Frederick A. Bode, 1969; David L. Carlton, 1977; Ruth F. Claus, 1975; Daniel W. Crofts, 1968; Robert F. Engs, 1972; Barbara J. Fields, 1978; James R. Green, 1972; F. Sheldon Hackney, 1966; Steven H. Hahn, 1979; Thomas Holt, 1973; Frank J. Huffman, 1974; J. Morgan Kousser, 1971; Marc W. Kruman, 1978; John L. McCarthy, 1970; Richard L. McCormick, 1976; William S. McFeely, 1966; Geraldine M. McTigue, 1975; Bruce Palmer, 1972; Robert Dean Pope, 1976; Lawrence N. Powell, 1976; Daniel T. Rodgers, 1973; Richard Skolnik, 1964; J. Mills Thornton III, 1974; Bert H. Thurber, 1973; Michael S. Wayne, 1979; and John A. Williams, 1966. The Johns Hopkins list supplied by Comer Vann Woodward and supplemented by *Doctoral Dissertations Accepted by American Universities*, vols. 15–22, and *Index to American Doctoral Dissertations*, 1957–1965; the Yale University list supplied by Registrar, Department of History, Yale University, and supplemented by *Index to American Doctoral Dissertations*.

6. Woodward quotes Toynbee on this score in several places, first and most prominently, *Origins*, viii.

7. Mortimer J. Adler, *The Paideia Experiment: An Educational Manifesto* (New York: Macmillan, 1982).

8. George Brown Tindall, *South Carolina Negroes, 1877–1900* (1952; 2d ed., Baton Rouge: Louisiana State University Press, 1966).

9. Edward L. Ayers, *The Promise of the New South: Life after Reconstruction* (New York: Oxford University Press, 1992). See also Ayers, "Narrative Form in Origins of the New South," in *Woodward*, 37–46; and on a different but related point, Joel R. Williamson, "C. Vann Woodward and the Origins of a New Wisdom," in *Woodward*, 203–26.

10. Phrase quoted on dust cover, Joel R. Williamson, *The Crucible of Race: Black-White Relations in the American South since Emancipation* (New York: Oxford University Press, 1984); see also Williamson, "C. Vann Woodward," in *Woodward*, 203–26; M. E. A. Bradford, "The Strange Career of C. Vann Woodward," in *Woodward*, 253–65; John Shelton Reed, *Southern Folk, Plain & Fancy: Native White Social Types*, Lamar Memorial Lectures No. 29 (Athens: University of Georgia Press, 1986); Reed, *The Enduring South: Subcultural Persistence in Mass Society* (Chapel Hill: University of North Carolina Press, 1972); Eugene D. Genovese, *The Southern Front: History and Politics in the Cultural War* (Columbia: University of Missouri Press, 1995).

11. Woodward, *American Counterpoint: Slavery and Racism in the North-South Dialogue* (Boston: Little, Brown, 1971).

12. Charles R. Crowe, "Tom Watson, Populists, and Blacks Reconsidered," *Journal of Negro History* 55(April 1970): 99–116; Barton C. Shaw, *The Wool-Hat Boys: Georgia's Populist Party* (Baton Rouge: Louisiana State University Press, 1984);

and Carl N. Degler, "Review of *Mary Chesnut's Civil War,*" *American Historical Review* 87(February 1982): 262–63. For a very thorough review of recent controversies concerning Chesnut, see Michael P. Johnson, "Mary Chesnut's Autobiography and Biography: A Review Essay," *Journal of Southern History* 47(November 1981): 585–92.

13. Charles A. Beard and Mary Ritter Beard, *The Rise of American Civilization,* 2 vols. (rev. ed., New York: Macmillan, 1939). For classroom purposes, young Woodward used the Beardian textbook Curtis Putnam Nettles, *The Roots of American Civilization* (New York: Appleton-Century-Crofts, 1938).

14. David Morris Potter, *The South and Sectional Conflict* (Baton Rouge: Louisiana State University Press, 1968), esp. 3–34; Ulrich Bonnell Phillips, "The Central Theme of Southern History," *American Historical Review* 34(October 1928): 30–43.

15. Eugene D. Genovese, *The Political Economy of Slavery: Studies in the Economy and Society of the Slave South* (1961; rev. ed., New York: Random House Vintage, 1967); Cf. a much more complex variation on these themes, Elizabeth Fox-Genovese and Genovese, *Fruits of Merchant Capital: Slavery and Bourgeois Property in the Rise and Expansion of Capitalism* (New York: Oxford University Press, 1983).

16. James Tice Moore, "Redeemers Reconsidered: Change and Continuity in the Democratic South, 1870–1900," *Journal of Southern History* 44(August 1978): 357–78; William J. Cooper, Jr., *The Conservative Regime: South Carolina, 1877–1890* (Baltimore: The Johns Hopkins University Press, 1968); Jonathan M. Wiener, *Social Origins of the New South: Alabama, 1860–1885* (Baton Rouge: Louisiana State University Press, 1980); Carl N. Degler, *Place Over Time: The Continuity of Southern Distinctiveness,* Walter Lynwood Fleming Memorial Lecture, 1976 (1977; reprint ed., Athens: University of Georgia Press, 1997). See general discussion on this issue by Moore and by Degler in *Woodward,* 95–117 and 118–42, respectively.

17. Hackney, "Origins," in *Woodward,* 69–94; Ayers, *The Promise of the New South.*

18. Richard H. King, *A Southern Renaissance: The Cultural Awakening of the American South, 1930–1955* (New York: Oxford University Press, 1980); Gaines M. Foster, "Woodward and Southern Identity," in *Woodward,* 56–68; and Michael O'Brien, "From a Chase to a View: The Arkansan," in *Woodward,* 234–53. See Reed, *Southern Folk, Plain & Fancy* and *The Enduring South.*

19. Samuel S. Hill, *Religion and the Solid South* (New York: Abingdon Press, 1972); John B. Boles, ed., *Masters and Slaves in the House of the Lord* (Lexington: University Press of Kentucky, 1988); Boles, "Evangelical Protestantism in the Old South: From Religious Dissent to Cultural Dominance," in *Religion in the South,* Porter L. Fortune Symposium on the South, 1985, ed. Charles Reagan Wilson (Jackson: University Press of Mississippi, 1985), 13–34; Boles, "The Discovery of Southern Religious History," in *Interpreting Southern History: Historiographical Essays in Honor of Sanford W. Higginbotham,* ed. Boles and Evelyn Thomas Nolen (Baton Rouge: Louisiana State University Press, 1987), 510–48; Eugene D. Genovese, *Roll Jordon, Roll: The World the Slaves Made* (New York: Pantheon Books,

1974), and Genovese, *The Slaveholders' Dilemma: Freedom and Progress in Southern Conservative Thought, 1820–1860* (Columbia: University of South Carolina Press, 1992); and Donald G. Matthews, *Religion in the Old South* (Chicago: University of Chicago Press, 1977).

20. Reed, *The Enduring South*; see also reports on polls, *Southern Cultures*, vols. 1–4, 1994–1998. The oversight on Woodward's part of the importance of religion in Southern history, and even reform, has been noted by Wayne Flynt in "Dissent in Zion: Alabama Baptists and Social Issues, 1900–1914," *Journal of Southern History* 35(November 1969): 523–42.

21. David Hackett Fischer, *Historians' Fallacies: Toward a Logic of Historical Thought* (New York: Harper and Row, 1970), 149ff.

Chapter 11. John Hope Franklin:
Southern History in Black and White

1. John Hope Franklin, "The Practice of History," in Franklin, *Race and History: Selected Essays, 1938–1988* (Baton Rouge: Louisiana State University Press, 1989), 71. Franklin has made similar statements on several occasions: "You can't have Jim Crow history any more than you can have Jim Crow anything else. That's what I've tried to do in my books and my teaching, to talk about the Southern scene as a whole," quoted in "Our Changing Region," *Southern Living* 25(June 1990): 148; "I do not teach black history at the University [of Chicago]. I teach the history of the South—black and white," quoted in August Meier and Elliott Rudwick, *Black History and the Historical Profession, 1915–1980* (Urbana: University of Illinois Press, 1986), 120. For better or worse, Franklin has not been able to shake the general impression that he is a *black* historian. With apparent exasperation he told an interviewer in 1990: "It's often assumed that I'm a scholar of Afro-American history, but the fact is I haven't taught a course in Afro-American history for some 30-odd years. They say I'm the author of 12 books on black history, when several of those books focus mainly on whites. I'm called a leading *black* historian, never minding the fact that I've served as president of the American Historical Association, the Organization of American Historians, the Southern Historical Association, Phi Beta Kappa, and on and on. The tragedy is that black scholars so often have their specialties forced on them. My specialty is the history of the South, and that means I teach the history of whites and blacks." Quoted in "That's History, Not Black History," *New York Times Book Review* 95(3 June 1990): 13.

2. For the circumstances surrounding Franklin's (reluctant) acceptance of the commission that established him as the leading scholar of African-American history, see Meier and Rudwick, *Black History and the Historical Profession*, 117–18. On the critical reception of the first edition of *From Slavery to Freedom: A History of Negro Americans* (New York: Alfred A. Knopf, 1947) see Earl E. Thorpe, *Black Historians: A Critique* (New York: William Morrow and Co., 1971), 181. The reviewer in the *Journal of Negro History* was both on and wide of the mark when he asserted of the first edition: "It is a solid work destined to be used for some time to come. It may never be on the list of best-sellers, for it is not that sort of book,

but I dare say that it will be used when many of the best-sellers have been forgotten." Williston H. Lofton, "Review of *From Slavery to Freedom*," *Journal of Negro History* 33(April 1948): 225–26. See also Franklin's essay "A Brief History of the Negro in the United States," in *The American Negro Reference Book*, ed. John P. Davis (Englewood Cliffs, N.J.: Prentice-Hall, 1966), 1–95. For an incisive and succinct survey of the concerns and phases of African-American historiography, see Franklin's essay "On the Evolution of Scholarship in Afro-American History," in *The State of Afro-American History: Past, Present, and Future*, ed. Darlene Clark Hine (Baton Rouge: Louisiana State University Press, 1986), 13–22.

3. Meier and Rudwick, *Black History and the Historical Profession*, 121. See also William M. Banks, *Black Intellectuals: Race and Responsibility in American Life* (New York: W. W. Norton, 1996), 131.

4. Williams also authored *A History of Negro Troops in the War of the Rebellion*, published in 1887 by Harper and Brothers.

5. John Hope Franklin, *George Washington Williams: A Biography* (Chicago: University of Chicago Press, 1985), 240–41. The book is dedicated to four of Williams's "warm admirers" and notable African-American scholars in their own right: W. E. B. Du Bois, Carter G. Woodson, Charles H. Harris, and Rayford W. Logan.

6. Ibid., 133, 107, 115.

7. George M. Frederickson, "Pioneer" [John Hope Franklin], *New York Review of Books* 40(23 September 1993): 30.

8. John Hope Franklin, "A Life of Learning," The Charles Homer Haskins Lecture (14 April 1988), in Franklin, *Race and History*, 286.

9. Ibid., 286–88. In his public lectures (as distinct from his essays and monographs) Franklin has made more trenchant and critical comments on the American racial situation, its origins, and prospects. See especially *Racial Equality in America* (Columbia: University of Missouri Press, 1993) and *The Color Line: Legacy for the Twenty-First Century* (Columbia: University of Missouri Press, 1993).

10. Franklin is reported to have said, "Every person in the United States ought to recognize the fact that this [the enslavement of African-Americans] was a despicable act on the part of our Founding Fathers and all the people who came before us." Martin Walker, "Clinton Ponders Apology for Slavery," *The Guardian* 18 June 1997.

11. Curiously, Franklin has so far escaped the attentions of a biographer, but he is now working on his autobiography, having recently published that of his father: John Hope Franklin and John Whittington Franklin, eds., *My Life and an Era: The Autobiography of Buck Colbert Franklin* (Baton Rouge: Louisiana State University Press, 1997).

12. John Herbert Roper, "John Hope Franklin," in *Encyclopedia of Southern Culture*, ed. Charles Reagan Wilson and William Ferris (Chapel Hill: University of North Carolina Press, 1989), 208.

13. Franklin, "A Life of Learning," 278.

14. Asked on the 1997 PBS television documentary "First Person Singular:

John Hope Franklin" whether he felt in retrospect that his father's decision to leave "the relative safety of an all-black town" for the racial violence that engulfed Tulsa in 1921 had been a mistake, Franklin responded: "The more you study these small communities like Rentiesville, even if they are homogeneous, the more you become convinced that they are not the answer to the problems of race, ethnicity or any other division. I would not countenance, would not be interested in the kind of experimentation that would suggest that an all-black community or even an all-black school would be good for self-esteem or for preparation to live in the larger community." "Q & A with Historian John Hope Franklin," South Carolina Educational TV transcript, n.d., in possession of author.

15. Reflecting on this, many years later, Franklin confessed, "I am not altogether proud of going to Convention Hall; there are times, even now, while enjoying a symphony or an opera, when I reproach myself for having yielded to the indignity of racial segregation. I can only say that in the long run it was my parents who knew best, though later I made a conscious effort to regain my self-respect." "A Life of Learning," 280–81.

16. Franklin's first impressions of and subsequent meetings with Du Bois are recollected in "W. E. B. Du Bois: A Personal Memoir," *Massachusetts Review* 31(Autumn 1990): 409–28.

17. Meier and Rudwick, *Black History and the Historical Profession,* 117.

18. Franklin, "A Life of Learning," 285.

19. Franklin, "Their War and Mine," *Journal of American History* 77(September 1990): 578. Angered at his rejection by the War Department, Franklin wrote an essay "History—Weapon of War and Peace," which W. E. B. Du Bois, about to retire as editor of *Phylon,* recommended to his successor for publication. Franklin writes self-disparagingly of this article that it "was wide-ranging, ostentatiously learned [and] written in a style that seemed imitative of Du Bois himself. I quoted John Fiske, the Count de Gobineau . . . Alfred Mahan, and dropped in a few other names such as Johann Droysen, Thomas Macaulay, Von Treitschke, and Houston Stewart Chamberlain," and also "denounced the way in which historians had, on many occasions, prostituted themselves to narrow, selfish, nationalistic ends." Franklin, "W. E. B. Du Bois," 417.

20. Franklin, "Their War and Mine," 579.

21. Franklin wrote, "If the war had not ended when it did, and if the archives had not been closed for the celebration of the victory of good over evil and democracy over totalitarianism, and had not a gracious and generous archivist invited me there when it was closed, I might never have completed that book." Ibid., 579.

22. John Hope Franklin, "The Dilemma of the Negro Scholar," in *Race and History,* 304. C. Vann Woodward discovered that he and Franklin could not dine together on Saturdays in Washington, D.C., when they were both researching at the Library of Congress and government offices were closed. Franklin remembered that Woodward asked him, "What will you do?" and his reply was: "I eat a big breakfast, I come late [to the archives], I bring a piece of candy, and, when I can't stand it, I go home"—for an early dinner. Woodward reportedly replied: "I

don't think I could be a historian if I couldn't eat dinner!" John Herbert Roper, *C. Vann Woodward, Southerner* (Athens: University of Georgia Press, 1987), 167. Franklin also recounts this episode, and adds that he informed his white friend: "I assured him that for a Negro scholar searching for truth, the search for food in the city of Washington was one of the *minor* inconveniences." "The Dilemma of the Negro Scholar," 305.

23. Franklin, "A Life of Learning," 290.

24. Franklin, "Our Changing Region," 150.

25. Ben Stocking, "A New Campaign in a Long War," *Raleigh News and Observer*, 19 July 1997, 14A. Franklin also takes a mischievous and gleeful delight in reversing the conventions of Southern (if not also Northern) racial "etiquette." On one hilarious occasion, when this (white) author offered to help him carry bags of groceries from a Durham, North Carolina, supermarket, he replied—to the consternation and confusion of the white customers waiting at the checkout—"OK, *boy!*"

26. Meier and Rudwick, *Black History and the Historical Profession*, 120–21. Fitchett was an African-American sociologist who had studied free blacks in Charleston.

27. Not all Southern white historians sympathized with the integration of the profession. Interviewed by Peter Applebome, for a profile marking his eightieth birthday, Franklin recounted a conversation he had, as a young professor at North Carolina College for Negroes, with Charles S. Sydnor of the University of Mississippi (on the campus of Duke University), in which Sydnor said, "Franklin, I hear you were against segregation," to which Franklin replied in the affirmative. Baffled, Sydnor exclaimed, "I don't understand. You've got a very nice job over there at the North Carolina College for Negroes, and if we had desegregation, you'd be out of a job. Why would you want anything like that?" "Keeping Tabs on Jim Crow: John Hope Franklin," *New York Times Magazine* (23 April 1995): 36–37.

28. Roper recounts that at the Williamsburg meeting, "by the peculiar workings of Southern manners, those who objected to an integrated program blamed Woodward more than they blamed Franklin," and were less concerned with the contents of the program than over where Franklin would eat and sleep. Woodward sardonically replied that he would probably sleep "in a pup tent." Asked where he would eat, Woodward replied: "Oh, he's very resourceful, he'll probably bring K-rations." In the event, Franklin lodged with the family of historian Douglas Adair, "sleeping and taking his meals in seclusion from other conference delegates." *C. Vann Woodward, Southerner*, 165–67.

29. C. Vann Woodward, *Thinking Back: The Perils of Writing History* (Baton Rouge: Louisiana State University Press, 1986), 88–90.

30. Carter G. Woodson, "Review of *The Free Negro in North Carolina*," *Journal of Negro History* 28(October 1943): 482–85. Woodson offered two mild criticisms of Franklin's study: the discussion of Native American–African-American relations might have been profitably extended, and more attention should have been given to the anti-slavery movement in North Carolina. Franklin was "not to be held

accountable for not making his dissertation an anti-slavery treatise" but "must be blamed for not showing more clearly the bearing of the movement on the Free Negroes of North Carolina," 484.

31. Blanche H. Clarke, "Review of *The Free Negro in North Carolina*," *Journal of Southern History* 9(August 1943): 411–13.

32. John Hope Franklin, "Slavery and the Martial South," *Journal of Negro History* 37(January 1952): 36–53; reprinted in Franklin, *Race and History*, 92–103. Quotation on p. 103.

33. William Archibald Dunning, *Reconstruction: Political and Economic* (New York: Columbia University Press, 1907), 212.

34. John Hope Franklin, "Whither Reconstruction Historiography?" *Journal of Negro Education* 17(Fall 1948): 444–61, reprinted in Franklin, *Race and History*, 24–40. Quotation on p. 26.

35. John Hope Franklin, "Mirror for Americans: A Century of Reconstruction History," *American Historical Review* 85(February 1980): 1–14, reprinted in Franklin, *Race and History*, 386–98.

36. Franklin, "Whither Reconstruction History?" 28.

37. Ibid., 33. In his 1979 essay "*The Birth of a Nation*: Propaganda as History," Franklin observed that Coulter's book perpetuated the Thomas Dixon/D. W. Griffith depiction of Reconstruction: "the unwashed, drunken, corrupt black legislators; the innocent disfranchised whites; and the resort to desperate measures by the Klan to save the South from complete disaster." Franklin, *Race and History*, 23. He also noted that Alistair Cooke's popular coffeetable book on American history and the television programs based on it "follow, to an incredible degree, the argument set forth in *Birth of a Nation*," 23.

38. Eric Anderson and Alfred A. Moss, Jr., eds., *The Facts of Reconstruction: Essays in Honor of John Hope Franklin* (Baton Rouge: Louisiana State University Press, 1991), ix-x.

39. John Hope Franklin, *Reconstruction after the Civil War* (Chicago: University of Chicago Press, 1961), 118. For an insightful discussion of education in the former Confederate states, see Franklin's essay "Jim Crow Goes to School: The Genesis of Legal Segregation in the South," *South Atlantic Quarterly* 58(Spring 1959): 225–35.

40. Franklin, *Reconstruction after the Civil War*, 126.

41. Ibid., 123.

42. Ibid., 194. The central assertions of "the *revisionist synthesis*" that challenged the Dunning/Coulter viewpoint are ably summarized in Carl H. Moneyhon's essay "The Failure of Southern Republicanism, 1867–1876," in Anderson and Moss, eds., *The Facts of Reconstruction*, 100–102.

43. Edgar Allan Toppin, "Review of *Reconstruction after the Civil War*," *Journal of Negro History* 47(January 1962): 57–59, passim.

44. Avery O. Craven, "Review of *Reconstruction after the Civil War*," *Journal of Southern History* 28(May 1962): 255–56, passim; Franklin, *Reconstruction after the Civil War*, vii–viii (Boorstin quoted).

45. John Hope Franklin, "Review of Kenneth Stampp's *The Era of Reconstruction, 1865–1877*," *Journal of Negro History* 50(October 1965): 286–88, passim.

46. John Hope Franklin, *The Emancipation Proclamation* (Garden City, N.Y.: Doubleday, 1963), x, 132.

47. John Hope Franklin, *A Southern Odyssey: Travelers in the Antebellum North* (Baton Rouge: Louisiana State University Press, 1976), 243, 285.

48. John Hope Franklin, "As For Our History," reprinted in Franklin, *Race and History*, 63, 70.

49. Franklin, *Race and History*, 352.

50. Drew Gilpin Faust, "Unpolluted by Passion," *New York Times Book Review* (3 June 1990): 13.

51. John Hope Franklin and Loren Schweninger, *Runaway Slaves: Rebels on the Plantation* (New York: Oxford University Press, 1999), 243 (quoted).

52. Ibid., 248 (quoted).

Chapter 12. A. Elizabeth Taylor: Searching for Southern Suffragists

1. Columbus (Ga.) *Ledger*, 24 October 1983 (thanks to Martha H. Swain for sharing a photocopy of this story); Columbus (Ga.) *Enquirer*, 26 December 1978; William B. Hesseltine and Louis Kaplan, "Women Doctors of Philosophy in History," *Journal of Higher Education* 14, no. 5(1943): 255.

2. A. Elizabeth Taylor, "A Lifelong Interest," in *Citizens at Last: The Woman Suffrage Movement in Texas*, ed. Ruthe Winegartern and Judith N. McArthur (Austin, Texas: Ellen C. Temple Publishing, 1987), 3; Carol K. Bleser, ed., "The Three Women Presidents of the Southern Historical Association: Ella Lonn, Kathryn Abby Hanna, and Mary Elizabeth Massey," *Southern Studies* 20(Summer 1981): 119 (Massey quotation). Virginia Van der Veer Hamilton recalled the obstacles to women in the historical profession in "Clio's Daughters: Whence and Whither," a chapter in *Taking Off the White Gloves: Southern Women and Women Historians*, ed. Michelle Gillespie and Catherine Clinton (Columbia: University of Missouri Press, 1998).

3. Taylor, "A Lifelong Interest," 3–5.

4. Anne Firor Scott, ed., *Unheard Voices: The First Historians of Women in the South* (Charlottesville: University Press of Virginia, 1993), 1–59. Also cited: Virginia Gearhart Gray, "Activities of Southern Women: 1840–1860," *South Atlantic Quarterly* 27(1928): 264–79; Marjorie Stratford Mendenhall, "Southern Women of a 'Lost Generation,'" *South Atlantic Quarterly* 33(1934): 334–53; Guion Griffis Johnson, *Antebellum North Carolina: A Social History* (Chapel Hill: University of North Carolina Press, 1937); and Eleanor M. Boatright, "The Political and Civil Status of Women in Georgia, 1783–1860," *Georgia Historical Quarterly* 25(1941): 301–24.

5. A. Elizabeth Taylor's works include: "A Short History of the Woman Suffrage Movement in Tennessee," *Tennessee Historical Quarterly* 2(September 1943): 195–215; "The Origins of the Woman Suffrage Movement in Georgia," *Geor-*

gia Historical Quarterly 28(June 1944): 63–79; "Revival and Development of the Woman Suffrage Movement in Georgia," *Georgia Historical Quarterly* 42(December 1958): 339–54; "The Last Phase of the Woman Suffrage Movement in Georgia," *Georgia Historical Quarterly* 43(March 1959): 11–28; "The Woman Suffrage Movement in Texas," *Journal of Southern History* 17(May 1951): 194–215; "The Woman Suffrage Movement in Arkansas," *Arkansas Historical Quarterly* 15(Spring 1956): 17–52; "The Woman Suffrage Movement in Florida," *Florida Historical Quarterly* 36(July 1957): 42–60; *The Woman Suffrage Movement in Tennessee* (New York: Bookman, 1957); "The Woman Suffrage Movement in Mississippi, 1890–1920," *Journal of Mississippi History* 30(February 1968): 1–34; "The Woman Suffrage Movement in North Carolina," *North Carolina Historical Review* 38(January and April 1961): 45–62, 173–89; "South Carolina and the Enfranchisement of Women: The Early Years," *South Carolina Historical Magazine* 77(April 1976): 115–26; "South Carolina and the Enfranchisement of Women: The Later Years," *South Carolina Historical Magazine* 80(October 1979): 298–310; "Woman Suffrage Activities in Atlanta," *Atlanta Historical Journal* 23(Winter 1980): 45–54; "Tennessee: The Thirty-Sixth State," in *Votes for Women! The Woman Suffrage Movement in Tennessee, the South, and the Nation,* ed. Marjorie Spruill Wheeler (Knoxville: University of Tennessee Press, 1995), 53–70. Taylor was also a contributor to the *Encyclopedia of Southern History, Encyclopedia of Southern Culture, Dictionary of North Carolina Biography, Dictionary of Georgia Biography, Notable American Women,* and *Handbook of Texas* (*TWU Update,* 18 October 1993, p. 7, A. Elizabeth Taylor Papers, Texas Woman's University).

6. *Dissertation Abstracts* shows no previous dissertations and only two master's theses, both completed at the University of Chicago in 1913: Gertrude May, "A History of the Woman Suffrage Movement in Illinois," and Nelle E. Bowman, "A Short History of Woman Suffrage in California."

7. Taylor, "A Lifelong Interest," 6, 8; interview with Martha Swain and Dorothy DeMoss, 13 November 1998.

8. Hesseltine and Kaplan, "Women Doctors of Philosophy in History," 254–59.

9. A. Elizabeth Taylor, "Regulations Governing Student Life at the Judson Female Institute during the Decade Preceding the Civil War," *Alabama Historical Quarterly* 3(1941): 23–31, "The Origin and Development of the Convict Lease System in Georgia," *Georgia Historical Quarterly* 26(1942): 113–29, and "The Abolition of the Convict Lease System in Georgia," *Georgia Historical Quarterly* 26(1942): 273–88.

10. Interview with Martha Swain and Dorothy DeMoss, 13 November 1998.

11. Taylor, "A Lifelong Interest," 6–7.

12. See Judith N. McArthur, "Minnie Fisher Cunningham's Back Door Lobby in Texas: Political Maneuvering in a One-Party State," in *One Woman, One Vote: Rediscovering the Woman Suffrage Movement,* ed. Marjorie Spruill Wheeler (Troutdale, Ore.: NewSage Press, 1995): 315–31.

13. Taylor to Beatrice Blackmar Gould, 6 July 1945, *National Woman's Party*

Papers (Bethesda, Md.: University Publications of America, 1977–1981), part 1, series 1, reel 87; Taylor to Martha Swain, 14 August 1977, Martha Swain Papers, Texas Woman's University, Denton. I am indebted to Professor Swain for granting me access to this collection, which is closed to the public. Decades later Taylor herself could not remember exactly when she was president of the Texas NWP, only that it was "a year or two in the 1940s." Thomas C. Pardo, ed., *The National Woman's Party Papers, 1913–1974: A Guide to the Microfilm Edition* (Microfilm Corp. of America, 1979), 642, identifies her as state chair of the Texas branch without designating a term. Membership lists are incomplete, but she is recorded as a dues-paying member in 1947 (reel 126). As late as 1957 the chair of the Committee on Endorsements asked her to help generate support from Texas for the ERA; see Emma E. Newton to Taylor, 8 March 1957, *NWP Papers*, part 1, series 1, reel 103.

14. Sidney R. Bland, "'Mad Women of the Cause'": The National Woman's Party in the South," *Furman University Bulletin* 26(December 1980): 82–91, and "Fighting the Odds: Militant Suffragists in South Carolina," *South Carolina Historical Magazine* 82(January 1981): 32–43.

15. Taylor, *The Woman Suffrage Movement in Tennessee*, 56; Anita Shafer Goodstein, "A Rare Alliance: African American and White Women in the Tennessee Elections of 1919 and 1920," *Journal of Southern History* 64(May 1998): 219–46.

16. Taylor's review of Kraditor's book (*Journal of American History* 52[March 1966]: 855), entirely ignores the chapter on Southern suffragists and race.

17. Taylor, "A Lifelong Interest," 8–9; Jacquelyn Dowd Hall and Anne Firor Scott, "Women in the South," in *Interpreting Southern History: Historiographical Essays in Honor of Sanford W. Higginbotham*, ed. John B. Boles and Evelyn Thomas Nolen (Baton Rouge: Louisiana State University Press, 1987), 454.

18. Taylor to Mary Elizabeth Massey, 6 May 1963, Mary Elizabeth Massey Papers, Winthrop University, Rock Hill, South Carolina; interview with Martha Swain and Dorothy DeMoss, 13 November 1998; Martha Swain to Judith McArthur, 17 August 1998.

19. Taylor to Martha Swain, 14 August 1977 (quotation) and 17 November 1992, Swain Papers; telephone interview with Mollie C. Davis, 20 November 1998. Taylor was elected vice president of SAWH in 1977, which would have elevated her to the presidency as she was preparing for retirement; she declined to serve.

20. "SHA Participation List as of 1986," Swain Papers; "Report of the Ad Hoc Committee on the Status of Women in the Southern Historical Association," 15 October 1982, and "Supplement to the Report," 25 October 1982, Southern Historical Association Records, No. 4030, Southern Historical Collection, University of North Carolina at Chapel Hill. The other members of the three-woman committee were La Wanda Cox and Mollie C. Davis.

21. Taylor to Martha Swain, 20 May, 17 June (quotation), 1982, Swain Papers; *On Campus*, Winter 1979, Swain Papers.

22. Taylor to Dewey Grantham, 27 May 1987; Grantham to Taylor, 10 June 1987; Taylor to Martha Swain, 15 June 1987: all in Swain Papers.

23. Taylor to Martha Swain, 15 July 1987 (first quotation); Taylor to Seetha

Srinivasan, 15 July 1987 (second quotation); Taylor to Swain, 27 January 1988, 18 March 1989, 30 November 1989, 25 April 1991: all in Swain Papers.

24. Paul E. Fuller to Judith McArthur, 29 December 1998; Taylor to Martha Swain, 17 November 1992, Swain Papers. "The Woman Suffrage Movement in Texas" was reprinted in Meckler's *History of Women in America*, ed. Nancy F. Cott (Westport, Conn.: Meckler Publishing Co., 1991).

25. Taylor to Martha Swain and Dorothy DeMoss, 4 August 1988 (quotation); Taylor to Swain, 30 April 1988, 30 November 1989: all in Swain Papers; Taylor obituary, *Journal of Southern History* 60(February 1994): 193–94.

26. Taylor to Martha Swain, 25 August 1993, Swain Papers; Wheeler, *Votes for Women*, xii.

Chapter 13. David M. Potter:
Lincoln, Abundance, and Sectional Crisis

1. David M. Potter, *The South and the Sectional Conflict* (Baton Rouge: Louisiana State University Press, 1968), vi.

2. Ibid., v.

3. Ibid., vi.

4. Wood Gray, "Review of *Lincoln and His Party in the Secession Crisis*," *American Historical Review* 48(April 1943): 591–92.

5. Kenneth M. Stampp, "Review of *Lincoln and His Party in the Secession Crisis*," *Mississippi Valley Historical Review* 29(December 1942): 438–39.

6. David M. Potter, *Lincoln and His Party in the Secession Crisis* (1942; reprint, New Haven: Yale University Press, 1962), xxiv–xxviii.

7. Boyd C. Shafer, "Review of *People of Plenty: Economic Abundance and the American Character*," *American Historical Review* 60(January 1955): 381.

8. Fred A. Shannon, "Review of *People of Plenty: Economic Abundance and the American Character*," *Mississippi Valley Historical Review* 41(March 1955): 733–34.

9. David M. Potter, *People of Plenty: Economic Abundance and the American Character* (Chicago: University of Chicago Press, 1954), 112.

10. Ibid., 165.

11. David M. Potter, "Horace Greeley and Peaceable Secession," 220, in Potter, ed., *The South and Sectional Conflict* (Baton Rouge: Louisiana State University Press, 1968).

12. Chase C. Mooney, "Review of *The South and Sectional Conflict*," *Journal of American History* 56(September 1969): 382.

13. David M. Potter, *The Impending Crisis, 1848–1861*, ed. Don E. Fehrenbacher (New York: Harper and Row, 1976), 84–85.

14. Maurice G. Baxter, "Review of *The Impending Crisis, 1848–1861*," *Journal of American History* 63(December 1976): 720.

15. David M. Potter, *History and American Society: Essays of David M. Potter*, ed. Don E. Fehrenbacher (New York: Oxford University Press, 1973).

16. Ibid., 303 (quoted).

17. David M. Potter, *The South and the Concurrent Majority*, ed. Don E. Fe-

hrenbacher and Carl N. Degler (Baton Rouge: Louisiana State University Press, 1972).

18. David M. Potter, *Freedom and Its Limitations in American Life,* ed. Don E. Fehrenbacher (Stanford, Calif.: Stanford University Press, 1976).

19. Potter, *The South and Sectional Conflict,* vi.

20. Ibid.

Chapter 14. David Herbert Donald:
Southerner as Historian of the Nation

1. David H. Donald, "The Southernization of America," *New York Times,* 30 August 1976.

2. David Herbert Donald, *Lincoln's Herndon* (New York: Alfred A. Knopf, 1948), 54.

3. David Herbert Donald to Jean Harvey Baker, 8 June 1998, in possession of the author.

4. Nicholas Lemann, *The Promised Land: The Great Black Migration and How It Changed America* (New York: Alfred A. Knopf, 1991); Robert Brandfon, *Cotton Kingdom of the New South: A History of the Yazoo Mississippi Delta from Reconstruction to the Twentieth Century* (Cambridge: Harvard University Press, 1967), 22–38.

5. James C. Cobb, *The Most Southern Place on Earth: The Mississippi Delta and the Roots of Regional Identity* (New York: Oxford University Press, 1992).

6. David Herbert Donald to Jean Harvey Baker, 8 June 1998.

7. The quotation is from T. S. Eliot's poem "Four Quartets," in *Four Quartets* (New York: Harcourt Brace, 1974).

8. David Herbert Donald, *Look Homeward: A Life of Thomas Wolfe* (Boston: Little, Brown, 1987), xv.

9. David Donald, "Acceptance of the Lincoln Prize," 1996, in possession of the author.

10. David Herbert Donald, "The Scalawag in Mississippi Reconstruction," *Journal of Southern History* 10(November 1944): 447–60.

11. Ibid., 460.

12. David Herbert Donald, "The Confederate as Fighting Man," *Journal of Southern History* 25(May 1959): 178–93.

13. David Herbert Donald, "Died of Democracy," in David Herbert Donald, ed., *Why the North Won the Civil War* (Baton Rouge: Louisiana State University Press, 1960), 89–90.

14. Richard F. Bensel, *Yankee Leviathan: The Origins of Central State Authority in America, 1859–1877* (New York: Cambridge University Press, 1990).

15. David Herbert Donald, *Liberty and Union* (Lexington, Mass.: D. C. Heath, 1978), ix.

16. David Herbert Donald, "The Proslavery Argument Reconsidered," *Journal of Southern History* 37(February 1971): 3–18.

17. David Herbert Donald, "Reconstruction," in *Interpreting American History:*

Conversations with Historians, ed. John Garraty (New York: Macmillan, 1970): 1, 341–67.

18. David Herbert Donald, *The Politics of Reconstruction, 1863–1877* (Cambridge: Harvard University Press, 1984); Jean Harvey Baker to Glenn Feldman, 9 November 1999 (e-mail message), in possession of the editor. See also Eric Foner, *Reconstruction: America's Unfinished Revolution, 1863–1877* (New York: Harper and Row, 1988).

19. Donald, *Lincoln's Herndon,* vii.

20. David Herbert Donald, *Lincoln Reconsidered: Essays on the Civil War Era* (New York: Alfred A. Knopf, 1956, 1961).

21. David Herbert Donald, *Charles Sumner and the Coming of the Civil War* (New York: Alfred A. Knopf, 1960, 1965).

22. David Herbert Donald to Jean Harvey Baker, 23 June 1998, in possession of the author.

23. Donald, *Look Homeward,* 434.

24. David Herbert Donald, *Lincoln* (New York: Simon and Schuster, 1995), 14.

Chapter 15. Kenneth Stampp's Peculiar Reputation

1. [James Oakes writes: "These observations are based on various conversations between Stampp and myself." They were confirmed in a letter from Kenneth Stampp to James Oakes, 20 October 1998, in Oakes's possession—Ed. note.]

2. Kenneth M. Stampp, *The Peculiar Institution: Slavery in the Antebellum South* (New York: Alfred A. Knopf, 1956).

3. Stanley Elkins, *Slavery: A Problem in American Intellectual and Institutional Life* (Chicago: University of Chicago Press, 1959), 21–22.

4. Stampp, *The Peculiar Institution,* vii–viii, 331, 350. See also p. 10: "[I]t is impossible to make valid generalizations about races as such"; p. 14: The Negro's "involvement in the Southern tragedy was not as a Negro but as the embodiment of the South's peculiar institution—as a type of labor and as a species of property. Not the Negro but slavery was the Old South's great affliction—the root of its tragedy."

5. See, for example, the foreword to Eugene D. Genovese's 1966 edition of Ulrich B. Phillips, *American Negro Slavery: A Survey of the Supply, Employment, and Control of Negro Labor as Determined by the Plantation Regime* (1918; Baton Rouge: Louisiana State University Press, 1966), x–xx. On the question of slave docility and resistance, for example, Genovese writes that "so long as we remain on the level on which Phillips placed the discussion and Stampp chose to keep it, we cannot get much further along," p. xviii.

6. Stampp's major works include: *Indiana Politics during the Civil War* (Indianapolis: Indiana Historical Bureau, 1949); *And the War Came: The North and the Secession Crisis, 1860–1861* (Baton Rouge: Louisiana State University Press, 1950 and 1970); *The Era of Reconstruction, 1865–1877* (New York: Vintage Books, 1965); *The Imperiled Union: Essays on the Background of the Civil War* (New York: Oxford

University Press, 1980); *America in 1857: A Nation on the Brink* (New York: Oxford University Press, 1990).

7. Stampp, *The Peculiar Institution*, 3.

8. Ibid., 34–85. Quotation on p. 34.

9. Ibid., 54.

10. Raymond A. Bauer and Alice H. Bauer, "Day to Day Resistance to Slavery," *Journal of Negro History* 27(October 1942): 388–419; Herbert Aptheker, *American Negro Slave Revolts* (New York: Columbia University Press, 1943).

11. Stampp, *The Peculiar Institution*, 86, 91–92, and in general 86–104.

12. Ibid., 178.

13. Ibid., 162, and in general 141–91.

14. Ibid., 192–236.

15. Ibid., 235–36.

16. Ibid., 237–78, 242.

17. Ibid., 279–321. On slave nutrition, Richard Sutch's chapter in Paul A. David et al., *Reckoning with Slavery: A Critical Study in the Quantitative History of American Negro Slavery* (New York: Oxford University Press, 1976), argues that the slave diet was adequate in calories but deficient in certain basic nutrients; Robert William Fogel, *Without Consent or Contract: The Rise and Fall of American Slavery* (New York: W. W. Norton, 1989), 132–47, concludes that "the nutritional deficiencies of early childhood, rather than the overwork or underfeeding of adults, were the main cause of the relatively high death rate of U.S. slaves."

18. Stampp, *The Peculiar Institution*, 340, 367, and in general 322–82. The subsequent scholarship on antebellum slave culture has been vast, but among the more important studies see John Blassingame, *The Slave Community: Plantation Life in the Antebellum South* (New York: Oxford University Press, 1972, 1979); Eugene D. Genovese, *Roll, Jordan, Roll: The World the Slaves Made* (New York: Pantheon Books, 1974); Lawrence W. Levine, *Black Culture and Black Consciousness: Afro-American Folk Thought from Slavery to Freedom* (New York: Oxford University Press, 1977).

19. Stampp, *The Peculiar Institution*, 383–418. The most thorough argument for the profitability and long-term viability of the slave economy is in Fogel, *Without Consent or Contract*, 60–113. Gavin C. Wright, *The Political Economy of the Cotton South: Households, Markets, and Wealth in the Nineteenth Century* (New York: W. W. Norton, 1978), is the best econometric case for the structural weaknesses of the plantation system in the Old South. But not even Wright disputes that slavery was profitable.

20. Stampp, *The Peculiar Institution*, 399–400.

21. Ibid., 423.

22. The sharpest critique of Stampp is Eugene D. Genovese, *The World the Slaveholders Made: Two Essays in Interpretation* (New York: Pantheon Books, 1969), 142–50. Somewhat less inflammatory is Gaines Foster, "Guilt Over Slavery: A Historiographical Analysis," *Journal of Southern History* 56(November 1990): 665–94.

23. Genovese, *Roll, Jordan, Roll*; Bertram Wyatt-Brown, *Southern Honor: Ethics and Behavior in the Old South* (New York: Oxford University Press, 1982); Mechal Sobel, *The World They Made Together* (Princeton: Princeton University Press, 1987).

24. Stampp, *The Peculiar Institution*, 430.

Chapter 16. Continuity and Change: George Brown Tindall and the Post-Reconstruction South

1. Elizabeth Jacoway, Dan T. Carter, Lester C. Lamon, and Robert C. McMath, eds., *The Adaptable South: Essays in Honor of George Brown Tindall* (Baton Rouge: Louisiana State University Press, 1991), 285 (quote). For a list of Tindall's principal writings, see pp. 291–93 of *The Adaptable South*.

2. Tindall's writings are examined in all of the historiographical essays covering the post-Reconstruction period in John B. Boles and Evelyn Thomas Nolen, eds., *Interpreting Southern History: Historiographical Essays in Honor of Sanford W. Higginbotham* (Baton Rouge: Louisiana State University Press, 1987). See the essays by George C. Rogers, Jr., LaWanda Cox, Harold D. Woodman, Richard L. Watson, Jr., Hugh Davis Graham, and Dan T. Carter.

3. Jacoway et al., *The Adaptable South*, 269 (quote).

4. Ibid., 265–66, 277. After his military service, Poole became a federal district attorney in San Francisco and, later, a federal circuit judge.

5. Ibid., 2, 266, 268–69.

6. Ibid., 2; John Hope Franklin, *From Slavery to Freedom: A History of Negro Americans* (New York: Alfred A. Knopf, 1947); George B. Tindall, "Southern Negroes Since Reconstruction: Dissolving the Static Image," in *Writing Southern History: Essays in Historiography in Honor of Fletcher M. Green*, ed. Arthur S. Link and Rembert W. Patrick (Baton Rouge: Louisiana State University Press, 1965), 339, 346–48, 353–54. For background on Fletcher Green, see pp. vi–vii. In addition to Tindall, other Green students included John G. Barrett, James C. Bonner, Charles E. Cauthen, J. Isaac Copeland, Horace H. Cunningham, Herbert J. Doherty, Jr., Paul M. Gaston, Allen J. Going, Dewey W. Grantham, Ernest M. Lander, Jr., Malcolm Cook McMillan, Mary Elizabeth Massey, Edwin A. Miles, Hugh F. Rankin, Charles G. Sellers, Jr., A. Elizabeth Taylor, Bennett H. Wall, and Vernon L. Wharton.

7. George Brown Tindall, *The Ethnic Southerners* (Baton Rouge: Louisiana State University Press, 1976), 92, 98, 101, 105, 108. The chapter on Howard Odum originally appeared as "The Significance of Howard W. Odum to Southern History: A Preliminary Estimate," *Journal of Southern History* 24(August 1958): 285–307. See also Jacoway et al., *The Adaptable South*, 276–77.

8. Tindall, "Southern Negroes Since Reconstruction," 337. Also, George B. Tindall, "The Campaign for the Disfranchisement of Negroes in South Carolina," *Journal of Southern History* 15(May 1949): 212–34. See also Jacoway et al., *The Adaptable South*, 2–3, 270–71.

9. Vernon L. Wharton, *The Negro in Mississippi, 1865–1890* (1947; reprint, New York: Harper Torchbooks, 1965); Tindall, "Southern Negroes Since Reconstruction," 354–55; Jacoway et al., *The Adaptable South*, 283. Vernon Wharton completed his dissertation in 1939 and published it in 1947.

10. George Brown Tindall, *South Carolina Negroes, 1877–1900* (Columbia: University of South Carolina Press, 1952), vii–viii, 9.

11. Ibid., 12, 14, 17, 21–22, 26, 36, 38, 53, 69, 73.

12. Ibid., 39–40, 74, 82, 91.

13. Ibid., 54–64, 78, 81.

14. Ibid., 77, 83–84, 229–30, 253, 298–99.

15. Ibid., 88–89, 258–59, 301-02.

16. Ibid., 104–10, 122–24, 137–49.

17. Ibid., 186–87, 190, 203, 208, 282.

18. Ibid., 203-05.

19. Ibid., 246–47.

20. Ibid.

21. Ibid.

22. Ibid., 209, 215, 217, 219, 267, 276.

23. C. Vann Woodward, *The Strange Career of Jim Crow*, 3d ed. (New York: Oxford University Press, 1974); Tindall, "Southern Negroes Since Reconstruction," 355; Jacoway et al., *The Adaptable South*, 2–3, 283.

24. Tindall, *The Ethnic Southerners*, 59–60, 84–86. This essay was originally published as "The Central Theme Revisited," in *The Southerner as American*, ed. Charles G. Sellers (Chapel Hill: University of North Carolina, 1960).

25. Tindall, *The Ethnic Southerners*, 65–71.

26. Ibid., 71–72.

27. Ibid., 74–77, 80, 84.

28. Ibid., 81–82, 84, 86–87.

29. George Brown Tindall's "Mythology: A New Frontier in Southern History" originally appeared in *The Idea of the South: Pursuit of a Central Theme*, ed. Frank E. Vandiver (Chicago: University of Chicago Press, 1964). See Tindall's *The Ethnic Southerners*, 35–36.

30. Tindall, *The Ethnic Southerners*, 35, 37–38, 42.

31. Jacoway et al., *The Adaptable South*, 5–6, 281; David M. Potter, "The Emergence of the New South: An Essay Review," *Journal of Southern History* 34(August 1968): 421–23; George Brown Tindall, *The Emergence of the New South, 1913–1945* (Baton Rouge: Louisiana State University Press, 1967).

32. Tindall, *The Emergence of the New South*, ix, x.

33. Ibid., 10, 143.

34. Ibid., 190–91, 207, 214, 287, 289.

35. Ibid., 32, 69, 219, 223, 230.

36. Ibid., 254, 257, 276.

37. Ibid., 232–33, 246, 251–52.

38. Ibid., III, 355, 389, 632. In 1930, the region's population was 69.7 percent rural; 42.8 percent of its work force labored on farms at a per capita income of $189 in contrast to the $484 for nonfarm occupations.

39. Ibid., 393, 403, 427–28.

40. Ibid., 435, 441. The NIRA set up the National Recovery Administration (NRA).

41. Ibid., 478, 480, 487, 492.

42. Ibid., 505, 512–13, 521–22, 531, 538.

43. Ibid., 541, 544–45, 547, 549, 556.

44. Ibid., 59–64, 572–73.

45. Ibid., 618.

46. Ibid., 621, 627, 633, 649.

47. Ibid., 687, 691–92.

48. Ibid., 712–16, 726.

49. Ibid., 731.

50. George Brown Tindall, *The Disruption of the Solid South*, Mercer University Lamar Memorial Lectures, No. 14 (Athens: University of Georgia Press, 1972) and *The Persistent Tradition in New South Politics* (Baton Rouge: Louisiana State University Press, 1975); Jacoway et al., *The Adaptable South*, 11, 289–90; Tindall, *The Ethnic Southerners*, 21.

Chapter 17. Anne Firor Scott:
Writing Women into Southern History

1. Anne Firor Scott, ed., *Unheard Voices: The First Historians of Southern Women* (Charlottesville: University Press of Virginia, 1993), reference to Link and Patrick (editors of *Writing Southern History: Essays in Historiography in Honor of Fletcher M. Green*, Baton Rouge: Louisiana State University Press, 1965) is on p. 196; see also Jacquelyn Dowd Hall and Anne Firor Scott, "Women in the South," in *Interpreting Southern History: Historiographical Essays in Honor of Sanford W. Higginbotham*, ed. John B. Boles and Evelyn Thomas Nolen (Baton Rouge: Louisiana State University Press, 1987), 454; Edgar T. Thompson, *Perspectives on the South: Agenda for Research* (Durham: Duke University Press, 1967); Anne Firor Scott, *The Southern Lady: From Pedestal to Politics, 1830–1930* (Chicago: University of Chicago Press, 1970; reprint with an afterword by the author, Charlottesville: University Press of Virginia, 1995); all citations are to first edition, unless otherwise indicated.

2. Anne Firor Scott, *Making the Invisible Woman Visible* (Urbana: University of Illinois Press, 1984), xii, xx; Ann Evory, ed., *Contemporary Authors: A Bio-Bibliographical Guide to Current Authors and Their Work* (Detroit: Gale Research Co., 1st revision series, 1973, 1978), v, 33–36, 703.

3. Jane Addams, *Democracy and Social Ethics*, ed. Anne Firor Scott (Cambridge: Harvard University Press, 1964); Scott, *Invisible Woman*, xix–xxiii; Anne Firor Scott, "The 'New Woman' in the New South," *South Atlantic Quarterly*

61(Autumn 1962): 417–83, and "After Suffrage: Southern Women in the 1920s," *Journal of Southern History* 30(August 1964): 298–318.

4. Scott, *Southern Lady*, 17. See also Anne Firor Scott, "Women's Perspective on the Patriarchy in the 1850s," *Journal of American History* 61(June 1974): 52–64; Dorothy Ann Gay, "The Tangled Skein of Romanticism and Violence in the Old South: The Southern Response to Abolitionism and Feminism, 1830–1861" (Ph.D. diss., University of North Carolina, 1975); and Joel R. Williamson, *The Crucible of Race: Black-White Relations in the American South Since Emancipation* (New York: Oxford University Press, 1984), 34–35.

5. Scott explored the assumptions that prevented historians from seeing women in her presidential address for the Organization of American Historians; see "On Seeing and Not Seeing: A Case of Historical Invisibility," *Journal of American History* 71(June 1984): 7–21. Arthur S. Link was the first historian to explore Southern Progressivism in "The Progressive Movement in the South, 1870–1914," *North Carolina Historical Review* 23(April 1946): 172–95. C. Vann Woodward developed a thesis that Southern Progressivism was "for whites only" in *Origins of the New South, 1877–1913* (Baton Rouge: Louisiana State University Press, 1951), and it remained unchallenged until recently.

6. Hall and Scott, "Women in the South," 460–62, 469, 475. Julia Cherry Spruill, *Women's Life and Work in the Southern Colonies* (Chapel Hill: University of North Carolina Press, 1938).

7. Gerda Lerner, *The Majority Finds Its Past: Placing Women in History* (New York: Oxford University Press, 1979), 162.

8. Barbara Welter, "The Cult of True Womanhood: 1820–1860," *American Quarterly* 18(Summer 1966): 151–74; Gerda Lerner, "The Lady and the Mill Girl: Changes in the Status of Women in the Age of Jackson," *Mid-continent American Studies Journal* 10(Spring 1969): 5–15; Scott, *Southern Lady*, 4–21.

9. Scott, *Southern Lady*, 22–44, quotation is on p. 31. See also Catherine Clinton, *The Plantation Mistress: Woman's World in the Old South* (New York: Pantheon Books, 1982), 16–29, 151–56; Elizabeth Fox-Genovese, *Within the Plantation Household: Black and White Women of the Old South* (Chapel Hill: University of North Carolina Press, 1988), 115–30; Sally G. McMillen, *Motherhood in the Old South: Pregnancy, Childbirth, and Infant Rearing* (Baton Rouge: Louisiana State University Press, 1990).

10. Scott, *Southern Lady*, 46–63, quotation is on p. 48; and Scott, "Women's Perspective on the Patriarchy."

11. Fox-Genovese, *Within the Plantation Household*, 345–49; C. Vann Woodward, ed., *Mary Chesnut's Civil War* (New Haven: Yale University Press, 1981); C. Vann Woodward and Elisabeth Muhlenfeld, eds., *The Private Mary Chesnut: The Unpublished Civil War Diaries* (New York: Oxford University Press, 1984); Jean E. Friedman, *The Enclosed Garden: Women and Community in the Evangelical South, 1830–1900* (Chapel Hill: University of North Carolina Press, 1985), 88.

12. Clinton, *Plantation Mistress*, 182–98, quotations are on pp. 189 and 185;

Suzanne Lebsock, *The Free Women of Petersburg: Status and Culture in a Southern Town, 1784–1860* (New York: W. W. Norton, 1984), 138–41, quotation is on p. 139; Friedman, *Enclosed Garden*, 87–91, quotations are on pp. 89 and 87; Elizabeth Varon, *We Mean to Be Counted: White Women and Politics in Antebellum Virginia* (Chapel Hill: University of North Carolina Press, 1998), 41–70, quotation is on p. 43.

13. Fox-Genovese, *Within the Plantation Household*, 334–71, quotation is on p. 334.

14. Scott, *Southern Lady* (1995 edition), 273–74.

15. Scott, *Southern Lady*, 79–102, quotation is on p. 79.

16. Ibid., 102–33.

17. Lebsock, *Free Women*, 247–49, quotation is on p. 247; LeeAnn Whites, *The Civil War as a Crisis in Gender: Augusta, Georgia, 1860–1890* (Athens: University of Georgia Press, 1995), 136; Joan E. Cashin, "Into the Troubled Wilderness: The Refugee Experience in the Civil War," in *A Woman's War: Southern Women, Civil War, and the Confederate Legacy*, ed. Edward D. C. Campbell, Jr., and Kym S. Rice (Richmond and Charlottesville: Museum of the Confederacy and the University Press of Virginia, 1996), 29–54, quotation is on p. 53. George C. Rable, *Civil Wars: Women and the Crisis of Southern Nationalism* (Urbana: University of Illinois Press, 1989), 265–88, quotation is on p. 267; Friedman, *Enclosed Garden*, 92–109; Gaines M. Foster, *Ghosts of the Confederacy: Defeat, the Lost Cause, and the Emergence of the New South* (New York: Oxford University Press, 1987), 30–33, quotation is on p. 31; Drew Gilpin Faust, *Mothers of Invention: Women of the Slaveholding South in the American Civil War* (Chapel Hill: University of North Carolina Press, 1996), 248–57, and "'Ours as Well as That of the Men': Women and Gender in the Civil War," in *Writing the Civil War*, ed. James M. McPherson and William J. Cooper, Jr. (Columbia: University of South Carolina Press, 1998), 236. See also Catherine Clinton, *Tara Revisited: Women, War, and the Plantation Legend* (New York: Abbeville Press, 1995). See also Mary Martha Thomas, *The New Woman in Alabama: Social Reforms and Suffrage, 1890–1920* (Tuscaloosa: University of Alabama Press, 1992).

18. *Journal of Southern History* 62(May 1996): 382–85, quotation is on p. 384; Faust, *Mothers of Invention*, 253; Scott, *Southern Lady* (1995 edition), 275–76, quotation is on p. 276.

19. Scott, *Southern Lady*, 106–211, quotations are on pp. 150, 176, and 226.

20. Examples of recent scholarship include Anastatia Sims, *The Power of Femininity in the New South: Women's Organizations and Politics in North Carolina, 1880–1930* (Columbia: University of South Carolina Press, 1997); Elizabeth Hayes Turner, *Women, Culture, and Community: Religion and Reform in Galveston, 1880–1920* (New York: Oxford University Press, 1997); Judith N. McArthur, *Creating the New Woman: The Rise of Southern Women's Progressive Culture in Texas, 1893–1918* (Urbana: University of Illinois Press, 1998); Sandra G. Treadway, *Women of Mark: A History of the Women's Club of Richmond, 1894–1994* (Richmond: Library of Virginia, 1995); Joan Marie Johnson, "'This Wonderful Dream Nation!' Black and

White South Carolina Women and the Creation of a New South, 1898–1930" (Ph.D. diss., University of California at Los Angeles, 1977); and Sarah Wilkerson-Freeman, "Women and the Transformation of American Politics: North Carolina, 1898–1940" (Ph.D. diss., University of North Carolina, 1995). See also Mary Martha Thomas, ed., *Stepping Out of the Shadows: Alabama Women, 1819–1990* (Tuscaloosa: University of Alabama Press, 1995).

21. Sims, *Power of Femininity*, 128–37; Elna C. Green, *Southern Strategies: Southern Women and the Woman Suffrage Question* (Chapel Hill: University of North Carolina Press, 1997), 70–72, quotation is on p. 70. See also Foster, *Ghosts of the Confederacy*, and Karen L. Cox, "Women, the Lost Cause, and the New South: The United Daughters of the Confederacy and the Transmission of Southern Culture, 1894–1919" (Ph.D. diss., University of Southern Mississippi, Hattiesburg, 1997).

22. Jacquelyn Dowd Hall, "'The Mind That Burns in Each Body'": Women, Rape, and Racial Violence," in *Powers of Desire: The Politics of Sexuality*, ed. Elizabeth Ann Snitow, Christine Stansell, and Sharon Thompson (New York: Monthly Review Press, 1983), 328–46, quotation is on p. 337; Sims, *Power of Femininity*, 2, 33–41; Marjorie Spruill Wheeler, *New Women of the New South: The Leaders of the Woman Suffrage Movement in the Southern States* (New York: Oxford University Press, 1993), 3–19, quotation is on p. 18. See also Donald G. Matthews and Jane Sherron DeHart, *Sex, Gender, and the Politics of ERA: A State and the Nation* (New York: Oxford University Press, 1990), 6–8; Glenda Elizabeth Gilmore, *Gender and Jim Crow: Women and the Politics of White Supremacy in North Carolina, 1896–1920* (Chapel Hill: University of North Carolina Press, 1996), 82–89; and Williamson, *Crucible of Race*, 190–93.

23. Aileen S. Kraditor, *The Ideas of the Woman Suffrage Movement, 1890–1920* (New York: Columbia University Press, 1965; reprint with a preface by the author, New York: W. W. Norton, 1981), 163–218; Scott, *Southern Lady*, 182–83; Suzanne Lebsock, "Woman Suffrage and White Supremacy: A Virginia Case Study," in *Visible Women: New Essays on American Activism*, ed. Nancy A. Hewitt and Suzanne Lebsock (Urbana: University of Illinois Press, 1993), 62–100, quoted phrases are on p. 79; Green, *Southern Strategies*, xiii, 10–12, 91–98, quotations are on pp. 94 and 93. See also Gilmore, *Gender and Jim Crow*, 203–11. See also Suzanne Lebsock's essay in Michelle Gillespie and Catherine Clinton, eds., *Taking Off the White Gloves: Southern Women and Women Historians* (Columbia: University of Missouri Press, 1998).

24. Wheeler, *New Women of the New South*, 100–32, quotations are on pp. 127 and 126. See also Sims, *Power of Femininity*, 155–88.

25. *Journal of Southern History* 62(May 1996): 385. The phrase about the paradox of Southern women's reform that Scott quotes appears in Faust, *Mothers of Invention*, 253.

26. Williamson, *Crucible of Race*, 124–30; LeeAnn Whites, "Rebecca Lattimer Fulton and the Problem of 'Protection' in the New South," in *Visible Women*, ed. Hewitt and Lebsock, 41–61.

27. Anne Firor Scott, "Most Invisible of All: Black Women's Voluntary Associations," *Journal of Southern History* 56(February 1990): 3–22, quotation is on p. 22; *Southern Lady* (1995 edition), 280–82.

28. In addition to *The Southern Lady, Making the Invisible Woman Visible,* and *Unheard Voices* (previously cited) Scott's books include *Natural Allies: Women's Associations in American History* (Urbana: University of Illinois Press, 1991); *Virginia Women: The First Two Hundred Years,* with Suzanne Lebsock (Williamsburg: Colonial Williamsburg Foundation, 1985); *Women in American Life: Selected Readings* (New York: Houghton-Mifflin, 1979); *Women and Men: Changing Roles, Relationships, and Perspectives,* with Libby A. Cater (New York: Praeger, 1977); *One Half the People: The Fight for Woman Suffrage,* with Andrew Mackay Scott (Philadelphia: J. B. Lippincott, 1975); and *The American Woman: Who Was She?* (New York: Prentice-Hall, 1970). Anne Firor Scott also contributed the essay "Unfinished Business" to Gillespie and Clinton, *Taking Off the White Gloves: Southern Women and Women Historians.*

29. Scott, *Southern Lady* (1995 edition), 287.

Chapter 18. "Ethos Without Ethic": Samuel S. Hill and Southern Religious History

1. Samuel S. Hill, Jr., *Southern Churches in Crisis* (New York: Holt, Rinehart, and Winston, 1967), 8. Material in quotation marks not Hill's words.

2. Ibid., 6.

3. Samuel Hill, Jr., "The Southern Baptists: Need for Reformation, Redirection," *Christian Century* 80(9 January 1963): 39–42, "Southern Protestantism and Racial Integration," *Religion in Life* 30(Summer 1964): 421–29, *Southern Churches in Crisis,* and with Edgar T. Thompson, Anne Firor Scott, Charles Hudson, and Edwin Gaustad, *Religion and the Solid South* (Nashville: Abingdon Press, 1972).

4. W. J. Cash, *The Mind of the South* (New York: Vintage Books, 1941), 58.

5. John B. Boles, "The Discovery of Southern Religious History," in *Interpreting Southern History: Historiographical Essays in Honor of Sanford W. Higginbotham,* ed. John B. Boles and Evelyn Thomas Nolen (Baton Rouge: Louisiana State University Press, 1987), 510.

6. Hill, *Southern Churches in Crisis,* 73.

7. Ibid., 23.

8. Samuel S. Hill, Jr., "Religion," in *Encyclopedia of Southern Culture,* ed. Charles Reagan Wilson and William Ferris (Chapel Hill: University of North Carolina Press, 1989), 1269.

9. Samuel S. Hill, Jr., *The South and the North in American Religion* (Athens: University of Georgia Press, 1980), 10–11.

10. Hill, *Southern Churches in Crisis,* 24.

11. Hill, *The South and the North in American Religion,* and "Florida," in *Religion in the Southern States: A Historical Study,* ed. Samuel S. Hill, Jr. (Macon: Mercer University Press, 1983).

12. Hill, introduction to *Religion in the Southern States,* 1.

13. Hill, *The South and the North in American Religion*, 139.

14. Hill, *Southern Churches in Crisis*, 77.

15. Samuel S. Hill, Jr., "Historical Survey," in *Religion in the Southern States*, 395.

16. Hill, *Southern Churches in Crisis*, 65.

17. Ibid., 25.

18. Donald G. Matthews's *Religion in the Old South* (Chicago: University of Chicago Press, 1977) built effectively on Hill's emphasis on what it felt like to be a converted person.

19. Hill, *The South and the North in American Religion*, 22–23.

20. Hill, "Historical Survey," 389–90.

21. For the various religious responses white evangelicals made to the civil rights movement, see Charles Marsh, *God's Long Summer: Stories of Faith and Civil Rights* (Princeton: Princeton University Press, 1997). See also Andrew Michael Manis, *Southern Civil Religions in Conflict: Black and White Baptists and Civil Rights, 1947–1957* (Athens: University of Georgia Press, 1987).

22. See Kerner Commission, *Report*, with an introduction by Tom Wicker (New York: Dutton, 1968).

23. Hill et al., *Religion and the Solid South*, 25 (first quotation), 48 (second quotation).

24. Ibid., 29.

25. Hill, *The South and the North in American Religion*, 7.

26. Hill, *Southern Churches in Crisis*, 112.

27. Samuel S. Hill, Jr., introduction to John Lee Eighmy, *Churches in Cultural Captivity: A History of the Social Attitudes of Southern Baptists*, with revised introduction, conclusion, and bibliography by Samuel S. Hill, Jr. (Knoxville: University of Tennessee Press, 1987), xiv. For Wayne Flynt's arguments, see "Dissent in Zion: Alabama Baptists and Social Issues, 1900–1914," *Journal of Southern History* 35(November 1969): 523–42, "Baptists and Reform," *Baptist History and Heritage* 7(October 1972): 211–22, "Alabama White Protestantism and Labor, 1900–1914," *Alabama Review* 25(July 1972): 192–217, and *Alabama Baptists: Southern Baptists in the Heart of Dixie* (Tuscaloosa: University of Alabama Press, 1998).

28. Hill, *Religion and the Solid South*, 34.

29. Hill, *Southern Churches in Crisis*, 191.

30. Ibid.

31. Ibid., 197.

32. Samuel S. Hill, Jr., ed., *Encyclopedia of Religion in the South* (Macon: Mercer University Press, 1997).

33. Samuel S. Hill, Jr., "Florida," 57–76.

34. Samuel S. Hill, Jr., ed., *Varieties of Southern Religious Experience* (Baton Rouge: Louisiana State University Press, 1988).

35. Hill, "Florida," 64, 68.

36. Hill, *Varieties of Southern Religious Experience*, 226.

37. Hill, *Southern Churches in Crisis*, 190.

38. Hill, "Historical Survey," 401.

39. Hill, "Religion," 1270.

40. Samuel S. Hill, Jr., *One Name but Several Faces: Variety in Popular Christian Denominations in Southern History* (Athens: University of Georgia Press, 1996), 12.

41. Samuel S. Hill, Jr., "Religion and Politics in the South," in *Religion in the South,* ed. Charles Reagan Wilson (Jackson: University Press of Mississippi, 1985), 143; Hill and Dennis E. Owen, *The New Religious-Political Right in America* (Nashville: Abingdon, 1982). The introduction to the Hill and Owen volume notes that Owen did more of the research and writing than Hill.

42. Hill, *One Name But Several Faces,* 108.

Select Bibliography

Books

Adler, Mortimer J. *The Paideia Experiment: An Educational Manifesto.* New York: Macmillan, 1982.

Anderson, Eric, and Alfred A. Moss, Jr., eds. *The Facts of Reconstruction: Essays in Honor of John Hope Franklin.* Baton Rouge: Louisiana State University Press, 1991.

Anderson, Jervis A. *A. Phillip Randolph: A Biographical Portrait.* Berkeley: University of California Press, 1986.

Aptheker, Herbert. *American Negro Slave Revolts.* New York: Columbia University Press, 1943.

Ayers, Edward L. *The Promise of the New South: Life after Reconstruction.* New York: Oxford University Press, 1992.

Bailey, Fred A. *William Edward Dodd: The South's Yeoman Scholar.* Charlottesville: University Press of Virginia, 1997.

Baker, Jean H. *Mary Todd Lincoln: A Biography.* New York: W. W. Norton, 1987.

Banks, William M. *Black Intellectuals: Race and Responsibility in American Life.* New York: W. W. Norton, 1996.

Bartley, Numan V. *The Creation of Modern Georgia.* Athens: University of Georgia Press, 1990.

———. *From Thurmond to Wallace: Political Tendencies in Georgia, 1948–1968.* Baltimore: Johns Hopkins University Press, 1970.

———. *The New South, 1945–1980.* Baton Rouge: Louisiana State University Press, 1995.

———. *The Rise of Massive Resistance: Race and Politics in the South during the 1950s.* Baton Rouge: Louisiana State University Press, 1969.

Bartley, Numan V., and Hugh Davis Graham. *Southern Politics and the Second Reconstruction.* Baltimore: Johns Hopkins University Press, 1975.

Beard, Charles A., and Mary Ritter Beard. *The Rise of American Civilization.* 2 vols. New York: Macmillan, 1939.

Bell, Bernard W., Emily Grosholz, and James B. Stewarts, eds. *W. E. B. Du Bois on Race and Culture: Philosophy, Politics, and Poetics.* New York: Routledge, 1996.

Bensel, Richard F. *Yankee Leviathan: The Origins of Central State Authority in America, 1859–1877.* New York: Cambridge University Press, 1990.

Berlin, Ira. *Slaves Without Masters: The Free Negro in the Antebellum South.* New York: Pantheon Books, 1974.

Blackwell, James E., and Morris Janowitz, eds. *Black Sociologists: Historical and Contemporary Perspectives.* Chicago: University of Chicago Press, 1974.

Blassingame, John. *The Slave Community: Plantation Life in the Antebellum South.* New York: Oxford University Press, 1972.

Bode, Frederick A., and Donald E. Ginter. *Farm Tenancy and the Census in Antebellum Georgia.* Athens: University of Georgia Press, 1986.

Boles, John B., ed. *Masters and Slaves in the House of the Lord.* Lexington: University Press of Kentucky, 1988.

Boles, John B., and Evelyn Thomas Nolen, eds. *Interpreting Southern History: Historiographical Essays in Honor of Sanford W. Higginbotham.* Baton Rouge: Louisiana State University Press, 1987.

Bolton, Charles C. *Poor Whites of the Antebellum South: Tenants and Laborers in Central North Carolina and Northeast Mississippi.* Durham: Duke University Press, 1994.

Bolton, S. Charles. *Arkansas, 1800–1860: Remote and Restless.* Fayetteville: University of Arkansas Press, 1998.

Brandfon, Robert. *Cotton Kingdom of the New South: A History of the Yazoo Mississippi Delta from Reconstruction to the Twentieth Century.* Cambridge: Harvard University Press, 1967.

Breisach, Ernst. *Historiography: Ancient, Medieval, and Modern.* Chicago: University of Chicago Press, 1994.

Bynum, Victoria E. *Unruly Women: The Politics of Social and Sexual Control in the Old South.* Chapel Hill: University of North Carolina Press, 1992.

Carey, Anthony Gene. *Parties, Slavery, and the Union in Antebellum Georgia.* Athens: University of Georgia Press, 1997.

Carlton, David L. *Mill and Town in South Carolina, 1880–1920.* Baton Rouge: Louisiana State University Press, 1982.

Carter, Dan T. *From George Wallace to Newt Gingrich: Race in the Conservative Counterrevolution, 1963–1994.* Baton Rouge: Louisiana State University Press, 1996.

———. *The Politics of Rage: George Wallace, the Origins of the New Conservatism, and the Transformation of American Politics.* New York: Simon and Schuster, 1995.

———. *Scottsboro: A Tragedy of the American South.* Baton Rouge: Louisiana State University Press, 1969.

———. *When the War Was Over: The Failure of Self-Reconstruction in the South, 1865–1867.* Baton Rouge: Louisiana State University Press, 1985.

Cash, W. J. *The Mind of the South.* New York: Alfred A. Knopf, 1941.

Cecil-Fronsman, Bill. *Common Whites: Class and Culture in Antebellum North Carolina.* Lexington: University Press of Kentucky, 1992.

Clark, Blanche Henry. *Tennessee Yeomen, 1840–1860.* Nashville: Vanderbilt University Press, 1945.

Clark, Thomas D., and John D. W. Guice. *Frontiers in Conflict: The Old Southwest, 1795–1830.* Albuquerque: University of New Mexico Press, 1989.

Clarke, John Henrik, et al. *W. E. B. Du Bois: Black Titan.* Boston: Beacon Press, 1970.

Clayton, Bruce. *The Savage Ideal: Intolerance and Intellectual Leadership in the South, 1890–1914.* Baltimore: Johns Hopkins University Press, 1972.

——. *W. J. Cash: A Life.* Baton Rouge: Louisiana State University Press, 1991.

Clayton, Bruce, and John A. Salmond. *Debating Southern History: Ideas and Action in the Twentieth Century.* Lanham, Md.: Rowman & Littlefield, 1999.

Clinton, Catherine. *The Plantation Mistress: Woman's World in the Old South.* New York: Pantheon Books, 1982.

——. *Tara Revisited: Women, War, and the Plantation Legend.* New York: Abbeville Press, 1995.

Cobb, James C. *The Most Southern Place on Earth: The Mississippi Delta and the Roots of Social Identity.* New York: Oxford University Press, 1992.

Cobb, James C., and Michael V. Namorato, eds. *The New Deal and the South.* Jackson: University Press of Mississippi, 1984.

Collingwood, R. G. *The Idea of History.* Oxford: Clarendon Press, 1946.

Collins, Bruce. *White Society in the Antebellum South.* New York: Longman, 1985.

Conkin, Paul K. *The Southern Agrarians.* Knoxville: University of Tennessee Press, 1988.

Cooper, William J., Jr. *The Conservative Regime: South Carolina, 1877–1890.* Baltimore: Johns Hopkins University Press, 1968.

——. *The South and the Politics of Slavery, 1828–1856.* Baton Rouge: Louisiana State University Press, 1978.

Coulter, E. Merton. *The Civil War and Readjustment in Kentucky.* Chapel Hill: University of North Carolina Press, 1926.

——. *Georgia: A Short History.* Chapel Hill: University of North Carolina Press, 1933.

——. *Negro Legislators in Georgia during the Reconstruction Period.* Athens: *Georgia Historical Quarterly,* 1968.

——. *The South during Reconstruction, 1865–1877.* Baton Rouge: Louisiana State University Press, 1947.

Coulter, E. Merton, Albert B. Saye, and Spencer B. King, Jr. *History of Georgia.* New York: American Book Company, 1954.

Cummings, Milton C., Jr., ed. *V. O. Key, Jr. and the Study of American Politics.* Washington: American Political Science Association, 1988.

Dailey, Jane, Glenda Elizabeth Gilmore, and Bryant Simon, eds. *Jumpin' Jim Crow: Southern Politics from Civil War to Civil Rights.* Princeton: Princeton University Press, 2000.

David, Paul A., et al. *Reckoning with Slavery: A Critical Study in the Quantitative History of American Negro Slavery.* New York: Oxford University Press, 1976.

Degler, Carl N. *Place Over Time: The Continuity of Southern Distinctiveness.* Baton Rouge: Louisiana State University Press, 1977.

Dillon, Merton L. *Ulrich Bonnell Phillips: Historian of the Old South.* Baton Rouge: Louisiana State University Press, 1985.

Dittmer, John. *Local People: The Struggle for Civil Rights in Mississippi.* Urbana: University of Illinois Press, 1994.

Donald, David Herbert. *Charles Sumner and the Coming of the Civil War.* New York: Alfred A. Knopf, 1960.

———. *Liberty and Union.* Lexington, Mass.: D. C. Heath, 1978.

———. *Lincoln.* New York: Simon and Schuster, 1995.

———. *Lincoln Reconsidered: Essays on the Civil War Era.* New York: Alfred A. Knopf, 1956.

———. *Lincoln's Herndon.* New York: Alfred A. Knopf, 1948.

———. *Look Homeward: A Life of Thomas Wolfe.* Boston: Little, Brown, 1987.

———. *The Politics of Reconstruction, 1863–1877.* Cambridge: Harvard University Press, 1984.

———. *Why the North Won the Civil War.* Baton Rouge: Louisiana State University Press, 1960.

Du Bois, W. E. B. *The Autobiography of W. E. B. Du Bois: A Soliloquy on Viewing My Life from the Last Decade of Its First Century.* New York: International Publishers, 1968.

———. *Black Reconstruction in America, 1860–1880.* 1935. Reprint. New York: Atheneum, 1992.

———. *Darkwater: Voices from Within the Veil.* New York: Schocken Books, 1969.

———. *The Negro Artisan.* Atlanta: Atlanta University Press, 1902.

———. *The Negroes of Farmville, Virginia.* Washington: U.S. Government Printing Office, Bulletin No. 14 of the U.S. Department of Labor, 1898.

———. *The Philadelphia Negro: A Social Study.* 1899. Reprint. Philadelphia: University of Pennsylvania Press, 1996.

———. *The Souls of Black Folk.* Chicago: A. C. McClurg, 1903.

———. *The Suppression of the African Slave-Trade to the United States of America, 1638–1870.* New York: Russell and Russell, 1965.

Du Bois, W. E. B., and Augustus Dill, eds. *The Negro American Artisan.* Atlanta: Atlanta University Press, 1912.

Dunning, William Archibald. *Reconstruction: Political and Economic.* New York: Columbia University Press, 1907.

Eagles, Charles W., ed. *The Mind of the South Fifty Years Later.* Jackson: University Press of Mississippi, 1992.

Egerton, John. *Speak Now Against the Day: The Generation before the Civil Rights Movement in the South.* New York: Alfred A. Knopf, 1994.

Eighmy, John Lee. *Churches in Cultural Captivity: A History of the Social Attitudes of Southern Baptists.* Knoxville: University of Tennessee Press, 1987.

Elkins, Stanley. *Slavery: A Problem in American Intellectual and Institutional Life.* Chicago: University of Chicago Press, 1959.

Escott, Paul D. *Many Excellent People: Power and Privilege in North Carolina, 1850–1900.* Chapel Hill: University of North Carolina Press, 1985.

———, ed. *W. J. Cash and the Minds of the South.* Baton Rouge: Louisiana State University Press, 1992.

Eskew, Glenn T. *But for Birmingham: The Local and National Movements in the Civil Rights Struggle.* Chapel Hill: University of North Carolina Press, 1997.

Fairclough, Adam. *Race and Democracy: The Civil Rights Struggle in Louisiana, 1915–1972.* Athens: University of Georgia Press, 1995.

Faust, Drew Gilpin. *Mothers of Invention: Women of the Slaveholding South in the American Civil War.* Chapel Hill: University of North Carolina Press, 1996.

Feldman, Glenn. *From Demagogue to Dixiecrat: Horace Wilkinson and the Politics of Race.* Lanham, Md.: University Press of America, 1995.

———. *Politics, Society, and the Klan in Alabama, 1915–1949.* Tuscaloosa: University of Alabama Press, 1999.

Fifteen Southerners. *Why the South Will Survive: Fifteen Southerners Look at Their Region a Half Century after "I'll Take My Stand."* Athens: University of Georgia Press, 1981.

Fischer, David Hackett. *Historians' Fallacies: Toward a Logic of Historical Thought.* New York: Harper and Row, 1970.

Flynt, Wayne. *Alabama Baptists: Southern Baptists in the Heart of Dixie.* Tuscaloosa: University of Alabama Press, 1998.

———. *Dixie's Forgotten People: The South's Poor Whites.* Bloomington: Indiana University Press, 1979.

———. *Poor but Proud: Alabama's Poor Whites.* Tuscaloosa: University of Alabama Press, 1989.

Fogel, Robert W. *Without Consent or Contract: The Rise and Fall of American Slavery.* New York: W. W. Norton, 1989.

Fogel, Robert W., and Stanley L. Engerman. *Time on the Cross.* Boston: Little, Brown, 1974.

Foner, Eric. *Reconstruction: America's Unfinished Revolution, 1863–1877.* New York: Harper and Row, 1988.

Ford, Lacy K., Jr. *Origins of Southern Radicalism: The South Carolina Upcountry, 1800–1860.* New York: Oxford University Press, 1988.

Foster, Gaines M. *Ghosts of the Confederacy: Defeat, the Lost Cause, and the Emergence of the New South, 1865–1913.* New York: Oxford University Press, 1987.

Fox-Genovese, Elizabeth. *Within the Plantation Household: Black and White Women in the Old South.* Chapel Hill: University of North Carolina Press, 1988.

Franklin, John Hope. *The Color Line: Legacy for the Twenty-First Century.* Columbia: University of Missouri Press, 1993.

———. *The Emancipation Proclamation.* Garden City, N.Y.: Doubleday, 1963.

———. *From Slavery to Freedom: A History of American Negroes.* New York: Alfred A. Knopf, 1947.

———. *George Washington Williams: A Biography.* Chicago: University of Chicago Press, 1985.

———. *The Historian and Public Policy.* Chicago: University of Chicago Press, 1974.

———. *The Militant South, 1800–1861.* New York: Beacon Press, 1956.

———. *Race and History: Selected Essays, 1938–1988.* Baton Rouge: Louisiana State University Press, 1989.

———. *Racial Equality in America.* Columbia: University of Missouri Press, 1993.

———. *Reconstruction after the Civil War.* Chicago: University of Chicago Press, 1961.

———. *A Southern Odyssey: Travelers in the Antebellum North.* Baton Rouge: Louisiana State University Press, 1976.

Franklin, John Hope, and John Whittington Franklin, eds. *My Life and an Era: The Autobiography of Buck Colbert Franklin.* Baton Rouge: Louisiana State University Press, 1997.

Franklin, John Hope, and Loren Schweninger. *Runaway Slaves: Rebels on the Plantation.* New York: Oxford University Press, 1999.

Frederickson, George M. *The Black Image in the White Mind: The Debate on Afro-American Character and Destiny, 1817–1914.* New York: Harper and Row, 1971.

Frederickson, Kari. *The Dixiecrat Revolt and the End of the Solid South, 1932–1968.* Chapel Hill: University of North Carolina Press, forthcoming.

Friedman, Jean E. *The Enclosed Garden: Women and Community in the Evangelical South, 1830–1900.* Chapel Hill: University of North Carolina Press, 1985.

Gaston, Paul. *The New South Creed: A Study in Southern Mythmaking.* New York: Alfred A. Knopf, 1970.

Genovese, Eugene D. *A Consuming Fire: The Fall of the Confederacy in the Mind of the White Christian South.* Athens: University of Georgia Press, 1998.

———. *The Political Economy of Slavery: Studies in the Economy & Society of the Slave South.* New York: Pantheon Books, 1965.

———. *In Red and Black: Marxian Explorations in Southern and Afro-American History.* New York: Vintage Books, 1971.

———. *Roll Jordan Roll: The World the Slaves Made.* New York: Pantheon Books, 1974.

———. *The Slaveholders' Dilemma: Freedom and Progress in Southern Conservative Thought, 1820–1860.* Columbia: University of Missouri Press, 1991.

———. *The Southern Front: History and Politics in the Cultural War.* Columbia: University of Missouri Press, 1995.

———. *The Southern Tradition: The Achievements and Limitations of an American Conservatism.* Cambridge: Harvard University Press, 1994.

———. *The World the Slaveholders Made: Two Essays in Interpretation.* New York: Pantheon Books, 1969.

Genovese, Eugene D., and Elizabeth Fox-Genovese. *Fruits of Merchant Capital: Slavery and Bourgeois Property in the Rise and Expansion of Capitalism.* New York: Oxford University Press, 1983.

Gillespie, Michelle, and Catherine Clinton, eds. *Taking Off the White Gloves:*

Southern Women and Women Historians. Columbia: University of Missouri Press, 1998.

Gilmore, Glenda Elizabeth. *Gender and Jim Crow: Women and the Politics of White Supremacy in North Carolina, 1896–1920.* Chapel Hill: University of North Carolina Press, 1996.

Gilroy, Paul. *The Black Atlantic: Modernity and Double Consciousness.* Cambridge: Harvard University Press, 1993.

Grantham, Dewey W. *Southern Progressivism: The Reconciliation of Progress and Tradition.* Knoxville: University of Tennessee Press, 1983.

——. *The Life and Death of the Solid South: A Political History.* Lexington: University Press of Kentucky, 1988.

Green, A. Wigfall. *The Man Bilbo.* Westport, Conn.: Greenwood Press, 1963.

Green, Dan S., and Edwin D. Driver, eds. *W. E. B. Du Bois on Sociology and the Black Community.* Chicago: University of Chicago Press, 1978.

Green, Elna C. *Southern Strategies: Southern Women and the Woman Suffrage Question.* Chapel Hill: University of North Carolina Press, 1997.

Grob, Gerald R., and George Athan Billias. *Interpretations of American History: Patterns and Perspectives.* New York: Free Press, 1982.

Gutman, Herbert G. *The Black Family in Slavery and Freedom, 1750–1925.* New York: Pantheon Books, 1976.

——. *Slavery and the Numbers Game: A Critique of* Time on the Cross. Urbana: University of Illinois Press, 1975.

Hackney, Sheldon. *Populism to Progressivism in Alabama.* Princeton: Princeton University Press, 1969.

Hahn, Steven. *The Roots of Southern Populism: Yeoman Farmers and the Transformation of the Georgia Upcountry, 1850–1890.* New York: Oxford University Press, 1983.

Hall, Jacquelyn Dowd. *Revolt Against Chivalry: Jesse Daniel Ames and the Women's Campaign Against Lynching.* New York: Columbia University Press, 1979.

Hall, Jacquelyn Dowd, James Leloudis, Robert Korstad, Mary Murphy, Lu Ann Jones, and Christopher Daly. *Like a Family: The Making of a Cotton Mill World.* Chapel Hill: University of North Carolina Press, 1987.

Harlan, Louis R. *Booker T. Washington: The Making of a Black Leader, 1856–1901.* New York: Oxford University Press, 1983.

Harris, J. William. *Plain Folk and Gentry in a Slave Society: White Liberty and Black Slavery in Augusta's Hinterlands.* Middletown, Conn.: Wesleyan University Press, 1985.

Havard, William C., Jr., ed. *The Changing Politics of the South.* Baton Rouge: Louisiana State University Press, 1972.

Heard, Alexander. *A Two-Party South?* Chapel Hill: University of North Carolina Press, 1952.

Heidler, David S. *Pulling the Temple Down: The Fire-eaters and the Destruction of the Union.* Mechanicsburg, Pa.: Stackpole Books, 1994.

Heidler, David S., and Jeanne T. Heidler. *Old Hickory's War: Andrew Jackson and the Quest for Empire.* Mechanicsburg, Pa.: Stackpole Books, 1996.

Hill, Samuel S., Jr. *One Name but Several Faces: Variety in Popular Christian Denominations in Southern History.* Athens: University of Georgia Press, 1996.

——. *Religion and the Solid South.* New York: Abingdon Press, 1972.

——. *The South and the North in American Religion.* Athens: University of Georgia Press, 1980.

——. *Southern Churches in Crisis.* New York: Holt, Rinehart, and Winston, 1967.

——, ed. *Encyclopedia of Religion in the South.* Macon: Mercer University Press, 1997.

——, ed. *Religion in the Southern States: A Historical Study.* Macon: Mercer University Press, 1983.

——, ed. *Varieties of the Southern Religious Experience.* Baton Rouge: Louisiana State University Press, 1988.

Hill, Samuel S., Jr., and Dennis E. Owen. *The New Religious-Political Right in America.* Nashville: Abingdon Press, 1982.

Hill, Samuel S., Jr., Edgar T. Thompson, Anne Firor Scott, Charles Hudson, and Edwin Gaustad. *Religion and the Solid South.* Nashville: Abingdon Press, 1972.

Hine, Darlene Clark, ed. *The State of Afro-American History: Past, Present, and Future.* Baton Rouge: Louisiana State University Press, 1986.

Hobson, Fred C., Jr. *Serpent in Eden: H. L. Mencken and the South.* 1974. Reprint. Baton Rouge: Louisiana State University Press, 1978.

——. *Tell About the South: The Southern Rage to Explain.* Baton Rouge: Louisiana State University Press, 1983.

Hyde, Samuel C., Jr., ed. *Plain Folk of the South Revisited.* Baton Rouge: Louisiana State University Press, 1997.

Jacoway, Elizabeth, Dan T. Carter, Lester C. Lamon, and Robert C. McMath, eds. *The Adaptable South: Essays in Honor of George Brown Tindall.* Baton Rouge: Louisiana State University Press, 1991.

Johnson, Guion Griffis. *Antebellum North Carolina: A Social History.* Chapel Hill: University of North Carolina Press, 1937.

Jordan, Terry C. *Trail to Texas: Southern Roots of Western Cattle Ranching.* Lincoln: University of Nebraska Press, 1981.

Katz, Michael B., and Thomas J. Sugrue, eds. *W. E. B. Du Bois, Race, and the City: The Philadelphia Negro and Its Legacy.* Philadelphia: University of Pennsylvania Press, 1988.

Kelley, Robin D. G. *Hammer and Hoe: Alabama Communists during the Great Depression.* Chapel Hill: University of North Carolina Press, 1990.

Key, V. O., Jr. *American State Politics: An Introduction.* New York: Alfred A. Knopf, 1956.

——. *Politics, Parties, and Pressure Groups.* New York: Thomas Y. Crowell, 1942.

———. *A Primer of Statistics for Political Scientists.* New York: Thomas Y. Crowell, 1954.

———. *Public Opinion and the American Democracy.* New York: Alfred A. Knopf, 1961.

———. *The Responsible Electorate: Rationality in Presidential Voting, 1936–1960.* Cambridge: Harvard University Press, 1966.

———. *Southern Politics in State and Nation.* New York: Alfred A. Knopf, 1949.

———. *The Techniques of Political Graft in the United States.* Chicago: University of Chicago Libraries, 1936.

King, Richard H. *A Southern Renaissance: The Cultural Awakening of the American South, 1930–1955.* New York: Oxford University Press, 1980.

Kirby, Jack Temple. *Darkness at the Dawning: Race and Reform in the Progressive South.* Philadelphia: J. B. Lippincott, 1972.

Kolchin, Peter. *American Slavery, 1619–1877.* New York: Hill and Wang, 1993.

———. *First Freedom: The Responses of Alabama's Blacks to Emancipation and Reconstruction.* Westport, Conn.: Greenwood Press, 1972.

Kousser, J. Morgan. *The Shaping of Southern Politics: Suffrage Restriction and the Establishment of the One-Party South, 1880–1910.* New Haven: Yale University Press, 1974.

Kraditor, Aileen S. *The Ideas of the Woman Suffrage Movement, 1890–1920.* New York: Columbia University Press, 1965.

Lamis, Alexander P. *The Two-Party South.* New York: Oxford University Press, 1984.

Lawson, Steven F., and Charles Payne. *Debating the Civil Rights Movement.* Lanham, Md.: Rowman & Littlefield, 1998.

Lebsock, Suzanne. *The Free Women of Petersburg: Status and Culture in a Southern Town, 1784–1860.* New York: W. W. Norton, 1984.

Lemann, Nicholas. *The Promised Land: The Great Black Migration and How It Changed America.* New York: Alfred A. Knopf, 1991.

Lerner, Gerda. *The Majority Finds Its Past: Placing Women in History.* New York: Oxford University Press, 1979.

Levine, Lawrence W. *Black Culture and Black Consciousness: Afro-American Folk Thought from Slavery to Freedom.* New York: Oxford University Press, 1977.

Lewis, David Levering. *W. E. B. Du Bois: Biography of a Race, 1868–1919.* New York: Henry Holt, 1993.

Link, Arthur S., and Rembert W. Patrick, eds. *Writing Southern History: Essays in Historiography in Honor of Fletcher M. Green.* Baton Rouge: Louisiana State University Press, 1965.

Link, William A. *The Paradox of Southern Progressivism, 1880–1930.* Chapel Hill: University of North Carolina Press, 1983.

McArthur, Judith N. *Creating the New Woman: The Rise of Southern Women's Progressive Culture in Texas, 1893–1918.* Urbana: University of Illinois Press, 1998.

McCurry, Stephanie. *Masters of Small Worlds: Yeoman Households, Gender Rela-

tions, and the Political Culture of the Antebellum South Carolina Lowcountry.
New York: Oxford University Press, 1995.

McMillan, Malcolm Cook. *Constitutional Development in Alabama, 1798–1901: A Study in Politics, the Negro, and Sectionalism.* Chapel Hill: University of North Carolina Press, 1955.

McMillen, Neil. *The Citizens' Council: Organized Resistance to the Second Reconstruction, 1954–64.* Urbana: University of Illinois Press, 1971.

McMillen, Sally G. *Motherhood in the Old South: Pregnancy, Childbirth, and Infant Rearing.* Baton Rouge: Louisiana State University Press, 1990.

McPherson, James M., and William J. Cooper, Jr., eds. *Writing the Civil War.* Columbia: University of South Carolina Press, 1998.

McWhiney, Grady. *Cracker Culture: Celtic Ways in the Old South.* Tuscaloosa: University of Alabama Press, 1988.

Manis, Andrew Michael. *Southern Civil Religions in Conflict: Black and White Baptists and Civil Rights, 1947–1957.* Athens: University of Georgia Press, 1987.

Marable, Manning. *W. E. B. Du Bois: Black Radical Democrat.* Boston: Twayne, 1986.

Marsh, Charles. *God's Long Summer: Stories of Faith and Civil Rights.* Princeton: Princeton University Press, 1997.

Martin, Tony. *Race First: The Ideological and Organizational Struggles of Marcus Garvey and the Universal Negro Improvement Association.* Westport, Conn.: Greenwood Press, 1976.

Matthews, Donald G. *Religion in the Old South.* Chicago: University of Chicago Press, 1977.

Matthews, Donald G., and Jane Sharon DeHart. *Sex, Gender, and the Politics of ERA: A State and a Nation.* New York: Oxford University Press, 1990.

Meier, August. *Negro Thought in America, 1880–1915: Racial Ideologies in the Age of Booker T. Washington.* Ann Arbor: University of Michigan Press, 1973.

Meier, August, and Elliott Rudwick. *Black History and the Historical Profession, 1915–1980.* Urbana: University of Illinois Press, 1986.

Mencken, H. L. *Prejudices: Second Series.* New York: Alfred A. Knopf, 1920.

Miller, Randall M., and John David Smith, eds. *Dictionary of Afro-American Slavery.* New York: Greenwood Press, 1988.

Minchin, Timothy J. *Hiring the Black Worker: The Racial Integration of the Southern Textile Industry, 1960–1980.* Chapel Hill: University of North Carolina Press, 1999.

Mitchell, Broadus. *Alexander Hamilton.* 2 vols. New York: Macmillan, 1957, 1962.

———. *Depression Decade from New Era through New Deal, 1929–1941.* New York: Rinehart and Winston, 1947.

———. *Frederick Law Olmstead, A Critic of the Old South.* Baltimore: Johns Hopkins University Press, 1924.

———. *The Rise of Cotton Mills in the South.* Baltimore: Johns Hopkins University Press, 1921.

——. *William Gregg, Factory Maker of the Old South.* Chapel Hill: University of North Carolina Press, 1928.

Mitchell, Broadus, and George Sinclair Mitchell. *The Industrial Revolution in the South.* Baltimore: Johns Hopkins University Press, 1930.

Mitchell, Broadus, and Louise Pearson Mitchell. *American Economic History.* Boston: Houghton Mifflin, 1947.

Mooney, Chase C. *Slavery in Tennessee.* Bloomington: Indiana University Press, 1957.

Morgan, Chester M. *Redneck Liberal: Theodore Bilbo and the New Deal.* Baton Rouge: Louisiana State University Press, 1985.

Morrison, Joseph L. *W. J. Cash, Southern Prophet: A Biography and Reader.* New York: Alfred A. Knopf, 1967.

Myrdal, Gunnar. *An American Dilemma: The Negro Problem and American Democracy.* 2 vols. New York: Harper and Brothers, 1944.

Nelson, Bruce. *Divided We Stand: American Workers and the Struggle for Black Equality.* Princeton: Princeton University Press, forthcoming.

Nettles, Curtis Putnam. *The Roots of American Civilization.* New York: Appleton-Century-Crofts, 1938.

Oakes, James. *The Ruling Race: A History of American Slaveholders.* New York: Alfred A. Knopf, 1982.

——. *Slavery and Freedom: An Interpretation of the Old South.* New York: W. W. Norton, 1990.

Obadele-Starks, Ernest. *Black Unionism in the Industrial South.* College Station: Texas A & M University Press, 2000.

Odum, Howard W. *American Social Problems: An Introduction to the Study of the People and Their Dilemmas.* New York: Henry C. Holt, 1945.

——. *Southern Regions of the United States.* Chapel Hill: University of North Carolina Press, 1936.

Osterweis, Roger G. *The Myth of the Lost Cause, 1865–1900.* Hamden, Conn.: Archon Books, 1973.

Ownby, Ted. *Subduing Satan: Religion, Recreation, and Manhood in the Rural South, 1865–1920.* Chapel Hill: University of North Carolina Press, 1990.

Owsley, Frank L. *Plain Folk of the Old South.* Baton Rouge: Louisiana State University Press, 1949.

——. *State Rights in the Confederacy.* Chicago: University of Chicago Press, 1931.

Owsley, Harriet Chappell, ed. *The South: Old and New Frontiers; Selected Essays of Frank Lawrence Owsley.* Athens: University of Georgia Press, 1969.

Parish, Peter J. *Slavery: History and Historians.* New York: Harper and Row, 1989.

Phillips, Kimberley L. *AlabamaNorth: African-American Migrants, Community, and Working-Class Activism in Cleveland, 1915–45.* Urbana: University of Illinois Press, 1999.

Phillips, Ulrich Bonnell. *American Negro Slavery: A Survey of the Supply, Employ-

ment, and Control of Negro Labor as Determined by the Plantation Regime. New York: D. Appleton, 1918.

Potter, David M. *History and American Society: Essays of David M. Potter,* ed. Don E. Fehrenbacher. New York: Oxford University Press, 1973.

——. *The Impending Crisis, 1848–1861.* New York: Harper and Row, 1976.

——. *Lincoln and His Party in the Secession Crisis.* 1942. Reprint. New Haven: Yale University Press, 1962.

——. *People of Plenty: Economic Abundance and the American Character.* Chicago: University of Chicago Press, 1954.

——. *The South and Sectional Conflict.* Baton Rouge: Louisiana State University Press, 1968.

Rabinowitz, Howard N. *Race Relations in the Urban South, 1865–1890.* New York: Oxford University Press, 1978.

Rable, George C. *Civil Wars: Women and the Crisis of Southern Nationalism.* Urbana: University of Illinois Press, 1989.

Rampersad, Arnold. *The Art and Imagination of W. E. B. Du Bois.* Cambridge: Harvard University Press, 1976.

Reed, John Shelton. *The Enduring South: Subcultural Persistence in Mass Society.* Chapel Hill: University of North Carolina Press, 1972.

——. *One South: An Ethnic Approach to Regional Culture.* Baton Rouge: Louisiana State University Press, 1982.

——. *Southern Folk, Plain & Fancy: Native White Social Types.* Athens: University of Georgia Press, 1986.

Reed, John Shelton, and Daniel Joseph Singal, eds. *Regionalism in the South: Selected Papers of Rupert B. Vance.* Chapel Hill: University of North Carolina Press, 1982.

Riley, Franklin L. *School History of Mississippi.* Richmond: B. F. Johnson, 1915.

Riley, Franklin L., J. A. C. Chandler, and J. G. de Roulhac Hamilton. *Our Republic: A History of the United States for Grammar Grades.* Richmond: Riley and Chandler, 1910.

Robinson, Armstead L., and Patricia Sullivan, eds. *New Directions in Civil Rights Studies.* Charlottesville: University Press of Virginia, 1991.

Robinson, Cedric. *Black Marxism: The Making of the Black Radical Tradition.* London: Zed Books, 1983.

Rodriguez, Junius P., ed. *The Historical Encyclopedia of World Slavery.* Santa Barbara: ABC-CLIO, 1997.

Roediger, David R. *The Wages of Whiteness: Race and the Making of the American Working Class.* New York: Verso, 1991.

Rogers, William Warren, Sr. *The One-Gallused Rebellion: Agrarianism in Alabama, 1865–1896.* Baton Rouge: Louisiana State University Press, 1970.

Roper, John Herbert. *C. Vann Woodward, Southerner.* Athens: University of Georgia Press, 1987.

——, ed. *C. Vann Woodward: A Southern Historian and His Critics.* Athens: University of Georgia Press, 1997.

Rudwick, Elliott. *W. E. B. Du Bois: Voice of the Black Protest Movement.* 1960. Reprint. Urbana: University of Illinois Press, 1982.

Schrecker, Ellen W. *No Ivory Tower: McCarthyism and the Universities.* New York: Oxford University Press, 1986.

Scott, Anne Firor. *The American Woman: Who Was She?* New York: Prentice-Hall, 1970.

———. *Making the Invisible Woman Visible.* Urbana: University of Illinois Press, 1984.

———. *Natural Allies: Women's Associations in American History.* Urbana: University of Illinois Press, 1990.

———. *The Southern Lady: From Pedestal to Politics, 1830–1930.* Chicago: University of Chicago Press, 1970.

———. *Women in American Life: Selected Readings.* New York: Houghton-Mifflin, 1979.

———, ed. *Unheard Voices: The First Historians of Women in the South.* Charlottesville: University Press of Virginia, 1993.

Scott, Anne Firor, and Libby A. Carter. *Women and Men: Changing Roles, Relationships, and Perspectives.* New York: Praeger, 1977.

Scott, Anne Firor, and Suzanne Lebsock. *Virginia Women: The First Two Hundred Years.* Williamsburg, Va.: Colonial Williamsburg Foundation, 1985.

Scott, Anne Firor, and Andrew Mackay Scott. *One Half the People: The Fight for Woman Suffrage.* Philadelphia: J. B. Lippincott, 1975.

Sellers, Charles G., ed. *The Southerner as American.* Chapel Hill: University of North Carolina Press, 1960.

Shaw, Barton C. *The Wool-Hat Boys: Georgia's Populist Party.* Baton Rouge: Louisiana State University Press, 1984.

Silver, James W. *Mississippi: The Closed Society.* New York: Harcourt, Brace, and World, 1963.

———. *Running Scared: Silver in Mississippi.* Jackson: University Press of Mississippi, 1984.

Simkins, Francis Butler. *The South, Old and New: A History, 1820–1947.* New York: Alfred A. Knopf, 1947.

Sims, Anastatia. *The Power of Femininity in the New South: Women's Organizations and Politics in North Carolina, 1880–1930.* Columbia: University of South Carolina Press, 1997.

Singal, Daniel J. *The War Within: From Victorian to Modernist Thought in the South, 1919–1945.* Chapel Hill: University of North Carolina Press, 1982.

Sobel, Mechal. *The World They Made Together.* Princeton: Princeton University Press, 1987.

Spruill, Julia Cherry. *Women's Life and Work in the Southern Colonies.* Chapel Hill: University of North Carolina Press, 1938.

Stampp, Kenneth M. *America in 1857: A Nation on the Brink.* New York: Oxford University Press, 1990.

——. *And the War Came: The North and the Secession Crisis, 1860–1861*. Baton Rouge: Louisiana State University Press, 1950.

——. *The Era of Reconstruction, 1865–1877*. New York: Vintage Books, 1965.

——. *The Imperiled Union: Essays on the Background of the Civil War*. New York: Oxford University Press, 1980.

——. *Indiana Politics during the Civil War*. Indianapolis: Indiana Historical Bureau, 1949.

——. *The Peculiar Institution: Slavery in the Antebellum South*. New York: Alfred A. Knopf, 1956.

Stein, Judith. *The World of Marcus Garvey: Race and Class in Modern Society*. Baton Rouge: Louisiana State University Press, 1986.

Stephenson, Wendell Holmes. *Southern History in the Making: Pioneer Historians of the South*. Baton Rouge: Louisiana State University Press, 1964.

Sullivan, Patricia. *Days of Hope: Race and Democracy in the New Deal Era*. Chapel Hill: University of North Carolina Press, 1996.

Sundquis, Eric J., ed. *W. E. B. Du Bois: The Oxford Reader*. New York: Oxford University Press, 1996.

Sydnor, Charles S. *American Revolutionaries in the Making: Political Practices in Washington's Virginia*. New York: Free Press, 1952.

——. *The Development of Southern Sectionalism, 1819–1848*. Baton Rouge: Louisiana State University Press, 1948.

——. *A Gentleman of the Old Natchez Region: Benjamin L. C. Wailes*. Durham, N.C.: Duke University Press, 1938.

——. *Gentlemen Freeholders: Political Practices in Washington's Virginia*. Chapel Hill: University of North Carolina Press, 1952.

——. *Mississippi History*. New York: Rand McNally, 1930.

——. *Political Leadership in Eighteenth-Century Virginia*. Oxford: Clarendon Press, 1951.

——. *Slavery in Mississippi*. New York: D. Appleton-Century, 1933.

Taylor, A. Elizabeth. *The Woman Suffrage Movement in Tennessee*. New York: Bookman, 1957.

Taylor, William R. *Cavalier and Yankee: The Old South and American National Character*. New York: George Braziller, 1961.

Thomas, Mary Martha. *The New Woman in Alabama: Social Reforms and Suffrage, 1890–1920*. Tuscaloosa: University of Alabama Press, 1992.

——, ed. *Stepping Out of the Shadows: Alabama Women, 1819–1990*. Tuscaloosa: University of Alabama Press, 1995.

Thompson, Edgar T. *Perspectives on the South: Agenda for Research*. Durham: Duke University Press, 1967.

Thornton, J. Mills III. *Politics and Power in a Slave Society: Alabama, 1800–1860*. Baton Rouge: Louisiana State University Press, 1978.

Thorpe, Earl E. *Black Historians: A Critique*. New York: William Morrow, 1971.

——. *The Mind of the Negro: An Intellectual History of Afro-Americans*. Baton Rouge: Louisiana State University Press, 1961.

Tindall, George Brown. *The Disruption of the Solid South.* Athens: University of Georgia Press, 1972.

———. *The Emergence of the New South, 1913–1945.* Baton Rouge: Louisiana State University Press, 1967.

———. *The Ethnic Southerners.* Baton Rouge: Louisiana State University Press, 1976.

———. *The Persistent Tradition in New South Politics.* Baton Rouge: Louisiana State University Press, 1975.

———. *South Carolina Negroes, 1877–1900.* Columbia: University of South Carolina Press, 1952.

Treadway, Sandra G. *Women of Mark: A History of the Women's Club of Richmond, 1894–1994.* Richmond: Library of Virginia, 1995.

Trotter, Joe W. *Coal, Class, and Color: Blacks in Southern West Virginia, 1915–1932.* Urbana: University of Illinois Press, 1990.

Turner, Elizabeth Hayes. *Women, Culture, and Community: Religion and Reform in Galveston, 1880–1920.* New York: Oxford University Press, 1997.

Twelve Southerners. *I'll Take My Stand: The South and the Agrarian Tradition.* New York: Harper and Brothers, 1930.

Vance, Rupert B. *All These People: The Nation's Human Resources in the South.* Chapel Hill: University of North Carolina Press, 1945.

———. *Human Factors in Cotton Culture: A Study in the Social Geography of the American South.* Chapel Hill: University of North Carolina Press, 1929.

———. *Human Geography of the South: A Study in Regional Resources and Human Adequacy.* Chapel Hill: University of North Carolina Press, 1932.

———. *Research Memorandum on Population Redistribution Within the United States.* New York: Social Science Research Council, 1938.

Vance, Rupert B., and Nicholas Demerath, eds. *The Urban South.* Chapel Hill: University of North Carolina Press, 1954.

Vandiver, Frank E., ed. *The Idea of the South: Pursuit of a Central Theme.* Chicago: University of Chicago Press, 1964.

Varon, Elizabeth. *We Mean to Be Counted: White Women and Politics in Antebellum Virginia.* Chapel Hill: University of North Carolina Press, 1998.

Wade, Richard C. *Slavery in the Cities: The South, 1800–1860.* New York: Oxford University Press, 1964.

Wharton, Vernon L. *The Negro in Mississippi, 1865–1890.* Chapel Hill: University of North Carolina Press, 1947.

Wheeler, Marjorie Spruill. *New Women of the New South: The Leaders of the Woman Suffrage Movement in the Southern States.* New York: Oxford University Press, 1993.

———, ed. *One Woman, One Vote: Rediscovering the Woman Suffrage Movement.* Troutdale, Ore.: NewSage Press, 1995.

———, ed. *Votes for Women: The Woman Suffrage Movement in Tennessee, the South, and the Nation.* Knoxville: University of Tennessee Press, 1995.

White, John. *Black Leadership in America, 1895–1968.* New York: Longman, 1985.

Whites, LeeAnn. *The Civil War as a Crisis in Gender: Augusta, Georgia, 1860–1890.* Athens: University of Georgia Press, 1995.

Wiener, Jonathan M. *Social Origins of the New South: Alabama, 1860–1885.* Baton Rouge: Louisiana State University Press, 1980.

Williams, George Washington. *A History of Negro Troops in the War of the Rebellion.* New York: Harper and Brothers, 1887.

Williamson, Joel R. *The Crucible of Race: Black-White Relations in the American South since Emancipation.* New York: Oxford University Press, 1984.

Wilson, Charles Reagan, ed. *Religion in the South.* Jackson: University Press of Mississippi, 1985.

Wilson, Charles Reagan, and William Ferris, eds. *Encyclopedia of Southern Culture.* Chapel Hill: University of North Carolina Press, 1989.

Wilson, Francine Rusan. *The Segregated Scholars: Black Social Scientists and the Development of Black Labor Studies, 1895–1950.* Charlottesville: University Press of Virginia, forthcoming.

Winegartern, Ruthe, and Judith N. McArthur, eds. *Citizens at Last: The Woman Suffrage Movement in Texas.* Austin, Texas: Ellen C. Temple, 1987.

Woodward, C. Vann. *American Counterpoint: Slavery and Racism in the North-South Dialogue.* Boston: Little, Brown, 1964.

———. *The Battle for Leyte Gulf.* 1947. Reprint. New York: W. W. Norton, 1965.

———. *Bougainville Landing and the Battle of Empress Augusta Bay.* Washington: Government Printing Office, ca. 1947.

———. *The Burden of Southern History.* Baton Rouge: Louisiana State University Press, 1960.

———. *Kolombangara and Vella Lavella.* Washington: Government Printing Office, 1947.

———. *Origins of the New South, 1877–1913.* Baton Rouge: Louisiana State University Press, 1951.

———. *Responses of Presidents to Charges of Misconduct.* New York: Delacorte, 1974.

———. *Reunion and Reaction: The Compromise of 1877 and the End of Reconstruction.* Boston: Little, Brown, 1951.

———. *The Strange Career of Jim Crow.* 3d rev. ed. New York: Oxford University Press, 1978.

———. *Thinking Back: The Perils of Writing History.* Baton Rouge: Louisiana State University Press, 1986.

———. *Tom Watson: Agrarian Rebel.* New York: Macmillan, 1938.

———, ed. *Mary Chesnut's Civil War.* New Haven: Yale University Press, 1981.

Woodward, C. Vann, and Elisabeth Muhlenfeld, eds. *The Private Mary Chesnut: The Unpublished Civil War Diaries.* New York: Oxford University Press, 1984.

Wright, Gavin C. *Old South, New South: Revolutions in the Southern Economy since the Civil War.* New York: Basic Books, 1986.

———. *The Political Economy of the Cotton South: Households, Markets, and Wealth in the Nineteenth Century.* New York: W. W. Norton, 1978.

Wright, Louis B. *Culture on the Moving Frontier.* New York: Harper Torchbooks, 1961.

Wyatt-Brown, Bertram. *Southern Honor: Ethics and Behavior in the Old South.* New York: Oxford University Press, 1982.

———. *Yankee Saints and Southern Sinners.* Baton Rouge: Louisiana State University Press, 1985.

Articles, Dissertations, and Unpublished Papers

Bailey, Fred A. "Free Speech and the 'Lost Cause' in Arkansas." *Arkansas Historical Quarterly* 55(December 1996): 143–66.

———. "Free Speech and the 'Lost Cause' in the Old Dominion." *Virginia Magazine of History and Biography* 103(April 1995): 237–66.

———. "Free Speech and the 'Lost Cause' in Texas: A Study of Censorship and Social Control in the New South." *Southwestern Historical Quarterly* 47(January 1994): 453–79.

———. "Free Speech at the University of Florida: The Enoch Marvin Banks Case." *Florida Historical Quarterly* 71(July 1992): 1–17.

———. "Mildred Lewis Rutherford and the Patrician Cult of the Old South." *Georgia Historical Quarterly* 78(Fall 1994): 509–54.

———. "Plain Folk and Apology: Frank L. Owsley's Defense of the South." In *Perspectives on the American South*, ed. James C. Cobb and Charles Reagan Wilson. New York: Gordon and Breach, 1987.

———. "Textbooks of the Lost Cause: Censorship and the Creation of Southern State Histories." *Georgia Historical Quarterly* 75(Fall 1991): 507–33.

———. "Thomas Nelson Page and the Patrician Cult of the Old South." *International Social Science Review* 72(Fall 1997): 110–21.

———. "Thomas Perkins Abernethy: Defender of Aristocratic Virtue." *Alabama Review* 45(April 1992): 83–102.

———. "William E. Dodd: The South's Yeoman Historian." *North Carolina Historical Review* 66(July 1989): 301–20.

Balsamo, Larry Thomas. "Theodore G. Bilbo and Mississippi Politics, 1877–1932." Unpublished Ph.D. dissertation, University of Missouri, 1967.

Bartley, Numan V. "The South and Sectionalism in American Politics." *Journal of Politics* 38(August 1976): 239–57.

Bauer, Raymond A., and Alice H. Bauer. "Day to Day Resistance to Slavery." *Journal of Negro History* 27(October 1942): 388–419.

Bland, Sidney R. "Fighting the Odds: Militant Suffragists in South Carolina." *South Carolina Magazine* 82(January 1981): 32–43.

———. "'Mad Women of the Cause': The National Woman's Party in the South." *Furman University Bulletin* 26(December 1980): 82–91.

Bleser, Carol K., ed. "The Three Women Presidents of the Southern Historical Association: Ella Lonn, Kathryn Abby Hanna, and Mary Elizabeth Massey." *Southern Studies* 20(Summer 1981): 101–21.

Boatwright, Eleanor M. "The Political and Civil Status of Women in Georgia, 1783–1860." *Georgia Historical Quarterly* 25(December 1941): 301–24.

Boles, John B. "The Discovery of Southern Religious History." In *Interpreting Southern History: Historiographical Essays in Honor of Sanford W. Higginbotham*, ed. John B. Boles and Evelyn Thomas Nolen, pp. 510–48. Baton Rouge: Louisiana State University Press, 1987.

———. "Evangelical Protestantism in the Old South: From Religious Dissent to Cultural Dominance." In *Religion in the South*, ed. Charles Reagan Wilson. Jackson: University Press of Mississippi, 1985.

———. "The 'New' Old South." Paper presented at the Annual Meeting of the Alabama Association of Historians. Orange Beach, Alabama, 4 February 2000.

Bolton, S. Charles. "Inequality on the Southern Frontier: Arkansas County in the Arkansas Territory." *Arkansas Historical Quarterly* 41(Spring 1982): 51–66.

Bonner, James C. "Plantation and Farm: The Agricultural South." In *Writing Southern History: Essays in Historiography in Honor of Fletcher M. Green*, ed. Arthur S. Link and Rembert W. Patrick. Baton Rouge: Louisiana State University Press, 1965.

Bowman, Nelle E. "A Short History of Woman Suffrage in California." Unpublished Ph.D. dissertation, University of Chicago, 1913.

Brinkley, Alan. "The New Deal and Southern Politics." In *The New Deal and the South*, ed. James C. Cobb and Michael V. Namorato. Jackson: University Press of Mississippi, 1984.

Burnham, Walter Dean. "V. O. Key, Jr. and the Study of Political Parties." In *V. O. Key, Jr. and the Study of American Politics*, ed. Milton C. Cummings, Jr. Washington: American Political Science Association, 1988.

Campbell, Randolph B. "Planters and Plain Folk: Harrison County, Texas as a Test Case." *Journal of Southern History* 40(August 1974): 369–98.

———. "Planters and Plain Folk: The Social Structure of the Antebellum South." In *Interpreting Southern History: Historiographical Essays in Honor of Sanford W. Higginbotham*, ed. John B. Boles and Evelyn Thomas Nolen. Baton Rouge: Louisiana State University Press, 1987.

Cashin, Joan E. "Into the Troubled Wilderness: The Refugee Experience in the Civil War." In *A Woman's War: Southern Women, Civil War, and the Confederate Legacy*, ed. Edward D. C. Campbell, Jr., and Kym S. Rice, pp. 29–54. Richmond and Charlottesville: Museum of the Confederacy and the University Press of Virginia, 1996.

Clayton, Bruce. "No Ordinary History: W. J. Cash's The Mind of the South," In *The Mind of the South Fifty Years Later*, ed. Charles W. Eagles, pp. 3–22. Jackson: University Press of Mississippi, 1992.

———. "W. J. Cash and the Creative Impulse." *Southern Review* 24(1988): 777–90.

Cobb, James C. "Beyond Planters and Industrialists: A New Perspective on the South." *Journal of Southern History* 54(February 1988): 45–68.

Coles, Harry L., Jr. "Some Notes on Slaveownership and Landownership in Louisiana, 1850–1860." *Journal of Southern History* 9(August 1943): 381–94.

Conkin, Paul K. "Hot, Humid, and Sad." *Journal of Southern History* 64(February 1998): 3–22.

Coulter, E. Merton. "Aaron Alpcoria Bradley: Georgia Negro Politician during Reconstruction Times." *Georgia Historical Quarterly,* part I, 51(March 1967): 15–41, part II, 51(March 1967): 154–74, and part III, 51(September 1967): 264–306.

———. "Henry M. Turner: Georgia Negro Preacher-Politician during the Reconstruction Era." *Georgia Historical Quarterly* 48(December 1964): 371–410.

———. "Tunis G. Campbell: Negro Reconstructionist in Georgia." *Georgia Historical Quarterly,* part I, 51(December 1967): 401–24, and part II, 52(March 1968): 16–52.

———. "What the South Has Done about Its History." *Journal of Southern History* 2(February 1936): 3–28.

Cox, Karen L. "Women, the Lost Cause, and the New South: The United Daughters of the Confederacy and the Transmission of Southern Culture, 1894–1919." Unpublished Ph.D. dissertation, University of Southern Mississippi, 1997.

Crowe, Charles R. "Tom Watson, Populists, and Blacks Reconsidered." *Journal of Negro History* 55(April 1970): 99–116.

Dew, Charles B. "The Slavery Experience." In *Interpreting Southern History: Historiographical Essays in Honor of Sanford W. Higginbotham,* ed. John B. Boles and Evelyn Thomas Nolen. Baton Rouge: Louisiana State University Press, 1987.

Donald, David Herbert. "The Confederate as Fighting Man." *Journal of Southern History* 25(May 1959): 178–93.

———. "The Proslavery Argument Reconsidered." *Journal of Southern History* 37(February 1971): 3–18.

———. "Reconstruction." In *Interpreting American History: Conversations with Historians,* ed. John Garraty, pp. 341–67. New York: Macmillan, 1970.

———. "The Scalawag in Mississippi Reconstruction." *Journal of Southern History* 10(November 1944): 447–60.

Du Bois, W. E. B. "Reconstruction and Its Benefits." *American Historical Review* 15(July 1910): 781–99.

Faust, Drew Gilpin. "'Ours as Well as That of the Men': Women and Gender in the Civil War." In *Writing the Civil War,* ed. James M. McPherson and William J. Cooper, Jr., pp. 248–57. Columbia: University of South Carolina Press, 1998.

Feldman, Glenn. "C. Vann Woodward: Liberalism, Iconoclasm, Irony, and *Belles-Lettres* in Southern History." *Southern Humanities Review* 29(Spring 1995): 127–44.

———. "Race, Class, and New Directions in Southern Labor History." *Alabama Review* 51(April 1998): 96–106.

Flynt, Wayne. "Alabama's White Protestantism and Labor, 1900–1914." *Alabama Review* 25(July 1972): 192–217.

——. "Baptists and Reform." *Baptist History and Heritage* 7(October 1972): 211–22.

——. "Dissent in Zion: Alabama Baptists and Social Issues, 1900–1914." *Alabama Review* 35(November 1969): 523–42.

Foster, Gaines M. "Guilt Over Slavery: A Historiographical Analysis." *Journal of Southern History* 56(November 1990): 665–94.

Franklin, John Hope. "Jim Crow Goes to School: The Genesis of Legal Segregation in the South." *South Atlantic Quarterly* 58(Spring 1959): 225–35.

——. "Mirror for Americans: A Century of Reconstruction History." *American Historical Review* 85(February 1980): 1–14.

——. "Slavery and the Martial South." *Journal of Negro History* 37(January 1952): 36–53.

——. "Their War and Mine." *Journal of American History* 77(September 1990): 576–79.

——. "W. E. B. Du Bois: A Personal Memoir." *Massachusetts Review* 31(Autumn 1990): 409–28.

——. "Wither Reconstruction Historiography?" *Journal of Negro Education* 17(Fall 1948): 445–61.

Gambino, Ferruccio. "W. E. B. Du Bois and the Black Proletariat in Black Reconstruction." In *American Labor and Immigration History, 1877–1920: Recent European Research*, ed. Dirk Hoerder. Urbana: University of Illinois Press, 1983.

Gay, Dorothy Ann. "The Tangled Skein of Romanticism and Violence in the Old South: The Southern Response to Abolitionism and Feminism, 1830–1861." Unpublished Ph.D. dissertation, University of North Carolina, 1975.

Genovese, Eugene D. "Foreword: Ulrich Bonnell Phillips and His Critics." In *American Negro Slavery: A Survey of the Supply, Employment, and Control of Negro Labor as Determined by the Plantation Regime*, by Ulrich B. Phillips, 1918. Rev. ed., Baton Rouge: Louisiana State University Press, 1987.

——. "Race and Class in Southern History: An Appraisal of the Work of Ulrich Bonnell Phillips." *Agricultural History* 41(October 1967): 300–329.

Giroux, Vincent A., Jr. "Theodore G. Bilbo: Progressive to Public Racist." Unpublished Ph.D. dissertation, Indiana University, 1984.

Goodstein, Anne Shafer. "A Rare Alliance: African American and White Women in the Tennessee Elections of 1919 and 1920." *Journal of Southern History* 64(May 1998): 219–46.

Gray, Virginia Gearhart. "Activities of Southern Women: 1840–1860." *South Atlantic Quarterly* 27(July 1928): 264–79.

Hall, Jacquelyn Dowd. "'The Mind That Burns in Each Body': Women, Rape, and Racial Violence." In *Powers of Desire: The Politics of Sexuality*, ed. Elizabeth Ann Snitow, Christine Stansell, and Sharon Thompson, pp. 328–46. New York: Monthly Review Press, 1983.

Hall, Jacquelyn Dowd, and Anne Firor Scott. "Women in the South." In *Interpreting Southern History: Historiographical Essays in Honor of Sanford W. Higgin-*

botham, ed. John B. Boles and Evelyn Thomas Nolen, pp. 454–509. Baton Rouge: Louisiana State University Press, 1987.

Hamilton, Virginia Van der Veer. "Clio's Daughters: Whence and Whither." In *Taking Off the White Gloves: Southern Women and Women Historians,* ed. Michelle Gillespie and Catherine Clinton. Columbia: University of Missouri Press, 1998.

Hill, Samuel S., Jr. "Religion and Politics in the South." In *Religion in the South,* ed. Charles Reagan Wilson. Jackson: University of Mississippi Press, 1985.

———. "Southern Protestantism and Racial Integration." *Religion in Life* 30(Summer 1964): 421–29.

Hofstadter, Richard. "U. B. Phillips and the Plantation Legend." *Journal of Negro History* 29(April 1944): 109–24.

Jacoway, Elizabeth. "The South's Palladium: The Southern Woman and the Cash Construct." In *W. J. Cash and the Minds of the South,* ed. Paul D. Escott, pp. 112–33. Baton Rouge: Louisiana State University Press, 1992.

Johnson, Joan Marie. "'This Wonderful Dream Nation!': Black and White South Carolina Women and the Creation of a New South, 1898–1930." Unpublished Ph.D. dissertation, University of California at Los Angeles, 1977.

Johnson, Michael P. "Mary Chesnut's Autobiography and Biography: A Review Essay." *Journal of Southern History* 47(November 1981): 585–92.

Key, V. O., Jr. "The Erosion of Sectionalism." *Virginia Quarterly Review* 31(Spring 1955): 161–79.

———. "The Future of the Democratic Party." *Virginia Quarterly Review* 28(Spring 1952): 161–75.

Lawson, Steven F. "Freedom Then, Freedom Now: The Historiography of the Civil Rights Movement." *American Historical Review* 96(April 1991): 456–71.

Lebsock, Suzanne. "Woman Suffrage and White Supremacy: A Virginia Case Study." In *Visible Women: New Essays on American Activism,* ed. Nancy A. Hewitt and Suzanne Lebsock, pp. 62–100. Urbana: University of Illinois Press, 1993.

Lerner, Gerda. "The Lady and the Mill Girl: Changes in the Status of Women in the Age of Jackson." *Mid-continent American Studies Journal* 10(Spring 1969): 5–15.

Lincoln, C. Eric. "Mind and Countermind: A Personal Perspective on W. J. Cash's *The Mind of the South.*" In *W. J. Cash and the Minds of the South,* ed. Paul D. Escott, pp. 226–42. Baton Rouge: Louisiana State University Press, 1992.

Linden, Fabian. "Economic Democracy in the Slave South: An Appraisal of Some Recent Views." *Journal of Negro History* 31(April 1946): 140–89.

Link, Arthur S. "The Progressive Movement in the South, 1870–1914." *North Carolina Historical Review* 23(April 1946): 172–95.

McArthur, Judith N. "Minnie Fisher Cunningham's Back Door Lobby in Texas: Political Maneuvering in a One-Party State." In *One Woman, One Vote: Redis-*

covering the Woman Suffrage Movement, ed. Marjorie Spruill Wheeler, pp. 315–31. Troutdale, Ore.: NewSage Press, 1995.

McCurry, Stephanie. "The Two Faces of Republicanism: Gender and Proslavery Politics in Antebellum South Carolina." *Journal of American History* 78(March 1992): 1245–64.

McDonald, Forrest, and Grady McWhiney. "The Antebellum Southern Herdsman: A Reinterpretation." *Journal of Southern History* 41(May 1975): 147–66.

———. "The South from Self-Sufficiency to Peonage: An Interpretation." *American Historical Review* 85(December 1980): 1095–118.

May, Gertrude. "A History of the Woman Suffrage Movement in Illinois." Unpublished Ph.D. dissertation, University of Chicago, 1913.

Mencken, H. L. "The Sahara of the Bozart." *New York Evening Mail* (13 November 1917). Reprinted in *Prejudices: Second Series,* by H. L. Mencken, pp. 136–37, 139, and 153. New York: Alfred A. Knopf, 1920.

Mendenhall, Marjorie Stratford. "Southern Women of a 'Lost Generation.'" *South Atlantic Quarterly* 33(October 1934): 334–53.

Moneyhon, Carl H. "Economic Democracy in Antebellum Arkansas, Phillips County, 1850–1860." *Arkansas Historical Quarterly* 40(Summer 1981): 154–72.

Moore, James Tice. "Redeemers Reconsidered: Change and Continuity in the Democratic South, 1870–1900." *Journal of Southern History* 44(August 1978): 357–78.

Owsley, Frank L. "The Fundamental Cause of the Civil War: Egocentric Sectionalism." *Journal of Southern History* 7(February 1941): 3–18.

———. "The Pattern of Migration and Settlement on the Southern Frontier." *Journal of Southern History* 11(May 1945): 145–76.

———. "The War of the Sections." *Virginia Quarterly Review* 10(October 1934): 630–35.

Owsley, Frank L., and Harriet C. Owsley. "The Economic Basis of Society in the Late Antebellum South." *Journal of Southern History* 6(February 1940): 24–45.

———. "The Economic Structure of Rural Tennessee, 1850–1860." *Journal of Southern History* 8(May 1942): 161–82.

Painter, Nell Irvin. "Race, Gender, and Class in *The Mind of the South*." In *W. J. Cash and the Minds of the South*, ed. Paul D. Escott, pp. 88–111. Baton Rouge: Louisiana State University Press, 1992.

Phillips, Ulrich Bonnell. "The Central Theme of Southern History." *American Historical Review* 34(October 1928): 30–43.

———. "The Plantation Product of Men." In the Proceedings of the Second Annual Session of the Georgia Historical Association. Atlanta: Georgia Historical Association, 1918.

Rodgers, Daniel T. "Republicanism: The Career of a Concept." *Journal of American History* 79(June 1992): 11–38.

Saucier, Bobby W. "The Public Career of Theodore G. Bilbo." Unpublished Ph.D. dissertation, Tulane University, 1971.

Schaefer, Donald. "Yeomen Farmers and Economic Democracy: A Study of

Wealth and Economic Mobility in the Western Tobacco Region, 1850–1860." *Explorations in Economic History* 15(October 1978): 421–37.

Scott, Anne Firor. "After Suffrage: Southern Women in the 1920s." *Journal of Southern History* 30(August 1964): 298–318.

———. "Most Invisible of All: Black Women's Voluntary Associations." *Journal of Southern History* 56(February 1990): 3–22.

———. "The 'New Woman' in the New South." *South Atlantic Quarterly* 61(Autumn 1962): 417–83.

———. "On Seeing and Not Seeing: A Case of Historical Invisibility." *Journal of American History* 71(June 1984): 7–21.

———. "Women's Perspective on the Patriarchy in the 1850s." *Journal of American History* 61(June 1974): 52–64.

Shalope, Robert. "Republicanism and Early American Historiography." *William and Mary Quarterly* 39(April 1982): 334–56.

Silver, James W. "Mississippi: The Closed Society." *Journal of Southern History* 30(February 1964): 3–34.

Smith, John David. "E. Merton Coulter, the 'Dunning School,' and *The Civil War and Reconstruction in Kentucky.*" *Register of the Kentucky Historical Society* 86(Winter 1988): 52–69.

Sydnor, Charles S. "The Beginning of Printing in Mississippi." *Journal of Southern History* 1(February 1935): 49–55.

———. "The Free Negro in Mississippi before the Civil War." *American Historical Review* 32(July 1927): 769–88.

———. "Historical Activities in Mississippi in the Nineteenth Century." *Journal of Southern History* 3(May 1937): 139–60.

———. "A Slave Owner and His Overseers." *North Carolina Historical Review* 14(January 1937): 31–38.

———. "The Southern Experiment in Writing Social History." *Journal of Southern History* 11(November 1945): 455–68.

Taylor, A. Elizabeth. "The Last Phase of the Woman Suffrage Movement in Georgia." *Georgia Historical Quarterly* 43(March 1959): 11–28.

———. "A Lifelong Interest." In *Citizens at Last: The Woman Suffrage Movement in Texas,* ed. Ruthe Winegartern and Judith N. McArthur. Austin, Texas: Ellen C. Temple, 1987.

———. "The Origins of the Woman Suffrage Movement in Georgia." *Georgia Historical Quarterly* 28(June 1944): 63–79.

———. "Revival and Development of the Woman Suffrage Movement in Georgia." *Georgia Historical Quarterly* 42(December 1958): 339–54.

———. "A Short History of the Woman Suffrage Movement in Tennessee." *Tennessee Historical Quarterly* 2(September 1943): 195–215.

———. "South Carolina and the Enfranchisement of Women: The Early Years." *South Carolina Historical Magazine* 77(April 1976): 115–26.

———. "South Carolina and the Enfranchisement of Women: The Later Years." *South Carolina Historical Magazine* 80 (October 1979): 298–310.

———. "Tennessee: The Thirty-Sixth State." In *Votes for Women: The Woman Suffrage Movement in Tennessee, the South, and the Nation,* ed. Marjorie Spruill Wheeler, pp. 53–70. Knoxville: University of Tennessee Press, 1995.

———. "Woman Suffrage Activities in Atlanta." *Atlanta Historical Journal* 23(Winter 1980): 45–54.

———. "The Woman Suffrage Movement in Arkansas." *Arkansas Historical Quarterly* 15(Spring 1956): 17–52.

———. "The Woman Suffrage Movement in Florida." *Florida Historical Quarterly* 36(July 1957): 42–60.

———. "The Woman Suffrage Movement in Mississippi, 1890–1920." *Journal of Mississippi History* 30(February 1968): 1–34.

———. "The Woman Suffrage Movement in North Carolina." *North Carolina Historical Review* 38(January and April 1961): 45–62, 173–89.

———. "The Woman Suffrage Movement in Texas." *Journal of Southern History* 17(May 1951): 194–215.

Tindall, George Brown. "Business Progressivism: Southern Politics in the Twenties." *South Atlantic Quarterly* 62(Winter 1963): 92–106.

———. "The Campaign for the Disfranchisement of Negroes in South Carolina." *Journal of Southern History* 15(May 1949): 212–34.

———. "The Central Theme Revisited." In *The Southerner as American,* ed. Charles G. Sellers. Chapel Hill: University of North Carolina Press, 1960.

———. "Mythology: A New Frontier in Southern History." In *The Idea of the South: Pursuit of a Central Theme,* ed. Frank E. Vandiver. Chicago: University of Chicago Press, 1964.

———. "The Significance of Howard W. Odum to Southern History: A Preliminary Estimate." *Journal of Southern History* 24(August 1958): 285–307.

———. "Southern Negroes since Reconstruction: Dissolving the Static Image." In *Writing Southern History: Essays in Historiography in Honor of Fletcher M. Green,* ed. Arthur S. Link and Rembert W. Patrick, pp. 337–61. Baton Rouge: Louisiana State University Press, 1965.

Trotter, Joe W. "African-American Workers: New Directions in U.S. Labor Historiography." *Labor History* 35(Fall 1994): 495–523.

Vance, Rupert B. "A Karl Marx for Hill Billies: Portrait of a Southern Leader." *Social Forces* 9(December 1930): 80–90.

———. "The Old Cotton Belt." In *Migration and Economic Opportunity,* ed. Carter Goodrich et al., pp. 124–63. Philadelphia: University of Pennsylvania Press, 1936.

———. "Region." In *International Encyclopedia of the Social Sciences,* ed. David L. Sills, vol. 13, pp. 377–82. New York: Crowell, Collier, and Macmillan, 1968.

———. "The Urban Breakthrough in the South." *Virginia Quarterly Review* 31(Spring 1955): 223–32.

Watson, Harry L. "Conflict and Collaboration: Yeomen, Slaveholders, and Politics in the Antebellum South." *Social History* 10(October 1985): 273–98.

Welter, Barbara. "The Cult of True Womanhood: 1820–1860." *American Quarterly* 18(Summer 1966): 151–74.

Whites, LeAnn. "Rebecca Lattimer Fulton and the Problem of 'Protection' in the New South." In *Visible Women: New Essays on American Activism,* ed. Nancy A. Hewitt and Suzanne Lebsock, pp. 41–61. Urbana: University of Illinois Press, 1993.

Wilkerson-Freeman, Sarah. "Women and the Transformation of American Politics: North Carolina, 1898–1940." Unpublished Ph.D. dissertation, University of North Carolina, 1995.

Winters, Donald L. "'Plain Folk' of the Old South Reexamined: Economic Democracy in Tennessee." *Journal of Southern History* 53(November 1987): 565–86.

Woodward, C. Vann. "The Elusive Mind of the South." In *American Counterpoint: Slavery and Racism in the North-South Dialogue,* by C. Vann Woodward. Boston: Little, Brown and Company, 1971.

Woodward, Michael Vaughan. "E. Merton Coulter and the Art of Biography." *Georgia Historical Quarterly* 64(Summer 1980): 159–71.

———. "The Publications of E. Merton Coulter to 1 July 1977." *Georgia Historical Quarterly* 61(Fall 1977): 268–78.

Wright, Gavin C. "'Economic Democracy' and the Concentration of Agricultural Wealth in the Cotton South, 1850–1860." *Agricultural History* 44(January 1970): 63–93.

Contributors

Texas native SUSAN YOUNGBLOOD ASHMORE is assistant professor in the Oxford College of Emory University. Her 1999 Ph.D. dissertation at Auburn University was entitled "Carry It On: The War on Poverty and the Civil Rights Movement in Alabama, 1964–1969." Professor Ashmore's work has appeared in the *Alabama Review*, and she has presented papers at the annual meetings of the Southern Historical Association, the Southern Women's History Association, and the Alabama Women's History Forum.

Professor and chair of the Department of History at Abilene Christian University, FRED ARTHUR BAILEY is the author of *William Edward Dodd: The South's Yeoman Scholar* (1997) and *Class and Tennessee's Confederate Generation* (1987). He received his Ph.D. in history from the University of Tennessee in 1979 and is at work on a book tentatively entitled *The Southern Quest for a Suitable Past: Historiography and Social Control, 1890–1980*.

JEAN H. BAKER is professor of history at Goucher College and has written widely on nineteenth-century politics. She is the author of *The Stevensons of Illinois: A Biography of an American Family* (1996), *Mary Todd Lincoln: A Biography* (1987), *Affairs of Party: The Political Culture of Northern Democrats in the Mid-Nineteenth Century* (1982), *Ambivalent Americans: The Know-Nothing Party in Maryland* (1976), and *The Politics of Continuity: Maryland Political Parties from 1850 to 1870* (1973). Professor Baker received her doctorate in history from The Johns Hopkins University in 1971.

ANTHONY GENE CAREY is associate professor of history at Auburn University and book review editor for the *Alabama Review*. He is also assistant dean of the College of Arts and Humanities. Carey wrote *Parties, Slavery, and the Union in Antebellum Georgia* (1997) and received his Ph.D. in history under the guidance of James L. Roark at Emory University in 1992.

The Harry A. Logan, Sr., Professor of History at Allegheny College, BRUCE CLAYTON is the author and editor of many books on the South, including *Debating Southern History: Ideas and Action in the Twentieth Century* (1999) and *Varieties of Southern History: New Essays on a Region and Its People* (1996), both edited with John A. Salmond. Clayton's other books include *Praying for Base Hits: An American Boyhood* (1998), *W. J. Cash: A Life* (1991), and *Savage Ideal: Intolerance and Intellectual Leadership in the South, 1890–1914* (1972). He was a Woodrow Wilson scholar and earned his doctoral degree in history at Duke University in 1966 working under Robert F. Durden and Richard L. Watson.

GLENN FELDMAN, a native of Birmingham, is assistant professor at the Center for Labor Education and Research in the School of Business at the University of Alabama at Birmingham. He is the author of *Politics, Society, and the Klan in Alabama, 1915–1949* (1999), which was nominated for the Charles S. Sydnor Award and the Robert F. Kennedy Memorial Book Award. He is also the author of *From Demagogue to Dixiecrat: Horace Wilkinson and the Politics of Race* (1995), and is editing, with Kari Frederickson, *Sowing the Seeds: Race, Rights, and Reaction in the American South, 1940–1956*. Professor Feldman holds five degrees, including a Ph.D. in history from Auburn University (1996), where he studied under Wayne Flynt.

Former editor of the *Florida Historical Quarterly*, KARI FREDERICKSON is an assistant professor of history at the University of Alabama. Frederickson received her doctorate in history from Rutgers University in 1996. Her revised dissertation, *The Dixiecrat Revolt and the End of the Solid South, 1932–1968*, is forthcoming from the University of North Carolina Press. Professor Frederickson is also the author of *Crusaders Against Modernity: The Ideology and Legacy of the Ku Klux Klan of the 1920s*, forthcoming from M. E. Sharpe, and is editing, with Glenn Feldman, a book entitled *Sowing the Seeds: Race, Rights, and Reaction in the American South, 1940–1956*.

A leading figure in Southern and women's history, JACQUELYN DOWD HALL is Julia Cherry Spruill Professor of History at the University of North Carolina at Chapel Hill. Professor Hall received her doctorate in history from Columbia University in 1974 and has since served as director of the Southern Oral History Program at the University of North Carolina and the Duke University–University of North Carolina Center for Research on Women. Her 1979 book, *Revolt Against Chivalry: Jessie Daniel Ames and the Women's Campaign Against Lynching*, won the Bancroft Dissertation Award, the Lillian Smith Award, and the Francis B. Simkins Award. For coauthoring *Like a*

Family: The Making of a Southern Cotton Mill World (1987), Hall received the Albert J. Beveridge Award, the Philip Taft Labor History Prize, and the Merle Curti Social History Award.

Both DAVID S. and JEANNE T. HEIDLER reside in Colorado Springs, Colorado, where Jeanne is professor and director of American history at the United States Air Force Academy, the first female and first civilian ever to hold that post. David taught history along with Jeanne at Salisbury State University and later at the University of Southern Colorado, but is currently devoting full time to research and writing. The Heidlers coedited the *Encyclopedia of the War of 1812* (1997) and coauthored *Old Hickory's War: Andrew Jackson and the Quest for Empire* (1996), a History Book Club Alternate Selection. They are currently coauthoring a work tentatively entitled *Andrew Jackson and the American Character.* In addition, David wrote *Pulling the Temple Down: The Fire-Eaters and the Destruction of the Union* (1994). The Heidlers received their doctorates at Auburn University.

JUDITH N. McARTHUR is the author of *Creating the New Woman: The Rise of Southern Women's Progressive Culture in Texas, 1893–1918* (1998), coauthor with Orville Vernon Burton of *A Gentleman and an Officer: A Military and Social History of James B. Griffin's Civil War* (1996), and coeditor with Ruthe Winegarten of *The Woman Suffrage Movement in Texas* (1987). She received her doctoral degree in history at the University of Texas in 1992 and is currently a lecturer in history at the University of Houston-Victoria.

JAMES OAKES is graduate school professor of the humanities in the Ph.D. in history program at the City University of New York, Graduate Center. He is also the author of *Slavery and Freedom: An Interpretation of the Old South* (1990) and *The Ruling Race: A History of American Slaveholders* (1982). Dr. Oakes received his Ph.D. from the University of California at Berkeley in 1981, was an NEH fellow, and has taught at Purdue, Princeton, and Northwestern universities.

TED OWNBY is the editor of *Interaction of Black and White Cultures in the Antebellum South* (1993) and the author of *American Dreams in Mississippi: Consumers, Poverty, and Culture, 1830–1998* (1999) and *Subduing Satan: Religion, Recreation, and Manhood in the Rural South, 1865–1920* (1990). He received his doctorate from The Johns Hopkins University in 1987, where he studied under John Higham. Dr. Ownby has been a member of the history department and the Center for the Study of Southern Culture at the University of Mississippi since 1988.

JOHN SHELTON REED is the foremost living Southern sociologist. He has taught at the University of North Carolina at Chapel Hill and is the author of many books, including: *The Enduring South: Subcultural Persistence in Mass Society* (1972), *One South: An Ethnic Approach to Regional Culture* (1982), *Southerners, the Social Psychology of Sectionalism* (1983), *Southern Folk, Plain & Fancy: Native White Social Types* (1986), *Surveying the South: Studies in Regional Sociology* (1993), *My Tears Spoiled My Aim and Other Reflections on Southern Culture* (1993), and *Kicking Back: Further Dispatches from the South* (1995).

Louisianan JUNIUS P. RODRIGUEZ is general editor of *The Chronology of World Slavery* (1999) and *The Historical Encyclopedia of World Slavery* (1997). He is also the author of *"Ripe for Revolt": Louisiana and the Tradition of Slave Insurrection, 1803–1865*, forthcoming from the Louisiana State University Press. An associate professor of history at Eureka College, Rodriguez earned his doctorate from Auburn University in 1992, where he worked with Civil War historian James Lee McDonough.

Richardson professor of history at Emory and Henry College, JOHN HERBERT ROPER is the author of *C. Vann Woodward, Southerner* (1987) and *U. B. Phillips: A Southern Mind* (1984), as well as the editor of *C. Vann Woodward: A Southern Historian and His Critics* (1997), *Paul Green's War Songs: A Southern Poet Looks at the Great War* (1994), and *Georgia and State Rights by U. B. Phillips* (1984). A native South Carolinian, Roper received his doctoral degree in history at the University of North Carolina at Chapel Hill in 1977, where Joel Williamson served as his major professor. Professor Roper is currently working on intellectual biographies of Paul Green and Benjamin E. Mays.

A professor of history at Georgia Southern University, ANASTATIA SIMS earned her Ph.D. in history at the University of North Carolina at Chapel Hill in 1985. A native of Mobile, she is the author of *The Power of Femininity in the New South: Women and Politics in North Carolina, 1880–1930* (1997) and co-editor, with Janet Coryell, Thomas Appleton, and Sandra Treadway, of *Dealing with the Powers That Be: Negotiating Boundaries of Southern Womanhood* (forthcoming from the University of Missouri Press). Dr. Sims's work has appeared in a number of journals and in Marjorie Spruill Wheeler's edited anthology, *One Woman, One Vote: Rediscovering the Woman Suffrage Movement* (1995), which was published to accompany the PBS documentary of the same name.

DANIEL JOSEPH SINGAL is professor of history at Hobart and William Smith Colleges, where he has taught since 1980. He received his Ph.D. in history at Columbia University in 1976 and his revised dissertation, *The War Within: From Victorian to Modernist Thought in the South, 1919–1945* (1982), won the Ramsdell and Emerson awards and the Francis B. Simkins and Fred W. Morrison prizes. He coedited, with John Shelton Reed, *Regionalism in the South: Selected Papers of Rupert B. Vance* (1982) and edited *Modernist Culture in America* (1989). He has also authored the *Guide to the Microfilm Edition of the Southern Tenant Farmers Union Papers* (1972) and *William Faulkner: The Making of a Modernist* (1997).

JOE W. TROTTER is Mellon Bank Professor of History at Carnegie-Mellon University. He is the author of *Black Milwaukee: The Making of an Industrial Proletariat, 1915–1945* (1985), *Coal, Class, and Color: Blacks in Southern West Virginia, 1915–1932* (1990), *African Americans in Depression and War, 1929–1945* (1995), and, with Earl Lewis, *Blacks in the Industrial Age: A Documentary History* (1996). Dr. Trotter is also the editor of *The Great Migration in Historical Perspective: New Dimensions of Race, Class, and Gender* (1991). He received his Ph.D. in history from the University of Minnesota in 1980.

British native JOHN WHITE is Reader in American Studies at the University of Hull, England. His books include *Slavery in the American South* (1970), *Reconstruction after the American Civil War* (1977), *Black Leadership in America, 1895–1968* (1985), and *Billie Holiday: Her Life and Times* (1987), and he also coedited *American Studies: Essays in Honour of Marcus Cunliffe* (1990). Professor White is presently editing a collection of essays on the Montgomery Bus Boycott and Southern civil rights and is completing a biography of Montgomery civil rights activist E. D. Nixon. He completed his doctoral degree at the University of Hull.

Index

Oklahoma, 79; Booker T. Washington High School, 154; Oklahoma City, 156; Rentiesville, 154; Tulsa, 154
"Old Cotton Belt, The" 84
Old Massa's People, 40
Old South. *See* Antebellum South
Old World's New World, The, 138
Olmstead, Frederick Law, 115
Omnibus Bill, 186–87
One Name but Several Faces: Variety in Popular Christian Denominations in Southern History, 257–58
One-Party South. *See* "Solid South"
"Open Letter to the Southern People, An," 62
Oral history. *See* Interviews
Organization of American Historians (OAH), 153, 173, 189, 246, 290 (n. 1), 305 (n. 5)
Origins of the New South, 1877–1913, 29, 45, 138, 141, 143–45, 147, 288 (n. 9)
O'Shea Report, 99
Osterweis, Roger G.: and "Lost Cause" historiography, 266 (n. 4)
Our Republic, 94
Outsiders, 6, 50, 106–7, 256. *See also* Ethnicity; Nativism; *Reconstruction Syndrome;* "Siege Mentality"; Yankees
Ovington, Mary, 70
Owen, Dennis P.: and the "Religious Right," 258, 310 (n. 41)
Owen, Robert, 29
Ownby, Ted, 7; chapter on Samuel S. Hill, Jr. by, 247–59
Owsley, Frank Lawrence: chapter on by Anthony Gene Carey, 49–60; on Charles S. Sydnor, 106–7; criticism of, 272 (n. 19); Donald Winters, on, 54; on E. Merton Coulter's work, 43–44; Gavin C. Wright on, 54; and "Lost Cause" historiography, 3, 4, 6, 7, 9, 32, 89, 106, 107, 265 (n. 2), 278 (n. 4), 282 (n. 57); major works of, 271

(n. 1); on U. B. Phillips's work, 22, 50–51, 58; works of, 271 (n. 1)
Owsley, Harriet Chappell, 49–50
"Owsley School," 271 (n. 1)
Oxford University, 108, 184, 196, 178

Pacifism 26
Page, Thomas Nelson, 34, 120
Painter, Nell Irvin, 5, 121
Pan-African Congress, 71
Paris, 71
Parties. *See* Politics
Party of Lincoln, 130, 178–80, 230. *See also* Republican party
Party of Roosevelt, 130, 230. *See also* Democratic party
Passion (as relates to historiography), 8, 11, 17, 32–48, 88–111, 134, 164–65, 177–90, 245. *See also* "Dunning School"; "Lost Cause"; *Usable Past*
Paternalism, 22, 26, 30, 115, 117, 144, 228. *See also* Race; Racism
Patriarchy, 59, 142, 235, 239–41. *See also* Gender; Slavery
Patrician whites, 3, 4, 6, 88, 103
Patrick, Rembert W., 3, 174, 233
Patriotism, 6, 12. *See also* Confederate patriotic societies; Confederate patriotism; Military themes; Nativism
Patronage, 130–31
Patterson, John, 216
Paul, Saint, 15, 252
Payne, Daniel Alexander, 256
Peabody Fund, 25
Pearson, C. Chilton, 113
Pearson, Josephine, 169
Peculiar Institution, The, 202–11
Pennsylvania: Gettysburg, 34, 119, 146; Philadelphia, 65–67
Pentecostal churches, 257, 259. *See also* Holiness churches
People of Plenty: Economic Abundance and the American Character, 180–85, 189